C

Edited by Katie Pickles and Myra Rutherdale

Contact Zones
Aboriginal and Settler Women
in Canada's Colonial Past

UBCPress · Vancouver · Toronto

Library and Archives Canada Cataloguing in Publication

Contact zones : aboriginal and settler women in Canada's colonial past /
edited by Katie Pickles and Myra Rutherdale.

Includes bibliographical references and index.
ISBN-13: 978-0-7748-1135-4 (bound); 978-0-7748-1136-1 (pbk.)
ISBN-10: 0-7748-1135-8 (bound); 0-7748-1136-6 (pbk.)

1. Indian women – Canada – Social conditions – 19th century. 2. Indian women
– Canada – Social conditions – 20th century. 3. Women pioneers – Canada – Social
conditions – 19th century. 4. Women pioneers – Canada – Social conditions – 20th
century. 5. Indian women – Canada – History – 19th century. 6. Indian women –
Canada – History – 20th century. 7. Women pioneers – Canada – History – 19th
century. 8. Women pioneers – Canada – History – 20th century. I. Pickles, Katie
II. Rutherdale, Myra, 1961-

E78.C2C5655 2005   305.4'0971'09034   C2005-904004-1

Canada

UBC Press gratefully acknowledges the financial support for our publishing
program of the Government of Canada through the Book Publishing Industry
Development Program (BPIDP), and of the Canada Council for the Arts, and
the British Columbia Arts Council.

This book has been published with the help of a grant from the Canadian Federation
for the Humanities and Social Sciences, through the Aid to Scholarly Publications
Programme, using funds provided by the Social Sciences and Humanities Research
Council of Canada, and with the help of the K.D. Srivastava Fund.

Printed and bound in Canada by Friesens
Set in Stone by Artegraphica Design Co. Ltd.
Copy editor: Audrey McClellan
Proofreader: Sarah Munro
Indexer: Heather Ebbs

UBC Press
The University of British Columbia
2029 West Mall
Vancouver, BC V6T 1Z2
604-822-5959 / Fax: 604-822-6083
www.ubcpress.ca

Contents

Illustrations / vii

Acknowledgments / ix

Introduction / 1
Katie Pickles and Myra Rutherdale

**Part 1: Dressing and Performing Bodies:
Aboriginal Women, Imperial Eyes, and Betweenness**

1 Sewing for a Living: The Commodification of Métis Women's Artistic
Production / 17
Sherry Farrell Racette

2 Championing the Native: E. Pauline Johnson Rejects the Squaw / 47
Carole Gerson and Veronica Strong-Boag

3 Performing for "Imperial Eyes": Bernice Loft and Ethel Brant Monture,
Ontario, 1930s-60s / 67
Cecilia Morgan

4 Spirited Subjects and Wounded Souls: Political Representations
of an Im/moral Frontier / 90
Jo-Anne Fiske

Part 2: Regulating the Body: Domesticity, Sexuality, and Transgression

5 Metropolitan Knowledge, Colonial Practice, and Indigenous
Womanhood: Missions in Nineteenth-Century British Columbia / 109
Adele Perry

6 Creating "Semi-Widows" and "Supernumerary Wives": Prohibiting Polygamy in Prairie Canada's Aboriginal Communities to 1900 / 131
Sarah A. Carter

7 Intimate Surveillance: Indian Affairs, Colonization, and the Regulation of Aboriginal Women's Sexuality / 160
Robin Jarvis Brownlie

8 Domesticating Girls: The Sexual Regulation of Aboriginal and Working-Class Girls in Twentieth-Century Canada / 179
Joan Sangster

Part 3: Bodies in Everyday Space: Colonized and Colonizing Women in Canadian Contact Zones

9 Aboriginal Women on the Streets of Victoria: Rethinking Transgressive Sexuality during the Colonial Encounter / 205
Jean Barman

10 "She Was a Ragged Little Thing": Missionaries, Embodiment, and Refashioning Aboriginal Womanhood in Northern Canada / 228
Myra Rutherdale

11 Belonging – Out of Place: Women's Travelling Stories from the Western Edge / 246
Dianne Newell

12 The Old and New on Parade: Mimesis, Queen Victoria, and Carnival Queens on Victoria Day in Interwar Victoria / 272
Katie Pickles

Contributors / 293

Index / 296

Illustrations

29 / Embroidered mitten, ca. 1860

30 / Charles Napier Bell, 10 March 1871

33 / Watch pocket, 1859-60

35 / North West Mounted Police pad saddle, ca. 1880, Métis type

38 / Quillwork embroidered tea cozy, ca. 1913

52 / Pauline Johnson in Native dress, ca. 1902

55 / Pauline Johnson, poetess, Vancouver, 1903

111 / Map of colonial British Columbia

133 / Blackfoot women and their husband, late 1870s

141 / Wedding group at the Anglican mission on the Siksika Reserve, ca. 1900

144 / Cardston, Alberta women, ca. 1900

232 / Aklavik schoolgirls dressed up

241 / Mary Kendi, child, and nurse Prudence Hockin

251 / Maria Levy Septima Collis, 1842-1917

255 / Emily Carr in her studio

277 / IODE Badge

Acknowledgments

The process of writing the acknowledgments for a book represents the end of a long journey. This journey began when we first met in 1998 in Melbourne, Australia at an International Federation for Research in Women's History conference. We connected instantly. Our shared interest in women and colonization led to many long discussions over email and in person in Vancouver over the winter of 1998-99, when Katie was a visiting scholar at the University of British Columbia and Myra was teaching women's studies at Simon Fraser University. Excited about questions concerning gender, colonization, and embodiment in Canada we began work on this volume in the summer of 2000.

Conferences, study leaves, and research trips in Canada and around the world have brought contributors together to discuss the core concerns of this project. We owe a debt of gratitude to the authors of these essays who patiently supported all of our efforts to bring this volume together. They were a pleasure to work with.

In Canada, we are very fortunate to have the Social Sciences and Humanities Research Council, which so generously supports publishing endeavours such as this one.

We would like to thank Jean Wilson for her constant enthusiasm, and all of the staff at UBC Press for their hard work and support. The comments of the anonymous readers were also helpful. For the help with photographic reproduction and map making we would like to thank Ateffa Salihi at York University's Department of History, Elizabeth Wright of the University of North Carolina at Chapel Hill, Eric Leinberger at the University of British Columbia, Kelly-Ann Nolin at the Royal British Columbia Museum, Jeannie Hounslow at the City of Vancouver Archives, and Robin Weber at the Prince of Wales Northern Heritage Centre in Yellowknife.

Katie would like to thank the School of History at the University of Canterbury for its ongoing support of this project. Pauline Wedlake provided technical assistance. As heads of department, John Cookson, Miles Fairburn, and Peter Hempenstall granted the research and study leave that enabled her to spend valuable time in Canada which was financially supported by funds from the University of Canterbury and a Government of Canada Faculty Research Award. The Association for Canadian Studies in Australia and New Zealand (ACSANZ) provided an important forum for the discussion of the project, in particular at the "Canada in New Zealand" regional conference held at the University of Canterbury on 1 July 2001. Family, friends, and colleagues have offered valuable advice and assistance. In particular, Melissa Kerdemelidis, Michael McCosker, Philippa Mein Smith, Ann Parsonson, and Graeme Wynn all shared their expertise.

Myra would like to thank her family, who have continued to sustain her throughout. Rob has been a dear friend and companion and her son Andrew now knows much more than he may ever want to on the theme of gender and colonization. Jean and the late Jack Rutherdale have always been kind, supportive, and interested in her work. In the final stages of bringing this book together Myra was fortunate to take up a Canada Research Chair postdoctoral fellowship in Native/Newcomer relations at the University of Saskatchewan. Her year there was very rewarding. Work in Native/Newcomer history is especially supported at the University of Saskatchewan. Apart from the scholarship, she was well looked after by colleagues Whitney Lackenbauer, Bill and Marley Waiser, Lesley McBain, Keith and Teresa Carlson, and Mary and Jim Miller. The kindness, hospitality, and encouragement of Mary and Jim was deeply appreciated. Sadly, Mary died in December 2004 but her positive spirit and friendly nature will long be remembered. She was a kindred spirit. At her new academic home, York University's Department of History, Myra is particularly fortunate to have many engaged and engaging colleagues including Bettina Bradbury, Kate McPherson, Carolyn Podruchny, and Anne Rubenstein who have been especially welcoming. It is also a pleasure to acknowledge William Westfall, who was her dissertation supervisor at York, and who is now a dear colleague and friend.

In the end, this book owes much to the experiences of the Aboriginal and the settler women whose lives unfold in the following chapters.

Contact Zones

Introduction

Katie Pickles and Myra Rutherdale

Women's raced and classed bodies were a vital "contact zone" in the Canadian colonial past. During colonization, women and bodies mattered and were bound up in creating and perpetuating an often hidden, complex, contradictory, and fraught history.[1] Women occupied the spaces of colonial encounter between Aboriginals and newcomers as both colonizers and the colonized, transgressing restrictive boundaries and making history. In varied sites of encounter, Aboriginal women, white women travellers, missionaries, and settlers were all integral to the colonial project. Colonial relationships of power were expressed locally and in different times and places that were grounded in the materiality of women's day-to-day lives. By focusing on the nexus between women's bodies and colonization, this book reveals and interprets contact zones in English Canada's colonial past. It demonstrates the importance of women's history in expanding the understanding of imperialism and colonialism.

The book is divided into three thematic parts. The first part of *Contact Zones* focuses on Aboriginal women and the ways in which they contested the colonial quagmire so that they would not just survive, but also benefit from the changing circumstances of their own and their people's lives. Part 2 looks at the regulation of Aboriginal women's and girls' bodies by non-Aboriginal or Anglo-Canadian church and state authorities. The third part considers both Aboriginal and white women in publicly demarcated spaces. In each of these public encounters, preconceived ideas about whiteness and entitlement were reinforced and sometimes challenged. Throughout the collection, contributors grapple with the ongoing difficulty of writing women into history, incorporating feminist and postcolonial theory. The contributors employ a wide range of methods to make sense of their material, which ranges from personal testimonies to government records.

Contact Zones contributes to a large, diverse, and international historical literature on gender, race, and colonialism. Prominent journals have devoted special issues to research and discussion; scholars interested in gender and

race in the history of nation, empire, and colony have gathered at conferences; and edited collections and monographs have multiplied.[2] Anna Davin's
1978 article "Imperialism and Motherhood" initiated examination of the
crucial importance of gender in imperialism.[3] Subsequent work recovered
and celebrated white women's presence in imperialism.[4] But such an approach was considered problematic by those who linked gender and race
and thought white women complicit in imperial projects. Clearly it was
insufficient to uncritically recover and chronicle women's presence as colonizers. This realization led to recognition that some white women were in
agreement with racist practices and had economically and morally benefited from their beliefs.[5] As Anne McClintock explains in *Imperial Leather:
Gender, Race and Sexuality in the Colonial Contest,* white women were not
"the hapless onlookers of empire, but were ambiguously complicit both as
colonisers and colonized, privileged and restricted, acted upon and acting."[6] At the same time as women's historians were questioning the invisibility of women of colour, they were also unpacking the term "white" in
order to, as Vron Ware explains, "get away from the assumption that to be
White is to be normal, while to be not-White is to occupy a racial category
with all its attendant meanings."[7] This new awareness of "whiteness" as a
racialized term further complicated questions of privilege and colonial
citizenship. For example, in Canada white women were both powerful and
powerless. Their power rested in their whiteness, but they were constrained
by patriarchy.

The purpose of this book is to locate Canadian women's history within
colonial and imperial systems. To do so, the contributors build upon a large
and varied body of work dealing with themes in Canadian women's history
such as voluntary work, health, welfare, children, and education.[8] They also
add to the historiography on women's public and private lives, maternal
and equal rights feminism, and labour history.

In order to explore the social construction of femininity and masculinity,
with "gender as a category of analysis," women's history has moved well
beyond fixed, biologically grounded sex categories.[9] As the editors of *Gendered
Pasts: Historical Essays on Femininity and Masculinity in Canada* admonished
fellow scholars, it is important to remember that "however diverse the approach or conclusions of gender history, it is imperative that historians not
lose sight of the power relations that constitute, and are constituted by,
gender."[10] In short, while gendered identities can be and often are fluid,
they are also always full of power. Colonial relations were particularly loaded
with racialized and fluid power dynamics. Racial relations and constructions therefore form the centre of this book. While Canadian women's historians have actively revealed the histories of immigrant women and women
of colour,[11] most of this book focuses on Aboriginal women, with Anglo-
Canadian women also prominent.

Specifically, *Contact Zones* builds upon the work of Canadian scholars who have examined gender, empire, and contact zones. Mary-Ellen Kelm's study of Aboriginal health and healing in British Columbia during the first half of the twentieth century, for example, is concerned with the multiple implications of "colonizing bodies."[12] Karen Dubinsky, in her work on honeymooning and tourism at Niagara Falls, explores the connections between travel and race/ethnicity. Dubinsky identifies the fascination with which tourists gazed at and commented on North American Aboriginals and the ways they expected them to perform Indianness.[13] Gillian Whitlock's interpretation of the autobiographical writings of Susanna Moodie resituates the complex position of settler subjects.[14] There is now a large literature on topics as diverse as heroines and history, Anglican missionary women, imperial women, and captivity narratives.[15] From a range of perspectives, the contributors in this book pursue themes such as marriage, the power of state and church institutions, men's control over women's bodies, women's agency, and material culture.

Women's bodies have always been at the heart of feminism. While some scholars may credit social theorists with recognizing the importance of concepts of "embodiment," feminists have always been keenly aware of women's struggle to control their own bodies.[16] As Ruth Roach Pierson claims, "Women in the second half of the twentieth century have challenged the disembodiment implied by the airy Cartesian stance as sexist and racist." According to Pierson, the dichotomy between the mind and the body proposed by Descartes does not hold true for women: "Proof of our embodiment ... confronts us at every turn. But so does proof of our lack of control over that embodiment, and that is what women have sought to change."[17] By placing bodies at the centre of this text, we have revealed a new way of understanding the ways that colonial practices are carried out in day-to-day lived experiences in colonial contexts.

By engaging critically with the ideas of male social theorists, while attending to Audre Lorde's warning that "the master's tools will never dismantle the master's house,"[18] we can see how the scaffolding for much feminist thinking on the body has engaged with Foucault and Derrida.[19] Foucault's focus on the way that bodies respond to various regimes of domination, discipline, and normalization – or as he would have it, "the micropractices of everyday life" – resituated our understanding of knowledge/power relations and moved the body from the margins to the centre of social scientific research.[20] In general, feminist theorists have paid much attention to how knowledge/power is embodied.[21] However, as Donna Haraway reminds us, attention to bodies does not mean just the individual body. Collective experience must also be analyzed.[22] *Contact Zones* considers individual bodily experiences as well as the collective project so wonderfully rendered by Mary-Ellen Kelm's notion of "colonizing bodies."

In this book, feminist historical and theoretical literatures intersect with the literature on "contact zones," a term coined by Mary Louise Pratt in *Imperial Eyes: Travel Writing and Transculturation.* Pratt identified the "contact zone" as "the space of colonial encounters, the space in which peoples geographically and historically separated come into contact with each other and establish ongoing relations, usually involving conditions of coercion, radical inequality, and intractable conflict."[23] To some extent, Pratt extended the concept of the frontier. While an earlier idea of frontier was seen from the perspective of European expansion, Pratt's concept of "contact zone" emphasized "copresence, interaction, interlocking understandings and practices, often within radically asymmetrical relations of power."[24]

Imperial Eyes, together with other work, has moved us beyond linear narratives of progress, allowing for the disruption of the position of Aboriginal peoples as "Other," who at best might offer resistance to colonial powers. Australian historian Lynette Russell has noted that although the term is widely used throughout the historiography of Native/newcomer relations, "resistance" represents a very restricted category. Russell explains in her introduction to *Colonial Frontiers* that "cross-cultural encounters produce boundaries and frontiers. These are spaces both physical and intellectual, which are never neutrally positioned, but are assertive, contested, and dialogic. Boundaries and frontiers are sometimes negotiated, sometimes violent and often are structured by convention and protocol that are not immediately obvious to those standing on either one side or the other."[25] Similarly, imperial historian John MacKenzie argues for the plural and complex consideration of frontiers that are "hidden as well as visible, mentally and psychically constructed as well as geographically expressed and surveyed."[26]

Focusing on contact zones necessitates the consideration of metropolitan power and the significance of empires.[27] While Mary Louise Pratt questions cores and peripheries, Antoinette Burton suggests that just as colonies were sites of contact, so too was the United Kingdom.[28] In her introduction to *Gender, Sexuality and Colonial Modernities,* Burton acknowledges that "like colonial modernities themselves, the latest work on gender and empire must be considered as unfinished and therefore as open to re-interpretation as any other material practice or discursive regime."[29] Reflecting such sentiments, there is now a growing interest in the experiences of Indian, Canadian, and Australian women in the United Kingdom, with their position in the imperial metropolis and discourses of modernity providing key themes.[30]

Canada was colonized by two often conflicting imperial powers. Because of the divergent scholarship on English and French Canada, contributors to this book are concerned solely with British imperialism in constructing the colonial past. *Contact Zones* includes the regions of Pacific, western, and central Canada. There is still much to be learned about Atlantic Canada, and new directions are being forged by those interested in Quebec's colonial past.[31] Renewed interest in imperialism has forced Canadians in general, and all historians of women in Canada, to ask to what extent Canada was shaped by empire. How much of an influence was the British empire or British Canada? In light of a renewed consciousness about "white settler societies," Phillip Buckner has asked, "Whatever happened to the British Empire?" The question suggests that recent Canadian historians have downplayed the significance of the imperial experience.[32]

Dressing and Performing Bodies: Aboriginal Women, Imperial Eyes, and Betweenness

In 1980 Sylvia Van Kirk argued in *Many Tender Ties* that women played a central role in fur-trade society. Van Kirk emphasized the complexities of an "unusual society" in which many Aboriginal women were vital and active in the operation and success of the fur trade. Van Kirk also moved beyond viewing either Aboriginal or white women as passive victims and explored the "women in between" – Aboriginal women who married white men, and the white women who were threatened by these marriages.[33] With her themes of acculturation, contact zones, the politics of white womanhood, and the division between the colonized and the colonizer, Van Kirk was at the forefront of scholarship relevant to this volume.

The first part of *Contact Zones* shows that, far from being invisible, without agency or voice, Aboriginal women in Canada expressed their responses to colonization in ways that centred on the body, from dress to performativity. Informed by the work of Judith Butler, these authors take performance to mean the ways in which aboriginality was both discursively made and politically situated in the materiality of women's lives. Clothing, gesture, speech acts, and stage performances all tended to reconfigure relations between Aboriginal and non-Aboriginal in the Canadian contact zone. Often caught between two worlds, Aboriginal women bravely and creatively negotiated identity.

In "Sewing for a Living: The Commodification of Métis Women's Artistic Production," Sherry Farrell Racette alters how we interpret the day-to-day experiences of Métis women, many of whom used traditional artistic skills for economic gain by "dressing the West." She describes the extent to which fur traders and settlers relied on Métis women and argues that Métis and "half-breed" women were motivated to participate in the shifting economy and provide clothing for the various groups of newcomers who occupied the land. These women were crucial cultural brokers who ensured the comfort and survival of the American army, the North West Mounted Police, cowboys, and Aboriginals. Clothing served as a mediator, giving Métis women access to the economy. The bodies of newcomer men served as a stage upon which Métis women could perform their brilliant acts of artistry.

Dress is also a theme in Carole Gerson and Veronica Strong-Boag's "Championing the Native: E. Pauline Johnson Rejects the Squaw." Being of mixed ancestry (Iroquois and European), Johnson traversed two worlds. As Gerson and Strong-Boag note, she was often "viewed as a test of the outcome of racial mixing in border spaces." Johnson's power came partly because she could move between Aboriginal and newcomer worlds. Skeptical about the common view of Aboriginal women as victims, Gerson and Strong-Boag argue that Johnson "portrayed Native women as not only the equals of white women, but at times their superiors." They see Johnson herself as a woman who could negotiate a new understanding and garner from the newcomer society a level of respect for her own people, and for the women in her nation in particular. Gerson and Strong-Boag point out how self-conscious and deliberate Johnson was about creating her own identity. "Her success as a star of stage and salon depended in large part, as with other actresses of her day such as Sarah Bernhardt, on the vivid and implicitly erotic presence of comely female flesh. Johnson always paid close attention to costume and movement and understood full well that her attractive appearance was the source of much of her appeal."

In "Performing for 'Imperial Eyes': Bernice Loft and Ethel Brant Monture, Ontario, 1930s-60s," Cecilia Morgan provides a very different example of how two Native women disturbed racially based categorization and negotiated equitable status for Aboriginal Canadians through improved educational opportunities and living conditions. Their public appearances at historical society meetings, Canadian Clubs, Pauline Johnson's poetry readings, and harvest festivals often forced them into "playing Indian." Both were expected to present a "refined" and "authentic" Aboriginal womanhood, yet they most often delighted in moving beyond these images. "Rather than being fascinated by feathers and fringes, though," argues Morgan, "non-Native observers could be pleasantly surprised at the spectacle of an 'Indian' woman who wore a two-piece suit, nylon stockings, heels, and a carefully coiffed Western-style hairdo." Newspaper reporters categorized these women as somehow exotic, yet at the same time they were "proof of the efficacy of assimilationist strategies." Morgan not only demonstrates how Monture and Loft destabilized racial categories, but her work also reminds us of a major historiographical gap. The history of Native/newcomer relations in Ontario – and all of Canada – has often neglected individuals' stories, focusing instead on institutions and detrimental public policy.

In "Spirited Subjects and Wounded Souls: Political Representations of an Im/moral Frontier," Jo-Anne Fiske looks at the residential school, considering the impact of residential schooling upon generations of Aboriginal women and their families, and argues that "no true story of the residential school should be alleged; neither should we seek some fair balance of good and evil, of morality and immorality on a colonial frontier. Rather, we should seek to understand the postcolonial representations of the past and ask what they might offer to those who seek remedy for the harm they endured." She examines assumptions about relations between nuns and young girls in residential schools, inviting readers to reconsider the colonial encounter "as a clash of moral strangers and posit the im/moral frontier as a struggle to define the moral universe and to enforce others to abide within its *nomos* through control of material and symbolic resources." Fiske offers a unique perspective by arguing for lost motherhood as an area of mutuality between nuns and their wards. While children and nuns met as strangers, in the contact zone they shared a common link – they had each sacrificed their mothers. Fiske suggests that since nuns gave up their families and friendships to live in poverty, chastity, and obedience, they believed it was not asking too much of Aboriginal children that they should do the same. But survivors of the schools could not necessarily understand this sacrifice and have tried to recover from "spirit wounding," the trauma and harshness caused by the residential school experience and the hypocrisy they were exposed to.

Regulating the Body: Domesticity, Sexuality, and Transgression

The second part of *Contact Zones* asserts the importance of domesticity and family in the colonial process. A central theme here is sexuality, particularly the idea of Aboriginal women as sexually transgressive and therefore needing to be controlled. Domesticity and proper womanly behaviour were critical components in colonial relations.[34] Agents of church and state attempted to enact colonization by controlling and regulating women's bodies. The force with which imperial policy was applied to Aboriginal women was particularly harsh given the conditions and changes for women in Anglo-Canadian society. As these chapters show, Aboriginal women's transgressions from the norms of health, family, and sexuality were subject to harsh discipline. Colonial expansion was predicated in part on ideas about inferior and superior racial types, and European Canadians were generally considered racially superior to Aboriginal peoples.

In "Metropolitan Knowledge, Colonial Practice, and Indigenous Womanhood: Missions in Nineteenth-Century British Columbia," Adele Perry examines behavioural prescriptions as expressed by male missionaries in British Columbia between the 1840s and 1890s. She argues that many domestic ideals were like missionary baggage, transferred and transposed in new environments. But "metropolitan knowledge" was rarely adopted by Aboriginal women in British Columbia. Perry talks about "Christian conjugality," by which she means "lifelong, domestic, heterosexual unions sanctioned by colonial law and [the] Christian church." This discourse, she argues, was "a staple of the missionary program throughout nineteenth-century British Columbia." Mixed-race marriages were particularly worrisome to Christian missionaries, but more offensive were marriages not sanctioned by the church. And while church weddings were performed and "proper woman-hood" enforced, missionaries were most concerned to keep Aboriginal women in a state of working-class dependence. They wanted them to work but not become too independent. "Waged work gave Aboriginal women the dangerous independence that went with having ready cash income and the means to support themselves outside of male authority and the family."

Similarly, in "Creating 'Semi-Widows' and 'Supernumerary Wives': Pro-hibiting Polygamy in Prairie Canada's Aboriginal Communities to 1900," Sarah A. Carter examines the Department of Indian Affairs' (DIA) imposi-tion of Western discourses of sexuality, polygamy, and morality on prairie Aboriginal communities from 1870 to 1900. Placing polygamy in a North American and international context, she argues that "legal, political, and missionary authorities shared the view that a particular marriage model – of lifelong monogamy in the tradition of the Christian religion and English common law – symbolized the proper differences between the sexes and set the foundation for the way both sexes were to behave." Carter suggests that DIA officials hoped that polygamy would die out. They believed that they were "introducing a superior civilization, at the core of which were the 'proper' gender identities embedded in the cherished marriage model." Ar-guing that the interventions caused "turmoil and rupture," Carter points out that one of the outcomes of enforced monogamy and prohibition of polygamy, divorce, and remarriage (except in the event of the death of a spouse) was the appearance of a sector of society that was new to Plains people: impoverished single women, often mothers.

In exploring "Intimate Surveillance: Indian Affairs, Colonization, and the Regulation of Aboriginal Women's Sexuality" in Ontario during the first half of the twentieth century, Robin Jarvis Brownlie presents a compelling case to show the power individual Indian agents could have in the moral regulation and control of Aboriginal women's lives. Brownlie points out that not all agents behaved the same way, but they could each wield both the carrot and the stick: "An obvious mode of colonialism in DIA practice and discourse lay in agents' assumption of the right to regulate Aboriginal women's sexuality and enforce obedience to Euro-Canadian models of cor-rect gender expression. Indian agents had a unique ability to enforce these codes against women, especially through the use of financial control." For behaviour deemed incorrect, DIA agents could hold back treaty payments, take away children, and, especially painful during the Depression, refuse to grant relief. The DIA viewed with suspicion those who dared to resist. A familiar tactic used by DIA agents was to send children to residential schools. As well, they viewed mixed-race marriages favourably, as they fit with the DIA's objective of assimilation.

Joan Sangster's "Domesticating Girls: The Sexual Regulation of Aboriginal and Working-Class Girls in Twentieth-Century Canada" considers race and class in the Ontario Training School for Girls (OTSG), which opened in 1933. By then, training schools were well-established as a means of reforming the white working class and underclass. For Aboriginal Canadians, this was a time of increasing dependence on the state, the loss of self-sufficiency, and the beginning of a shift to the cities. As well as being subject to Indian agents' power to arrest, judge, and incarcerate, girls were trained as domestic workers in the belief that "honest labour was ... preventative and formative." Sangster's work is a reminder of the importance of interrogating class and capitalism within the matrix of colonial relations. She argues that "it is thus difficult to isolate one rationale for sexual regulation that trumps all others, because colonialism, gender, and class were closely intertwined, though they sometimes worked themselves out in contradictory ways." Like other contributors, Sangster finds that working-class families were also swept up in "a common project of regeneration, the goal of which was to create 'heteronorms' characterized by marriage and monogamy, male breadwinning/female domesticity, and premarital female sexual purity."

Bodies in Everyday Space: Colonized and Colonizing Women in Canadian Contact Zones

The geography of women's bodies in various Canadian temporal and spatial contact zones is the central theme of the third part of *Contact Zones*. The creation of civic, national, and imperial identity is explored within the context of developing ideas on Canadian mythmaking and national identity.[35] As Kathy Davis reminds us, "women's bodies have historically been used as a metaphor for nation – as, for example, Delacroix's famous rendition of Marianne as a bare-breasted, flag-bearing heroine, leading the French nation into battle."[36] In nationalist propaganda, white women have represented freedom and liberty, yet at the same time there is the recognition that women have not shared in the same freedom and liberty as men, and that not all women have shared power equally either. These are some contradictions played out in the chapters in this part, which show that danger, death, or, at the very least, reprimand was never far away for those who transgressed perceived norms.

In her examination of "Aboriginal Women on the Streets of Victoria: Rethinking Transgressive Sexuality during the Colonial Encounter," Jean Barman argues that the women in her study were not passive victims of colonization, but rather that racialized perceptions and the concomitant limited opportunities made it difficult for them to flourish in the local economy. The streets of nineteenth-century Victoria were a contact zone where a woman was defined as either "prostitute or crone." Barman tries to "understand what newcomers saw, why they saw what they saw, and what were the consequences for Aboriginal women." Aboriginal women's bodies were portrayed as sexually transgressive, and their claims to social spaces on streets, in dance halls, and even in their own homes were often greeted suspiciously. According to Barman, "all behaviour unlike that of women whence newcomers came was equated with prostitution, with a willingness to provide sexual favours if remunerated." As Perry notes and Barman reiterates, financially independent Songhees, Tsimshian, Haida, and other Aboriginal women "were almost inherently suspect at a time when females were expected to live visibly subservient to their fathers, husbands, or sons." Barman presents a classic case of a Euro-American double standard being introduced into the contact zone of late-nineteenth-century Victoria.

Myra Rutherdale's "'She Was a Ragged Little Thing': Missionaries, Embodiment, and Refashioning Aboriginal Womanhood in Northern Canada" examines how white Anglican missionaries in northern British Columbia, the Yukon, and the Northwest Territories wrote about Aboriginal women and children between 1870 and 1940. Health, hygiene, and sexuality were at the core of the mission program and were just as important as biblical scripture and religious training. Rutherdale focuses on contrasting images of clothing and appearance, and shows that while missionary women wanted to impose their clothing tastes on Aboriginal women, they also relied heavily on Aboriginal women to help them procure winter necessities. Aboriginal bodies were "cleaned, clothed, and medicated" in an effort to exact change and conformity. Clothing and comportment served as "markers of 'civilization'" – even representing conversion to Christianity. Rutherdale concludes that "it was often a question of the visibility of the body over the invisibility of the spirit." Missionaries were pleased to send mission newspapers photographs of Aboriginals who looked cleaned up and "civilized," as these were visible indicators of their success for the outside world. But these too may have been performed identities rather than fixed categories of conversion.

In "Belonging – Out of Place: Women's Travelling Stories from the Western Edge," Dianne Newell studies the literal "appearance" of colonizing white women on the margins of empire. She considers three white women travellers and their "belonging out of place" in the British Columbia coastal contact zone. She asks: "How did they position themselves in the environment (the point of view), acknowledge boundaries, and project a voice?" To answer these questions, Newell examines the published travel narrative of an 1890 steamboat excursion through the Inside Passage by well-connected New Yorker Mrs. Maria Septima Collis; the autobiographical story (based on her attempts in the late 1920s to "word" her North Coast field experiences as a painter) by British Columbia artist-writer Emily Carr; and the local coverage of the 1926 murder of Miss Loretta Chisholm, a young, single schoolteacher, near a northern salmon-canning centre. Newell sees the canneries as contradictory sites, "both at home (belonged) and out of place, not unlike the travelling women whose stories" she explores, and she finds that clothing and body language were read as markers of morality. While Chisholm was in many ways typical of her 1920s generation and was described as "a real lady," she was the one who was "out of place" in the BC coastal contact zone, not the young Aboriginal man accused of her murder. While Maria Collis was an aloof traveller, Chisholm settled, worked, and lived in the contact zone, and as a result she suffered grievous bodily harm.

In "The Old and New on Parade: Mimesis, Queen Victoria, and Carnival Queens on Victoria Day in Interwar Victoria," Katie Pickles examines patriotic celebrations in which Anglo-Canadian settler women were active in constructing colonial identity. While the celebrations included British and "oriental" symbols, in the patriotic display of Anglo-Canadian identity there was room for only assimilated Aboriginal Canadians. As Pickles shows, colonizing women could exert considerable influence on Anglo-Canadian identity. She focuses on the performance and activities of the Imperial Order Daughters of the Empire (IODE), dressing as, and keeping alive the memory of, the ultimate female imperialist role model, Queen Victoria. An older generation of female imperialists dressed as the Queen herself, while contemporary young women appeared as carnival queens, embodying civic, national, and imperial pride. Their symbolic crowning on the steps of the provincial parliament saw men with real power bowing down to glamorous young white women who pretended to be queens. Settler women's part in colonization was far removed from the experiences of Aboriginal women. Ending the collection with a chapter on settler women's power and whiteness is redolent of the way in which spaces for negotiating sexuality, race, gender, and class were gradually circumscribed by an increasingly harsh and pervasive white, elite, colonial system.

Contact Zones sets out to explore Canadian history in new ways. The history of colonization is a tense and difficult area to write about, but there are many vital and important stories, especially those of women, that need to be told. The contributors to *Contact Zones* resist homogenizing colonial experiences, instead offering diverse perspectives. Aboriginal and settler women, the state and society are all present and marshalled together around colonial themes. The material spans episodes that occurred in a variety of places and time periods, ranging from the late-nineteenth-century streets of Victoria to Ontario public gatherings, prairie homes, and mid-twentieth-century northern communities. Often outside the mainstream of Canadian historiography, the women's experiences uncovered in this volume serve as a potent reminder of the implications of colonization.

Notes

1   The ideas and phrasing are adapted from Judith Butler, *Bodies that Matter: On the Discursive Limits of "Sex"* (London and New York: Routledge, 1993). See Fiona Webster, "Do Bodies Matter? Sex, Gender and Politics," *Australian Feminist Studies* 17, 38 (2002): 191-205.

2   For example see *Women's Studies International Forum* 21, 3 (1998), a special issue on women, imperialism, and identity; "Feminisms and Internationalism," *Gender and History* 10, 3 (1998); "Reconstructing Femininities: Colonial Intersections of Gender, Race, Religion and Class," *Feminist Review* 65 (Summer 2000); *Canadian Woman Studies* 20, 2 (2000), a special issue on national identity and gender politics. Ruth Roach Pierson and Nupur Chaudhuri, eds., with the assistance of Beth McAuley, *Nation, Empire, Colony: Historicizing Gender and Race* (Bloomington, IN: Indiana University Press, 1998) is a selection of papers from the 1995 International Federation for Research in Women's History conference in Montreal. For edited collections see Tony Ballantyne and Antoinette Burton, eds., *Bodies in Contact: Rethinking Colonial Encounters in World History* (Durham: Duke University Press, 2005); Antoinette Burton, ed., *Gender, Sexuality and Colonial Modernities* (London: Routledge, 1999); Clare Midgley, ed., *Gender and Imperialism* (Manchester, UK: Manchester University Press, 1998); Julia Clancy-Smith and Frances Gouda, eds., *Domesticating the Empire: Race, Gender and Family Life in French and Dutch Colonialism* (Charlottesville, VA, and London: University of Virginia Press, 1998); and Nupur Chaudhuri and Margaret Strobel, eds., *Western Women and Imperialism: Complicity and Resistance* (Bloomington, IN: Indiana University Press, 1992).

3   Anna Davin, "Imperialism and Motherhood," *History Workshop Journal* 5 (Spring 1978): 9-66.

4   See Joanna Trollope, *Britannia's Daughters: Women of the British Empire* (London: Cresset, 1983); Claudia Knapman, *White Women in Fiji, 1835-1930: The Ruin of Empire?* (Sydney: Allen and Unwin, 1986); and Helen Callaway, *Gender, Culture and Empire: European Women in Colonial Nigeria* (Basingstoke, UK: Macmillan, 1987).

5   Margaret Strobel, *European Women and the Second British Empire* (Bloomington, IN: Indiana University Press, 1991), xi.

6   Anne McClintock, *Imperial Leather: Race, Gender and Sexuality in the Colonial Contest* (New York: Routledge, 1995), 6.

7   Vron Ware, *Beyond the Pale: White Women, Racism and History* (London: Verso, 1992), 18. See also Ruth Frankenberg, *White Women, Race Matters: The Social Construction of Whiteness* (Minneapolis: University of Minnesota Press, 1995).

8   See Kathryn McPherson, Cecilia Morgan, and Nancy M. Forestell, eds., *Gendered Pasts: Historical Essays in Femininity and Masculinity in Canada* (Don Mills, ON: Oxford University Press, 1999); Franca Iacovetta and Wendy Mitchinson, eds., *On the Case: Explorations in Social History* (Toronto: University of Toronto Press, 1998); Alison Prentice, Paula Bourne, Gail Cuthbert-Brandt, Beth Light, Wendy Mitchinson, and Naomi Black, *Canadian Women: A History* (Toronto: Harcourt Brace Jovanovich, 1986); Joy Parr and Mark Rosenfeld, eds., *Gender and History in Canada* (Mississauga, ON: Copp Clark, 1996); Franca Iacovetta and Mariana Valverde, eds., *Gender Conflicts: New Essays in Women's History* (Toronto: University of Toronto Press, 1992); The Clio Collective, *Quebec Women: A History* (Toronto: The Women's Press, 1987); Alison Prentice and Susan Mann Trofimenkoff, eds., *The Neglected Majority: Essays in Canadian Women's History,* vol. 2 (Toronto: McClelland and Stewart, 1985); Linda Kealey, ed., *A Not Unreasonable Claim: Women and Reform in Canada, 1880s-1920s* (Toronto: The Women's Press, 1979); and Alison Prentice and Susan Mann Trofimenkoff, eds., *The Neglected Majority: Essays in Canadian Women's History* (Toronto: McClelland and Stewart, 1977).

9   Joan Scott, *Gender and the Politics of History* (New York: Columbia University Press, 1988); Catherine Hall, *White, Male and Middle Class: Explorations in Feminism and History* (London and New York: Routledge, 1992).

10   McPherson, Morgan, and Forestell, *Gendered Pasts,* 11.

11   Jean Burnet, ed., *Looking into My Sister's Eyes: An Exploration in Women's History* (Toronto: Multicultural History Society of Toronto, 1986); Varpu Lindstrom, *Defiant Sisters: A Social History of Finnish Immigrant Women in Canada* (Toronto: Multicultural Historical Society of

Ontario, 1988); Franca Iacovetta, *Such Hardworking People: Italian Immigrants in Postwar Toronto* (Montreal and Kingston: McGill-Queen's University Press, 1992); Peggy Bistrow and Afua Cooper, *"We're Rooted Here and They Can't Pull Us Up": Essays in African Canadian Women's History* (Toronto: University of Toronto Press, 1994); Himani Bannerji, ed., *Returning the Gaze: Essays on Racism, Feminism and Politics* (Toronto: Sister Vision Press, 1993); Sherene Razack, *Looking White People in the Face: Gender, Race, and Culture in Courtrooms and Classrooms* (Toronto: University of Toronto Press, 1998).

12 Mary-Ellen Kelm, *Colonizing Bodies: Aboriginal Health and Healing in British Columbia, 1900-50* (Vancouver: UBC Press, 1998).

13 Karen Dubinsky, *The Second Greatest Disappointment: Honeymooning and Tourism at Niagara Falls* (Toronto: Between the Lines, 1999), 55-83.

14 Gillian Whitlock, *The Intimate Empire: Reading Women's Autobiography* (London and New York: Cassell, 2000), 38-65.

15 Karen Dubinsky, "Vacations in the 'Contact Zone': Race, Gender, and the Traveler at Niagara Falls," in *Nation, Empire, Colony* (see note 2), 251-69; Colin M. Coates and Cecilia Morgan, *Heroines and History: Representations of Madeleine de Verchères and Laura Secord* (Toronto: University of Toronto Press, 2002); Myra Rutherdale, *Women and the White Man's God: Gender and Race in the Canadian Mission Field* (Vancouver: UBC Press, 2002); Katie Pickles, *Female Imperialism and National Identity: Imperial Order Daughters of the Empire (IODE)* (Manchester, UK: Manchester University Press, 2002); Adele Perry, *On the Edge of Empire: Gender, Race, and the Making of British Columbia, 1849-1871* (Toronto: University of Toronto Press, 2001); Sarah Carter, *Capturing Women: The Manipulation of Cultural Imagery in Canada's Prairie West* (Montreal and Kingston: McGill-Queen's University Press, 1997).

16 On feminist theories of embodiment see Butler, *Bodies That Matter*; Judith Butler, *Gender Trouble: Feminism and the Subversion of Identity* (London and New York: Routledge, 1999); Elizabeth Grosz, *Space, Time and Perversion* (London and New York: Routledge, 1995); and Elspeth Probyn, *Carnal Appetites: Foodsexidentities* (London and New York: Routledge, 2000).

17 Ruth Roach Pierson, Marjorie Griffin Cohen, Paula Bourne, and Philinda Masters, *Canadian Women's Issues: Twenty-Five Years of Women's Activism in English Canada* (Toronto: Lorimer, 1993), 98.

18 Audre Lorde, "The Master's Tools Will Never Dismantle the Master's House," in C. Moraga and G. Anzaldua, *This Bridge Called My Back* (New York: Kitchen Table, Women of Color Press, 1981), 98-101.

19 For feminist postcolonial theorizing on bodies that engages with Lévi-Strauss, Fanon, and Derrida, see Radhika Mohanram, *Black Body: Women, Colonialism, and Space* (Minneapolis: University of Minnesota Press, 1999). See also Michel Foucault's books *Discipline and Punish* (New York: Vintage, 1979) and *The History of Sexuality, Volume 1: An Introduction* (New York: Vintage, 1980).

20 Kathy Davis, "Embody-ing Theory: Beyond Modernist and Postmodernist Readings of the Body," in *Embodied Practices: Feminist Perspectives on the Body*, ed. Kathy Davis, 1-7 (London: Sage, 1997), 7.

21 Nancy Duncan, ed., *Body Space: Destabilizing Geographies of Gender and Sexuality* (London and New York: Routledge, 1996); Susan Bordo, *Unbearable Weight: Feminism, Western Culture and the Body* (Berkeley: University of California Press, 1993).

22 Donna Haraway, *Modest_Witness@Second_Millennium.FemaleMan_Meets_OncoMouse: Feminism and Technoscience* (London and New York: Routledge, 1997); Donna Haraway, *Simians, Cyborgs and Women: The Reinvention of Nature* (London and New York: Routledge, 1991).

23 Mary Louise Pratt, *Imperial Eyes: Travel Writing and Transculturation* (London: Routledge, 1992), 6.

24 Ibid.

25 Lynette Russell, ed., "Introduction," in *Colonial Frontiers: Indigenous-European Encounters in Settler Societies*, 1-15 (Manchester, UK: Manchester University Press, 2001).

26 John MacKenzie, "General Editor's Introduction" in Russell, *Colonial Frontiers*, xi-xii, at xi.

27 See Ann Laura Stoler's influential work on how colonized bodies were shaped by the sexual policies of colonial states. Stoler extended Foucault's examination of the regulatory discourses of sexuality to race. Her work also allows Foucauldian ideas to be applied

to sexuality and colonization. Ann Laura Stoler, *Race and the Education of Desire: Foucault's History of Sexuality and the Colonial Order of Things* (Durham, NC: Duke University Press, 1995); Ann Laura Stoler, *Carnal Knowledge and Imperial Power: Race and the Intimate in Colonial Rule* (Berkeley: University of California Press, 2002). See also Mona Gleason, "Embodied Negotiations: Children's Bodies and Historical Change in Canada, 1930 to 1960," *Journal of Canadian Studies* 34, 1 (1999): 112-38; and June Hannam and Katherine Holden, "Heartland and Periphery: Local, National and Global Perspectives on Women's History," *Women's History Review* 11, 3 (2002): 341-49.

28 Antoinette Burton, *At the Heart of the Empire: Indians and the Colonial Encounter in Late-Victorian Britain* (Berkeley: University of California Press, 1998).

29 Burton, *Gender, Sexuality and Colonial Modernities*, 13.

30 Burton, *At the Heart of the Empire;* Cecilia Morgan, "Creating Transatlantic Worlds? Upper Canadian Aboriginal Peoples in Britain, 1830s-1870s" (paper presented to the Canadian Historical Association, 2003); and Angela Woollacott, *To Try Her Fortune in London: Australian Women, Colonialism and Modernity* (Oxford: Oxford University Press, 2001).

31 For some examples in English see Colin Coates, *The Metamorphoses of Landscape and Community in Early Quebec* (Montreal and Kingston: McGill-Queen's University Press, 2000); Coates and Morgan, *Heroines and History;* Carolyn Podruchny, "Festivities, Fortitude and Fraternalism: Fur Trade, Masculinity and The Beaver Club, 1785-1827," in *New Faces in the Fur Trade: Selected Papers of the Seventh North American Fur Trade Conference,* ed. William Wicken, Jo-Anne Fiske, and Susan Sleeper-Smith, 31-52 (East Lansing: Michigan State University Press, 1998); Carolyn Podruchny, "Baptizing Novices: Ritual Moments among French Canadian Voyageurs in the Montreal Fur Trade, 1780-1821," *Canadian Historical Review* 83, 2 (June 2002): 165-95.

32 Phillip Buckner, "Whatever Happened to the British Empire?" *Journal of the Canadian Historical Association* 4 (1994): 3-32; Phillip Buckner, ed., *Canada and the End of Empire* (Vancouver and Toronto: UBC Press, 2005).

33 Sylvia Van Kirk, *Many Tender Ties: Women in Fur-Trade Society in Western Canada, 1670-1870* (Winnipeg: Watson and Dwyer, 1980).

34 Margaret Jolly, "Colonizing Women: The Maternal Body and Empire," in *Feminism and the Politics of Difference,* ed. Sneja Gunew and Anna Yeatman, 103-27 (St. Leonard's, Australia: Allen and Unwin, 1993); and Kalpana Ram and Margaret Jolly, *Maternities and Modernities: Colonial and Postcolonial Experiences in Asia and the Pacific* (Cambridge: Cambridge University Press, 1998).

35 See Himani Bannerji, Shahrzad Mojab, and Judith Whitehead, eds., *Of Property and Propriety: The Role of Gender and Class in Imperialism and Nationalism* (Toronto: University of Toronto Press, 2001); Michael Dawson, *The Mountie from Dime Novel to Disney* (Toronto: Between the Lines, 1998); Daniel Francis, *National Dreams: Myth, Memory, and Canadian History* (Vancouver: Arsenal Pulp Press, 1997); Veronica Strong-Boag, Sherrill Grace, Abigail Eisenberg, and Joan Anderson, *Painting the Maple: Essays on Race, Gender, and the Construction of Canada* (Vancouver: UBC Press, 1997); and Andrew Parker, Mary Russo, Doris Summer, and Patricia Yaeger, eds., *Nationalisms and Sexualities* (London and New York: Routledge, 1992).

36 Kathy Davis, "Embody-ing Theory," 7.

Part 1
Dressing and Performing Bodies: Aboriginal Women, Imperial Eyes, and Betweenness

1
Sewing for a Living: The Commodification of Métis Women's Artistic Production
Sherry Farrell Racette

> My mother's name was Sauvé; she came from the North and was partly of Indian blood – Swampee. My father died when I was very young. He had been sick for a long time ... My mother had to support the family. She made fine moccasins and fine coats for other women.[1]

Charlotte Sauvé lived at the Red River Settlement in the mid-nineteenth century. Her son Norbert Welsh remembered the family she supported with her sewing as "seven children ... all small."[2] Charlotte's industrious application of her skills was not unusual. Johnny Grant described other hardworking women at Red River who "had a pleasant rivalry as to who made the finest garments for their husbands. They embroidered moccasins with silk or beads and also ornamented pieces of black cloth or leather which were used to carry a powder horn and a shot sack. Besides this they trimmed leather coats and gun covers, using porcupine quills sometimes with the silk and beads."[3] He noted that women also "tanned the hides and got the leather to make moccasins," did all their sewing by hand, and "in summer they helped in the hay-field and then in harvesting the grain."[4]

The women Johnny Grant described were dressing their husbands and children, wrapping them up in their finest silk and bead embroidery to present to an audience of friendly rivals who dressed their own families. Charlotte Sauvé, on the other hand, sewed to lighten the domestic burden of "other women" who could afford to purchase her goods. In 1868, when the Red River crops were devastated by a grasshopper plague, women organized to assist a community in profound crisis. Generally recognized as first-class needlewomen, prominent women formed a clothing club that divided the region into districts. Women such as Anne McDermott Bannatyne mobilized women in each area "to see that no one in her district went unclothed."[5]

The women of Red River are only one example of a female economy, which not only played a critical social role, but also occupied an essential niche within the overall economy of the fur trade and the myriad associated quasi-independent initiatives undertaken by free traders and family groups. In 1844 three women at Moose Factory were commissioned to make birchbark baskets, or rogans, for Governor George Simpson. The women, identified only as Mrs. Gladman, Mrs. Vincent, and Mrs. Flett, made several types of rogans, listed in the accounts only as "nest round, basket and flat" for a total cost of four pounds, five shillings.[6] The Gladman and Vincent families were related through marriage, suggesting the possibility of female kin-based work groups. Women organized their skills, time, and relationships to manufacture a range of products for a diverse market that included domestic consumption, exchange within and between communities, and consumption by other ethnic, and even international, markets.

Learning to Sew

The development of a skilled population of women was the result of home-based instruction and participation in the communal work of women, supplemented by exposure to the curriculum of early schools. Daughters learned from mothers, and those affiliated with fur-trade posts were also exposed to new techniques and markets.

Children of fur-trade families had access to a range of educational experiences. The active interest, financial support, and resources of a father determined the type of education a daughter received. Priority was often given to the education of sons, but the experiences of girls ranged from home schooling in the basics of literacy to the finest education available, according to the custom of the day. Montreal was an educational centre for fur trade children, particularly those of French-Canadian descent. British fathers often sent their children to England and Scotland. The three daughters of Elizabeth, a French-Sioux woman, and her husband Dr. David Mitchell, a surgeon in the British army at Michilimackinac, were sent to Europe for a "lady's education," while their brothers went to Montreal.[7] The loss of a father could dramatically alter the education of children. Unlike their older siblings, Thérèse and Madeline, the daughters of Jean Baptiste Marcot and his Odawa wife Migisan, were not sent to Montreal for an education because their father died when they were very young. They were raised according to the traditions of their mother's family and learned the business side of the fur trade through experience. Both sisters became successful fur traders. The Marcot sisters used their own resources to ensure that their children had access to at least a rudimentary education. Madeline's daughter, Josette Laframboise, was "at Montreal, at school" in 1809 when her father died, and her mother subsequently took over the family business.[8]

A tradition of woman-to-woman education had developed at Michilimackinac by the early nineteenth century, adding literacy to the traditional skills acquired through female mentorship. Thérèse Marcot Schindler and

Madeline Marcot Laframboise both became literate as adults and Madeline regularly gathered children at her home for instruction. Thérèse's daughter, Marienne Lasalière, was a student in a little school opened in 1802 by Angelique Adhemar.[9] Although the school was open for only a few years, Marienne Lasalière subsequently went on to open her own boarding school for the daughters of fur traders. According to Marienne's daughter, "the ... manager of the American Fur Company, persuaded my mother to open a school for the traders' daughters ... the first boarding school in the Northwest. It was not however, a school of the modern sort. The girls were taught to read, to write, and to sew, which latter accomplishment included the art of cutting and making their own clothes. In addition, they were taught general housekeeping."[10]

Cutting, which involved creating patterns to fit the intended wearer, and sewing clothes became a recognized area of female expertise. In January 1814 Robert Dickson sent John Lawe "Three dress'd Skins for a pr Capotes for me." In less than a month, Lawe's wife, Sophie Thérèse Rankin, had made and delivered the capote. Robert Dickson enthused to her husband: "My Capot is a famous one and fitts me to a hair. Thank your girl for the trouble she has had in making it so well. I would not change Coats with the Grand Turk."[11]

Early mission schools continued to integrate sewing into the curriculum for female students. In 1823 William Keating visited the Baptist missionary school on the St. Joseph River in what is now Michigan. He observed fifteen female students out of a total student population that ranged between forty and sixty children. He noted that "the females receive in the school the same instruction which is given to the boys, and are in addition to this, taught spinning, weaving, and sewing, both plain and ornamental; they were just beginning to embroider." He observed that the girls enjoyed embroidery, and needlework was used as a "reward and stimulus; it encourages their taste and natural imitation which is very great."[12] Local women were still teaching in the 1830s. Marienne Lasalière Fisher was teaching at the Michilimackinac Catholic mission in 1832, and by 1836 Elizabeth Grignon was teaching at Green Bay.[13]

The development of the mackinaw coat is credited to the industry and competence of the women of Michilimackinac. During a clothing shortage in the winter of 1811-12, Captain Charles Roberts at Fort St. Joseph, in protest at the threadbare state of his troops, made a "requisition to the storekeeper of the Indian department, a consignment of heavy blankets for the purpose of making them greatcoats."[14] John Askin hired a group of "half-breed women" who not only designed a garment that met the captain's requirements, but also delivered the order within two weeks. Roberts had ordered blue coats, but when the women ran out of blue blankets they completed the order with red coats and a few in plaid. Askin was soon inundated with requests for similar coats, including one from a dispatch runner who asked that his be cut above the knee.[15]

The Red River Settlement also became a site for the merger of indigenous knowledge, European notions of a lady's education, and the enduring demand for female production. From 1833 to 1835, English governess Mary Lowman included sewing and needlework in her program for girls at the Red River Academy. Following her marriage to retired Chief Factor James Bird, a male teacher changed the curriculum, causing John Dugald Cameron's daughter to complain, "Since Mr. Allen began to teach, none of them have been allowed the use of the needle."[16] Her father commented that he was "not sorry for" the change "as they all sew well enough – except some of the little ones." Seven daughters from the Campbell family "at one time traveled all the way from the Peace River to attend the Red River Academy."[17] Small groups of scholars attended schools such as the one established by Mrs. Ingham, who "opened a school in a house belonging to Mr. Logan. Among her pupils were: Harriet Sinclair, Annie McDermott, Barbara Logan and Caroline Pruden."[18] Matilda Davis, who had been educated in England, established a private school for girls at St. Andrews in the Red River Settlement around 1840.

Matilda Davis was the daughter of "John Davis and Nancy, a Half Breed."[19] Miss Davis' school offered full board for students from northern and western posts, and day instruction for local girls. The school's advertisement described a program consisting of "the usual branches of a solid English education, with French, Music, Drawing, Dancing, Plain and Ornamental Needle-work."[20] Many girls would return to the posts as the young wives of clerks and company officers, so sewing was an important part of the curriculum. Jane Bell Clark, the wife of the chief factor at Fort Carlton, wrote to both praise and encourage her daughter. "Miss Davis writes me you made all your own clothes this year and that you sew very neatly when you like."[21] Miss Davis herself excelled at the fine needlework she promoted, and her papers reveal that she had won "Best Silk Work Mottoes, 2nd Indian Shoes, 3rd Quilt Work" in local competitions. Her Hudson's Bay Company accounts show regular purchases of coloured seed beads and silk embroidery thread. One purchase in 1866 was noted as "Beads for Children." A list of the girls attending Miss Davis' school shows a preponderance of families long associated with the Hudson's Bay Company: Flett, Truthwaite, Dreaver, Murray, Clark, Black, Bunn, Cook, Bruce, Inkster, Christie, McKenzie, McKay, Hardisty, and Spencer.[22]

The schools operated by the Catholic Church served a different clientele. In 1829 Angelique and Marguerite Nolin, two Métis sisters from Pembina, opened the first school for girls in St. Boniface. Very little is known about the curriculum of early Catholic schools, but in 1826 Father Provencher wrote, "[I hired] our farmer's wife who is a Canadian [to] teach the girls of the school to work the flax and [buffalo] wool, in order that they might inspire in the others the desire to do so."[23] Weaving was still being taught in 1838 when the Hudson's Bay Company "began to pay the wages of two weaving instructors who taught the children of St. Boniface."[24] The school started by the Nolin sisters was taken over by the Sisters of Charity, or the Grey Nuns, in 1844. The Grey Nuns viewed sewing as a priority in their curriculum, and they had several women among them, particularly Mère Thérèse Coutlée and Soeur Lagrave, who excelled at floral embroidery, but they were not the first teachers to combine domestic skills and practical arts with literacy.[25]

The Red River Settlement was also not the only place to offer educational opportunities. In 1857 Father Georges Belcourt began to train Métis teaching sisters, the "Sisters of the Propogation of the Faith," for schools he established at Pembina and St. Joseph.[26] Two of the young Métisse teachers remembered by their students were Rachel Cavalier and Sister Ketchie.[27] The fledgling order was in existence only for three years. It was disbanded amid scandal and disgrace when three of the young women accused Father Belcourt of sexual misconduct.[28] Little information about Belcourt's schools has been found, but the presence of a group of local women teaching the children of families primarily engaged in hunting raises intriguing questions regarding their possible impact on the development and diffusion of art forms that thrived in that sector of the Métis collective.

At St. Paul, Minnesota, the Sisters of St. Joseph convent school attracted the daughters of American Fur Company employees, such as Celia Campbell, who attended for nine months in 1860 and learned "fancy needlework."[29] Susan Bordeaux Betteyloun described a school in Kansas, run by the Sisters of the Sacred Heart, where "hundreds of the children ... born of Indian mothers were brought to be cared for."[30] The girls' curriculum was based on "domestic arts," which included "sewing (plain and embroidery) ... and the painting of pictures on canvas, tapestry, and textiles."

Métis and mixed-race girls certainly had an early exposure to schools, but the duration and regularity of their instruction need to be carefully examined. How many girls actually attended school? In 1826 Provencher reported, "Our school is still going, but there are few pupils."[31] Many girls did not attend school. Female enrolment at local schools in the Red River Settlement in the last half of the nineteenth century was typically in the range of twenty to forty students per year. The 1873-74 attendance records for the Écoles de Saint Norbert indicate a fluctuating enrolment, which did not exceed twenty-eight in any month. In addition, attendance declined sharply in April and May, with entire families disappearing from the register.[32]

Schools did not merely serve as distribution points for European designs and sewing techniques. The curriculum was also moulded by local artistic traditions and the continuing importance of moccasins and other indigenous clothing forms as essential requirements for life in the West. The earliest surviving examples of floral work in the Red River region predate the arrival of the Grey Nuns in 1844.[33] An 1851 entry in the journal of the Mother Superior at St. Boniface also suggests a dynamic climate of exchange that took place outside the classroom. Soeur Lagrave, who worked at the St. Francois Xavier mission, decorated the interior of the new cathedral at St. Boniface with elaborate paintings of garlands and urns of flowers. These became a source of inspiration for "the native women, who enjoy silk-thread, bead and quill embroidery [and] came to copy these designs from the Cathedral."[34] These women came to view the visual spectacle of their own volition. Marie Rose Delorme, who spent four years at a St. Boniface convent, credited "the lessons learned at [her] mother's side" for her knowledge of traditional media and the skill that brought her renown as a mature artist.[35]

According to Madeline Mercredi Bird, the Holy Angels mission at Fort Chipewyan "didn't have real teachers in those days. The convent needed the girls to do all the work around the convent and to look after the priests' and brothers' clothing."[36] Madeline valued the practical experiences she had while a student there: "I learned everything at the convent, cooking bread, pastry and good meals, how to make butter, milk the cows and look after the chickens, how to do heavy laundry, decorate the altars, do beadwork, crochet, knitting, crafts and quilting."[37] With these skills she was able to sew her own wedding dress trimmed with handmade lace. However, her convent training was only one aspect of her education. She identified her mother and grandmother as important sources of knowledge:

> [My grandmother] used to stitch birchbark baskets and used roots for everything ... We used to collect all kinds of roots and tie them together. When she needed them to do crochet work she would soak them in water for awhile. Only she didn't use a store crochet hook, she crocheted with her fingers. She got along well with nature and nature gave her all the important things she needed ... She brought many of her secrets with her from her first home in St. Boniface ... She is the reason why I had such a good chance to learn so much of the early ways of survival and to make life more pleasant with flowers, decoration and fancy work on clothing.[38]

The womanly arts of practical and ornamental sewing were valued in both indigenous and European traditions and provided an area where values from diverse cultural heritages overlapped. William Keating observed that some might consider the fine needlework done by the girls at the mission school as "unsuitable to the situation which they are destined to hold in life," acknowledging the association of ornamental sewing with social status, leisure, and "ladies."[39] However, these girls would also have secured status in their pursuit of excellence in the traditional media of their mothers and grandmothers. While the domestic activities included in school curricula introduced girls to a range of skills and techniques, older, experienced women in the intimate circle of home and family provided the mentored learning that formed the principal vehicle for training, and sewing became a means to integrate the two knowledge systems.

Clothing Production at Fur-Trade Posts

The formative years of the fur trade saw the development of hybrid traditions that sprang from a social field crosscut by mercantile competition, economic necessity, basic survival needs, and cross-cultural dynamics. The Hudson's Bay Company employed its first tailor in 1706, and by the late eighteenth century, tailors were manufacturing clothing in western posts such as Manchester House and Edmonton. However, by the 1790s, Peter Fidler's rough journal at Chesterfield House revealed the presence of other sewers at the posts.[40] He documented the manufacture of sixty-three hide coats in addition to a hundred cloth coats made by the tailor. Post journals from York Factory and Churchill reveal that company employees had established relationships with First Nations women who contributed in a variety of ways to the daily life of each post. Between 1785 and 1786 the Hudson's Bay Company's London Committee received a series of complaints from Humphrey Marten at York Factory regarding Alfred Robinson, a young surgeon employed there. The complaints focused on Robinson's relationship with a young Cree woman. Although her name was not mentioned in the correspondence, she was probably Sehwahtahow, the maker of a long, painted, hide coat that Robinson brought back to England. The coat remained in the possession of his descendants, along with the memory and name of the woman who made it.[41] The number of hide coats that travelled to England with retiring fur traders indicates that Sehwahtahow was not alone.[42] The 1804-5 post journal at Fort Churchill documents women and the unidentified journal writer working side by side:

September 1st   Myself employed at times in cutting out Indian cloathing (having no Taylor) and the women belonging to the factory making the same, Snowshoes, shoes for the men and various things requisite.

October   Myself cutting out Indian cloathing and the women making these etc.

February   Myself cutting out and the Indian women making Indian cloathing, Shoes etc.[43]

The necessity of having women as companions and helpmates was an accepted aspect of fur-trade life. In 1809 Alexander Henry the Younger's list of the residents at Fort Vermillion included twenty-seven men with families and a combined total of sixty-seven children. Henry's journal described dances, weddings, and women who were usually "all busily employed" processing meat and hides, sewing, and procuring a significant amount of food.[44] However, as essential as a First Nations wife was, the daughters and grand-daughters of these unions became the preferred spouses. As Van Kirk's study of women in fur-trade society indicated, these women "supplanted" their mother's role for a complex array of reasons.[45] By the early decades of the nineteenth century, women living at fur-trade posts were predominantly of mixed descent, and their increased presence coincided with a decline in the employment of tailors.

By 1822 the Hudson's Bay Company's tendency to equate sewing with women's duty provided an opportunity to reduce expenditures. The minutes of the council for the Northern Department noted the presence of women's free labour in its decision to stop importing clothing for its workers (slops) and move to local manufacture.[46] "Our Slops are generally of good quality and by no means extravagantly priced, but as an other measure of Economy, we have it in contemplation to make up the Clothes principally at this place and at the English Establishments which ... would reduce the Expense very materially as the labour would actually cost nothing it being the duty of the Women at the different Posts to do all that is necessary in regard to Needle Work."[47] In addition to slops, hide coats in a variety of sizes were listed in the 1824 Moose Factory post inventory under "Goods of Country Manufacture."[48] The coats were among a repertoire of hybrid garments that combined indigenous aesthetics and function with trade goods and European clothing styles. Women created clothing that specifically addressed the challenges of a subarctic climate and occupational demands. Some garments, such as hide trousers, moccasins, mittens, warm coats, firebags, and leggings, were essential to survival. To be without them placed an individual's life in jeopardy.

By 1840 the female residents of fur-trade posts were described as "the only tailors and washer women in the country, and make all the mittens, moccasins, fur caps, deer skin coats etc., etc., worn in the land."[49] At York Factory in 1840, Letitia Hargrave described women sewing for her family needs: "An Indian half cast lady [who] took the ... opportunity to send 6 pairs of mocassins [sic] along with a request that we should send her tea and sugar in return. Another embroidered covers of fine scarlet cloth for the dogs that draw my cariole. Hargrave paid the cloth silk & ribbons & her return is to be a merino gown made in the London fashion."[50] Paul Kane noted that in 1846 the employment of the women at Fort Edmonton "consists of making moccasins and clothing for the men and converting the dried meat into pemmican."[51]

At Moose Factory, Samuel Taylor noted in his diary of February 1853 that his wife, Nancy McKay, had been issued the sewing that she was paid to do for the company.[52] He wrote, "The women of Moose Factory all got coverings, bags, nets and snowshoes on Friday 18th." Entries made in March 1856 provide greater detail regarding the items women were engaged to manufacture and the pressure they were under to complete the work within tight time constraints. "The women all got coverings, bags and shoes to make up on Monday the 10th. The women got their pay for making the company's coverings, shoes, bags, net, netting snowshoes, etc. etc. On Saturday the 29th the above work was not finished entirely yet. My wife finished all the above work and sent it all upon Monday 30th."[53]

Women were also considered essential members of long-distance expeditions. Sir John Franklin's expeditions included "the wives of three voyageurs, who were brought for the purpose of making shoes and clothes for the men."[54] Women also went on the expeditions led by John Rae, and George Simpson sent directions to Norway House regarding the role of women in Rae's 1847 expedition: "Three of the men attached to the expedition will be accompanied by their wives, as the services of the females may be useful in washing, making and mending people's clothes and moccasins, netting snowshoes ... and other necessary work; these women of course will have to be maintained as a charge on the expedition, to be moderately remunerated for any public service they may render, but to be paid by the people themselves for washing, etc."[55] Rae's list of "Articles Required for Arctic Expedition Summer 1853" included "60 pairs of good moose skin shoes," an indication of the volume of moccasins consumed during rigorous travel.[56]

By 1867, unmarried men such as Walter Traill were responsible for costs related to clothing care, and they contracted women living at posts to do their laundry, sew, and mend and make moccasins. Writing from Fort Ellice, Traill declared, "Truly our washing is our main expense for with the greatest economy, I am unable to reduce the cost of it to less than a fifth of my salary."[57] In 1879 at York Factory, George Simpson McTavish contracted Mrs. Sally Gunn to do his "washing, mending, making moccasins, mittens, leggings, ornamented with beads or silk, or anything necessary according to the custom of the country, for remuneration of one pound sterling." McTavish reported, "I got full value for my money, and during the years I was at York Factory, Sally never neglected me."[58] Walter Traill bemoaned the loss of his "washer woman" when she married suddenly, leaving him with no one to supply the clothing he required for the performance of his duties at Fort Qu'Appelle.[59] Traill illustrates how need and desire merged in fur-trader demand for Métis-style clothing. He not only dressed in the garb of the country, but also adapted his behaviour to incorporate Métis cultural performance into his own presentation of self. Isaac Cowie, another fur-trade consumer, described Traill as "a dashing horseman, clad in buckskin shirt and leggings, carrying a gun crossways in front in the bend of his left arm, and a quirt dangling from the wrist of his right," who on their first meeting proceeded to greet Cowie with a handshake on horseback, in "the fashion of the country."[60] This provides insight into the motivations of the predominantly male market for which Métis women sewed. The fur trader dressed for more than function. He was also attracted to the exotic and sought to emulate the physical ideal represented by the Métis hunters, runners, and voyageurs whose clothing he wore.[61]

A Female Economy: Self-Directed and Partnered Entrepreneurship
A series of women's accounts in the 1828 Abitibi post records, and the records of the women who produced birchbark baskets for George Simpson at Moose Factory in 1844, indicate that some women were marketing their goods and skills, providing sewing and artistic services beyond the confines of their resident post. The Officer's Shop Book at Abitibi provides a rare window into the economic lives of six women: Madame Gervais, Nancy Folds, Nanny Governor White, Betsy Pottinger, Mrs. Doré, and "Nancy Kirkness say Spence."[62] While the accounts do not specify that women were being paid for artistic and clothing production, it seems a reasonable conclusion. Nancy Kirkness Spence's account had the greatest volume of transactions. The items charged to her account, with few exceptions, were materials required to produce clothing and decorative objects, such as beads, cloth, scissors, thimbles, tape, and thread. Also noted are payments or transfers made by different men, most of them company officers not resident at Abitibi. Men's names listed beside the note "By transfer," with amounts entered as credits in Nancy Kirkness Spence's 1828 accounts, included:

W. Mittleberger
R.J. Hamlyn
James Hargrave
Joseph Charles
D.J. Jones
C. Cumming
D. Finlayson
John Charles
A. Stewart[63]

Other women's accounts were less active, but Nancy Folds received credit from "Ed. Ermatinger, C. Robertson, A. McDonald, W.G. Rae and Rob't. Miles." James Hargrave and R.J. Hamlyn appear in Nanny Governor White's account, and Betsy Pottinger received transfers from John Clarke, Joseph

McGillivray, and one entry noted as "Cash, Prompt Sales." These economic transactions, although tracked through company books, appear to be an example of female entrepreneurship.

In addition to dressing their own families and sewing "for the company" at fur-trade posts, Métis women also dressed a steady stream of men coming to the Northwest as travellers, adventurers, and hunters. Throughout the nineteenth century there were three basic paths of westward travel. The old water route from the east led from Lachine, through the Great Lakes to Fort William, down the Rainy River system to the Winnipeg River, and south to the mouth of the Red River on Lake Winnipeg. By 1859, travellers could take the train from Lachine to Chicago, and from there to Saint Cloud, Minnesota, continuing by land or water to Pembina and on to the Red River Settlement. A second route, by ship to York Factory, continued by York boat brigade to the same destination. The Red River Settlement served as a supply depot for incoming fur traders, exploring expeditions, hunters, and adventurers travelling westward from one Hudson's Bay Company post to another, visiting, in sequence, Fort Ellice, Fort Qu'Appelle, Fort Carlton, Fort Pitt, Fort Edmonton, and Jasper House. A third route came up the Missouri River from St. Louis and followed a similar string of American Fur Company posts: Fort Pierre, Fort Clark, Fort Union, and Fort Benton. Travellers were dependent on fur-company posts for supplies. Also to be found at the posts were Métis men who served as guides and hunters, and Métis women to manufacture the particular clothing required for the rigours of western travel.

The narratives of, and journals kept by, men who travelled north and west illustrate the regularity of such consumers. Women responded to the ready market, and by the mid-nineteenth century, Métis girls at Red River were the objects of admiration, described by Scottish fur trader and author Robert Ballantyne as "generally very pretty; they make excellent wives ... With beads, and brightly coloured porcupine's quills, and silk, they work the most beautiful devices on the moccasins, leggings and leathern coats worn by the inhabitants; and during the long winter months, they spin, and weave an excellent kind of cloth from the wool produced by the sheep of the settlement, mixed with that of the buffalo, brought from the prairies by the hunters."[64] J.J. Hargrave described "the making of Indian shoes or moccasins" as one of the settlement's "most common exercises of domestic manufacture."[65] In 1856 Dr. John Bunn at the Red River Settlement apologized to family friends in England for his inability to replace the gifts that his recently deceased stepmother, Phoebe Sinclair, had regularly supplied: moccasins, dolls, and birchbark baskets. The items he ordered "were not ready to time, as the demand is somewhat brisk by the number of visitors and passers-by."[66]

Travellers and newcomers generally emulated Métis dress, with its combination of indigenous and imported elements, as the most suited to the conditions of the country. In 1819 Father Dumoulin, a missionary at Pembina, wrote the bishop of Quebec, asking, "Is it necessary to be very particular about saying Mass in moccasins out here where nothing else is worn?"[67] The Earl of Southesk described the "quaint and pretty dress" of the Sisters of Charity at the Catholic mission at Red River in 1859. The sisters wore "moccasins instead of shoes, according to the universal custom of the country, to which even the bishops conformed."[68] It is possible that the sisters benefited, as did the priests, from a tradition described by Louis Schmidt in which Métis members of the Catholic community supported the mission. Hunters saved the finest cuts of meat, traders gave "sa meilleur piece de drap pour le missionaire" (the best piece of woolen cloth for the missionary) and women "rivalisaient de zèle et d'empressement pour confectionner les souliers et des mitaines du prêtre" (had a zealous rivalry, eager to make the shoes and mittens of the priest).[69] George Winship recalled his initial prejudice in 1867 "against the style of men's dress in vogue" at the Red River Settlement. His later adoption of Métis dress, which he described as "both comfortable and ornamental," was the result of its practicality coupled with his desire to emulate Métis men, who he felt "enjoyed life greatly," leading "an ideal life hunting, traveling and trading, being in the open and riding spirited horses."[70] "Before many months passed I was attired much the same as they including moccasins ... red sash and capeaux. I even began to speak with the accent of the native ... completely absorbed by my environment and made over into a child of the wild."[71]

The continuing importance of Métis dress was evident in 1870 when William Butler described himself as having "all the appliances of half-breed apparel ... possessed of ample stores of leggings, buffalo 'mitaines' and capotes, wherewith to face the biting breeze of the prairie and to stand at night the icy bivouac."[72] In 1871 Charles Napier Bell posed for a photograph he titled "In Prairie Hunter's Costume."[73] Wearing moccasins, fringed leather pants and jacket, fur hat, and gauntlets, Bell tucked a pistol, knife, and beaded firebag into his belt or sash and, holding a pair of snowshoes and a rifle, appeared ready for all the challenges of western travel. He used his gear from 1872 to 1873, trapping and hunting along the North Saskatchewan River.[74]

Market demand at the Red River Settlement was high, but not unique. Other locations served as gateways and supply depots. In 1851 Swiss artist Rudolph Kurz was employed as a clerk at Fort Union on the Missouri River, straddling the border between what is now North Dakota and Montana. His 17 November journal entry noted that he had "finally decided to order from Madame Bombarde a winter suit made of buckskin. Up to the present

Embroidered mitten or "mitaine" essential for winter travel in the North West, ca. 1860, "Chipewyan Halfbreeds," Fort Simpson, North West Territories. Caribou and moose hide, silk ribbon and embroidery thread, wool.
Bernard Rogan Ross Collection, A.848.7 © The Trustees of the National Museums of Scotland

time I have worn my summer clothes, with a buckskin shirt." Four days later he wrote, "Today I received my winter suit of calfskin, made with hood, 'metif fashion,' and sewed through with sinew."[75] The Madame Bombarde who made Kurz's winter suit was contracted, with her two daughters, to make clothing, while her husband, Alexis Labombarde, was contracted as a hunter, guide, and labourer. According to Kurz, the women were "employed regularly at the fort to make clothes for pay (credit on account)."[76] Items listed on an inventory made at Fort Union on 15 May 1851 may be examples of their artistic production:

Charles Napier Bell, 10 March 1871, "In Prairie Hunter's Costume"
Archives of Manitoba, N10514

1 pair Garnished Leather Pants $6.25
11 pairs Garnished Mockasins $5.50[77]

Madame Labombarde was born Nancy Kipling. Her 1885 scrip application provides a rare opportunity to hear her voice. It is written in the first
person and appears to have been dictated. "I was born at Winnipeg about
1810. My father was James Kipling. My mother was Marguerite Okenese.
My father was a halfbreed. My mother was an Indian."[78] Fur-trade records
and journals identify her father as John Kipling, also known as John Rem or
Ram Kipling to distinguish him from other men of the same name.[79] He was
described as a "native of Rupertsland," probably born on Hudson Bay. He
joined the service of the Hudson's Bay Company at Albany in 1798, working his way from middleman to steersman on the Albany boats. According
to his Hudson's Bay Company employment records, Kipling was steersman
at Norway House by 1811, but he was listed among the thirteen men at
Pembina for the 1811-12 outfit as "Kipling, John Ram," along with "Kipling,
John Sr., Kipling, John Jr."[80] He was at Pembina until 1815. The following
year he was interpreter at Turtle River. He was at "the Forks" from 1817 to
1819.[81] His employment with the Hudson's Bay Company ended in 1821.
The Kipling family remained on the high plains and reappears in the historical record living at Fort William, an old fort near Fort Union that was
used to house horses and the Métis families employed to care for them.

Nancy Kipling's scrip application provides an understated synopsis that
belies the drama of her life. "I married twice. The first time to Michel Gravel,
on the plains about 1825." She also named her two daughters from her first
marriage, Marguerite and Domitilde, born in 1826 and 1828. Her daughters'
scrip applications identified their father as a "Halfbreed."[82] He was employed
in 1828 and 1830 by the American Fur Company as a Cree interpreter.[83] By
the early 1830s he was working as a clerk. In 1834 Nancy accompanied her
husband to Fort Cass on the Yellowstone River, but returned to live in her
father's accommodations at Fort William. James Hamilton, who was in charge
at Fort Union, wrote "M. Gravelle did not like fort Cass quarters for his wife
and has sent her back here, Jack Ram's family will in a few days number
fourteen!!!"[84]

The 1835-36 journals kept by Francis A. Chardon and Charles Larpenteur
at Fort Union and Fort Clark documented a series of tragic events in Nancy's
life. In July 1835 tensions developed between Jean Baptiste Gardepie, who
shared quarters with the Kipling-Gravel family, and the Deschamps family,
which resulted in the death of François Deschamps Sr. In the fall of 1835,
Michel Gravel was killed by the Blackfoot while trapping beaver on Milk
River.[85] Tensions between the Gardepie and Deschamps families erupted on
the night of 28 June 1836 when Mother Deschamps urged her sons to avenge

their father's death. Charles Larpenteur was awakened when, he wrote, "[Nancy Kipling,] crying bitterly, informed me that Deschamps had killed her father and shot at her ... I was awakened by loud raps and voices at the door, which latter [sic] I could distinguish to be those of females, crying, 'Open the door! quick – they are fighting – they have killed my father!' They were the widow of Michel Gravel and her mother, the wife of Jack Rem."[86] Nancy lost both her father and husband in one year and witnessed the extermination of the Deschamps family, an extraordinary event that ended with the burning of old Fort William. Larpenteur recorded: "[It was] not a crueler death than they deserved, but much crueler than I wished to witness."[87] Nancy returned either to Pembina or the Red River Settlement later that year, where her baptism was entered in the Anglican register on 16 February 1836: "Nancy Keppling, An Adult Woman."[88] As a young widow with at least two small children, Nancy quickly remarried. According to her scrip deposition, she was married "to Alexis Labombarde at Red River, about 1835." Labombarde worked for the American Fur Company at Fort Union. Kenneth McKenzie mentioned him in 1834, writing, "I wish you to re-engage Labombarde before you come down."[89] Most records describe him as a "half-breed," although Nancy identified him as "a plain Indian" who "resided at various places throughout Manitoba and the Territories."[90] In fact, the Labombardes spent most of their time along the Upper Missouri.

In 1843 Alexis was at Fort Pierre, where he was engaged to assist John James Audubon's zoological expedition. Nancy, described by Audubon as "a good-looking young woman," accompanied them.[91] Edward Harris, a member of Audubon's party, acquired a finely quilled hide frock coat, wrap-around moccasins, a pouch with quilled strips and quill-wrapped fringe, and a pad saddle. These items are currently in the Montgomery Museum in Montgomery, Alabama, and were probably acquired from Nancy Labombarde. Harris' accounts indicate that he purchased elk and antelope hides and paid someone for "making moccasins."[92] Audubon also acquired a similar fitted coat with quilled decoration that is now in the collections of the American Museum of Natural History.[93]

Rudolph Kurz described a conflict between Nancy and her employer Edward Denig that resulted in her departure from Fort Union, which had served as her home base for more than twenty years. "Madame la Bombard ... refused Mr. Denig the loan of her dogs [he] retaliated by giving her no more work to do now she has to use her own supply of meat for food."[94] On 10 April 1852 Kurz noted Alexis Labombarde's arrival at a hunting camp "for the purpose of making an arrangement with Belhumeur whereby he could induce the latter to go along with his family to the Red River. In other words, La Bombarde is employed by Mr. Denig for another year but his family is not included in the contract. They must go. The metifs leave to-morrow with their horses."[95] The duration of Nancy Kipling Labombarde's residence along the Missouri River, the economic unit she formed with her two daughters, the presence of other Métis women in the community of itinerant workers along the network of American Fur Company posts, and the marked stylistic similarity of coats collected in the Upper Missouri region suggest an almost workshoplike environment.[96] Two decades of relative stability following her marriage to Alexis Labombarde provided her with economic security and safety, while her proximity to the American Fur Company provided the materials and market demand necessary for a voluminous output.

In 1859 the Earl of Southesk purchased both functional clothing and decorative items as he travelled westward. He noted that purchases made at the Red River Settlement, which included two fire bags and several watch pockets, were made by "half breed women." At Fort Carlton he contracted Mary

Watch pocket, 1859-60, Métis, acquired by James Carnegie, 9th Earl of Southesk at the Red River Settlement.
Earl of Southesk Collection, Kinnaird Castle, Brechin, Scotland

"Florida" Monkman Tait to do some unspecified sewing and make mocca-sins. In addition, Richard Hardisty "insisted on giving me three beautifully finished sets [of moccasins]" and "a leather hunting-shirt for wear in the Rocky Mountains, where the dead and rugged branches in the thick fir woods make a terrible havoc of all woolen clothes."[97] At Fort Edmonton, Southesk's party purchased further equipment, and while staying at an Iroquois Métis camp in the foothills along the Mcleod River, he noted that "the wife of one of the [half-breed] hunters has made me a gun-cover of moose leather, or-namented with fringes and narrow braidings of red and black cloth, after the picturesque fashion of the country."[98] On his return journey, the party was dressed in fresh winter clothing at Fort Pitt, which included "roomy flannel-lined, fingerless gloves, which we carried slung round our necks, that our hands might be slipped in and out as circumstances happened to require."[99]

Also travelling west in 1859 was Dr. Augustus Thibido of the Northwest Exploring Expedition. At the Red River Settlement on 12 August he hired Pierre Desnommé, who had just been with the Southesk party, as a guide. Thibido "agreed with the half-breed for his wife to make [him] a pair of buffalo skin breeches & shirt," which he received on 19 August, noting: "Got a full hunter suit of buffalo skin dressed from Pierre. Traded a hand-kerchief for a pair of moccasins."[100] Mrs. Desnommé was Madeleine Amyotte.[101] She created a complete outfit in less than a week. Another pair of travellers on the same route in 1862, Viscount William Milton and Dr. Walter Cheadle, contracted Judith Morin, the wife of their guide Louis Laronde, to make twelve pairs of moccasins, one caribou-skin hunting shirt, one pair of moose-skin breeches, and leggings at the Red River Settlement prior to setting out. They also traded their saddle for "an Indian pad" at a local store. They "discarded boots and coats, adopting the costume of the country, viz. mocasins [sic] and hunting-shirts of the Cariboo deer."[102]

Husbands and fathers often provided the intial contact with a potential customer. Southesk met Philip Tait's hunting party from Fort Carleton and camped nearby. He noted: "Tait himself paid me a special visit, accompa-nied by his six-year-old daughter whose bright black eyes and pleasant smiles seemed to bring sunbeams with them to my lonely tent."[103] It may have been this child who inspired Southesk to commission Mrs. Tait to make gifts for his own three children. Madeleine Amyotte Desnommé and Judith Morin Laronde secured their customers through their husbands' employ-ment as guides. In 1889 Baptiste Tastewich, identified as a "Half Breed Iroquois" by the man who proved to be his eager customer, greeted Warburton Pike, an English adventurer travelling through the Peace River district on his way to the barren grounds. Tastewich carried "a dozen pair of the best moose-skin moccasins from his daughters, who were beyond com-pare the belles of Hudson's Hope." Tastewich advised Pike not to travel and

made grim weather forecasts, recommending that the party "wait a fort-
night ... while he would make [Pike and his companions] five pairs of snowshoes." Like many travellers before him, Pike was feted with "a ball given
every night, and the moose-dance, rabbit-dance, and duck-dance were kept
up till the small hours." [104]

Women's production was important merchandise in free traders' economic
activity. In 1844 Peter Garrioch, a free trader, noted: "Sold one of my coats
for four robes. I still have three remaining, thank fortune." [105] A cart train of
a "dozen Métisse" traders arrived at Fort Berthold in 1851, where they were
described by Kurz as wanting "horses, either in exchange or by purchase ...
All were dressed in bright colors ... tobacco pouches, girdles, knife cases,
saddles, shoes, and whips were elaborately decorated with glass beads, porcupine quills, etc." He bartered for "some beautiful work at a reasonable
price ... a knife ... with its embroidered sheath ... a most beautifully ornamented pouch and whip ... six pairs of children's shoes, three pairs of larger
moccasins, one pair of gloves for winter lined with beaver and three
ceintures." [106] At St. Paul, Minnesota, the same year, Frank Blackwell Mayer
observed a cart train "laden with buffalo hides, pemmican ... embroidered
leather coats, moccasins, saddles, etc. These they sell or exchange at St. Paul
and return again to their secluded homes." [107] He described the three primary media used by Métis women: "beautiful garnished work of beads, porcupine quills and silk."

Some traders marketed women's production on a large scale. Louis Goulet
recalled his father conducting "a roaring business, specializing in buying

North West Mounted Police pad saddle, ca. 1880, Métis type
Royal Canadian Mounted Police Museum, Regina, Saskatchewan

and selling suits of moose, deer and cariboo hide."[108] Moise Goulet hired women to create clothing for him and travelled to different communities to purchase garments to market to the Hudson's Bay Company and American markets. Workers described as "les vieilles" (elderly women) were employed "sur une assez grande échelle" (on a grand scale) at hivernant (winter) camps. In 1867 the Goulet family left St. Norbert and travelled across the northern plains to the Judith Basin in Montana, intending to winter in the Saddle Lake region of Alberta and from there settle at St. Albert. That year Moise Goulet reportedly made five trips to Lac La Biche and two to Lesser Slave Lake, where "il revenait chaque fois chargé d'habits de peau d'orignal et de caribou, de peleteries surtout de loutre et de castor" (he returned each time, loaded with deer and elk hide clothing, fur pelts, especially otter and beaver).[109] As money was rarely used in these bartering exchanges, hide clothing served as both commodity and currency.

Métis women responded to the needs of the people they dressed and consciously created consumer desire for the goods they produced, often using the bodies of their own men for advertisement. The similarity of clothing and accessories worn by a range of men across a broad terrain, as documented in both visual records and museum collections, indicates the success of their project. But while the decline of the fur trade marked the end of the social and economic infrastructure created by the network of posts, it did not mark the end of women's production. The fur trade continued, very much as it always had, throughout the north, and the early years of the twentieth century saw women in other regions adapt to the dramatic shifts in their economy, transforming their production to suit new needs and new markets.

Marie Rose Delorme Smith, who by 1881 had married Charley Smith and settled on a ranch at Pincher Creek, Alberta, found that her sewing skills had increasing economic importance. The skills she had learned from her mother and at the convent in St. Boniface served a new purpose.[110] She was among a group of Métis women who competed for the prize money offered for fancy costume at the Calgary Stampede. The beaded glove or gauntlet with heavily embellished cuffs emerged at this time and became, with the fringed and beaded vest, essential elements of "cowboy" or western dress. Marie Rose described her "buckskin gloves [which] were very much sought after by the early settlers of our community from Mcleod River to Pincher Creek." The glove was not part of the traditional repertoire of garments. According to Marie Rose:

> When Arthur Rouleau was once returning from [Fort] MacLeod [sic], he lost one of a pair of brand new gloves. Disgustedly he threw the other glove on the table saying, "Here, Mrs. Smith, you may have this." I ripped the glove, cut a pattern from it and made my first pair of buckskin gloves, stitching

them by hand. Then I branched out making buckskin shirts and bedroom slippers, drawing my own beaded designs. When my husband saw how interested I had become in the buckskin work ... he ... brought me – yes – a brand new sewing machine. I thought then that the whole wide world was mine.[111]

Marie Rose received commissions to create beaded garments for hotel employees at Waterton National Park and even created garments worn by First Nations men and women to construct the images of "Indianness" used in postcards and performances created for consumption by tourists.[112]

In 1909 the Canadian Handicraft Guild, which took an active role in promoting and marketing traditional arts unique to Canada, began a working relationship with the Department of Indian Affairs. One of the Guild's members, Amelia Paget, initiated a project in 1913 that involved a Métis woman from the Qu'Appelle Valley who maintained her family with her artistic production. Paget described their meeting in her report:

> I left Edgeley towards the end of August and returned to the [Qu'Appelle Industrial] School. Here I made enquiries for the address of a certain French family, by name of Blondeau, whose women were noted years ago for the fancy work they did in quill, silk and beadwork, as well as for moccasin making. Finding that the three remaining members of the family, Madame Blondeau, and her aged sister Isabelle, and M[a]lanie the daughter still occupied the little cottage on their small holding directly across the Lake from the School, I rowed over to their place which is most beautifully situated on the South side of the Lake. Here I found that M[a]lanie was the sole support of her family, and that she earned every cent by her excellent work. Her mother and Aunt Isabelle were too old and feeble to help her in any way towards earning anything for their daily needs. But they had taught her their handicrafts, and what that meant to them nobody can ever fully realize. M[a]lanie was doing a beautiful piece of quill work (a tea-cozy) on smoked deerskin. As it was an order I could not obtain it for the Shop. It has been impossible for her to do any work except where the materials were provided, as of course she has not had the means to provide anything herself. I left some deerskin and beads with her to do some work for the Guild which she was delighted to get.[113]

A quillwork tea cozy associated with Malanie Blondeau is in the collection of the Glenbow Museum.[114] Given the volume of her output as the sole support of her family, it is probable that similar household articles in museum collections can be traced either to her hands or to other Métis women in the region.

Tea cozy, Métis, by Malanie Blondeau, mid-twentieth century. Cotton, buckskin, quills, rabbit skin, 27 × 29 cm.
Collection of Glenbow Museum, Calgary, Canada

Porcupine quillwork persisted as a preferred medium in the southeast corner of Saskatchewan, but the forms had shifted to accommodate a female consumer interested in objects that would beautify her home or her person. A quillwork sewing kit belonging to Rosalie Laplante Laroque of Lebret is in the collection of the Royal Saskatchewan Museum. The kit was in active use in the 1890s and was organized by a family member or curator into a framed display with samples of material and stitches used.[115] The persistence of quillwork in this sector of the Métis population can perhaps be related to their late movement toward settlement. The profound poverty that fell upon this community in the post-1885 era could also have been a factor. Quills, natural dyes, and hide could be obtained from nature, needing only an application of a woman's energy, knowledge, and artistic skill. Stroud and beads had to be purchased.

Malanie Blondeau was born in 1866, the daughter of Simon Blondeau and Françoise Desjarlais. Her mother and Aunt Isabella were the daughters of Antoine Desjarlais and Catherine Allary. The last of the Saskatchewan buffalo hunters, the Blondeaus were at the Battle of Grand Coteau in 1851.[116] Like other families in the region, they shifted between applying for treaty and scrip, following a survival strategy Simon Blondeau imposed on his children during the difficult transition years. Elder Lucy Desjarlais Whiteman recalled her family's experiences:

> The women never stopped talking about the lost lands. They were more bitter than the men who were told there was more land and they believed that. It's, Mr. Blondeau, my great grandpa wouldn't let the boys take treaty and yet he let the daughters take treaty. I don't know why. They had scrips for the boys and the girls took treaty. Grandma and her sister went down on treaty day with their carts and they sold their treaty because they got flour and sugar and things like that you know, groceries. That was government policy, they could do that, but they had nothing after that. They didn't understand.[117]

The artistic skill that enabled the three Blondeau women to maintain their tenuous hold on the small parcel of land they were living on in 1913 was to find a new application. Following her meeting with Malanie Blondeau, Amelia Paget embarked on an energetic campaign to get her hired "on the Staff of the School, to teach the little Indian girls." She gave Malanie her strongest endorsement, urging the Department of Indian Affairs to take "this opportunity of having such a splendid teacher, so competent in every way."[118] The Canadian Handicraft Guild followed up with correspondence urging the department to act. As a result, Duncan Campbell Scott replied that "while the school authorities, of course, are not called upon to furnish instruction of this kind ... I think that if the Department could secure the services of this girl at a small wage, say $15.00 or $20.00 a month it would be well to make the appointment in the interests of the children of the school."[119] As a result, the Qu'Appelle Industrial School was the only residential school in Canada with a budget line item for craft instruction in the annual reports of the Department of Indian Affairs. The budget item "Salary, M[a]lanie Blondeau, instructor in Indian handicraft," appeared continuously in the annual reports from 1914 to 1931.[120] On average she was paid $225.00 annually for eleven and a quarter months' work. During this time the school was involved, with great success, in the Regina Exhibition. A 1929 receipt found in the department's handicraft file documents the shipping of a thirty-eight-pound package to Lebret with materials for the teacher and her students.[121]

4	yds. red stroud	3.25	13.00
4	"blue"	3.60	14.40
150	bnchs. seed beads	.30	45.00
¼	lb. col. embry. silk	19.50	4.87
1⁄20	glovers needles	4.00	.20
			77.47
	Express Charges		1.73
			79.20

Perhaps the enjoyment of teaching and working with materials that she could not otherwise afford was some compensation for her small annual stipend.

Malanie Blondeau's impact on her young students throughout a teaching career that spanned almost two decades can perhaps be seen in the pronounced shift from the geometric patterns traditionally used on the central and southern plains. The use of floral designs was overwhelmingly identified as a relatively new phenomenon by the Cree elders interviewed by anthropologist David Mandelbaum in 1934-35. Fine Day said, "In my young days I didn't see very much beadwork. It was mostly porcupine quillwork. We never used floral designs then – all patterns were geometric. The floral designs came from the half-breed." Ask-kaw-taphi-tak (Sitting with Earth) of File Hills concurred, "In the old days there were no flower beadwork. This style was introduced by the Half Breeds."[122] Because she taught hundreds of girls over the course of her career, the impact of Malanie Blondeau and her curriculum would have been evident by the time of Mandelbaum's interviews.

As the twentieth century progressed, women's production became increasingly important as other sources of revenue failed. Their work often provided the sole support for their family, as it did for Malanie Blondeau. Celina Amyotte Poitras of Lebret described the Depression as a time when "there wasn't a speck of work for men [and] the kids really suffered ... I did a lot of sewing for people that's one thing I had to fall back on ... I had no electricity. I had coal oil lamps. I could hardly see because I had to sew at night, because I had babies and when they were asleep then I'd sew ... So we managed to live through [it]."[123]

From Their Hands
Women's production was a critical component of the economy in Métis communities. They converted the meat and hides, obtained through men's labour, into the commodities of pemmican, tanned robes, clothing, and decorative items. They continued subsistence production for their own needs while simultaneously producing for a market, managing both resources and the means of production.[124] The speed with which women like Madeleine Amyotte Desnommé and Nancy Kipling Labombarde could respond to a request for a complete outfit speaks to a high degree of organization and

preparation. Women were ready to manufacture, and not only did they respond to the customer on their doorstep, but they assertively marketed their goods. Women approached potential customers and brought goods to their homes or camps.[125] Husbands or fathers engaged as guides or working as traders also made initial contacts with potential customers. Men and women formed economic partnerships with complementary skill sets.

The clothing production of Métis women raises questions that are not easily answered and speaks to the complexity and variety of contexts in which they lived and worked. Sewing could be viewed as menial domestic labour, underpaid and undervalued. We can hear the implications of gender, race, and class in the phrase "my washer woman." Certainly echoes of subservience and exploitation can be found in the sparse historic record. The Hudson's Bay Company considered women's labour "free," equating the act of dressing men with women's duty. However, the HBC's own records also document women being paid in cash, goods, or credit for their work. In retrospect, and with some chagrin, Louis Goulet described the women employed by his father as showing "that other's people's labour pays best. I suppose if he'd lived in our times he wouldn't have been called a businessman, more likely a vile capitalist drinking other people's sweat."[126]

Yet is there not also power in the act of dressing? If the meaning of dress is constructed through multidirectional discourse between maker, wearer, and audience, "maker" holds an equal position in that communication, simultaneously initiating and responding with garments that attract the consumer. The volume of Métis women's production also speaks to their economic and aesthetic influence. While women across indigenous North America produced useful and beautiful clothing and other decorative items, no other group of women had their work commodified to the same extent.[127] Through a network of fur-trade posts and camps, Métis women dressed most of the men engaged in trade or seeking adventure in the West. The similarity of clothing and accessories worn by men across a broad terrain, as documented in both visual records and museum collections, indicates the success of their project. Beyond this sprawling domestic market, Red River cart trains piled with coats, saddles, and other desirable objects positioned women in a critical economic role that connected their communities to a global economy. Winnipeg and St. Paul, the centres of exchange, were only initial stops in their distribution to an interethnic and international market.

Frugality, efficiency, family labour units, and an acute sense of shifting market trends enabled Métis women to maintain access to consumers. The longevity and volume of their production, and their use of marketing strategies ranging from contractual arrangements with fur-trade companies to community-based entrepreneurship, suggest that much of the material in museum collections came from their hands. Sewing could be a desperate act, done by the light of a candle or kerosene lamp after the children were asleep, to secure the most basic of necessities. But collectively, Métis women can be seen as creators and manufacturers who used their work to inscribe their voices on the canvas of the male body.

Notes

1 Norbert Welsh with Mary Weekes, *The Last Buffalo Hunter* (New York: Thomas Nelson and Sons, 1939), 13-14.

2 In her scrip application filed in Manitoba, Charlotte identified herself as the daughter of Jean Baptiste Sauvé (French Canadian) and Marguerite (an Indian), born in 1808 on "the Polar Sea." Charlotte Walsh [Welsh] claim 994, Record Group (RG) 15, vol. 1324, series D-11-9-a, Library and Archives of Canada (LAC).

3 Johnny Grant, *Very Close to Trouble: The Johnny Grant Memoir,* ed. Lyndel Meikle (Pullman: Washington State University Press, 1996), 153.

4 Ibid., 154.

5 "Pioneer Women Played Their Part: The Days of Red River When Keeping Schools Supplied With Teachers Was a Problem," Manitoba History Scrapbook, M9, p. 84a (10 November 1928-27 August 1947), Manitoba Legislative Library. Anne Bannatyne was the daughter of Andrew McDermott (Irish) and Sarah McNab (Half Breed). Anne Bannatyne claim 1690, RG 15, vol. 1329, series D-11-8-a, LAC.

6 Mrs. Gladman and Mrs. Vincent were probably Mary Moore, the wife of George Gladman Sr., and Jane Renton, the first country wife of Thomas Vincent. E.E. Rich, ed., *John Rae's Correspondence with the Hudson's Bay Company on Arctic Exploration, 1844-1855* (London: The Hudson's Bay Record Society, 1853), 3. See Jennifer S. Brown, *Strangers in Blood: Fur Trade Company Families in Indian Country* (Vancouver: UBC Press, 1980), 75, 139-40, for a discussion of the Gladman and Vincent families.

7 Elizabeth Mitchell is identified as Odawa or Chippewa (Ojibwa) in various historical documents, but Elizabeth Fisher Baird remembered her as "mixed blood," speaking a mixture of French and a language that was neither Odawa or Chippewa, as did Julia Kinzie who described her as "an extremely pretty, delicate woman, part French and part Sioux, whose early life had been passed at Prairie du Chien." See Elizabeth Thérèse Fisher Baird, "Reminiscences of Early Days on Mackinac Island," in *Collections of the State Historical Society of Wisconsin (CSHSW),* vol. 14, 17-64 (Madison: State Historical Society of Wisconsin, 1898), 34, and Mrs. John H. Kinzie, *Wah-bun: The Early Days in the North West* (Philadelphia: J.B. Lippincott, 1873), 24.

8 Baird, "Reminiscences," 35, 38, 40.

9 Ibid., 20.

10 Ibid., 22. Marienne Lasalière was the daughter of Thérèse Marcot and her first husband, Pierre Lasalière. Her grandmother was Migisan, the daughter of Kewinaquot, an Odawa chief. Her stepfather, George Schindler, opened a school for boys following his retirement from active trade due to ill health. According to her daughter, Marienne opened her school around the same time. Schindler died in 1825.

11 Robert Dickson to John Lawe, 13 January 1814, Lac Puants; Robert Dickson to John Lawe, 6 February 1814, Winebagoe Lake, *CSHSW,* vol. 11 (1888): 283, 293.

12 William Keating, *Narrative of an Expedition to the Source of St. Peter's River, Lake Winepeek, Lake of the Woods, etc. Performed in the Year 1823* (1825; repr., Minneapolis: Ross and Haines, 1959), 153.

13 Father Baraga to Father Rese, 24 October 1832, Mackinaw, Michigan Territory [Wisconsin]; Father Sim Saénderl to Bishop Rese, 28 January 1836, Green Bay, Wisconsin, III-2-g, University of Notre Dame Archives, Notre Dame, Indiana.

14 H.J.L. Wooley, "The Origin of the Mackinaw Coat," *The Canadian Magazine* (January 1928): 25; "Mackinaw Coat Will Observe 139th Anniversary," *Indian Head News* (21 December 1950), Blankets Search File, HBCA.

15 This proved to be the most popular and enduring form of the coat, and plaid the most popular colour.

16 John D. Cameron to James Hargrave, 1 February 1835, Red River, in *The Hargrave Correspondence*, ed. G.P. Glazebrook (Toronto: Champlain Society, 1938), 71.

17 "Pioneer Women Played Their Part," 84a-b.

18 Ibid.

19 The heirs of Matilda Davis (deceased) claim 60, RG 15, vol. 1320, series D-11-8-a, LAC.

20 Davis Papers – Matilda Davis School, 1859-78, file No. 6, Barbara Johnstone Collections, P2343, Archives of Manitoba (AM).

21 Jane Bell Clark, 14 September 1865, Fort Carlton, box 1, file 1: Correspondence, Matilda Davis School Collection, MG2 C24, AM. Jane Bell Blanchard identified her mother as "Jane Bell (Half Breed)" in her scrip application. Jane Blanchard claim 1469, RG 15, vol. 1325, series D-11-8-b, LAC.

22 Accounts (n.d.), box 1, file 9; Accounts (1866-70), box 1, file 12; Accounts (1871-76), file 13; (1863) box 2, file 1 in Matilda Davis School Collection, MG2 C24, AM.

23 The Nolin sisters were still teaching at Baie St. Paul in the early 1830s. See Donald Chaput, "The Misses Nolin of Red River," *The Beaver* (Winter 1975): 14-17. Provencher's comments are in Grace Lee Nute, *Documents Relating to Northwest Missions, 1815-1827* (1943; repr., Ann Arbor, MI: University Microfilms International, Clarence Walworth Alvord Memorial Commission, 1981), 439.

24 See also W.B. Ready, "Early Red River Schools," *The Beaver* (December 1947): 34-36.

25 Jan Morier, "Métis Decorative Art and Its Inspiration," *Dawson and Hind* 8, 1 (1979): 28-32.

26 See Terrence G. Kardong, "Metis Sisters, 1857-1860," in *Beyond Red River*, 27-28 (Fargo, ND: Diocese of Fargo, 1988).

27 Michael Davis (1937), pp. 6-7; and Joseph Laframboise (1938), p. 2, in the Pioneer Biography Files, Works Project Administration Historical Data Project, State Historical Society of North Dakota.

28 Belcourt denied the charges and maintained that he had whipped them for disciplinary reasons before expelling them from the order (Kardong, "Metis Sisters," 28). According to Louis Goulet, "les vieux de la génération de mon père" (the old people of my father's generation) attributed the burning of the St. Boniface cathedral and other misfortunes as punishment for the treatment of Belcourt and the closure of the mission at St. Joseph. "Guillaume Charette – Louis Goulet manuscript," pp. 163-64, MG9 A6, AM.

29 Celia was the daughter of Dakota/French/Scottish parents, Scott and Margaret Campbell of Traverse des Sioux in present-day Minnesota. The Campbells were a prominent fur-trade family. Celia Campbell Stay Papers, "Massacre at Lower Sioux Agency," p. 4, MG1 A8, AM.

30 Susan Bordeaux was the daughter of James Bordeaux and Red Cormorant Woman, a Lakota. She grew up at Fort Laramie. Susan Bordeaux Bettelyoun and Josephine Waggoner, *With My Own Eyes: A Lakota Woman Tells Her People's History* (Lincoln: University of Nebraska Press, 1988), 35.

31 Nute, *Documents Relating to Northwest Missions*, 436.

32 Régistre Écoles de Saint Norbert, 1873-74, St. Boniface Historical Society.

33 A horse crupper with floral quillwork was collected in 1841 from the Red River region, cat. no. V-X-290, Canadian Museum of Civilization, Ottawa. The Samuel Black bag in the Pitt Rivers Museum was collected in 1842, cat. no. B.1.38, E.M. Hopkins Collection, Pitt Rivers Museum, Oxford.

34 *Chroniques des Soeurs Grises* as cited in Morier, "Métis Decorative Art and its Inspiration," 31.

35 Marie Rose Delorme Smith, "Eighty Years on the Plains," p. 2, file 4, M1154, Marie Rose Smith Fonds, Glenbow-Alberta Institute (GAI).

36 Madeline Bird, *Living Kindness: The Dream of My Life; The Memoirs of Métis Elder, Madeline Bird* (Yellowknife: Outcrop, 1991), 45.

37 Ibid., 21, 31.

38 Ibid., 63. Madeline Bird identified her grandmother as Charlotte Deschambeau.

39 Keating, *Narrative*, 152.

40 Edmonton Post Journal, 25 February 1796-8 March 1796, B.60/a/1; Manchester House Post Journal, 1786-89, B121/a/1-4; rough draft of Peter Fidler's Chesterfield House Journal, B.39/a/2-6, HBCA.
41 The coat, with accessories, is part of the James Robertson Collection (No. 1998.H267) at the Hancock Museum, University of Newcastle.
42 Most British museum collections have at least one of these coats. During the course of this study, eleven such coats were identified in five museum collections.
43 Fort Churchill Post Journal, 1804-5, B.42/a/130, Hudson's Bay Company Archives (HBCA), Winnipeg.
44 Alexander Henry, *The Journal of Alexander Henry the Younger, 1799-1814*, vol. 2 (Toronto: Champlain Society, 1992), 407-8, 418, 428-66.
45 Sylvia Van Kirk, *Many Tender Ties: Women in Fur-Trade Society in Western Canada, 1670-1870* (Winnipeg: Watson and Dwyer Publishing, 1980).
46 Slops was the term used for cheap work clothing worn by labourers.
47 R. Harvey Fleming, ed., *Minutes of Council Northern Department of Rupert Land, 1821-31* (Toronto: Champlain Society, 1940), 378.
48 Coats were listed as six-, five-, four-, and three-skin coats. Goods of Country Manufacture, Moose Factory Inventory 1824, 1824 Moose Factory Account Book, B.135/a/120, fo. 2, HBCA.
49 Robert M. Ballantyne, *Hudson Bay, or Everyday Life in the Wilds of North America* (London: Thomas Nelson and Sons, 1879), 53.
50 Margaret A. Macleod, *The Letters of Letitia Hargrave* (Toronto: Champlain Society, 1947), 73.
51 Paul Kane, *Wanderings of an Artist* (1858; repr., Edmonton: Hurtig, 1968), 93.
52 Jane Harriott identified her parents as Samuel Taylor (Scot) and Nancy McKay (Half Breed). Jane Harriott scrip affidavit, RG 15, vol. 1321, series D-11-8-a, LAC.
53 Samuel Taylor's Journal, pp. 11 and 21, Miscellaneous Diaries, Microfilm, R 2.47, Saskatchewan Archives Board (SAB).
54 Sir John Franklin, *Thirty Years in the Arctic Region* (New York: G. Casper, 1859), 115.
55 E.E. Rich, ed., *John Rae's Correspondence with the Hudson's Bay Company on Arctic Exploration, 1844-1855* (London: Hudson's Bay Record Society, 1953), 76.
56 Ibid., 333.
57 Walter Traill, *In Rupert's Land: Memoirs of Walter Traill* (Toronto: McClelland and Stewart, 1970), 99.
58 George Simpson McTavish, *Behind the Palisades: An Autobiography* (Victoria: E. Gurd, 1963), 42-43.
59 Traill, *In Rupert's Land*, 99.
60 Isaac Cowie, *Company of Adventurers* (1913; repr., Lincoln: University of Nebraska Press, 1993), 181-82.
61 Ruth P. Rubenstein describes physical strength and agility as the principal tenets of the masculine physical ideal. See Ruth P. Rubenstein, *Dress Codes: Meanings and Messages in American Culture* (Boulder, CO: Westview Press, 1995), 90-91. See also Elizabeth Vibert, "Real Men Hunt Buffalo: Masculinity, Race, and Class in British Traders' Narratives," in *Cultures of Empire: A Reader,* ed. Catherine Hall, 281-97 (London: Routledge, 2000).
62 Officer's Shop Book, 1828 Abitibi Accounts, B.1/d/1: 2-11, HBCA.
63 Nancy Kirkness say Spence account, B.1/d/1: 3-6, HBCA.
64 Robert M. Ballantyne, *Hudson Bay, or Everyday Life in the Wilds of North America* (London: W. Blackwood, 1848), 106-7.
65 Joseph James Hargrave, *Red River* (1871; repr., Altona, MB: Friesen Printers, 1977), 179.
66 Thomas Bunn maintained a lifelong correspondence with the Bayley family, supplying them with items made by his wife, Phoebe Sinclair, and receiving in return an annual box of magazines and newspapers. Denis Bayley, *A Londoner in Rupert's Land: Thomas Bunn of the Hudson's Bay Company* (Chichester, England: Moore and Rillyer, 1969), 95.
67 Nute, *Documents Relating to Northwest Missions*, 189.
68 The Earl of Southesk, *Saskatchewan and the Rocky Mountains: A Diary and Narrative of Travel, Sport and Adventure during a Journey through the Hudson's Bay Company Territories in 1859 and 1860* (1875; repr., Edmonton: Hurtig, 1969), 33.

69 Louis Schmidt (1912), Addenda to Louis Schmidt Mémoires, pp. 1-2, "Les Mémoires de Louis Schmidt," MG9 A31, AM.

70 George Winship (1914), "My First Flat-Boat Ride down the Red River, and Incidents Connected Therewith," p. 2, MG3 B15, AM.

71 Ibid., 6.

72 William Francis Butler, *The Great Lone Land: A Tale of Travel and Adventure in the North-West of America* (London: S. Low, Marston, Low, and Searle, 1875), 201.

73 "In Prairie Hunter's Costume," 10 March 1871, Charles Napier Bell Collection (2), neg. 10514, AM.

74 Charles Napier Bell, Manitoba Historical Society website (http://www.mhs.mb.ca/docs/ people/bell_cn.shtml).

75 Rudolph Friedrich Kurz, *Journal of Rudolph Kurz: An Account of His Experiences among Fur Traders and American Indians on the Misisippi and Upper Missouri Rivers during the Years 1846 to 1852,* Bulletin 115 (Washington: Smithsonian Institution, Bureau of American Ethnology, 1937), 229, 234.

76 Ibid., 252.

77 Inventory of Stock, the Property of Pierre Chouteau Jr. and Co. on hand at Fort Union, 15 May 1851, Montana Historical Society.

78 Nancy Kipling claim 107, RG 15, vol. 1329, series D-11-8-b, LAC.

79 John Ram Kipling Biographical Sheet; John Ram Kipling Search File, HBCA.

80 Pembina Miscellaneous Post Records, B160/d/1. HBCA.

81 This refers to the forks of the Assiniboine and Red rivers in present-day Winnipeg, Manitoba.

82 Marguerite Swain claim 1625, RG 15, vol. 1332, series D-11-8-b, LAC.

83 Annie Abel, ed., *Chardon's Journal at Fort Clark, 1834-1839* (1930; repr., Lincoln: University of Nebraska Press, 1997), 297-298, 354.

84 James Archdale Hamilton to Jacob Halsey, 17 September 1834, Fort Union, in Abel, *Chardon's Journal,* 288.

85 Charles Larpenteur, *Forty Years a Fur Trader on the Upper Missouri: The Personal Narrative of Charles Larpenteur, 1833-1872* (Minneapolis: Ross and Haines, 1962), 72-76.

86 Ibid., 80-84.

87 Ibid., 84.

88 Anglican Register, St. John's Baptisms, E.4/1a: fo. 126, AM.

89 Kenneth McKenzie to Samuel Tulloch, 8 January 1834, Fort Union, Fort Union Letter Book, Fort Union Historical Park Collection.

90 John J. Audubon and Edward Harris described him as "a half-breed" when he served their party as a guide in 1843. Edwin Morris identified him as "Alex La Bombarde, a halfbreed," when he served as guide and interpreter for the North West Mounted Police. See Maria R. Audubon, *Audubon and His Journals* (Gloucester, MA: Peter Smith, 1972), 529; John Francis McDermott, ed., *Up the Missouri with Audubon: The Journal of Edward Harris* (Norman: University of Oklahoma Press, 1951), 84; Edwin Morris (n.d.), "Lt. Col. Irvine and the North West Mounted Police," p. 9, MG12 B2 351, AM.

91 Audubon, *Audubon and His Journals,* 529.

92 Post accounts often show men who acquired outfits purchasing hide. McDermott, *Up the Missouri with Audubon,* 217.

93 Item No. 70, Department of Ornithology, American Museum of Natural History.

94 Kurz, *Journal,* 252.

95 Ibid., 324.

96 Most of the fitted hide coats for which the provenance is known belonged to men who spent time on the Upper Missouri and by necessity passed through Fort Pierre and Fort Union. This would include the Pierre Chouteau, Honore Picotte, and Robert Campbell coats at the Missouri Historical Society and Campbell House in St. Louis, Missouri.

97 The maker of the gifts is not mentioned, and the incident predates Hardisty's marriage in 1866 to Eliza McDougall, the daughter of a missionary. Richard Hardisty claim 1138, RG 15, vol. 1328, series D-11-8-b, LAC; Southesk, *Saskatchewan,* 131-32.

98 Southesk, *Saskatchewan,* 181.

99 Ibid., 292.

100   "Diary of Dr. Augustus J. Thibido of the Northwest Exploring Expedition," reprinted from the *Pacific North-West Quarterly* 31 (July 1940): 287-347, Pamphlet File: Western Canada – Descriptions and Travel, SAB.

101   Josette Desnommé Racette identified her parents as Pierre Desnommé and Madeleine Amiot. Josette Desnommé claim 89, RG 15, vol. 1327, series D-11-8-b, LAC.

102   W.B. Cheadle, *Cheadle's Journal of Trip Across Canada, 1862-1863* (Ottawa: Graphic Publishers, 1931), 45 and 47. Elise Chartrand identified her parents as Louis la Ronde and Judith Morin. Elise Chartrand scrip affadavit, RG 15, vol. 1319, series D-11-8-a, LAC.

103   Southesk's journey was taken on the advice of his physician following the death of his wife, for whom he grieved deeply. David Charles Carnegie, Earl of Southesk, personal communication, 24 April 2002; Southesk, *Saskatchewan*, 104.

104   Warburton Pike, *The Barren Ground of Northern Canada* (London: Macmillan, 1892), 233-36.

105   Peter Garrioch Journal, 1843-47, p. 10, MG2 C38, AM.

106   Kurz, *Journal*, 85-86.

107   Frank Blackwell Mayer, *With Pen and Pencil on the Frontier in 1851: The Diary and Sketches of Frank Blackwell Mayer* (St. Paul: Minnesota Historical Society Press, 1986), 238.

108   Louis Goulet, *Vanishing Spaces: Memoirs of Louis Goulet*, ed. Guillaume Charette, trans. Ray Ellenwood (Winnipeg: Edition Bois Brulés, 1980), 67.

109   Ibid.

110   Smith, "Eighty Years on the Plains," 2.

111   Ibid., 170.

112   Marie Rose kept copies of postcards that used her work, Marie Rose Smith Fonds, GAI.

113   Amelia M. Paget (1913), "Report on the Qu'Appelle Agencies," RG 10, file 40,000-9, vol. 7908, LAC.

114   Quillworked tea cozy, AR 12, GAI.

115   J.Z. Laroque donor file, Royal Saskatchewan Museum, Regina, Saskatchewan. Rosalie Laroque was born in 1845 at White Horse Plains, the daughter of Antoine Plante and Josette Gagnon. Rosalie Laroque claim 719, RG 15, vol. 1322, series D-11-8-a, LAC.

116   Malanie Blondeau claim 158, RG 15, vol 1325, series D-11-8-b, LAC. Simon Blondeau was born in 1826 on the Pembina River, Françoise Desjarlais was born the same year "west of Lake Manitoba." Simon Blondeau claim 2 and 148, vol. 1325; Françoise Desjarlais claim 33, RG 15, vol. 1327, series D-11-8-b, LAC. Françoise Blondeau hid her son Johnnie "in a hole she had dug" during the Battle of Grand Coteau. "Veteran of the West Laid to Rest," *Regina Leader Post*, 4 May 1941, Biography File – Blondeau, John, SAB.

117   Interview with Lucy Desjarlais Whiteman incorporated in Rita Shilling, *Gabriel's Children* (Saskatoon: Saskatoon Metis Society, Local 11, 1983), 90-91.

118   Amelia Paget, Report on Qu'Appelle Agencies, 5 September 1913, 3.

119   D.C. Scott to Mr. Pedley, 27 February 1913, Ottawa, RG 10, file 41,000-9, vol. 7908, LAC.

120   Qu'Appelle Industrial School, "Dominion of Canada Annual Report of the Department of Indian Affairs (1914-1931)," Library and Archives Canada web site (http://www.collectionscanada.ca/indianaffairs/index-e.html).

121   Hudson's Bay Company Shipping Receipt, 7 March 1929, RG 10, file 41,000-10 pt. 1, vol. 7908, LAC.

122   David Mandelbaum Field Notes (1934), Notebook 2, R-875, SAB.

123   Celina Amyotte Poitras, interview, 3 August 1982, Lebret, SK, IH-SD.73, Indian History Film Project, First Nations University of Canada Library Collection.

124   For a discussion of women's adaptations of gendered economic roles, see Lucy Eldersveld Murphy, "Autonomy and the Economic Roles of Indian Women of the Fox-Wisconsin Riverway Region, 1763-1832," in *Negotiators of Change: Historical Perspectives on Native American Women*, ed. Nancy Shoemaker, 72-89 (New York: Routledge, 1995), 76.

125   Southesk, *Saskatchewan*, 123-24.

126   Goulet, *Vanishing Spaces*, 51.

127   See Ruth Phillips and Christopher Steiner, eds., *Unpacking Culture: Art and Commodity in Colonial and Postcolonial Worlds* (Berkeley and Los Angeles: University of California Press, 1999), for a discussion of the commodification of First Nations artistic production and the creation of material for a tourist or souvenir market.

2
Championing the Native:
E. Pauline Johnson Rejects the Squaw
Carole Gerson and Veronica Strong-Boag

As many writers in this volume and elsewhere attest,[1] indigenous women in Canada, as in the imperial world more generally, have suffered oppression and diminution in all dimensions of experience and representation. Whether Indian, Inuit, or mixed race, they have commonly been reduced to shells of real human beings, existing primarily to service others. In particular, under the imperial gaze Native women have been regarded as symbols of sexual depravity and exploited labour, abused first by their own people and then by their European conquerors. Degraded and exploited, they became objects of others' actions and, despite their frequent appearance in colonial discourse, rarely the subjects of their own lives. As women or as Natives, they were considered worthy of respect only in special instances that suited the agenda of colonization, such as the story of Molly Brant.[2] Generally, however, their supposed deficiencies, moral and physical, became one more justification for imperial expansion.

In the late nineteenth and early twentieth centuries, while some Native women defied their detractors, few public voices on the national stage challenged the distortions that were so useful to imperial conquerors. One exception, we recently suggested in *Paddling Her Own Canoe: The Times and Texts of E. Pauline Johnson (Tekahionwake)*, was the Anglo-Mohawk writer and performer Pauline Johnson (1861-1913).[3] In her life and her publications, Johnson struggled to orchestrate a dramatically different vision. Through her own person as well as the characters presented in her writings and her stage performances, she portrayed Native women as not only the equals of white women, but at times their superiors. Virtuous, hard-working, and dignified, they were never "squaws," a derogatory but commonplace term that signalled sexual licence, indolence, and disrespect. As we have argued, Johnson's reclamation of the social value and moral character of Native women was courageous and not without influence. Later Iroquois commentators like Patricia Monture-Angus and Beth Brant would recognize that Johnson took up a highly unusual project in the colonial world:

the redemption of Native women from imperial calumny.[4] Current First Nations authors who have created literary subjectivity for Native women, such as Lee Maracle and Jeannette Armstrong, acknowledge Johnson's importance as an enabling foremother.[5]

In our discussion first of Johnson's performance as the Native female subject and then of her texts' treatment of the agency, affections, and labour of Native women, we extend our earlier arguments to highlight her efforts to dignify the person of Canada's prototypical "other." We therefore focus on Johnson as a cultural worker in several realms. We examine how her representation of the Indian woman on the stage was perceived through the imperial (mostly male) gaze of her reviewers in the press, and how her own writings attempted to correct literary stereotypes of the Indian maiden and matron. Created by authors who were, in the main, unthinkingly ethnocentric and white, prevailing romantic plot conventions depicted Native female characters shaped more by Anglo-Canadian narrative conventions than by sincere efforts to embody another culture in print.

With Johnson, consideration of embodiment begins with the woman herself. Her publicity photographs and public presentation communicated a vivid sense of her physicality to her international audience of viewers and readers. Her success as a star of stage and salon depended in large part, as with other actresses of her day such as Sarah Bernhardt, on the vivid and implicitly erotic presence of comely female flesh. Johnson always paid close attention to costume and movement and understood full well that her attractive appearance was the source of much of her appeal. Aging reduced her capital, as she explained when writing to a friend about her "actress's aversion to my years being made general knowledge."

The significance of appearance and its communication of the facts of race were very much part of Johnson's personal history. Indeed, with Johnson the term "personal history" is particularly oxymoronic, for her biography embodies the larger social history of her era. She was born in 1861 to an English mother and a mostly Mohawk father, at their stately home on the Six Nations Reserve west of Brantford. The offspring of controversial unions such as that of her parents testified to the physical unity of the human race, a matter then still in dispute among anthropologists.[6] Intermarriage also raised questions critical to the political geography of imperialism. To whom would the daughters and sons cleave? Or would they, as Métis leader Louis Riel hoped, emerge as a new people uniquely positioned to inherit both indigenous and imperial worlds? Like her sister and two brothers, and their counterparts the world over, Pauline would often be viewed as a test of the outcome of racial mixing in border spaces.

As a mixed-race woman in *fin de siècle* Canada who chose to embrace both her heritages, Johnson presented a complicated story of embodiment that hearkened back to first encounters between Europeans and Natives in North America. Her paternal great-grandfather, Tekahionwake, acquired the surname Johnson in the 1760s, when it was added to his baptismal name, "Jacob," by Sir William Johnson, superintendent of Indian Affairs in the American colony of New York. The official story is that Johnson's donation of his patronym was motivated by generosity; the unofficial rumour is that he was more than a godfather to the boy.[7] The lineage of Pauline's powerful paternal grandmother, Helen Martin, the matron of the Wolf clan, likewise incorporates colonial sexual history. Martin's own mother was Catherine Rollstone (or Ralston), a captive of German or Dutch origin, who chose to integrate fully into the culture of her Mohawk husband. Helen, following in maternal footsteps, strongly upheld Iroquois values and refused to speak English. Pauline Johnson's selection of "Rollstone" as her pseudonym for three early prose sketches published in the *Brantford Courier* in 1890 documents her own sense of identification with a foremother who had set a vivid and successful example of transgressing established cultural boundaries.[8]

The marriage of Pauline Johnson's parents in 1853 replicated this pattern of border crossing. Her mother, Emily Susanna Howells, came from an abolitionist Quaker family that had emigrated from Bristol, England, to Putnam, Ohio, an American centre of antislavery activity. On an extended visit to her sister, who had married the Anglican missionary at Six Nations, Emily fell in love with the young Mohawk translator who assisted her brother-in-law. Their unconventional marriage resulted in a goldfish-bowl existence for their children, who were carefully trained in both perfect English manners and respect for their Native heritage. Despite being generally admired as handsome and cultivated, they ultimately failed to integrate fully into either culture.[9]

In the course of her career, Pauline Johnson chose to accentuate her dual lineage in very public ways, including a standard costume change halfway through her performances. In December 1897, a review in the *Winnipeg Free Press* described the power of dress in facilitating her staged embodiment of contradictory identities, and the confusion she created for her captivated audience:

> In the first part of the programme she appeared in picturesque Indian costume, and in every gesture, in the glances of her eye, in the varying expressions of her face, and in the working of the different emotions and passions she was a pure Indian ... When Miss Johnson, in the second part of the programme, appeared in a rich and beautiful dress made in fashionable, civilized style, the impression upon the audience was entirely changed. People then thought she must surely be at least almost white, in her features and complexion they could see nothing of the Indian.[10]

This transition from "pure Indian" to "at least almost white" through a mere change of garment demonstrates the truth underlying the cliché that "clothes make the (wo)man." Johnson's use of Native apparel was further problematized by the association of fur and feathers with commercial performances by costumed "show Indians" in events such as the spectacles mounted by Buffalo Bill Cody. By the time Johnson took to the stage in the mid-1890s, imperial audiences were well accustomed to the transformation of old rivals into amusing entertainments located safely in a distant past, where they did not raise uncomfortable questions about abuse and dispossession.

Despite her insistence on her Iroquois heritage, Johnson's own buckskin dress did not replicate a specific tribal tradition but was a created artifact that offered her viewers a general sense of indigeneity in its assembly of fringed buckskin, beads, weapons, silver ornaments, and even a Sioux scalp.[11] By espousing this generic representation (to an audience that usually saw her costume as "genuine"), Johnson seemed to disregard authenticity and contribute to the homogenization of the Native in modern culture. However, this strategy may well have enhanced her political positioning. By claiming the universal Indian subject, her dramatic persona effectively engaged with the whole history of imperialism in North America. While Buffalo Bill's rodeolike troupe enacted anti-Indian episodes of American history, such as Custer's last stand, the daughter of Six Nations reversed both attitude and social class by presenting pro- and pan-Indian dramatic monologues in dignified venues like schools, drawing rooms, and church halls. Much like First Nations writers and performers such as Tomson Highway and Thomas King, who appear to have joined Canada's cultural establishment at the end of the twentieth century, Johnson played the "trickster," carefully manipulating her audiences in what art historian Ruth Phillips describes as "reverse appropriation of the stereotype."[12]

But for Johnson, existence as both "Indian" and "white" was only the beginning of a complicated story. In her cultural arithmetic, the sum of her own racial mixture created a third factor, completing the equation with "Canadian." By celebrating a multiple heritage, she claimed an inclusive nationality during an era characterized by racialized hierarchies and dichotomies. In particular, she argued that the authentic Canadian body was marked not by colour or language ("French and English and Red men are we") but by place of origin: "we were born in Canada, beneath the British flag."[13]

Her apparent disregard of religious difference, commonly embraced as crucial to group identity in her era and a source of blood feuds between the Orange and the Green in her home province of Ontario, was also significant. By celebrating the "pagan" and drawing little distinction between Catholic and Protestant missionaries, for example, she indicated that relationship to the land meant more than essentially arbitrary spiritual allegiances.[14] As Christie, the mixed-race heroine of "A Red Girl's Reasoning," observes with pride: "My people have no priest, and my nation cringes not to law. Our priest is purity, and our law is honour."[15] In her invocation of "the Manitou of all nations,"[16] Johnson envisioned a religious universe that would have done credit to her Quaker ancestry, however much it placed her at odds with the majority of her white contemporaries.

However, to be identified as "Indian" in Canada at the turn of the last century was to be stigmatized as a body, to represent a "memory site," to borrow Smaro Kamboureli's useful term, marked by a history of conquest and defeat.[17] The poetry of Duncan Campbell Scott, who was both Johnson's contemporary as a writer and the senior administrator in the Department of Indian Affairs during her adult years, invoked the common representation of Native women as living relics of an outmoded era. His portrayal of an old woman, "Watkwenies," now "wrinkled like an apple kept till May," suggested that the time of her people was a "perished day." More threatening still was Scott's youthful "Onondaga Madonna," whose baby, "paler than she," was "the latest promise of her nation's doom." The body of this young woman, standing "full-throated and with careless pose," tells the story of her people's apparent inability to participate in the nation to which the twentieth century would belong. With "the tragic savage lurking in her face," and her "rebel lips ... dabbled with the stains / Of feuds and forays and her father's woes," she is scarcely a citizen of the modern world.[18]

Given the racial tensions of the times, Pauline Johnson's dramatic self-insertion into her era's discourse of Aboriginal savagery and concomitant propagation of negative ethnic stereotypes puzzled her reviewers and interviewers. Who was this elegant young woman with drawing-room manners, who uttered war whoops on the stage and dressed so fashionably in private life? Journalists who met her, and acquaintances who later penned their memoirs, continually referred to the physical body of Pauline Johnson, as if her face and features held the key to her complex identity. Their interest in pinning down the precise details of her appearance reflected more than the usual journalistic practice of objectifying women by enumerating their physical attributes. In their attempts to define the colouring of her skin, eyes, and hair, they echoed the more academic theorizing that preoccupied contemporary race analysts and passed for the science of the day.[19]

All commentators on Pauline Johnson in the first years of her performing career agree that she was slender with a "straight, elastic figure" and a "graceful willowy form."[20] Such descriptions testify to childhood training in good posture while also participating in the discourse associated with the stereotype of the Noble Savage, who was usually seen as possessing natural strength and dignity. But was Johnson "tall" or "a little above middle height" or of "medium height"?[21] Were her eyes "grey" or "hazel" or "dark" or "deep" or "wild"?[22] Is there a qualitative difference between describing her as a "brunette," as glorying in "tresses woven of midnight,"[23] or as simply possessing

Pauline Johnson in Native dress, ca. 1902
BC Archives, A-09684

black hair? Still more suggestive were her audiences' various perceptions of her face and skin tone. Those who thought her lineage entirely Native saw her as "a full blooded and rarely handsome Mohawk Indian,"[24] whose "pure Indian blood shows in every feature of her round, dark, handsome and thoughtful face."[25] Others described her as possessing "beautifully clean cut features," an "oval face," "high cheek bones," and "clean-cut aquiline features."[26] Her skin varies from an "olive-red complexion" to "a clear olive complexion" to "clear dark skin."[27]

Their subject's personal presentation of the meaning of empire was so alien to the usual terms of distinction between Native and white that several journalists ran short of words. Retreating from the conventional distinctions between the civilized and the savage, they endeavoured to make sense of Pauline by referring to familiar variations among European cultures. Her long-time Brantford acquaintance, journalist Sara Jeannette Duncan, was typical in praising her former schoolmate as "charmingly bright in conversation [with] a vivacity of tone and gesture that is almost French."[28] Associations with specific European cultures invoked different implications in different contexts. The same "French" quality, which was attractive in parts of educated English Canada, was viewed with suspicion in journalistic Chicago (which had largely forgotten its own foundational links to the French empire in North America):

It takes a careful study of the square chin, high cheek bones, and dark hair to convince the casual observer that she really is of Indian stock ... Miss Johnson wears Frenchy looking gowns and neatly fitting shoes, she doesn't powder her face nor rouge her lips, but she curls her front hair and manicures her nails. In fact, she does pretty much everything that a real Indian would not be expected to do, and leaves undone everything that one would expect of a child of the Iroquois. And she talks like a Vassar graduate, only with a trifle more naiveté.[29]

This comparison to students at an elite eastern female college aligned Johnson with the intellectual New Woman, a surprisingly shrewd comparison to appear in a brash western metropolis.

Perhaps in answer to such curiosity and confusion about her origins, Johnson took considerable pains to describe two fictional mixed-race heroines in terms that accounted for herself as well. In "A Red Girl's Reasoning," Christie "looked much the same as her sisters, all Canada through, who are the offspring of red and white parentage": she was "olive-complexioned, grey-eyed, black-haired, with figure slight and delicate."[30] Her equally strong-minded counterpart Lydia, in "The Derelict," was "a type of mixed blood, pale, dark, slender, with the slim hands, the marvelously beautiful teeth of her mother's people, the ambition, the small tender mouth, the utter fearlessness of the English race."[31] Both characterizations also contain warnings: Christie has "the wistful, unfathomable expression in her whole face that ... is the forerunner too frequently of 'the white man's disease,' consumption."[32] In turn, Lydia's "strange, laughless eyes ... silent step [and] hard sense of honor, proclaimed her far more the daughter of red blood than of white."[33] These composites warned that mixed-blood Canadian women, whether real or fictional, were complex and unpredictable individuals who deserved attention and respect as full and unique human beings.

Johnson's direct repudiation of negative stereotypes began early in her career. Her 1892 essay "A Strong Race Opinion on the Indian Girl in Modern Fiction," published in Toronto's *Sunday Globe,* called for a fair deal for her compatriots. Deftly dissecting the shortcomings of contemporary Canadian authors, she derided their fictional representations of generic Indian maidens who inevitably yield to white rivals and appear to have been created only to be subjected to humiliation and elimination. Dismissing authors who avoided the problem of miscegenation by consigning Native women to lose alike in love and conquest, Johnson set her contemporaries the task of creating "real live" Indian girls, characters who both deserved respect and reflected the diversity of Native communities.[34] Unfortunately, her call appears to have fallen on deaf ears, but if others failed to rise to the challenge, Johnson carved out her own example of agency and success in the creation of several proactive fictional protagonists. Yet over time, constrained by literary conventions and popular markets as well as by common prejudice, she fell short of her ambitions. Captive to romantic conventions that diminished both women and Natives, her written representations of Native women would ultimately be more successful in confirming dignity than in acknowledging diversity.

Johnson's self-created mystique as a stage performer, honed before the critical eyes of Canadian, American, and British audiences, enhanced the power of her textual messages. The poetry and prose that appeared in newspapers, magazines, and her own collections likewise negotiated the contact zone inhabited by Natives and Europeans, as well as by women and men. As a cultural bohemian and New Woman of the late nineteenth century, she used her writing to foreground the questions of autonomy and independence, both erotic and economic, that she raised in her own person. Indeed, erotic independence had been her first venture beyond convention. During the late 1880s and early 1890s, before she developed her stage persona as Native, Pauline Johnson published a series of rather explicit love poems voicing a female perspective, thus earning the distinction of being Canada's very own "daughter of decadence," as we argue in *Paddling.*[35] As a younger woman, optimistic about the reception of her person and her politics, she directly tackled the question of Native women's passions and agency. Johnson's rejection of convention was most obviously signalled by her own location in many narratives. The author who appeared as both "master of rapid, paddle and Peterboro" and the much-in-demand mistress of "dear, athletic college boys" was clearly in charge of her own fate as well as that of others.[36] While Johnson often veiled her Nativeness in both her outdoor narratives and her erotic verse, those who knew her understood that the writer who claimed both the "shadow and the dreaming" was "one of them," the "superior" Iroquois.[37] The "I" imprinted in Johnson's prose and poetry was very clearly not the "squaw" of others' stories.

Pauline Johnson, poetess, Vancouver, 1903
City of Vancouver Archives, Port P1633N957

The unnamed speaker of "A Cry from an Indian Wife" (1885), Christie in "A Red Girl's Reasoning" (1893), Ojistoh and Dawendine in eponymous poems whose titles accentuate their heroines' agency (both 1895), and Esther in "As It Was in the Beginning" (1899) similarly convey their creator's early attachment to active expressions of womanhood.[38] These characters, whose vigour was further enhanced when brought to life in Johnson's stage performances, enjoy full subjectivity. As they negotiate the worlds of sentiment and action, they display both principles and passions. If seemingly traditional in their commitment to family life and heterosexuality, these first heroines also assert intellectual and sexual independence. The mixed-race Christie returns Charlie's love with a depth of feeling that might render other women pawns of the patriarchal order. When her young husband rejects her parents' "custom of the country" marriage as improper and thus betrays the old Indian-European alliance of near-equals, Christie demonstrates her overriding commitment to justice. She deliberately chooses the loneliness and poverty of life as an Ontario seamstress over the comfort of marriage with an oath-breaker. Unlike her "fair" husband, she masters the flesh to remain faithful to a higher truth. Unlike the usual depictions of her real-life sisters, she rejects submission to custom or men. Even as her love fills her with "agony," she insists that "neither church, nor law, nor even love can make a slave of a red girl."[39]

The strong sense of honour that motivates Christie recurs in the poem "Ojistoh." A regular feature of Johnson's later performance programs, it dramatizes a story of abduction and threatened rape, albeit safely transposed to the ancient conflict between Huron and Iroquois. While imperial commentators regularly assumed that Native women were promiscuous by nature, this poem insists upon their fidelity and majesty. Captured by her traditional enemy only after a fierce struggle, Ojistoh musters sufficient self-possession to enact time-honoured revenge. She seduces her captor in order to dispatch him with his own hunting knife, a motif recalling the Judeo-Christian story of Judith, whose beheading of her would-be seducer Holofernes inspired scores of European painters. Ojistoh likewise is no man's plaything; "like a northern gale," she will not be tamed.[40] Dawendine similarly becomes the agent of her own fate when she intervenes in male warfare. Beloved by a warrior from a feuding tribe, a man who killed her brother, she answers her mother's request to "sing and sue for peace between us" in order to "save thy brothers, save thy sire." By carrying the white wampum of peace to her would-be lover, Dawendine averts the potential tragedy suggested by the poem's echoes of *Romeo and Juliet*.[41] Here, the double agency of mother and daughter in resolving manmade conflict foreshadows Johnson's later stress on the value of girls and women as peacemakers in her stories adapted from the Salish of the West Coast.

In other stories, Johnson turned to a time when the outstanding foes of Natives were no longer one another. In "The Derelict" (1896) and "As It Was in the Beginning" (1899), Charlie's morally unreliable white brethren reappear. Both Cragstone and Laurence readily succumb to convention and prejudice. The former, an Anglican minister little better than a remittance man, is ironically "packed off north as a missionary for the Indians," whom Johnson clearly suggests are his moral superiors.[42] Here he meets and, for a time, fails a major test of manhood. Ultimately he remains faithful both to true love and to the spirit of the original Indian-European compact. In contrast, Lydia, another mixed-race heroine, embodies the best of both peoples, including "the hard sense of honor" that "proclaimed her far more the daughter of red blood than of white." She might be merely a "serving maid" while Cragstone is the son of a high-born mother, but the identity of the real aristocrat is never in doubt. Unlike her predecessor in "A Red Girl's Reasoning," Lydia forgives her lover when he is man enough to admit his error. Rejected by the Church, Cragstone finds a far better "haven" in "the world's most sheltered harbor" of "a woman's love."[43]

Salvation was, however, at best an uncertain outcome of Indian-white contact. Johnson returned to the more familiar unhappy resolution of the imperial story in "As It Was in the Beginning." Fresh from protestations of love to the mixed-race Esther, Laurence surrenders to the insistence of his clergyman uncle that he retract his pledge in favour of a respectable white girl with a "baby face," no match for the real womanhood of her rival. The treachery of yet another fair-haired young man, always a suspect character in Johnson's personal racial lexicon, destroys the Edenic promise of the match between childhood sweethearts. Like her counterparts in other stories, Esther is portrayed as deeply in thrall to her beloved, "the fullness of his perfect beauty ... his slender form, his curving mouth that almost laughed even in sleep, his fair, tossed hair, his smooth, strong-pulsing throat."[44] Earthly charms, however, fail in face of betrayal. The covenant now broken between woman and man, Native and white, it seems only just that the serpent's sting be ministered by the spurned lover who refuses the role of victim. Ultimately neither the church of the uncle nor passion for the nephew can make Esther meekly endure injustice.

The strength of Native women's affections is a recurring theme in Johnson's work. Family devotion structures many of her later stories and legends, most often in the form of the expected commitment of mothers to their children, but in one special instance the love of a daughter for her mother. The legend "The Grey Archway" recounts the story of a young woman who, in the course of selecting between two male rivals, resolves the equally difficult choice between lover and parent. Announcing that even he "cannot keep" her, Yaada invites her youthful sweetheart to join her in diving into the sea. There the two lovers, transformed into a pair of "silvery fish," survive to seek "the soul of the Haida woman – her mother," who was murdered by the young man's rival, a wicked old sorcerer.[45]

Johnson recalled more commonplace manifestations of Native women's fidelity and passion in stories of separated lovers from "The Pilot of the Plains" (1891) to "The Quill Worker" (1896), "The Legend of Qu'Appelle Valley" (1898), "The Call of the Old Qu'Appelle Valley" (1910), and "The Ballad of Yaada" (1913).[46] The women of these narratives, more ethereal and less grounded in earthly passions than Christie, Ojistoh, or Esther, wait, sometimes until death, for the men they have freely chosen. Like Neykia, "the Sioux chief's daughter," or Yakonwita, "guiding with her lamp of moonlight / Hunters lost upon the plains," they ignore other suitors' attempts to distract them or taunts that they have been betrayed. Their male choices, in turn, promise to live up to the standards set by their loyal lovers. Such commitment on both sides, however, often proves unavailing. With the exception of "The Quill Worker," who treasures an unnamed "young red hunter" who might well belong to her own tribe, the separation of women and men brings pain or death, especially when the relationship involves lovers identified with communities racialized as "Other," whether Native or European.

Similar plots occur in many cultures, in Europe as well as North America, as in Thomas Campbell's popular Scottish ballad "Lord Ullin's Daughter," in which a noble maiden's border-crossing for love reaps disaster.[47] Nevertheless, if Johnson's stories drew on colonial audiences' familiarity with the romance of star-crossed lovers, they were distinctive for incorporating Native women as equal actors and worthy objects of desire. These heroines fully meet the high standards of true love set by the conventions of the day. The obstacles to their happiness are natural, such as prairie snowstorms or illness, or manmade by wizards or warriors; above all, they are not created by the failings traditionally attributed to women in Western culture, such as inconstancy, gossip, cupidity, or jealousy. Countering the prevailing racist narratives that cast indigenous women as a source of weakness and evil in the meeting of races and communities, Johnson's female characters demonstrate strength and capacity, even when the outcome is ultimately tragic.

Notwithstanding her willingness to take risks in her depiction of female eroticism in her early poems, Johnson's treatment of sexuality and romantic love ultimately yielded to prevailing convention. As she aged and felt her vulnerability more keenly, her explorations of sexual or erotic independence and autonomy declined. The shift was especially evident in the first decade of the twentieth century, as she relinquished her *fin de siècle* bohemianism to forge a livelihood in the pages of family periodicals. While later stories range from Ontario to the British Columbia coast, the women are ultimately all cut from the same cloth. In order to give Native women dignity at a time when their social value and legal rights were under increased assault, Johnson sacrificed the individuality and tribal difference she had earlier celebrated. Generically beautiful, strong, quiet characters express their ethical principles in their way of life, rather than through their use of words. The question of overt sexuality, so clearly raised by Christie and Ojistoh, disappears, along with hints about the real-life exploitation of Native women.[48] The entire question of sexuality became too dangerous a zone for an aging and impoverished performer of Canada's racial history.

Hence, young Native women recede in Johnson's later texts, to be replaced by older, maternal figures. As early as 1896, in "Lullaby of the Iroquois,"[49] she invoked a universal nurturing script that linked mothers of every race. In the following decade, while writing for the Illinois-based *Mother's Magazine,* she consistently added Native figures to a domestic pantheon that was confirmed with the inauguration of Mother's Day in the United States in 1908. For all its apparent conformity to Euro-American conventions of the sanctity of the hearth, Johnson's contribution remains nonetheless distinctive: she placed the loving yet rigorous supervision of indomitable, if often silent, Indian matrons at the centre of a vital community. Iroquois and Mohawk women emerge as the epitome of generic Native values when Johnson describes them under such titles as "Mothers of a Great Red Race" (1908) and "Heroic Indian Mothers" (1908).[50] These articles present disciplined and competent figures, very different from the neglectful or overly indulgent parents portrayed by white critics, whose recurring mother-blaming proclivities readily extended to Native nations. As well, she insisted on the chastity of traditional Native courtship practices and the harmony of Indian marriages: "It is only when the conflicting results of attempting to emulate the white man's ways enter into the forest lodge, that domestic difficulties arise. Extravagance, social rivalry, whisky, love of display these are what strikes at the roots of Indian family felicity."[51]

The high standards of social and biological mothers in Johnson's stories affirmed a superior moral order that had strengthened Native communities in the past and promised to do so in the future. Like "Catharine of the Crow's Nest" (1910) and Maarda in "The Tenas Klootchman" (1911), who adopt orphans, including a white infant, her characters confront and overcome tragedy.[52] Nor are these proactive figures trapped in a world of oppressive tradition, as was often suggested by imperial detractors. In "Hoolool of the Totem Poles" (1911), for example, Johnson indicated that women could readily move with the times in service to their children.[53] In this case, an impoverished Haida widow creates miniature totems for the province's emerging tourist industry, and in the process secures her son's totemic heritage from greedy, white, artifact hunters. Like her Iroquois sisters, this West Coast mother is not one "to sit with idle hands and brains." Far from a remnant of "the glories of yesterday," she is fully capable of supporting her nation in "its turn of tide toward civilization and advancement."[54]

Johnson's determined effort to redeem the reputation of Native women included not only their child-rearing practices, but also the meaning and extent of their labours. Her 1888 poem "Workworn" echoed the insistence of early feminists on the value of women's work, despite its recurring dismissal by misogynist observers.[55] Johnson took this argument a step further than the great majority of her contemporaries, however, when she challenged commonplace depictions of Natives as lazy and improvident. She showed Native homemakers, much like other idealized colonial householders, toiling unceasingly to ensure the present and future well-being of their families. Her frequently reprinted article "The Iroquois Women of Canada" (1895) insisted on the up-to-date domestic skills of Native homemakers, as demonstrated at annual fairs and exhibitions. The more traditional daily tasks sketched in such accounts as "Winter Indoor Life of the Indian Mother and Child" (1908), "Outdoor Occupations of the Indian Mother and Her Children" (1908), and "The Stings of Civilization" (n.d.) matter-of-factly locate women's work at the centre of a healthy network of social relations.[56] Like the ideal settler women celebrated in the stories of Nellie McClung, Johnson's suffragist friend, Native women appear as full partners in a shared economic enterprise. Far from being mere beasts of burden, they both value themselves and are valued by others.

In stories like "The Potlatch" (1910),[57] "The King's Coin" (1909),[58] and "The Sea-Serpent" (1910),[59] unnamed Native mothers, with their seemingly menial home-based tasks and local knowledge in such realms as herbal medicine, prove critical to their sons' eventual triumph. Moreover, unlike the Anglo-Canadian son in "Her Dominion: A Story of 1867, and Canada's Confederation" (1907), Native offspring honour their parents.[60] Tenas Tyee, the valiant slayer of a mythic monster, the great sea-serpent, fully acknowledges his debt and leaves no doubt about the value of maternal support: "My mother, I could not have killed the monster of greed amongst my people had you not helped me by keeping one place for me at home fresh and clean for my return."[61] Her preparations might appear relatively inconsequential to the insensitive European eye, but in fact they symbolize the maternal contribution to the foundations of a male hero's spirituality and principles. In effect, this humble, unnamed mother enabled her son to become his nation's saviour. In harmony with their surroundings and their kin, it is Johnson's later female characters, idealized as mothers and daughters, rather than the male warriors who might attract more attention, who sustain the moral and physical foundations of life.

Johnson tended not to disseminate this provocative message very openly to her many young male readers in the pages of the American magazine *The Boys' World*, a sustaining market in her last years. While the majority of her stories for male juveniles feature Native youth, Indian mothers are significantly less visible than their white counterparts. On the other hand, Native mothers are not killed off in the English tradition of populating fiction with orphan heroes – rather, they are simply offstage, as in the case of the mother of "Maurice of His Majesty's Mails."[62] When seen, they remain silent because they do not speak English, as in "A Night with 'North Eagle.'"[63] In both cases, readers are left with the quiet confidence that Native women are hard at work, keeping the home fires burning for good sons.

Johnson's presentation of Native women's work was not restricted to the domestic realm. Like the Iroquois matrons she celebrated, Indian women, whatever their tribal affiliation, assume important public roles on occasion. As their choral counterparts do in classical Greek plays, they emerge as moral arbiters to demand justice and sometimes revenge. One of her first poems, "A Cry from an Indian Wife" (1885), a powerful response to the plight of the prairie tribes in the 1885 conflict, highlights the perspective of the tormented Native wife and mother. It is the female non-combatant, rather than the warrior or chief – the male figures given authority status in negotiations with imperial agents – who articulates the consequences of the "greed of white men's hands."[64] Attribution of moral leadership to women continued to characterize Johnson's writing throughout her career. The growing desperation of Indian communities was sharply sketched in two poems, "The Cattle Thief" (1894) and "The Corn Husker" (1896), which describe the famine stalking the original inhabitants of the land. Given Johnson's belief that female labour and female ethics stood at the heart of the Native world, it was not surprising that she assigned to women the task of condemning official Canadian policies. In the first poem, a daughter defends the body of her father, murdered by white "demons" who "robbed him first of bread."[65] In the second, the tragedy engulfing an entire people is embodied in the description of one old woman: "Age in her fingers, hunger in her face, / Her shoulders stooped with weight of work and years." Determinedly toiling in all-too-scanty fields, she offers living testimony to "might's injustice."[66] She also provides a contrast to the Sioux chief in "Silhouette" (1894). While the gaunt male representative of the destruction of Canada's First Nations stands still, looking impotently "towards the empty west, to see / The never-coming herd of buffalo," his female counterpart works to glean the harvest fields, in an image reminiscent of the biblical women labourers, Ruth and Naomi.[67]

As a corollary to her insistence on the high principles and significant economic contribution of Native women, Johnson took care to describe the respect in which women were held in their own communities. She supplied "a powerful contradiction to the widespread error, that Indian men look down upon and belittle their women."[68] Like many subsequent Native commentators, she argued that European newcomers threatened an older order in which women and men lived in harmony. For Johnson, that order was embodied most concretely in the power of Iroquois matrons to nominate chiefs. As she observed in "The Lodge of the Law-makers" (1906), disenfranchised white women were still waiting for the power that their Iroquois sisters had held for hundreds of years. Her characterization of prairie tribes, in the poems described above, suggests that she readily extended her argument to regions beyond Mohawk territory. In uncollected western stories, as well as those gathered in *Legends of Vancouver* (1911), she placed women at the centre of respectful coastal communities. While she did not specifically note the matrilineal organization of many British Columbia tribes, a social feature they shared with the Iroquois, she did not hesitate to credit Haida and Coast Salish women with important public authority.

As much as the men in their communities, Johnson's female characters emerge as custodians of truth and tradition. When her BC stories first appeared in *Mother's Magazine* and Vancouver's *Daily Province Magazine,* many were narrated by a woman, most likely Líxwelut, also known as Mary Agnes Capilano, from the reserve on the north shore of Burrard Inlet. However, the collection published in 1911 as *Legends of Vancouver* privileged a single male informant, Su-á-pu-luck, better known as Chief Joe Capilano, by changing the narrator in two legends[69] and omitting another three.[70] Only "The Lost Salmon-Run" retained its original female narrator, presumably because the issue of gender is central to the moral of the story.[71]

The custodian of many stories, Johnson's "old friend, the klootchman,"[72] was not only a storyteller but also "an indefatigable work-woman,"[73] whose labours would be central to the survival of her granddaughter. Similarly, in the original *Mother's Magazine* version of "The Recluse" (titled "The Legend of the Squamish Twins"), "Mrs. Chief" is both an industrious fisher of salmon and a fascinating teller of tales.[74] Equally important, she voices her nation's high regard for women. Even as Vancouver's newspapers were filled with derogatory portraits, these klootchmen, respected elders of their tribes, insisted on the value of the "girl-child." As the legend of the lost salmon run confirms, if individual Native tribes failed at times to appreciate women, the Great Tyee or god – perhaps much like Jesus, whom Johnson's white feminist contemporaries were also endeavouring to recuperate[75] – was ultimately far wiser. Long ago he taught the klootchman's people a hard lesson, leaving them to face starvation when they preferred a son to a daughter. In other legends, such as "The Two Sisters," fathers and chiefs who attend carefully to the wishes of their daughters experience peace rather than war.[76] With such parables, Johnson repudiated colonizers' commonplace assumptions about female inferiority in Native societies, thus effectively undermining one of the key justifications for European imperialism.

When we were children in the 1950s, we were told that Indian men were called "braves" and Indian women were called "squaws." While our progressive parents did not allow the use of the word "nigger" in common rhymes because it was derogatory, they had little notion that "squaw" was equally offensive. If we had had access to Johnson's fiction, we might have known better. In "A Red Girl's Reasoning," when Christie ends her marriage, she accuses her white husband of treating her as his "squaw," a word very difficult for her to utter: "The terrible word had never passed her lips before, and the blood stained her face to her very temples."[77] This message that First Nations cultural practices are never inferior to the normative practices of white society underlies all of Johnson's writing. Her texts, while sometimes appearing romantic and essentialist, also work as strategically crafted interventions in the ideological battle to legitimize the claims for respect of the First Nations in general, and of Aboriginal women in particular.

Notes

1 See, for example, Jean Barman, "Aboriginal Women on the Streets of Victoria: Rethinking Transgressive Sexuality during the Colonial Period" (this volume) and her earlier "Taming Aboriginal Sexuality: Gender, Power, and Race in British Columbia, 1850-1900," *BC Studies* 115/116 (Autumn/Winter 1997-98): 237-66; Adele Perry, *On the Edge of Empire: Gender, Race, and the Making of British Columbia, 1849-1871* (Toronto: University of Toronto Press, 2001); and Sarah Carter, *Capturing Women: The Manipulation of Cultural Imagery in Canada's Prairie West* (Montreal and Kingston: McGill-Queen's University Press, 1997).

2 On Molly Brant see Jean Johnston, "Molly Brant: Mohawk Matron," *Ontario History* 61, 2 (1964): 105-23; and Gretchen Green, "Molly Brant, Catharine Brant, and Their Daughters: A Study in Colonial Acculturation," *Ontario History* 81, 3 (September 1989): 235-50.

3 Veronica Strong-Boag and Carole Gerson, *Paddling Her Own Canoe: The Times and Texts of E. Pauline Johnson (Tekahionwake)* (Toronto: University of Toronto Press, 2000), 98.

4 See Angela Burke, "Ethel Brant Monture: Champion of Her People," *Star Weekly*, 3 October 1953; and Beth Brant, *Writing As Witness: Essay and Talk* (Toronto: Women's Press, 1994).

5 Lee Maracle, interview by Hartmut Lutz, in *Contemporary Challenges: Conversations with Canadian Native Authors*, 169-79 (Saskatoon: Fifth House, 1991). Armstrong's recent novel, *whispering in shadows* (Penticton, BC: Theytus Press, 2000), the story of an Okanagan woman artist and activist, opens with Johnson's poem "Shadowland."

6 See Veronica Strong-Boag, "'A People Akin to Mine': Indians and Highlanders within the British Empire," *Native Studies Review* 14, 1 (2001): 27-53.

7 See Clayton W. McCall, "Fresh Light on Pauline Johnson," unpublished ms., n.d., Johnson Collection, Vancouver City Archives. On William Johnson's legendary progeny, see Charlotte Gray, *Flint and Feather: The Life and Times of E. Pauline Johnson (Tekahionwake)* (Toronto: HarperFlamingo, 2002), 24.

8 "Charming Word Pictures: Etchings of a Muskoka Idler," *Brantford Courier*, 15 August, 23 August, 4 September 1890, are all signed "Rollstone."

9 See Sylvia Van Kirk's discussion of the difficulties of mixed-race children, "Tracing the Fortunes of Five Founding Families of Victoria," *BC Studies* 115/116 (Autumn/Winter 1997-98): 148-79. She suggests that boys faced considerably greater difficulty in integrating into Euro-Canadian society than did their sisters, an observation that also appears to hold true for Molly Brant's offspring (see Green, "Molly Brant, Catharine Brant, and Their Daughters"). Given the incomplete historical record on Pauline's siblings, it is difficult to fully reconstruct their stories, but it appears that Pauline and her sister Evelyn led less troubled lives than their brothers.

10 *Winnipeg Free Press*, 30 December 1897.

11 Strong-Boag and Gerson, *Paddling*, 109-11.

64   *Carole Gerson and Veronica Strong-Boag*

12 Ruth Phillips, "Performing the Native Woman: Primitivism and Mimicry in Early Twentieth-Century Visual Culture," in *Antimodernism and Artistic Experience: Policing the Boundaries of Modernity,* ed. Lynda Jessup, 26-49 (Toronto: University of Toronto Press, 2001), 28.
13 "The Good Old N.P." (1896) and "Canadian Born" (1897) in *E. Pauline Johnson, Tekahionwake: Collected Poems and Selected Prose,* ed. Carole Gerson and Veronica Strong-Boag, 119, 125 (Toronto: University of Toronto Press, 2002). Hereafter cited as *CPSP.*
14 See E. Pauline Johnson, "A Pagan in St Paul's Cathedral" (1906), *CPSP,* 213-15, at 213.
15 "A Red Girl's Reasoning" (1893), *CPSP,* 188-202, at 197.
16 "The Lodge of the Law-makers" (1906), *CPSP,* 215-18, at 214.
17 Smaro Kamboureli, *Scandalous Bodies: Diasporic Literature in English Canada* (Toronto: Oxford University Press, 2000), 177.
18 Carole Gerson and Gwendolyn Davies, eds., *Canadian Poetry: From the Beginnings through the First World War* (Toronto: McClelland and Stewart, 1994), 269-70.
19 Okanagan storyteller Harry Robinson's account of a Native who was displayed as a specimen in Europe in the late 1880s gives some insight into the "scientific" temperament of the age. See "Captive in an English Circus" in *Write It on Your Heart: The Epic World of an Okanagan Storyteller,* ed. Wendy Wickwire (Vancouver: Talonbooks/Theytus, 1989), 259.
20 *Hamilton Spectator,* 1 March 1892; *Terre Haute Gazette,* 1900; clippings in Johnson fonds, McMaster University.
21 Sara Jeannette Duncan, "Woman's World," *Toronto Globe,* 14 October 1886; *Montreal Gazette, Terre Haute Gazette,* 1900; clippings in Johnson fonds, McMaster University.
22 Duncan, "Woman's World"; *Ladies Pictorial Weekly,* 23 April 1892; *Montreal Gazette,* n.d.; *Hamilton Spectator,* 1 March 1892; *Times Literary Supplement,* 4 December 1913; Gilbert Parker, introduction to *The Moccasin Maker,* by E. Pauline Johnson, 9-12 (Toronto: Briggs, 1913), 12.
23 Parker, introduction to *The Moccasin Maker,* 12.
24 *Fredericton Daily Gleaner,* 20 November 1900.
25 *Globe,* 18 January 1892.
26 Duncan, "Woman's World"; *Montreal Gazette,* n.d.; *Hamilton Spectator,* 1 March 1892; Ernest Thompson Seton, introduction to *The Shagganappi,* by E. Pauline Johnson, 5-7 (Toronto: Briggs, 1913), 5.
27 Seton, introduction to *The Shagganappi,* 5; *Hamilton Spectator,* 1 March 1892; *Ladies Pictorial Weekly,* 23 April 1892.
28 Duncan, "Woman's World."
29 *Chicago Tribune,* 28 January 1897.
30 *CPSP,* 190.
31 *The Moccasin Maker,* 213.
32 E. Pauline Johnson, "A Red Girl's Reasoning," in *CPSP,* 188-202, at 190.
33 E. Pauline Johnson, "The Derelict" (1867), in *The Moccasin Maker,* 212-21 (Toronto: Briggs, 1913), at 213.
34 "A Strong Race Opinion on the Indian Girl in Modern Fiction" (1892), *CPSP,* 177-83.
35 *Paddling,* 144-45. The phrase comes from Elaine Showalter, *Daughters of Decadence: Women Writers of the Fin de Siècle* (New Brunswick, NJ: Rutgers University Press, 1993).
36 *CPSP,* 185; E. Pauline Johnson, "Striking Camp," *Saturday Night,* 29 August 1891, 7.
37 *CPSP,* 44, 203.
38 "A Cry from an Indian Wife" (1885), *CPSP,* 14-15; "A Red Girl's Reasoning" (1893), *CPSP,* 188-202; "Ojistoh (1895), *CPSP,* 114-16; "Dawendine" (1895), *CPSP,* 112-14; "As It Was in the Beginning" (1899), *CPSP,* 205-12.
39 *CPSP,* 201.
40 *CPSP,* 116.
41 *CPSP,* 113.
42 Johnson, "The Derelict," 213.
43 Ibid., 221.
44 *CPSP,* 212.
45 E. Pauline Johnson, "The Grey Archway" (1911), in *Legends of Vancouver,* 117-28 (Toronto: McClelland and Stewart, 1961).

46 "The Pilot of the Plains" (1891), *CPSP*, 205-12; "The Quill Worker" (1896), *CPSP*, 122-23; "The Legend of the Qu'Appelle Valley" (1898), *CPSP*, 126-28; "The Call of the Old Qu'Appelle Valley," *Daily Province Magazine*, 19 November 1910, 6, 11; "The Ballad of Yaada" (1913), *CPSP*, 162-63.

47 See Elizabeth Waterston, *Rapt in Plaid: Canadian Literature and Scottish Tradition* (Toronto: University of Toronto Press, 2001), 31-34. Waterston draws a connection between Johnson and Scottish literary figures, notably Robbie Burns.

48 See the discussion in Carol Ann Cooper, "'To Be Free on Our Lands': Coast Tsimshian and Nisga'a Societies in Historical Perspective, 1820-1900" (PhD dissertation, University of Waterloo, 1993), 182.

49 "Lullaby of the Iroquois" (1896), *CPSP*, 223-27.

50 "Mothers of a Great Red Race" (1908), *CPSP*, 223-27, and "Heroic Indian Mothers," *Mother's Magazine*, 3 September 1908, 23-24.

51 "Heroic Indian Mothers," 23.

52 "Catharine of the Crow's Nest" (1910), *The Moccasin Maker*, 86-101, and "The Tenas Klootchman" (1911), *The Moccasin Maker*, 201-11.

53 "Hoolool of the Totem Poles" (1911), *CPSP*, 257-62.

54 E. Pauline Johnson, "The Iroquois Women of Canada" (1895), *CPSP*, 203-5, at 204.

55 "Workworn" (1888), *CPSP*, 36. There is now a considerable literature on suffragist arguments about the value of women's work, both reproductive and productive. See, *inter alia*, Veronica Strong-Boag, "Pulling in Double Harness or Hauling a Double Load: Women, Work and Feminism on the Canadian Prairie," *Journal of Canadian Studies* 21, 3 (Fall 1986): 32-52.

56 "Winter Indoor Life of the Indian Mother and Child," *Mother's Magazine*, February 1908, 5, 54; "Outdoor Occupations of the Indian Mother and Her Children," *Mother's Magazine*, July 1908, 22-23; "The Stings of Civilization" (n.d.), *CPSP*, 283-87.

57 "The Potlatch" (1910), *CPSP*, 250-57.

58 "The King's Coin" (1909), *Boys' World*, 29 May, 4; 5 June, 4; 12 June, 4; 19 June, 4; 26 June, 4.

59 "The Sea-Serpent" (1910), *Legends of Vancouver*, 77-88.

60 "Her Dominion: A Story of 1867, and Canada's Confederation," *Mother's Magazine*, July 1907, 10-11; 40.

61 Johnson, *Legends of Vancouver*, 85.

62 "Maurice of His Majesty's Mails," *Boys' World*, 23 July 1906, 1-2; 7.

63 "A Night with 'North Eagle,'" *Boys' World*, 23 July 1906, 1-2; 7.

64 *CPSP*, 15.

65 "The Cattle Thief" (1894), *CPSP*, 97-99.

66 "The Corn Husker" (1896), *CPSP*, 121.

67 "Silhouette" (1894), *CPSP*, 104-5.

68 Johnson, "The Iroquois Women of Canada," *CPSP*, 205.

69 In *Mother's Magazine*, the "Legend of the Two Sisters" is told by "the quaint old Indian mother." However, in the version published in *Daily Province Magazine* as "The True Legend of Vancouver's Lions," she is replaced by "the chief," who remains the narrator in *Legends of Vancouver*.

70 Also narrated by "the old Klootchman" are stories that were never collected: "The Legend of the Seven Swans," "The Legend of the Ice Babies," and "The Legend of Lillooet Falls," the latter reprinted in *The Moccasin Maker*. Little is known about the editing of *Legends of Vancouver*, other than that it was prepared by a committee of Johnson's supporters to raise money for her medical and living expenses.

71 "The Lost Salmon Run" (1911), *Legends of Vancouver*, 39-52.

72 According to Johnson, "In the Chinook tongue, in general usage as a trade language on the Pacific coast, Klootchman means woman, and is a word used with great respect among the Indian tribes." *Mother's Magazine*, January 1909, 23.

73 Johnson, *Legends of Vancouver*, 53.

74 "The Recluse" (1911), *Legends of Vancouver*, 39-52; "The Legend of the Squamish Twins," *Mother's Magazine*, 23 July 1910, 16-17.

75 See Sharon Anne Cook, *"Through Sunshine and Shadow": The Woman's Christian Temperance Union, Evangelicalism and Reform in Ontario, 1874-1930* (Montreal and Kingston: McGill-Queen's University Press, 1995) on the liberalization of Protestant churches and their promise of spiritual and marital equality. See also Barbara Welter, "The Feminization of American Religion," in *Clio's Consciousness Raised*, ed. Mary Hartman and L. Banner, 137-55 (New York: Harper and Row, 1973); Ann Douglas, *The Feminization of American Culture* (New York: Knopf, 1977).
76 "The Two Sisters" (1911), *Legends of Vancouver*, 19-28.
77 *CPSP*, 198.

3
Performing for "Imperial Eyes": Bernice Loft and Ethel Brant Monture, Ontario, 1930s-60s
Cecilia Morgan

Indians Not Vanishing Race But Growing, Progressing, Club Hears.
The problems with which the Indians of the Twentieth Century are faced were ably presented to a large and appreciative audience of Canadian Club women when Mrs Ethel Brant Monture addressed their meeting on Wednesday afternoon at the Civic Centre. The attractive, smartly-dressed descendant of the famous Mohawk chief, Joseph Brant, spoke in a beautifully modulated voice and quite captivated her listeners with her charming, natural manner.[1]

The newspaper report went on to outline Monture's arguments about the need for education for "Indians." Those who had been the beneficiaries of non-Native education had gone on to make substantial educational and cultural contributions to Canadian society. Monture appreciated the "small rural schools that are available to Indian children," having attended one such institution herself. As in many of her public appearances, Monture stressed the desire and ability of Native Canadians to adapt to changing circumstances, saying: "Young Indian people of the Twentieth Century find that they cannot and do not wish to live in the past which is but a springboard to the future ... we must prove that we are a part of Canada." However, she also pointed to the "many beautiful Indian legends" and artistic accomplishments, and "encouraged them to be proud of their native birth."[2]

Monture's lecture to the Canadian Club women was one of many such talks delivered over four decades of work as a public lecturer, performer, and writer presenting Iroquois and First Nations history.[3] Furthermore, while she was often hailed by newspaper reporters as anomalous – a unique example of a "civilized Indian woman" who appeared in front of Euro-Canadian audiences – Monture was far from alone. Not only was she a contemporary of other Iroquois historians, educators, and activists such as Milton Martin, Elliott Moses, Harold Hill, and Alma Greene, but Monture was also joined – sometimes literally – in her performances of Native history by another Iroquois woman, Bernice Loft.[4] Throughout the 1930s, Loft spoke about Iroquois history and religion to Euro-Canadian service groups, churches, educational institutions, and girls' and women's organizations throughout Ontario and western New York.[5]

To date, the structure of Ontario historiography allows little room for individuals such as Monture and Loft. Aboriginal peoples rarely figure as historical actors in provincial narratives of the nineteenth century after the War of 1812 and generally are not visible in the twentieth century until the 1960s. What appearances they do make are in carefully delineated areas: disputes over natural resources, discussions of missionary work and education, and, in the twentieth-century context, confrontations and negotiations with Ottawa over its neocolonial policies.[6] Ontario historians often seem to make a tacit assumption that reservations and the state policy that governed them were, indeed, successful at controlling and containing Aboriginal peoples' bodies, keeping them carefully sequestered from the mainstream of Ontario society. However, while I do not want to minimize the colonizing power of the federal and provincial states and other forms of socioeconomic and cultural imperialism over the bodies of Ontario's First Nations, the performances of Monture and Loft suggest there may well be more to this particular narrative than we have assumed.

The performances of these two Iroquois women for the imperial eyes of the Euro-Canadian public pose challenges and questions with the potential to disturb the supposedly neatly delineated boundaries of neocolonialism in Ontario.[7] While they inherited a history of colonized peoples, women and men, who had appeared before imperial audiences in both colonial settings and European metropoles, Monture and Loft's performances of Iroquois identity cannot be reduced to – or dismissed as – simply the enactment of racist stereotypes of "Indians."[8] For one, as public figures, their bodies were not completely contained by the neocolonial state, despite its history of efforts to define and limit Aboriginal women's physical presence outside of reserves.[9] Monture and Loft also attempted to direct their careers and to use the lecture platforms on which they appeared as political stages, from which they (particularly Monture) could make calls for changes to mainstream Canadian society's treatment of Native peoples. This is not to argue that Monture and Loft were somehow free to move outside of racist and colonizing discourses, nor that their challenges to Canadian neocolonialism were not complicated by its structures and practices. Nor can I claim that I have achieved a definitive knowledge of Monture and Loft. Gaps, absences, and silences play a role in my narrative, despite my attempts to uncover and offer some understanding of their lives as they pertained to these performances.[10]

Notwithstanding such caveats, it is possible to gain some glimpses of Loft's and Monture's thoughts about their experiences, not least because both women maintained friendships with two non-Native women, and their correspondence with them has survived. Of course, the act of reading those letters cannot be undertaken simply as a straightforward and uncomplicated reading of their real selves divorced from their representations by others (such as newspaper reporters). The letters do, however, bear witness to these women's complicated struggles with performing the representative Iroquois woman, on and off stage. They also suggest the various ways in which both women attempted to negotiate the genre of such performance and its conventions.

Ethel Brant Monture, the elder of these two women, was born on the New Credit Reserve in 1894 and attended school in the area. In the 1920s she married Wilbur Monture, a Methodist lay preacher, and moved to another part of the Grand River territory. In the 1920s and 1930s she had two children, became active in the church and the Women's Institute, and founded the Women's Section of the Ontario Association of Agricultural Societies (1937-39).[11] She also began making public appearances at gatherings of the Brant Historical Society, reciting Pauline Johnson's poetry and sitting on the society's Johnson memorial committee.[12] Around 1939, Monture left her family and moved to Toronto and then, in 1945, to Rochester, in upstate New York, where she worked first in the Strong Memorial Hospital and then in a men's clothing store. She continued to develop her career as a lecturer and also devoted more time to researching Six Nations history.[13] In 1960 Monture returned to Toronto, where she worked as a staff member for the Canadian Council of Christians and Jews, an organization she respected "not only because of its interest in Canadian Indians but because this interest lack[ed] dogooder overtones of which her people [were] sensitive and resentful."[14] She collaborated with American author Harvey Chalmers on a biography of Joseph Brant and published her own biographical studies of Native leaders.[15] Monture helped found, and became a member of, the Indian Hall of Fame at Six Nations; she also was commemorated in the Ontario Agricultural Hall of Fame.[16] In 1967 she retired to Six Nations, where she died on 31 January 1977.

Bernice Loft was born in 1902 on Six Nations Reserve. Her father, William De-wau-se-ra-keh Loft, was a hereditary Mohawk chief who had attended the Mohawk Institute in Brantford. Loft's mother, Elizabeth Ann Johnson Loft, was a member of the Cayuga and a teacher, who taught her daughter both English and Iroquois crafts and medicine. Both parents instructed their three children in the Five Nations' dialects and the histories and traditions of the Confederacy; as well, Loft learned the Cayuga Longhouse religion of Handsome Lake and attended the local Anglican Sunday school. Loft also had a link to contemporary Aboriginal political activism; in the 1920s her father's brother, Frederick Ogilvie Loft, founded the first Canadian

pan-Native political organization, the League of Indian Nations. After gradu-
ating from high school, Loft became a teacher and subsequently taught in
one of the reserve's schools. However, her knowledge of Iroquois history,
religion, and narratives, as well as financial exigency, took Loft from the
local schoolhouse to lecture platforms and daises, which she toured throughout the 1930s. After her mother's death in 1934, Loft became the mainstay
of her elderly and ailing father. In 1937 Loft married the American Arthur
H. Winslow, who had come to nearby Galt to work and had visited the
Grand River Reserve as a curious tourist. The birth of her daughter, Dawn
Marie, in 1938 brought a lengthy halt to Loft's performances. After her
father's death in 1943, she and her family left the Grand River to live in
Whitman, Massachusetts, where she spent the rest of her life. Arthur's death
in 1962, though, left Loft free to resume her work as a lecturer and orator
for summer camps, where she reminded her audiences of the Iroquois role
in creating Canada and of the history that both she and her non-Iroquois
listeners shared. Loft died recently in the Boston-area nursing home where
she had lived since the mid-1990s.[17]

Both women were born into what has been described as the nadir of
Native-white relations at the national level in Canada. From the 1880s until the 1930s, the Dominion government sought to entrench imperial rule
over Aboriginal peoples with its violent repression of the 1885 Riel upris-
ing, the consolidation of the residential school system, systematic attempts
to outlaw Aboriginal culture (for example, the suppression of the potlatch
and Plains peoples' spiritual practices), and the Department of Indian Affairs' expansion of Indian agents' powers on reserves.[18] The state also sought
to create fundamental shifts in the nature of band governance, as it man-
dated elections for communities in eastern and central Canada.[19] On the
Six Nations Reserve, the divisions between those who supported a council
made up of hereditary chiefs and those who favoured elections were intense. The debate was only partly resolved in 1924 with the imposition of
the latter, an act carried out by the local superintendent with the assistance
of the RCMP. Yet while the tensions over reserve governance were acute
(and are still felt today), Monture and Loft also spent their childhood, adolescence, and young adulthood in a community that experienced a greater
degree of agricultural success and economic prosperity than its prairie or
northern Ontario counterparts.[20] Notwithstanding the Six Nations' concerns
about their lack of political autonomy, they appear to have had more control over social welfare, education, and physical infrastructure (such as roads
and sewers) than other First Nations peoples during this period.[21] As well,
Monture and Loft participated in a rich and varied associational life that
offered a range of activities: traditional Longhouse religious life, Sunday
schools and church socials, temperance work, and annual agricultural
shows.[22] And as their biographical sketches indicate, neither Loft nor Monture

was completely isolated from non-Native society. Loft's descriptions of her home life with William in the 1930s include numerous references to visits by anthropologists and writers eager to mine their expertise on the Iroquois.[23] In turn, Monture's participation in the Brant Historical Society was not an individual act but was part of a larger influx of the Six Nations into the society's meeting rooms, tea parties, and, by the 1940s, executive council positions.[24]

Such associational life also included a history of the Six Nations' own performances at the Grand River, ones which displayed both Iroquois and Euro-Canadian markers of identity. From the early 1860s on, Queen Victoria's birthday was celebrated by the council and community as "Bread and Cheese Day," which grew from the dispensation of food to the community's sick and poor to a day on which all received bread and cheese, listened to speeches by both chiefs and Brant County officials, and pledged loyalty to the crown. The annual fall fairs' ploughing matches, as well as the related exhibition of agricultural produce and the juried competition that evaluated it, were also particular performances of the community's agricultural history and expertise. Longhouse religious practices involved ritual display and ceremony, such as the Thanksgiving or Harvest Ritual and the New Year's Celebration. As well as pageants, rituals, and other types of publicly enacted social ceremonies, the Six Nations also had a long-standing history of public, political rhetoric that was enacted in council meetings and in dealings with Euro-Canadian officials.[25]

But when Monture and Loft performed outside the Grand River Reserve, they walked onto a stage on which certain kinds of generic conventions and tropes defined such performances, playing to packed audiences in Wild West shows and colonial exhibitions since the mid-nineteenth century.[26] However, the kinds of performance venues and circuits that Monture and Loft frequented had more in common with Pauline Johnson's recital platforms and drawing-room appearances. Furthermore, both Monture and Loft were directly inspired by Johnson's legacy. Monture's first recorded presentation to the Brant Historical Society was in September 1934, where she "recited very splendidly three poems," including Johnson's "The Song My Paddle Sings," all of which were "enthusiastically received."[27] On a return visit in 1950, Monture told the society of her speaking tour in the western provinces, where she had addressed thirty "women's Canadian Clubs."[28] By April 1952, Monture had become a "prominent lecturer and authority on Indian matters" in the society's eyes when she appeared before them to describe her ancestor, Joseph, and to correct the "many discrepancies recorded of Indian history."[29] Monture's stock does seem to have risen over the years, for in 1958 the historical society invited her to speak at its fiftieth anniversary banquet. She agreed to waive her usual fee of $60 but asked that they pay her expenses of $15 (an offer they accepted).[30] As well as historical societies (in both southern Ontario and the United States), Monture's customary speaking venues were women's organizations, secular and denominational; Canadian Clubs; high schools; and, in the 1950s, CBC television and radio broadcasts. Monture also taught at various summer schools, including one run for children by the Suffolk Museum at Stony Brook, New York, in 1959, where she was billed as a "well-known national lecturer and author on Indian culture."[31]

Thus Monture presented herself, and was presented by her supporters to the public, as an expert, an authority, although as I will discuss later, she lacked access to the kinds of funds and connections that would have allowed her to concentrate solely on her work. And her speaking engagements were not limited to discussions of the past, even though Iroquois history was a central focus of all her work. Monture also used the lecture platform as a vehicle to demonstrate Native ingenuity, intelligence, and resourcefulness. In short, like Johnson, she intended to show their fitness to be full citizens of both Aboriginal and non-Native Canadian society. In 1963 Monture spoke on behalf of the National Indian Council of Canada to the Royal Commission on Bilingualism and Biculturalism, where she told the commissioners that "Canada is a tri-cultural country," one "indelibly" marked by Native people. "We feel that until we are taking our full share at all levels we are in many ways a wasted people." However, while making a claim to full citizenship, Monture went on to explain the unique position of Aboriginal peoples in Canada: "Indians possess a culture quite distinct from the biculturalism of French Canadians through which is woven a pattern of Canadian rights."[32] A year later, at an "Indian folk school" held in the southwestern Ontario town of Petrolia, Monture's keynote speech focused on issues such as representations of Native peoples in school textbooks (a favourite subject for both Monture and other Aboriginal activists in Ontario) and on the need for an "overhauling" of the Department of Indian Affairs. "We would welcome thorough research into the operation of the Indian administration to determine what is necessary to improve it," she told her audience.[33]

Much of Monture's analysis of the problems faced by Native communities centred on the need for improvements in education; she laid claim to the resources of non-Native Canadian society in order to improve Aboriginal peoples' lives and communities. Her "College for Indian Youth," a 1940 *Maclean's* article, discussed the importance of the extension courses run by agricultural colleges on Six Nations. Here Native boys learned about crop and livestock management, while girls studied various dimensions of household and domestic management. Monture was particularly proud of their accomplishments in dressmaking, claiming that their struggles with tissue-paper patterns and sewing machines led them to "find self-expression in making a truly pretty dress. This bolstering of the ego is one of our best by-products."[34] While Monture admired these courses for their ability to equip Six Nations young women and men with Euro-Canadian tools, she did not see aquiring new economic skills as replacing long traditions. On the contrary, she described the gala night that ended the course as an occasion when "stately old racial customs" were practised, noting that "here we see, in the bearing of these young people, the self-esteem of our race."[35]

Monture also turned her attention to the situation of Aboriginal women. In "Ontario Indian Reservations Have Fine Institutes," a piece that explored the work of Women's Institutes on reserves, she told her readers that Native women had taken such a "splendid adaptable program" and tailored it to their own needs, providing social services to the elderly and disabled, supervising school curricula and its implementation for Native children, beautifying communities, and developing a leadership that placed Native women firmly within the nation's life. Native women had educated themselves about public health, housing improvements, child psychology, and – tellingly – "Constitutional laws as applied to Reservations." They corresponded with a world outside the borders of Canada as they wrote to like-minded women in Mexico and Britain. The institutes also sought to maintain certain kinds of Native practices and knowledge by appropriating the strategies and methodologies of non-Native society. They had preserved oral histories, "the choicest form of Historical Research," in writing. As well, Monture believed the reserve institutes ensured that "old crafts" could become a "profitable sideline for the women" by exercising strict controls over quality: "Romance and sentiment may be worth a nickel, but it's really hard to get a dime for them if they are poorly made." In Monture's account it was Native women, not their Euro-Canadian counterparts, who were responsible for adapting a non-Native institution to their own needs: the institute's success was not a result of mainstream society's beneficence and paternalism. A typical meeting was marked by the pleasure taken by participants, many of whom had walked over five miles to attend. It might be in either an Aboriginal language or a mixture of Native and English speech, and "everyone takes part and everyone takes responsibility." Substantial amounts of food were provided "to keep a woman stepping briskly on her homeward walk," and "it is an honour to entertain the Institutes, so meetings are usually held in homes."[36]

At first glance, Monture might seem to a twenty-first-century critic to be delivering mixed messages to her readers, being ambivalent about political strategies, and not arguing strongly enough for specifically Aboriginal practices and values. However, as much as she called for education for Native peoples (and that demand could be seen as simply reminding Euro-Canadian society of a promise made but hardly kept), she also argued for the education of non-Natives and critiqued mainstream Canadian society sharply for its ignorance of her peoples and its racism. Asked in 1964 if she thought there was an "Indian problem," Monture replied, "Oh no, we've never thought WE were a problem. We've always looked on you whites as the problem!"[37] In her submission to the Centennial Commission, the federal body set up to organize events marking Canada's one-hundredth anniversary, Monture told her readers that "through the years we have been surveyed by an endless parade of observers. We have been simpered over as the 'dear dead race' by sentimentalists who see us as a romantic hangover. Or again we break out from the printed page as wooden cigar adornments, seldom as human beings intent on holding to a country and an identity. The writer, always of another race, uses the yardstick of his own values and understanding."[38] Monture's words take on added power when we consider their audience: a group of non-Natives, themselves intent on constructing and celebrating a particular kind of Canadian identity.

Moreover, Monture stringently objected to the kinds of performances of Native masculinity present in Canadian popular culture, ones that were repeated and reiterated in the images of "scalping and savage" Native men that she felt were endemic to many school textbooks. In her work on Brant, Crowfoot, and Oronhyatekha, she created historical portraits of men who were more than such a stereotype; for her, these men were skilled and eloquent diplomats, politicians, and rhetoricians, intelligent and wise leaders of their people.[39] As well, they were devoted husbands and fathers, who came from societies where family and community ties were valued; societies, moreover, where women had important roles and made essential political, social, and cultural contributions.[40] Monture also was fascinated by these men's roles as cultural and political mediators, and she quite likely identified with them in this role.[41]

But unlike Oronhyatekha, who posed in Mohawk ceremonial dress and in his Independent Order of Foresters' uniform, Monture rarely appeared in Native dress for her talks. Except for the occasions when she actually played Johnson – such as a 1955 pageant at the Grand River – she generally did not, for example, dress in the kind of Aboriginal bricolage designed and displayed by Johnson. Monture's own performances, official and informal, were usually delivered in Euro-Canadian feminine garb; indeed, newspaper interviews remarked on her chic, well-groomed appearance that was combined with her "Indian" features. "The inherent refined dignity of the Indian is very apparent in Mrs. Monture [who] was dressed in a simple blue suit, with a silver brooch," commented one writer.[42] It is possible that the press's close attention to her appearance may have been a twentieth-century manifestation of the Victorian fetishization of Native peoples' bodies. Rather than being fascinated by feathers and fringes, though, non-Native observers could be pleasantly surprised at the spectacle of an "Indian" woman who wore a two-piece suit, nylon stockings, heels, and a carefully coiffed Western-style hairdo. The press's treatment of Monture exoticized her while simultaneously suggesting that here, indeed, was proof of the efficacy of assimilationist strategies.

Yet as her remarks about the positive effects of Aboriginal girls learning to construct their own European-style clothes indicate, Monture herself was a willing participant in her image as a chic and sophisticated urbanite. After helping to open an Indian centre in Toronto during the mid-1960s, Monture remarked that she was "proud of [the] innate fashion sense" of the young Native women she had met in that city, who enjoy a shopping spree with their first paycheque. Many young Native women, Monture declared, "are fashionably well-dressed and well-groomed."[43] Monture's family remembered her as having attended Sunday service in the 1920s in a "red velvet dress, with her long dark hair tightly braided."[44] Monture's wardrobe was one of the subjects she discussed with her friend, Victoria University Coleridge scholar Kathleen Coburn, particularly when she was setting off on a lecture tour and was concerned about appearing "smart."[45] "I know," she wrote Coburn, "I have the failing of being uneasy and low if I am not well-groomed and in moderate style but maybe that is something I should give up. But happily detergents are here and I am near Lake Ontario. But I might as well face it – I love to look well. But so did my ancestors – Joseph loved his spotless shirts and his Catherine had beautifully fitted 'leggins.'"[46]

Monture's public performances, then, linked historical knowledge to contemporary activism and were complex enactments of modernity and of colonial hybridity – or movement through "space and time" – as she invoked Six Nations' history and criss-crossed the Canadian/United States' border.[47] She argued strenuously that Aboriginal peoples were capable of cultural adaptation and amalgamation, but that neither process should be mistaken for assimilation. She frequently hinted that, far from being frozen or dying (a favourite Euro-Canadian trope for Native peoples and their societies), the Six Nations possessed a living and dynamic culture, capable of incorporating useful aspects of mainstream "Canadian" social and cultural practices, but as a means of enhancing, not destroying, those of the Iroquois. Unlike her contemporary Elliott Moses, Monture refused to pathologize Aboriginal peoples' practices and values or to accept assimilation as an inevitable, albeit tragic fate.[48] Even if she did not perform Native identity on the lecture platform in the same manner as Johnson or, as we shall see, Loft, an important aspect of that performance was Monture's claim to descent from Brant. And frequently her credentials as an expert included that of genealogical authenticity, as she was invariably billed as Brant's descendant. While Monture usually only stated her genealogy without explaining explicitly its significance, it is likely that for her this was yet another means of reminding non-Native Canadians of the living and dynamic nature of Native peoples. It showed that Brant and all he stood for were not accessible only in the pages of history books. Rather, Brant and the Six Nations lived on and could not be dismissed as having no meaning or significance for modern Canadian society. It could even be said that his legacy of leadership transcended gendered bodies, as he was embodied in the body of an Iroquois woman. Of course, Monture's own narratives of Native peoples' significance had their own silences and gaps; while she was certainly aware of racism, she preferred celebratory narratives of Aboriginal agency and disliked dwelling on neocolonial state policies and procedures.[49]

We might wonder, too, why her promoters felt it was necessary to stress her authenticity, why they linked her ability to speak the truth about her people to bloodlines. Was she seen as an "exceptional Indian" by virtue of both her appearance and her genealogy? Was their reception of her performance tinged with an antimodernist pleasure in her authenticity, a pleasure that prevented her audiences from seeing her as both Aboriginal and modern?[50] If such was the case, Monture's correspondence with her non-Native friends and patrons holds few hints that she reacted on a personal level to such stereotypes. Given Monture's apparent self-possession, it may have been simply too painful and too much of a risk for her to expose to non-Natives the psychic cost of colonialism. Monture may not have felt sufficient intimacy with and trust toward Coburn or the American scholar of Iroquois history, Paul Wallace (unlike Loft who, as we shall see, did speak of such things to her friend Celia File).[51]

Monture was not reticent about her financial struggles and her need for institutional support to carry out her research and writing. When she wrote to Wallace about his contacts at the American Philosophical Society (APS) in the 1950s, Monture inquired about the possibility of a society grant and informed him of her application for a Guggenheim fellowship.[52] When her application for the latter was rejected, Monture wrote breezily but with an underlying wistfulness to Wallace: "No, I did not achieve a Guggenheim! Cannot seem to worry about it but it would have been wonderful I think although it is hard to imagine having it since I have always had to be concerned about ways and means. Anyway, that is clear. I shall not have to worry about G-n-h-m ways and means!"[53] More disappointment was to follow, for in 1953 Wallace informed Monture that while the APS would buy her work (a biography of Brant) upon completion, at present the society could not consider a "grant-in-aid." Funds were short at the time, and they were unsure of her scholarly credentials. Wallace advised her to submit a "finished chapter of the Brant biography, well organized, with bibliography, documentation and a clear outline of how you intend to proceed," accompanied by a supporting letter from "someone like Dr. Vail of the New York Historical Society" who would vouch for Monture's qualifications (according to Wallace, Vail would be quite happy to do so). "These men of science at the APS are hard-boiled and take little on spec. They are a splendid group to be connected with, and they are deeply interested in what you are doing. But it is one of the rules of the game with them that you must prove that you can get along (in scholarly work) without help before they will give you any."[54]

Performances, therefore, of genealogy and authenticity were not enough for Philadelphia's "men of science." Nor did they carry sufficient weight for Monture to receive much support from Canadian organizations, despite the number of letters Coburn wrote on her behalf.[55] In Coburn's letters, Monture was cited first and foremost for her genealogy, as a descendant of Joseph Brant and a relation of Pauline Johnson: "She comes therefore of outstandingly intelligent and capable Indian stock, a fact obvious to anyone who meets her."[56] But Coburn also mentioned Monture's long-standing interest in Native history and "problems of the Indians," and the work she had already completed: her CBC broadcasts, the first volume of Brant's life, and her lecture tours for the Canadian Clubs. Coburn made no secret of Monture's lack of a university education, for its absence prevented her from receiving funds that would support her work. However, she made it clear Monture had "worlds more experience and training than many persons who have more paper certificates."[57] Moreover, Monture had access to reserves across North America and the knowledge that these locations contained, while simultaneously being "very much persona grata in anthropological and historical societies."[58] Overall, she concluded, Monture's "humanity and sense of humour, as well as her Indian wisdom, will enable her to do more effective pieces of writing, I believe, than many persons with higher academic qualifications."[59] Coburn also believed that Monture had more to offer the Canadian reading public than her history of Brant, as she frequently told the funding agencies that she had encouraged Monture to write her own "very good" story because there had to that point been "no account of what it means to be brought up on an Indian Reserve." In her 1965 letter to the Centennial Commission's Publication Programme, Coburn stated that while Monture's passion for her people and devotion to their history made her "more eager to write about them, than an impersonal account," such "objectivity will be impossible and that much the more potent and valuable thing Mrs Monture could do would be to fuse those two stories into one, frankly, told in the first person singular."

I do not know if Coburn told Monture of her recommendations to the commission, but it is unlikely, for Monture might not have taken kindly the suggestion that she was incapable of objectivity. After all, her public life was devoted to the demolition of what she perceived to be biased, subjective, and untrue histories. Yet it is worth reflecting on Coburn's desires for Monture's work. The Subaltern Studies Collective and feminist scholars, amongst others, have long made us aware of how the notion of "objective location" can be used to disqualify marginalized groups from writing "their" own histories. To be sure, twenty-first-century scholars (including myself) would have prized Monture's narrative. But what does Monture's desire to not write about herself say about Monture? Caution is needed in the face of Monture's reticence on this topic. Yet her reticence – or silence – about her own personal struggles might be construed as an attempt to move beyond a state of painful "compulsory visibility," to shift the audience's focus from Monture as an (always raced, always gendered) individual to a collectivity, the Iroquois.[60] Their history, she argued, made it impossible to see them as pathetic victims. In speaking of her history, it seems that Monture was also speaking of herself, albeit not strictly or solely as an Iroquois woman. In performing that history – whether reciting Pauline Johnson, writing about Oronhyatekha, or lecturing about Brant – Monture was also struggling to perform a subjectivity that was linked to, although not confined by, a particular kind of memory and historical narrative. Monture's life and work remind us of the performed nature of history, a performance enacted in social, cultural, and political contexts through the mechanisms of repetition and reenactment, which are subject to reworking, negotiation, and, at times, contestation.[61]

Monture's appearances, both off and on the lecture platform, suggest her desire to craft and control her public persona as much as possible. While Loft, as I shall explore later, privately agonized over such matters, observers' coverage of her public appearances in the 1930s created a picture of calm and self-possession. Her close friend, the historian and high-school teacher Celia File, described Loft upon first meeting as being "charming" and having a "wonderful personality – beautiful voice – [an] educated, refined public speaker."[62] An interview conducted with both Loft and File at a tea given in their honour by a University of Toronto professor described Loft as an "eloquent woman whose English, spoken in a softly modulated voice, is a pleasure to the ear" and characterized her as "probably the best versed woman in the history, traditions, religions, and customs of the Indians of Canada." But, similar to the way in which Monture used history to make contemporary political arguments, Loft also "spoke as one of a long line of women who have, for generations, enjoyed the franchise, 'for,' she said, with a twinkle in her sloe brown eyes, 'despite all the talk of Indian women being slaves of the wigwam it has been the Indian law and custom that the women elect the chiefs,'" who were chosen for their loyalty and character. "It makes me smile," Loft added, "when I hear women talking about the franchise, but I feel sorry, sometimes, when I think how they use it – or fail to use it. They could do so much."[63]

Loft herself was certainly not impervious to the public's reception of her work. For one, she used others' descriptions to promote herself and cited accolades from the *London Evening Advertiser,* the *Simcoe Reformer,* and the *Napanee Beaver* in her program; she also included lists of endorsements from the Boy Scouts, a United Church minister, and Lt. Col. Morgan, the

superintendent at Six Nations.⁶⁴ In this material Loft did not have to speak
or make claims for her expertise and knowledge; others, most notably non-
Native experts, adjudicated her authority and did so for her. File, for example, told the Ontario public that Loft's father was Chief Sah-re-ne-wah-ne,
that she was descended from Brant, and that her home at Six Nations had
been a meeting place for all six tribes. Thus Loft spoke all Iroquois languages and had learned all her people's histories, traditions, and folklore.
Another paragraph informed potential audiences that "outstanding ethnolo-
gists" from the Smithsonian had seen her father as the "most reliable authority on the Reserve" and that his knowledge had been passed on to her.
Because of her background, Loft was "well suited" to interpret her people's
"legends" to white Canadians. But such an interpretation was a gendered
performance, at least in the eyes of Loft's supporters. As well as Loft's embodiment of Iroquois history and culture, she also was a "lady of culture
and refinement, with the grace and dignity and the fine musical voice peculiar to women of her race. Her charming personality makes her addition-
ally attractive."⁶⁵

The program suggests how Loft – and also Monture, about whom similar
things were said – had to participate in the drama of playing Indian. In this
role Loft had to appear both a refined and "authentic" representation of
Iroquois womanhood, her authority verified by the Smithsonian's scholars
in order to garner bookings.⁶⁶ It would be naive to assume that Loft had no
hand in making decisions about her program copy, if for no other reason
than she was acutely self-conscious about her presentation and aware of her
need to satisfy her audiences. Loft read her reviews and frequently commented on them in her correspondence with File. A description of Loft by a
St. Catharines' newspaper as a "lovely, cultured, soft-voiced Indian girl"
made her want "to keep that, to merit that. Surely even that is something
for our race, something accomplished."⁶⁷ A Hamilton reporter, "who fan-
cies himself quite a critic," was kind, "but I also got my fiercest criticism,"
wrote Loft. "[He] said I did not have the histrionic ability of Frances Nickawa
but that she was almost neurotic in her intensity. So where does that leave
me?" Yet while Loft was perturbed by these comments, she was not silenced.
She went on to tell File that the reporter had made a "bad mistake," as he
claimed that her solos were "very well-rendered but would have been much
better enjoyed if not given in the Indian language and had they been intel-
ligible to the audience." However, "Pale Moon," "Indian Dawn," and "By
the Waters of Minnetonka" had all been sung in English.⁶⁸

While critics, both informed and ignorant, were a problem, Loft was even
more demanding of herself. "What I know of Indian history and customs is
only a smattering. I'm ashamed to get up and speak about it, when I think
of how little I do know," she told File in 1934. Possibly a performance in
which Loft had stage fright and was "weary with sorrow" in the aftermath

of her mother's death precipitated this confession. She had appeared last on the program and thus did a reading instead of telling the "story of the wampum." She wrote: "I found myself speaking very slowly and distinctly, so I knew the ability to think on my feet was nil – and the heat of the Klieg lights centred on me was awful besides. The program had already been too long, and I didn't seem to give a damn." Her audience was "kindness itself," but Loft told File, "[I] was a big disappointment to myself and a 'flop' in truth ... I never felt myself to be such a regular wash-out at that time."[69] When appearing in Brockville, Loft was tired, had a headache, and did not recite "The Cattle Thief" as she could not be heard in the gallery. She told File that she knew her voice was *rotten,* even though the review stated otherwise.[70]

Not all of Loft's unhappiness with certain performances was caused by her own self-doubt, for she also was a keen and critical assessor of audiences' reactions. In Buffalo in 1936, Loft spoke primarily to church groups and was told by one minister that she "brought a totally different slant of the Indian race to him (Bologna, or is it Baloney!)." On this tour she found that her audiences were "as in Canada like doubting Thomases, and then wax enthusiastic." But even that enthusiasm might ring hollow to Loft. "Today I had an awful feeling after speaking and could have cried for I realized I was so wandering and incoherent to me, but they were all so pleased. I still feel blue, and could cry my head off. I guess I must be an ass. I think I'll cultivate a poker face for Beulah said the women said my face – eyes and expression – said so much they had to watch me every minute. How awful! Do they know when I feel devilish! Several women cried and there was nothing to cry about."[71] While Loft often wrote jokingly about her "devilish" – and, as she dubbed them, "Mohawk" – tendencies, the degree to which audience misinterpretations and the trickery of performance unsettled her was not limited to this one appearance. Loft wrote that the Hamilton reporter who made incorrect statements about her singing also said that "it was an enjoyment just to look at me with the rich natural colouring of youth. And I had rouge and powder on. I almost don't know whether I'm me or not. Whether Bunny's powder puff is fore or aft or betimes?"[72] A sense of dislocation might, of course, be integral to the act of performance; as Della Pollock has argued, performers encounter a "split role as subject and object."[73] And this was not an atypical reflection by Loft on the threat that the demands of performance posed to her identity and sense of a unified self. Her anxiety also came from the demands of touring; her letters to File are filled with longing for "the peace of home and Dad's homely philosophy."[74]

Loft was at times more satisfied by her appearances and wrote: "The work helps when I get up and be Indian and can lose myself in things Indian."[75] Her own ambitions and financial need, coupled with the knowledge that she was perceived as a "representative" of the Iroquois, pushed Loft back onstage. "Somehow I want to be a success now and a big one. I may never feel at home and it may always be hard but people have said again and again as you that I seemed a Missionary for our race."[76] But it was precisely the exigencies of having to be an "Indian" for a non-Native society that tormented Loft "because first and foremost," she wrote, "when I go to speak – my Indian blood stands out and is proclaimed. I am then of necessity a little bit aloof from your people."[77] "I wish I could run from this being peddled on a block as it were and the people wondering and looking rather askance at me if they can find time to have me."[78]

Furthermore, being "peddled" was not just a matter of being commodified in her public appearances. Loft's poverty made it difficult for her to stay in hotels while touring, so she often was billeted with local hosts. Longing for her own home, Loft did not find the houses of the white women with whom she stayed to be domestic havens. She confessed to File, "I never can feel quite myself or at home in all the places I go. Perhaps for one of your race it would be easier to fit in and enjoy things but I never can just make myself at home."[79] The religiosity and respectability of "Mrs. L" in Brockville particularly grated on Loft's nerves, as did her expectation that Loft would accompany her on social visits to her friends' homes and express gratitude toward her. "In one home finally I *revolted* from being sweet and humbly grateful – and didn't say a word. And Mrs. L with a very sweet smile at me said 'Oh no she is not grateful.' Perhaps it was sarcastic because I'd failed to come across."[80] "I think," Loft mused to File in another letter about Mrs. L, "if she does too much for me I'll never be allowed to forget it – and her generosity to the poor Indian will always be the subject of some heartrending later. I can see her telling people I bade her adieu with tears rolling down my face."[81]

And it was not just Mrs. L's expectation that her benevolence would be properly appreciated by Loft that raised the latter's ire. Loft also questioned the honesty and motives of Mary Edgar, who ran the girls' summer camp at which Loft appeared. In July 1936 Loft was astonished to hear that Edgar was offering her only ten dollars a week and expenses for the summer, despite having promised her twenty. Writing to File, Loft said, "[I] was fairly stunned for I thought of all I owed you [Celia File] ... and I managed to gasp out I think we agreed on twenty. I supposed even idealists have an eye out for themselves." She remembered the advice of another, non-Native lecturer to always get written agreements: "And I said what an awful recommendation for your race – I can't conceive of Miss Edgar not living up to her word and I'd never think of asking for one. I think she thought she was providing a beautiful holiday for an Indian – but evidently she did not realize just how poor I was."[82] While Loft was not impervious to the gendered racism of white men, the genteel nature of her recitals often brought her directly into contact with white women whose behaviour, in her eyes, left much to be desired. After she had married and moved to Galt, Loft was invited to speak at a tea held at a "grand" house, with a maid and "some *very* society-like" women. When introductions were made, Loft waited for the women to shake her hand, but then forgot and, as she wrote to File:

> [I] extended my hand to a stately lady, she just looked at and ignored my hand, for about a full minute. Did I feel funny? I suppose she was putting the Indian in her place. Then I found afterwards even $$ and a name didn't give her and her fellows true courtesy. They asked me straight out like this that they supposed I would be glad to or like to speak for the IODE joint groups here. And then that awful Mohawk in me quietly said that though I had yet failed to find, save one or two egotists, any public speaker who loved to speak, that for most of them it was an ordeal and a discipline, but that if they cared to hear the Indian's story I should be very glad to come to them. You know after that they thawed out and were more respectful, but *inwardly* I was hurt and resented this discourtesy and rather despised them. I wouldn't breathe this to anyone but you, but you can see how hard it is to climb in this city. Money and position seem to count most.[83]

If "position" did not matter much to Loft, money certainly did. She often referred to her financial state of affairs as a reason for taking up her performing career. The incident in Mrs. L's friend's home made Loft feel that her "Mohawk pride and independence are dragged in the dust for the *sake* of keeping a home going," but she tried, she said, "to think of father and his dependence upon me at such times, and God keep me, I hope I'll win through to a different life some day. I can't quit now!" Loft's fees were a frequent topic in her correspondence with File: they were never adequate, at times were paid grudgingly, and were the source of constant worry.[84] Moreover, touring the province and appearing in public meant that Loft also had to worry about her appearance. Unlike Monture, in her performance Loft wore "Indian" dress that appears, judging from her descriptions, to have been similar to that of Johnson's and which included a buckskin, fringed tunic that File purchased for her from Malabar's, the Toronto costume house. Such an outfit had, for at least one member of her audience, the potential to blur the lines between authenticity and fabrication. She commented that Loft's tunic – which she believed to be "authentic" – reminded her of one she had rented from Malabar's for a production of *Hiawatha*. "Maybe it was the same one," Loft told File, "but did I let a peep out of me. I didn't dare say what I thought – I could almost feel you pinching me – and later on, when we were alone, having a good laugh."[85]

However, it was her offstage appearances, in which Loft had to worry about the trappings of Euro-Canadian femininity, that caused her more anxiety about money. An invitation to travel to Ottawa with her cousin (and pupil) Ella Monture and stay with her uncle Gilbert Monture, who would introduce her to various contacts for future performances, created a flurry of anxieties for Loft. "I'm caught at a bad time," she wrote, "with only one decent slip, not much undies, and only one pair of socks I'm not scared to wear ... I will have to stick to black. I still have my big black hat to wear, I think everybody knows it." She felt she would come off badly in comparison with her cousin, as Ella was always "nicely dressed."[86] The cost of tending to her appearance plagued Loft throughout the 1930s, as she grumbled to File after giving up half an appearance fee to the Pauline Johnson Memorial Fund at Six Nations, telling her: "I want a new dress, shoes, slip, and here Pauline Johnson gets it and she's dead."[87] While Monture also discussed her appearance in Euro-Canadian clothing, she rarely expressed the degree of anxiety about it that Loft felt, possibly because her financial situation was less straitened than Loft's. Moreover, Monture rarely expressed the same degree of doubt about her work in non-Native society, nor did she write about her personal experiences of racism.[88] Yet Loft's concerns over her need for slips, shoes, dresses, and permanent waves were not trivial, nor can they be dismissed as simply the quirks of personal vanity. She was acutely self-conscious of being "an ambassador" for her race and having to appear as a respectable Native woman who, when required, could adopt the costumes and props of genteel Euro-Canadian femininity.

But as well as anxieties over Euro-Canadians' perceptions of her, Loft also felt that her role as an "ambassador" had created jealousies and misconceptions about her within her own community. When her father was quite ill and had to be hospitalized, Loft found out that her neighbours were gossiping about the overly large number of "white people" they believed were in and out of the family's home.[89] Three months later, Loft confided to File that she was still helping her neighbours as her father had done, writing wills, deeds, letters, and grocery lists for those who did not write English. She tried to gain some perspective on the rumours, thinking that she had overreacted. "Perhaps the malicious comment of one woman hurt," she told File, "that I was selling my race." Yet, while she was encouraged by others telling her to keep on with her work, she thought that, just as she was "aloof" from whites, now it was "almost the same with [her] people."[90]

If Loft felt she received contradictory and ambivalent messages from the community about her performances, she had few doubts about her feelings toward Monture. In 1937 the two women appeared together at a recital sponsored by the Guelph Junior Institute. In their shared dressing room, Loft was "amused" by Monture "immediately beginning a recital of Indian successes to tell me I was not the only pebble on the beach." Loft believed that Monture had refused to sit with her and the event's organizer on the platform "because my Indian outfit looked so much nicer than hers."

Monture's recital of "Canadian Born" "filled me with a great amazement: she was so colourless." However, at the end of the recital, Loft was asked to speak at the Canadian Club in Guelph, "so I won."[91] As Loft's terse dismissal of this situation indicates, the neocolonial, commercial context in which they performed might have exacerbated the rivalry between the two women. There may have been little room, so far as audience demand was concerned, for more than one living embodiment of Native authenticity and expertise. However, Loft also disliked Monture's political strategies and felt that Monture was overly conciliatory when speaking to non-Native audiences. Loft described a 1938 appearance in Brantford to which she had gone in a belligerent mood, but which, she felt, was kindly received by the white audience. "I knew Moses and Mrs Monture always just *pat pat pat*," she wrote. "Do you know I honestly believe they admired me for being frank."[92]

In many ways Monture and Loft resemble those Native Americans, identified by Frederick Hoxie as travellers, who launched "journeys of discovery" between 1900 and 1930. These travellers were "intellectuals, religious reformers, and political leaders [who] ... struggled to define and defend areas where their voices would be heard by whites and yet remain recognizable to their kinsmen."[93] Both women deployed their bodies in performance in this struggle and drew upon Native history to remind their Ontario audiences that colonialism was far from being over; that it was being repeated and reenacted, and that Aboriginal peoples' relationship to Canada was, in British historian Antoinette Burton's words, "unfinished business."[94] To be sure, their performances were fraught with perils. Like their contemporaries in the United States, who were also engaged in "playing Indian" in order to reshape the category, Monture's and Loft's performances suggest just how little cultural capital Native peoples had. As Coburn's comments about Monture's "innate" "Indian" disposition, and Loft's observations about her audience's reactions, suggest, this was an "ambiguous and dangerous exercise," one that might simply reinforce certain non-Native notions of "the Indian."[95]

However, despite the imperial and gendered kinds of pleasure, desire, and fantasy that they might have embodied for their audiences, Monture and Loft's own writings remind us that performance is not unidirectional. Performances are not undertaken just for the sake of audiences, but are also embarked upon by performers who have their own motivations, their own fantasies and desires to fulfill.[96] Their writings also remind us that, despite these women's similarities, Monture and Loft cannot be easily assimilated into a totalizing and homogenizing category of colonized women. Such an act strips them of their own psychic and subjective complexities that cannot be reduced solely to the relations of gender, class, and race.[97] Neither woman, for example, reacted in identical or predictable ways to the exigencies of performing for imperial eyes. Monture and Loft thus serve as warnings that feminist scholarship needs to tread carefully, lest we perpetuate those ways of seeing and thinking about embodied contact that comprise such a significant part of the ongoing, not-yet-ended, work of colonialism.

Notes

1 "Proud, Able, People. Indians Not Vanishing Race but Growing, Progressing, Club Hears," source unknown, Ethel Brant Monture file, Woodland Cultural Centre.
2 Ibid.
3 Ethel Brant Monture biography, prepared by the Woodland Cultural Centre staff, Ethel Brant Monture file, Woodland Cultural Centre. See also "Ethel Brant Monture: Lecturer, Author, Expert on Indian Culture," in *Significant Lives: Profiles of Brant County Women*, 101-3 (Brantford: The University Women's Club of Brantford, 1997).
4 Milton Martin was a member of the Canadian armed forces during the First World War. After the war he became a public school teacher, principal, and secretary of the Ontario Public School Men Teacher's Federation. He was a vociferous critic of the representation of Aboriginal people in school textbooks (Colin M. Coates and Cecilia Morgan, *Heroines and History: Representations of Madeleine de Verchères and Laura Secord* [Toronto: University of Toronto Press, 2002], 190-91). Harold Hill and Elliott Moses were both active in the Brant Historical Society; for discussions of their work, see Cecilia Morgan, "History and the Six Nations: Complicating the Imagined Community, 1890s-1960s" (paper presented to the Third Conference on Contemporary Canadian Issues: Nationalism, Citizenship, and National Identity in Canada, Canadian Studies, Mount Allison University, 11-13 November 1999). The work of the Mohawk writer Alma Greene (1896-1984) is discussed in Penny Petrone, *Native Literature in Canada: From the Oral Tradition to the Present* (Toronto: Oxford University Press, 1990), 110, 115, and is excerpted in Daniel David Moses and Terry Goldie, eds., *An Anthology of Canadian Native Literature* (Toronto: Oxford University Press, 1992), 46-51.
5 Loft's career as a performer will be discussed more extensively in this chapter. See, however, George Beaver, Bryan Winslow Colwell, Donald Smith, and Robert Stacey, *Iroquois Fires: The Six Nations Lyrics and Lore of Dawendine (Bernice Loft Winslow)* (Ottawa: Penumbra Press, 1995).
6 Some recent entries in the field that suggest new developments are Janet E. Chute, *The Legacy of Shingwaukonse: A Century of Native Leadership* (Toronto: University of Toronto Press, 1998); Robin Brownlie, "Work Hard and Be Grateful: Native Soldier Settlers in Ontario After the First World War," in *On the Case: Explorations in Social History*, ed. Franca Iacovetta and Wendy Mitchinson, 181-203 (Toronto: University of Toronto Press, 1998); Joan Sangster, "Criminalizing the Colonized: Ontario Native Women Confront the Criminal Justice System, 1920-1960," *Canadian Historical Review* 80, 1 (March 1999): 32-60; Edward S. Rogers and Donald B. Smith, eds., *Aboriginal Ontario: Historical Perspectives on the First Nations* (Toronto: Dundurn Press, 1994).
7 My treatment of the concept of "performance" draws from both the literature on Aboriginal peoples who worked in that capacity (see note 8) and some of Judith Butler's arguments about the performativity of gender, particularly her point that "gender is an identity tenuously constituted in time, instituted in an exterior space through a *stylized repetition of acts*" (*Gender Trouble: Feminism and the Subversion of Identity* [London and New York: Routledge, 1990], 140). For an illuminating analysis that deploys Butler's theoretical insights, see Kathryn McPherson, "'The Case of the Kissing Nurse': Femininity, Sexuality, and Canadian Nursing, 1900-1970," in *Gendered Pasts: Historical Essays in Femininity and Masculinity in Canada*, ed. Kathryn McPherson, Cecilia Morgan, and Nancy M. Forestell, 179-98 (Don Mills, ON: Oxford University Press, 1999).
8 For explorations of the complex nature of these acts, see Veronica Strong-Boag and Carole Gerson, *Paddling Her Own Canoe: The Times and Texts of E. Pauline Johnson (Tekahionwake)* (Toronto: University of Toronto Press, 2000); Karen Dubinsky, "Vacations in the 'Contact

Zone': Race, Gender, and the Traveler at Niagara Falls," in *Nation, Empire, Colony: Historicizing Gender and Race,* ed. Ruth Roach Pierson and Nupur Chaudhuri, 251-59 (Bloomington, IN: Indiana University Press, 1998); Patricia Jasen, *Wild Things: Nature, Culture, and Tourism in Ontario, 1790-1914* (Toronto: University of Toronto Press, 1995); Peter Geller, "'Hudson's Bay Company Indians': Images of Native People and the Red River Pageant, 1920," in *Dressing in Feathers: The Construction of the Indian in Popular Culture,* ed. S. Elizabeth Bird, 65-77 (Boulder, CO: Westview Press, 1996); Paige Raibmon, "Theatres of Contact: The Kwakwaka'wakw Meet Colonialism in British Columbia and at the Chicago World's Fair," *Canadian Historical Review* 81, 2 (June 2000): 157-90; Bunny McBride, "The Spider and the WASP: Chronicling the Life of Molly Spotted Elk," in *Reading beyond Words: Contexts for Native History,* ed. Jennifer S.H. Brown and Elizabeth Vibert, 403-27 (Peterborough, ON: Broadview Press, 1996).

9 Sarah Carter, "Categories and Terrains of Exclusion: Constructing the 'Indian Woman' in the Early Settlement Era in Western Canada," in *Gender and History in Canada,* ed. Joy Parr and Mark Rosenfeld, 30-49 (Mississauga, ON: Copp Clark, 1996).

10 While I have chosen to emphasize "what is known," there are areas that I cannot explore or analyze, such as Monture's decision to leave Six Nations, given a lack of sources and a desire to respect her and her family's privacy. See McBride, "The Spider and the WASP," for a discussion of how a non-Native scholar attempted to write about a Native American woman.

11 "Ethel Brant Monture," *Significant Lives.*

12 Minute Book 1, entries for 14 September 1934 and 25 May 1937, Brant Historical Society Records, Brant County Historical Museum.

13 This sketch is drawn from the Woodland Cultural Centre biography and from "Ethel Brant Monture," *Significant Lives.* The records of the Brant Historical Society show that Monture returned from time to time to the Brantford area, as she addressed the society's meetings on a number of occasions (Minute Book 1, 19 September 1941, 16 September 1942; Minute Book 2, 16 April 1952). Further information about Monture's career in the 1950s and 1960s may be found in her correspondence with Kathleen Coburn, the Victoria University Coleridge scholar. See "Monture, Ethel Brant, 1955-59," file 3, box 07, series 1, and "Monture, Ethel: Indians [1965-72]," file 06, box 009, series 1, of the Kathleen Coburn Papers, Special Collections, E.J. Pratt Library, University of Toronto.

14 "Red Threads of Continent Society Topic," coverage of a talk given by Monture to the Etobicoke Historical Society, n.p., n.d., Ethel Brant Monture file, Woodland Cultural Centre.

15 Harvey Chalmers and Ethel Brant Monture, *West to the Setting Sun* (New York: Twayne Publishers, 1965); Ethel Brant Monture, *Famous Indians: Brant, Crowfoot, Oronhyatekha* (Toronto: Clarke, Irwin, 1960).

16 "Ethel Brant Monture Named to Agricultural Hall of Fame," *Brantford Expositor,* 23 January 1984, Ethel Brant Monture file, Woodland Cultural Centre.

17 This sketch of Loft has been drawn from George Beaver, Bryan Winslow Colwell, Donald Smith, and Robert Stacey, *Iroquois Fires: The Six Nations Lyrics and Lore of Dawendine (Bernice Loft Winslow)* (Ottawa: Penumbra Press, 1995).

18 Olive Patricia Dickason, *Canada's First Nations: A History of Founding Peoples from Earliest Times* (Toronto: McClelland and Stewart, 1992), 306-28.

19 Ibid., 320-21.

20 Sally M. Weaver, "The Iroquois: The Grand River Reserve in the Late Nineteenth and Early Twentieth Centuries, 1875-1945," in *Aboriginal Ontario* (see note 6), 213-57, at 247-48.

21 Ibid., 224-32.

22 Ibid., 213-23.

23 Bernice Loft to Celia B. File, 18 February 1934, file 5.24, box 5, Celia B. File papers 1887-1973, Lennox and Addington Historical Society Museum.

24 Cecilia Morgan, "History and the Six Nations: Complicating the Imagined Community, 1890s-1960s," unpublished paper presented to the 3rd Conference on Contemporary Canadian Issues: Nationalism, Citizenship, and National Identity in Canada, Canadian Studies, Mount Allison University, 11-13 November 1999.

25 Weaver, "The Iroquois," 221-23.
26 For discussions of these displays, see Daniel Francis, *The Imaginary Indian: The Image of the Indian in Canadian Culture* (Vancouver: Arsenal Pulp Press, 1993). For a more complicated exploration, see Raibmon, "Theatres of Contact," and L.G. Moses, *Wild West Shows and the Images of American Indians, 1883-1933* (Albuquerque: University of New Mexico Press, 1996).
27 Minute Book 1, 14 September 1934, Brant Historical Society Records, Brant County Historical Museum.
28 Minute Book 2, 15 March 1950, ibid.
29 Ibid., 16 April 1952.
30 Minute Book 3, 12 April 1958, ibid.
31 "Summer Program at Suffolk Museum," 1 July to 22 August 1959, file 3, box 07, Coburn Papers.
32 Canada, Royal Commission on Bilingualism and Biculturalism, *Minutes of the Royal Commission on Bilingualism and Biculturalism* (Ottawa: Queen's Printer, 1963), 144. While a full discussion of Monture's and Loft's identities as Canadians is beyond the scope of this chapter, it is worth noting the potential complications of their national subjectivities, given their histories of border-crossing and, indeed, of spending parts of their lives in the United States. (In Loft's case, at least one of her brothers lived in Buffalo.) However, it is also worth noting that the Mohawk had a long history of using their decision to maintain their alliance with Britain in order to become Canadians, while still maintaining their Mohawk identity. For a discussion of the latter, see Cecilia Morgan, "'A Wigwam to Westminster': Performing Mohawk Identity in Imperial Britain, 1890s-1900s," *Gender and History* 15, 2 (August 2003): 319-41. I would like to thank *Contact Zones'* anonymous reader for reminding me of this important point.
33 "Indian Folk School 'Unqualified Success,'" *London Free Press,* 23 March 1964, Ethel Brant Monture file, Woodland Cultural Centre.
34 Ethel Brant, "College for Indian Youth," *Maclean's Magazine,* 15 April 1940. My thanks to Don Smith for forwarding this article to me.
35 Ibid.
36 Ethel Brant, "Ontario Indian Reservations Have Fine Institutes," 8 July 1940, Ethel Brant Monture file, Woodland Cultural Centre.
37 "She's Gone Fishing, Leaving 'White Problems' Temporarily," no publisher, n.d., Elliott Moses papers, vol. 1, file 13, "Clippings, 1888-1930," MG30, C169, National Archives of Canada.
38 Ethel Brant Monture, "The Six Nations of the Grand River," n.d., file 06, box 009, series 1, Coburn papers.
39 Ethel Brant Monture, *Famous Indians,* 55-59, 69, 89, 93, 127, 132, 140-42, 152-57.
40 Ibid., 58-59.
41 Ibid., 69.
42 "She's Gone Fishing, Leaving 'White Problems' Temporarily." This was an interview conducted with Monture when she chaired sessions of the National Indian Council, probably in 1964. Monture also supported Kahn-Tineta Horn in the latter's clash with William Wuttunee and Alanis Obomsawin at the council's 1964 meeting (Elliott Moses papers, ibid.).
43 Ibid.
44 "Ethel Brant Monture," *Significant Lives,* 102.
45 Monture to Coburn, 18 June 1954, file 3, box 007, Coburn papers. It is not clear from their correspondence how Coburn and Monture met; it may have been through Monture's lectures to university women's clubs.
46 Monture to Coburn, 5 August 1955, ibid.
47 My concept of colonial hybridity has been drawn from Angela Woollacott, "The Colonial Flaneuse: Australian Women Negotiating Turn-of-the-Century London," *Signs* 25, 3 (Spring 2000): 761-87; and Antoinette Burton, *At the Heart of the Empire: Indians and the Colonial Encounter in Late-Victorian Britain* (Berkeley: University of California Press, 1998).
48 For a discussion of Moses' ambivalence toward Iroquois culture, see Morgan, "History and the Six Nations."

49 To date, for example, I have not found that Monture had anything to say about residential schools.

50 For discussions of antimodernism in twentieth-century Canada, see Ian McKay, *The Quest of the Folk: Antimodernism and Cultural Selection in Twentieth-Century Nova Scotia* (Montreal and Kingston: McGill-Queen's University Press, 1994); also Donald A. Wright, "W.D. Lighthall and David Ross McCord: Antimodernism and English-Canadian Imperialism, 1880s-1914," *Journal of Canadian Studies* 32, 2 (Summer 1997): 134-153; and Renato Rosaldo, "Imperialist Nostalgia," *Representations* 26 (Spring 1989): 107-122.

51 While certainly having a greater degree of economic security and privilege than Loft, File was the breadwinner of her family. Her teaching jobs across southern Ontario meant that she spent much time living away from her husband. Loft and File met in the late 1920s when the latter was conducting research on the Six Nations. See Cecilia Morgan, "Reaching beyond White Womanhood? Celia B. File and Bernice Loft Winslow in 1930s' Ontario" (paper presented to the 80th annual meeting of the Canadian Historical Association, May 2001).

52 Paul A.W. Wallace to Monture, 1 October 1951, 21 October 1951, 7 November 1951, 25 February 1952; Monture to Wallace, 4 November 1951, 2 March 1952. Originals in the collection of the American Philosophical Society. My thanks to Don Smith for his generosity in sharing copies of this correspondence.

53 Monture to Wallace, 26 May 1952, ibid.

54 Wallace to Monture, 8 June 1953, ibid.

55 See, for example, Coburn to H.G. Hindmarsh, 15 June 1953; Coburn to Arthur Meighen, 19 June 1953; Coburn, "Statement About Ethel Brant Monture," n.d., file 3, series 1, box 07, Kathleen Coburn Papers, E.J. Pratt Library, University of Toronto. See also Coburn to the Centennial Commission's Publication Programme, 16 December 1965, file 6, series 1, box 009, Coburn papers, E.J. Pratt Library. Hindmarsh was the president of the *Toronto Daily Star*, and Coburn wrote to him concerning the *Star*'s Atkinson Charitable Foundation.

56 Coburn, "Statement About Ethel Brant Monture."

57 Coburn to H.G. Hindmarsh, 15 June 1953.

58 Coburn, "Statement About Ethel Brant Monture."

59 Ibid.

60 For the Subaltern Studies Collective, see the eight-volume collection edited by Ranajit Guha, *Subaltern Studies: Writings on South Asian History and Society* (New Delhi: Oxford University Press, 1982-84). Inspired by the writings of Italian Marxist Antonio Gramsci, this group of Marxist South Asian historians has focused on the subaltern groups, such as peasants and workers, whose perspectives and experiences, they argue, have been ignored or treated inadequately by Eurocentric historians. Robyn Wiegman's *American Anatomies: Theorizing Gender and Race* (Durham, NC: Duke University Press, 1995) explores how American culture produces gendered and racialized categories, meanings, and identities that are attached to, and performed on and through, bodies.

61 I do not want to suggest that other kinds of categories or attachments – age or religion, for example – are irrelevant, merely that in this case gender and race seem particularly important.

62 "Minutes of Tyendinaga," talk given by Celia B. File to Lundy's Lane Historical Society, 9 October 1934, file 115, box 2, Celia B. File papers 1887-1973, Lennox and Addington Historical Society Museum.

63 Elizabeth Gowan, "Franchise Ancient Right of Women of Six Nations. Daughter of Chief Loft Glories in Heritage of Her People. Character Fate. Speaks Many Tongues but Prefers Indian As Interpretive," n.p., n.d., file 117 (press clippings), box 2, Celia B. File papers. Yet another interviewer shaped for his readers an image of a "well educated, posed and dignified" daughter of a "Grand River chief." "She talks in an almost academic English, with a slight Irish brogue that cannot be explained," *Globe and Mail* reporter Ken W. McTaggart told his readers (n.d., file 117, box 2, Celia B. File papers).

64 "Program for Bernice Minton Loft, 'Dawendine,'" file 5.28, Loft correspondence, box 3, Celia B. File papers.

65 Ibid.

66 See Philip J. Deloria, *Playing Indian* (New Haven and London: Yale University Press, 1998), 122-25, for a discussion of Native Americans' performances as "Indians."

67 Loft to File, 21 February 1937, file 5.28, Loft correspondence, box 3, Celia B. File papers.

68 Loft to File, ? November 1935, ibid.

69 Loft to File, 18 February 1934, ibid.

70 Loft to File, ? November 1935, ibid.

71 Loft to File, 14 May 1936, ibid.

72 Loft to File, ? November 1935, ibid.

73 Della Pollock, "Introduction: Making History Go," in *Exceptional Spaces: Essays in Performance and History*, ed. Della Pollock, 1-45 (Chapel Hill: University of North Carolina Press, 1998), 6.

74 Loft to File, ? November 1935, file 5.28, Loft correspondence, box 3, Celia B. File papers.

75 Loft to File, 26 January 1936, ibid.

76 Ibid.

77 Loft to File, 21 February 1937, ibid. She also wrote File about the need to keep her hair tidy and of the need to have permanent waves done while touring, as marcel sets "are no good" (Loft to File, 22 January 1936, ibid.).

78 Loft to File, ? November 1935, ibid.

79 Loft to File, 22 January 1936, ibid.

80 Ibid.

81 Loft to File, ? November 1935, ibid.

82 Loft to File, 7 July 1936, ibid.

83 Loft to File, 5 March 1935, ibid.

84 Loft to File, 16 January 1936, 26 January 1936, 14 May 1936, 7 July 1936, ibid.

85 Loft to File, n.d., ibid.

86 Loft to Ka-noe-rohn-kwa, 21 June 1937, file 106, box 1, Celia B. File papers. Ka-noe-rohn-kwa, or "Loving Heart," was File's Mohawk name, given her by the community of Tyendinaga. See Morgan, "Reaching beyond White Womanhood."

87 Loft to File, 5 March 1938, file 5.29, box 3, Celia B. File papers.

88 It is possible that Monture's audience for her letters shaped her choice of subjects. She appears to have depended on Coburn for her patronage and might not have wanted to upset her.

89 Loft to File, 1 December 1936, file 5.28, box 3, Celia B. File papers.

90 Loft to File, 21 February 1937, ibid.

91 Loft to File, 14 June 1937, ibid.

92 Loft to File, 4 February 1938, ibid. Loft was referring to Elliott Moses, a politically active member of the Delaware from Six Nations. For further discussion of Moses, see Morgan, "History and the Six Nations."

93 Frederick E. Hoxie, "Exploring a Cultural Borderland: Native American Journeys of Discovery in the Early Twentieth Century," *Journal of American History* 79, 3 (December 1992): 969-95, at 994.

94 Antoinette Burton, "Introduction: The Unfinished Business of Colonial Modernities," in *Gender, Sexuality and Colonial Modernities*, ed. Antoinette Burton, 1-16 (London: Routledge, 1999).

95 See Deloria, *Playing Indian*, 122-26, on the US situation.

96 Pollock, "Introduction: Making History Go," 8.

97 Wiegman, *American Anatomies*, 192; also Sara Suleri, "Woman Skin Deep: Feminism and the Postcolonial Condition," in *Colonial Discourse and Post-Colonial Theory: A Reader*, ed. Patrick Williams and Laura Chrisman, 244-57 (New York: Columbia University Press, 1994).

4
Spirited Subjects and Wounded Souls: Political Representations of an Im/moral Frontier
Jo-Anne Fiske

For well over a century, women religious devoted themselves to a sacrificial life that has become understood as an aberrant act of chastity and charity. The rise of Aboriginal nationalism, as claimed within postcolonial discourses of legal subjects seeking collective and individual redress, has rejected the harsh religiosity of colonial education. In the search to understand the etiology of colonial violence, women religious have been under scrutiny for their founding beliefs in a life of holiness and redemption. As women who forsook and were forsaken by their mothers, they are represented as motherless daughters who involuntarily visited cruelty upon the children they were to nurture in the name of universal love of Christ and civilization.

Psychological narratives grant new meanings to the absence of the maternal figure and reconstitute age-old criticisms, some might say slanders, of chaste celibates who live beyond male control as the spiritual daughters of the Roman Catholic Church. While symbolic of a psychology of pathology, the motherless daughter does not, however, evoke universal condemnation. Rather, she is open to both sympathy and condemnation for the involuntary consequences of her motherlessness. And notwithstanding the cruelty of the colonial institution in which she served, in the eyes of some she remains a woman of heroic virtue and a compassionate maternal symbol.

Within these multiple layers of expression and the many quests for personal understanding of a troubled past, no true story of the residential school should be alleged; neither should we seek some fair balance of good and evil, of morality and immorality on a colonial frontier. Rather, we should seek to understand the postcolonial representations of the past and ask what they might offer to those who seek remedy for the harm they endured.

When I began my most recent study of the impact of residential schooling upon generations of Aboriginal women and their families, I was frequently asked: "Will you tell the true story of what happened to 'the children?" When I demurred that this was the wrong question, indeed an impossible question, I was often then cautioned to "tell both sides of the story, the good and the bad." While this chapter is a response to both of these concerns it does not constitute "the" answer to either. For neither is an appropriate starting point to understand the complex, contrary, and all too frequently painful narratives of self that emerge from the memoirs and research undertaken by former staff, students, and teachers of the Canadian colonial educational establishments that have come to be known as the "residential schools for Indian children."

Consideration of the residential school within Marc Augé's concept of the "anthropological place," characterized by the embodiment of social identity, representation of the past, and the history of a people and their place, affords a more appropriate vantage point from which to interrogate the moral relations of the colonial frontier.[1] As an "anthropological place," the residential school speaks to the paradox of being a place that displaces, a historic site that constituted the destruction of history, and hence a site that marks shifts to new subjectivities and identities. Following Augé's lead with respect to the particularities of place, we can reconsider the specificities of social identities as they become understood, rather than resorting to the ethnopornography of a simplified dichotomy of good/evil.

This leads us in turn to two points of theoretical consideration. First, the search for identity and authenticity as part of a project of an alternative modernity, that is, as a project for the future, and thus implicitly the quest is one of rights and difference. Second, shifting representations of the im/moral encounters of colonial strangers constitute "symbolic capital"[2] of the "politics of recognition."[3] As others have made clear, whenever we address the politics of "morphological categories" in conjunction with "subjects of rights," we are obliged to examine those ethnosociologies through which difference is articulated, as well as the structures and processes through which rights are sought.[4]

Colonialism has been represented as an encounter of cultural strangers.[5] Indeed, anthropologists have given priority to understanding colonial relations within a wide frame of narratives of cultural conflict, embracing the notion that colonized people suffer socially and psychologically as a consequence of a disrupted *nomos,* and experience anomie from the loss or delegitimation of enduring values and expressive traditions. I prefer to reconsider the colonial encounter as a clash of moral strangers and posit the im/moral frontier as a struggle to define the moral universe and to enforce others to abide within its *nomos* through control of material and symbolic resources. I stress moral encounters because, as Mercer and Julien, as cited by Kulick, have noted: "Traditional notions of sexuality are deeply linked to race and racism because sex is regarded as that thing which par excellence is a threat to the moral order of Western civilisation. Hence, one is civilised at the expense of sexuality, and sexual at the expense of civilisation. If the black, the savage, the nigger is the absolute Other of civility it must follow that he is endowed with the most monstrous and terrifying proclivity."[6]

Overdetermination of sex shaped the very conception of Christian colonial schooling, so much so that female sexuality was greatly feared from the outset. Indeed, acceptance of female students rested on the perception of their inherent immorality, which was to be controlled through their internalization of duties appropriate to Christian motherhood.[7] Without religious constraints placed on the females, missionaries argued that "it would be difficult to make the next generation respectable," but "under the control of the nuns, Indian girls would make noble women and good mothers and lead happy and respectable lives."[8] Nor has this fear diminished among current sympathizers of the school regime. Catholic historian Raymond Huel, for example, not only suggests that some "parents actually attempted to subvert schools by sending only females," but also argues that the "Oblates had to be very careful in accepting female students. Parents were known to hide the fact that their daughters were pregnant, allow them to be recruited by residential schools and then when the female's condition became obvious, blame the institutions for what had happened."[9]

As Huel's remarks exemplify, within the uneasy relations of the postcolonial state, representations of the im/moral frontier now resonate as a multivocal struggle for individual and collective legitimacy. This struggle is expressed in the continuing quest for self, for, as Fanon asserted, "because it is a systematic negation of the other person and a furious determination to deny the other person all attributes of humanity, colonialism forces the people it dominates to ask the question constantly: 'In reality, who am I?'"[10] However, to know one's colonized self, one must also "know" the other. Identities are always relational and inventive, hence narratives of the emergent postcolonial self resonate with the query: "In reality, who were they?"

Who "they" were can be explicated by setting the site of the narrated self, in this case the residential school, within a moral universe, contexualized by a "moment" in life that transforms the subject. As I hope to demonstrate, such is the nature of the stories emanating from the current moral crisis of colonial education as exposed in the disclosures of rampant abuse of schoolchildren and counter-narratives of benign, if not merciful, care of little children brought to God.

Working from the premises that "we do not *have* identities, we only invent them," and that the way in which we do so constitutes, in part, the politics of recognition, I approach these narratives within a frame that allows me to identify two "conversational communities" that inhabited the remembered school and then moved through successive conversational communities in the quest for meaning.[11] One marks the school as the site of sacrifice; the other relives the school as a site of terror. Both seize upon the same life moment – the separation of mothers and daughters – to explicate their self-understanding.

I locate my interpretations within a framework of discursive decon-struction. Following Goodrich, I attempt to formulate and substantiate the complex relationship of structural features, or regularities, of systems of communication as discursive formations, and to explicate their agency or manifestation in empirical practice.[12] Within this frame, I find the work of Carol Smart properly directs me to a theory of discourse that seeks to under-stand how individuals draw upon levels of ideology and rhetoric to place themselves in society and culture. More specifically, I seek neither to ground an historic truth in concepts of right and wrong, or fact and fiction, nor to construct an objective tale of balanced good and evil. Rather, I pursue the manner in which cultural narratives offer the foundation of identity and the categorization of social subjects by "thinking about subjects who are con-tinually being constituted and who constitute themselves through language/ discourse."[13] That is, I take as my starting point that the subject is a politi-cally situated discursive arrangement. This allows me to take up my second consideration respecting representation of difference, namely, to ask: How are these newly constituted subjects – and their rights – positioned within ethnonational political discourses that insist upon valorization of differ-ence and recognition of differential rights?

Through stories we come to know who we are. Mothers and the mother-less daughters exist in and through stories told by and about them. Thus, taking up the theme of motherless daughters, I locate collections of per-sonal tales within broader cultural narratives that give meaning to the nar-rators' experiences. I am concerned with understanding the semantics of motherhood and motherlessness as they are expressed through particular economies of representation, especially the representations of the relation-ship of the maternal to the soul and body, the spiritual and sexual, the sacrificial and heroic.

In narratives of residential schooling, images of "motherless daughters" are applied to both teaching sisters of the residential school staffs and the children who resided in these isolated schools for long periods of time. These images derive their meanings from three distinct cultural narratives: Catho-lic narratives of heroic virtue and sanctity, which place the maternal prin-ciple in "the mother church" and the "family of God"; psychological narratives that attribute psychopathologies to an absence of loving experi-ences with a maternal figure; and Aboriginal narratives that honour a life-long relationship of mother and daughters while locating the maternal principle within a concept of "mother earth." Each of these narratives, moreover, sustains conflicting understandings of the maternal principle and of the sociopsychological consequences of the absence of a mother figure throughout young women's lives. Narratives grounded in psychological precepts are drawn from psychoanalytical concepts of childhood trauma in which the loss of a mother, whether through death, lifelong severance, or long-term alienation, is seen as a defining moment in identity formation. As will be demonstrated below, narratives of former students echo psychological assertions that the unmothered child remains vulnerable throughout adulthood to emotional and social dysfunction. Loss of mother is not an event from which daughters recover, but a lifelong wound that undermines self-esteem and identity. Psychoanalytical theorists further argue that mother loss in childhood can inhibit psychosexual development; without the role model of the mother and mature attachment to her, the daughter may repress her sexual feelings, fail to resolve sexual yearnings for her father, or be trapped in a level of sexual development that precludes healthy adult relations. Just as the universalism of psychoanalytical theory presumes that mother loss incurs the same trauma and psychosexual development in girls and women regardless of culture difference, and therefore can explain the lifelong trauma of residential schooling, so, in narratives of former school residents, mother loss accounts for physical and sexual violence visited upon them by women religious.[14]

Culture of Sacrifice and Herocity

The organizing symbols of heroic virtue and sacrifice shape narratives of women religious on the im/moral frontier into a genre of biographies and autobiographies that conforms to an established hagiography. Like the sanctified women they seek to emulate, many of whom in modern times were foundresses of religious congregations, sisters on the im/moral frontier tell a life story that commences with an early commitment to the church; highlights the wrenching renunciation of their family, experienced first as they enter the convent as novices, and then as they depart for distant missions; mourns the separation of the sisters from each other and their beloved Mother, who leads their community; and closes with tales of heroism in the face of challenges and hardships that signify a career of service and dedication to poverty, charity, and chastity.[15]

The distinct culture of motherhood and sacrifice the Catholic missionaries brought to the colonial frontier created a racialized ethos of benevolence and social progress that spawned the residential schools for Aboriginal children. Colonial education signified the greatest effort of the church and state to transform entirely the identity and life way of Aboriginal children with a view to moulding them in the image of the colonists while never allowing them full participation in the emerging frontier society. Racialized practices of institutionalized reforms established the context for the sisters' missions: the impoverished, isolated residential schools that often became the only refuge for the poor, the orphaned, and the socially isolated.

The women religious, as the nuns/sisters are known to the church, organize their social and spiritual identities around imitation of Christ and the saints. To imitate Christ is to live a life of sacrifice and extraordinary moral discipline. Faith, hope, and charity underscore all other exemplars of a religious life, the greatest of which is charity, love of God. Renunciation of family ties is expressive of this love. As Christ did, so women religious renounce marriage, an act that has been described as "the first station, as it were, for our departure to Christ."[16]

Sacrifice of family ties marks a moment of intense sorrow, which in earlier times was observed by elaborate rites of passage in which a grieving mother melodramatically beseeched her daughter not to enter the convent.[17] While no such rituals are enacted today, women religious frequently reminisce about their own moment of parting and the loneliness they endured as novices, awaiting the moment when they would see their mothers again. For some the waiting was as long as seven years; for others it was shorter. Still others, as was more common in the past when the mission fields were so far from home or were located in the war front, never saw their families again.[18] Whatever their circumstances, the daughters accepted their vocation willingly in images of "canonized men and women who are asked by God to renounce for his sake all legitimate family ties and to follow unconditionally, though with a breaking heart, the Will of God clearly manifested to them."[19]

Mothers and daughters commit themselves to mutual sacrifice when they sever their ties with each other. When the daughter enters the convent, she may be denied her own mother's personal love, but she accepts that God will supply the love and care her mother can no longer offer through the divine love represented by the Holy Church herself, and through her relationship with the Mother Superior, prayer, and the nurture of her religious community, which gradually becomes her "big family." In the process, the "motherless" daughter adopts a new identity as a servant of God, the spiritual daughter to the "maternal affection" of the Mother Superior. In terms of endearment and honour, she may present herself to her "venerable," dearest," "most revered," or "most honoured Mother" as a "loving child," "a most submissive child," or as one of her "missionary children." Her assignments for service – obedience as they are known – may then take her to distant mission fields. In the nineteenth century, and even early in the twentieth century, this meant that many families were lost to one another forever, for many sisters never returned to their homelands, not even for a visit.[20]

The mothers find their solace in knowing that, through the good works of the daughters, their mutual sacrifice will be known as a response to God's care. Their role model is the Virgin Mary, onto whom sorrowing mothers may graft their own suffering in empathy with the Virgin's release of her son to God's purpose. Mothers come to understand that their daughters' holy vocation is a gift and the call of God by which their own virtue as a woman/mother has been received by the church as a sacrifice in the love of Christ. In this way, mothers and daughters represent themselves as members of a family called by God for his service and greater good.

From the onset of their decision to enter into their vows, the lives of women religious are shaped by their efforts to achieve herocity through endurance of suffering that goes beyond the normal expectations of laity. Their models for doing so are not their mothers – nor icons of motherhood that represent social practice – but the virgin martyrs of ancient times and the saints, among whom mothers and married women are least represented. Chaste celibacy has long been held as the route to sainthood.[21] Thus motherhood, symbolically represented by "the mother church" and revered through devotion to the Virgin Mary, is ambivalently represented within Catholic culture, which cannot connect sanctity with sexuality. Childbearing is not sacrificial in a pure way, for it is tainted by bodily sin and carnal knowledge. Thus, the mutual sacrifice of mother and daughter is, for some, one way to atone for Eve's sin. Carried further, a sense of pure motherhood is grafted onto the sanctification of the founding mothers of religious orders, such as Mother Marguerite d'Youville, foundress of the Grey Nuns, who was pronounced "Mother of Universal Charity" at her beatification in 1959 and was canonized in 1993.

The religious community thus represents a family, and each of its daughters must prepare for a second sacrifice as they separate from each other to undertake service in distant mission fields. This second separation is no easier than the first and is described in poignant terms of enduring sorrow and heartache, of sacrifice that can only have meaning within the solace of the Holy Mother Church and the charity for which it is made.

Seen from this perspective, the motherless daughters offer an ambivalent model for their child wards to emulate. Amongst former residents of the colonial schools who speak of their experiences, some perceive the nuns' sacrifice of their mothers as unequivocal evidence of their love and charity. Indeed, for those like Charles Kennedy, cited by Agnes Sutherland, the sacrifice of family and loss of a mother explains the compassion and positive discipline he experienced while residing at a remote school in the north. Sisters are represented by Kennedy, and others who share his view, as amazing women who left their mothers to serve the poor, who took care of children without judgment at any time and under any conditions. For some who are devout, the sisters are seen as obeying the command "to be fruitful and multiply" through their care of the motherless children in the schools, particularly through their spiritual teaching. Kennedy honours the hardships endured by the sisters as a sacrifice to God for the children: "She made a promise to serve God and His people and she meant business ... She didn't even have a decent place to rest and sleep. She just had a little miserable cubicle."[22] Another former student, speaking at a residential school reunion, was equally sympathetic. When asked for her views on the women who left their mothers in France to work in British Columbia, she replied, "Their mothers gave them [their daughters] to us because God asked them to. God knew we needed them."[23]

Separation from family, in particular from mothers, is seen by students praising their former teachers as a common bond between long-term child residents and the teaching staff. Whether the sisters are seen as sacrificial victims, torn from their mothers by the church's demand, or as courageous and willing servants of God, former students may evoke a sense of shared experiences as orphans (for indeed, many of the sisters on the frontiers had lost their mothers at an early age) or as children sacrificed by their own families in order to fulfill a community's need for educated young people. In the words of Charles Kennedy, "The years have not dimmed my memory of the kind and motherly sisters who devoted their whole life to the care of the unfortunates, the orphans and the children of single parents ... We were lonesome for our parents and friends we left behind to stay in the mission school. So were the sisters lonesome for their loved ones far away. We saw our families once in a while but they never saw theirs. "[24]

The Catholic doctrine of sacrifice and self-discipline merged with the austerity of school routines, which were ordered by devotion to prayer, hard work, self-sacrifice, and sustained physical denial (fasting, thirsting) and pain. Within the culture of devotion, women religious undergo self-mortification by applying the "discipline" – a small whip – to themselves. They inflict agony on themselves in order to suffer as Christ and the martyrs suffered. In seeking to ensure that their wards would not be denied the right to know Christ and realize salvation themselves, and in order to maintain their wards' possibilities of achieving holiness, women religious asked their students to make the same sacrifices they willingly made: loneliness, thirsting, fasting, silence, isolation, whipping, and sustained physical immobility prostrate before the altar or posed in imitation of the crucified Christ. Some converts of the school have come to accept these painful inflictions in the same light as the women religious: as punishments and denials necessary to moral formation and spiritual devotion. "Poor old Lejac," an elder mourned when she listened to younger women protesting stringent restrictions placed on girls at this school. "They made us understand. We took our punishments so we could know God."[25]

Acceptance of Catholicism does not necessarily lead to appreciation or defence of the sisters or the spiritual goals that the sisters claim directed them to the missions and a vocation of teaching. Personal agony and psychological stresses, most explicitly those attributed to the loss of language and culture, lead some former students to understand the cruelty and loneliness of their school years as a direct, but unintended, consequence of the religious practice of separating mothers and daughters. Their personal explanations vary, but carry common themes and motifs. In the eyes of these former residents, daughters denied their mothers lack compassion and wisdom. Women cannot be "fully human" without the love and guidance of their mothers and grandmothers. Thus, these former residents say the sisters' "cruelty" in casting aside their mothers is "inhuman" and cannot be accepted as a sacrifice to God, for God "loves everybody" and "knows you belong to your mother."[26]

In this view of the spiritual subject, "it does not make sense" for the nuns to "call each other sisters and mothers." Abstractions of motherhood symbolized by the church and the role of the leader of the religious community are not accepted as meaningful to those who mourn an absence of maternal figures. "What can they know about being mothers when they left them behind when they [the sisters] were so young?" The seemingly unnatural departure from their mothers is compounded by the sisters' equally unnatural vow to deny their own potential motherhood. While upholding a love of Christ and a commitment to the church, these former students reject the renunciation of family as an appropriate, or God-desired, sacrifice. In consequence, they can accept, and even be personally grateful for, the charitable calling of the sisters to compassionate teaching and nursing, while insisting that "their job was an impossible situation ... Not having children they didn't know tolerance."[27] They can express fondness for the sisters who treated them well and pity for the ones who were unkind. "We pitied them," recalled an elder who had attended the Lejac school. "They had no one to turn to. No wonder some of them could be so mean."[28]

Inability to accept the denial of mothers and motherhood as a meaningful spiritual sacrifice leads even the most sympathetic of the sisters' critics to link chaste celibacy to school tyrants. These speakers are deeply suspicious of the intent of harsh discipline and deprivation and either have no knowledge of the spiritual economy that guided their teachers or find the spiritual practices incomprehensible. Acts of self-mortification and self-denial, upon which women religious create their own subject positions as women of heroic virtue, become an abusive disciplinary routine for children in a seemingly inhospitable context. Without an acceptance of the Catholic principles of sacrifice and mortification, and without a shared conception of the coherent spiritual subject who possesses the right to know salvation, former students view harsh punishments as capricious or revengeful actions of unfulfilled women, which are recalled as being unnecessarily severe or, worse, as life-threatening and soul-wounding.

The moral virtues of the saints, which offer images of self-discipline and abnegation in heroic degree to the sisters, may either be unknown or unacceptable to students. Many former students (and the descendants of former students) claim to find unintelligible the church's expectation that by turning their bodies into objects of self-mortification, the sisters either wished, or achieved, the liberation of their spirits in true imitation of Christ in his humanity. Thus, the stories sisters tell of their own and each other's life sacrifices fail to be edifying. Rather, skeptical former students can readily dismiss the entire genre of tales that emulate hagiography as self-serving apologies for sisters who failed to behave in accordance with humanistic ideals of compassion and mercy. Tales of the "unsung heroes of untold adventures," such as those related by Sister Agnes Sutherland, who praises her own community of women as "giants in faith and commitment" who survived "untold sacrifices" and "awesome obstacles," not only pass over the violence and pain of the schools, but also allege that "troublemakers" or publicity seekers unfairly target the schools and their missionaries.[29] The seemingly deliberate dismissal of former students' concerns underlies rejection of the sisters' narratives of radical forms of poverty, chastity, and obedience. The very actions of renunciation that are meant to distinguish the lives of the religious from those of the laity are reconstrued as evidence of the failure of the religious to achieve holiness through charitable love for the poor and for Christ.

Other former students, working within the narratives of their own cultural legacy, are at best perplexed, at worst dismayed, by the values placed on separation of young women from their mothers and on the subsequent self-mortification and suffering desired by the sisters. Perceiving motherhood to be the basis of social order, as well as the spiritual expression of holism, symbolized by the universal (animistic) existence of soul and the maternal principle of mother earth, these students seek to express their own painful memories of loneliness, boredom, cultural alienation, and personal mental and physical abuse within their own cultural narratives. The statement "Poor things they took them from their mothers" takes on added meanings in this narrative, for not only are the young sisters now represented as victims of an aberrant institution that places its own interests before family and community, but they are also portrayed as wounded souls separated from the culture and language of their mothers and foremothers. Without a community of true female kin to guide them, the motherless daughters are likened to canoes without paddles, adrift in stormy waters. Maternity is likened to the earth upon whose breast we all feed. Nurture of the mother ensures in turn the nurture of her children. Just as we cannot live (spiritually or biologically) without earth, so we cannot live fully without our mothers. Thus, the markers of holiness to which the sisters aspire are repudiated. Holistic abstractions of a maternal principle reject the subject identity that places women religious apart from the laity, betwixt venerated saints and recipients of charity. Rather, this expression of motherhood celebrates one's own family and the "natural" bonds of maternal kin. Mothers are honoured when they sacrifice themselves to their children, not for sacrificing their children to God. Insofar as this narrative merges in a syncretic representation of religious faith, it does so by honouring meaningful acts of goodness and kindness expressed within a loving demeanour.

Contradictions between the practice and ideology of Christian benevolence are neutralized as former students relate memory tales within an age-old genre that teaches lessons of wisdom and reflection and that stresses humour and love. By honouring their own struggles and hardships within the culture of their foremothers, balanced with ideals of Christian love, former students can take pride in their transitional position between the life way of their parents and grandparents and that of their children and grandchildren, who are now able to "walk in two worlds," having excelled within the technical/intellectual world of professional accomplishment as teachers, lawyers, politicians, and health practitioners. Syncretic religious beliefs provide a moral discourse that is attached to the power of the creator and resonates with a confidence in Aboriginal identity. As benevolent persons secure in the maternal principles of their culture, they come to understand their tormentors and oppressors as individuals who strayed from their Catholic belief and who failed as moral guardians because, lacking maternal wisdom and discipline, they fell prey to individual weaknesses and twisted characters.

Culture of Sexual Pathology

The profession of celibacy is perhaps the least understood act of sacrifice and the one that raises the greatest public doubts and skepticism concerning sisters' private behaviour. These doubts and dismissals are expressed in apocryphal tales of secret pregnancies, ghastly orgies, unwanted babies either raised in secret or given up for adoption, numerous abortions, and even infanticides. Presumed evidence for these allegations has been advanced through suggestion that absences attributed to familial visits in distant lands are in fact trips taken to secretly give birth to priests' babies. Other stories insinuate, usually long after a mission is closed, the finding of unmarked graves of infants or the remains of infants hidden in building structures.[30]

Such tales are not new, but they represent, in current terms, the centuries-old struggle to come to terms with the isolation of professed virgins from the public male gaze. Incredulous responses to the profession of chastity are given shape by contemporary psychological narratives that impute sexual pathology to the religious practice of self-mortification and/or to the absence of a maternal figure in a woman's adolescence and early adulthood. Women's chaste lives are no longer understood as being analogous to Christ's passion and death, but are read as tales of shattered subjectivity. Such readings prompt a questioning of the subjectivity of the mothers who cast aside their daughters. "What mother would give up her daughter? How could she [the daughter] ever learn to love after her mother did that?"[31] In this way, the motherless daughter comes to represent an outrage of common sense and natural parental feelings. The heartless mother is simultaneously evoked to represent a monstrous femininity expressed in self-abnegation transmitted to her children.

Psychological narratives construe motherhood, and maternal love, within a symbolic system of universal psychosexual development. In broad terms, female psychosexual development is explained as being sado-masochistic in consequence of the penetrative sexual act. In popular renditions of this narrative, all actions of moral virtue, self-mortification, self-denial, renunciation of companionable kin ties, etc., signify sexual repression and are therefore liable to be interpreted as perverse. Assumptions of sado-masochism represent sacrificial subjects as pathological sexual subjects.

Psychological narratives of repression and perversion resonate with tales of childhood sexual trauma. Unlike narratives of stoic suffering and personal achievement, which encode a stable spiritual subject, tales of trauma describe discontinuity and instability. Trauma engendered by violent and cultural abuses marks the rupture of innocence. Loss of innocence indexes loss of a unified sexual subject with an intact, positive cultural and psychosexual identity, and the creation of a violated sexual subject incapable of healthy psychosexual relations. The rupture of innocence resulting from the harshness of colonial education has been widely felt, leading to a psychological categorization of common symptoms of trauma as the "mission [or residential] school syndrome," a condition sharing characteristics with post-traumatic stress disorder. Conceptualizing adult social stresses and interpersonal difficulties as symptomatic of childhood trauma gives structure to remembered experiences within a confessional narrative. In this discourse, trauma, not sacrifice, makes the person who she or he is.

Constructs of the universal sexual subject reject the possibility that similar acts – such as wrenching separation of daughter from mother or forced isolation from one's cultural legacy – will carry culturally specific meanings and subjective consequences. Thus mother/daughter separation is traumatic for all; self-mortification is self-abuse, and extraordinary moral discipline is an abusive perversion of an obligation to nurture the young. In consequence, this cultural narrative offers an unsympathetic view of the voluntarily motherless daughter. It lacks empathy for the sisters' circumstances and disregards the presumptions of herocity and sacrifices that give their life stories meaning. Insofar as it offers a space for shared meaning, it does so through assumptions of shared trauma of orphanhood, maternal and cultural. It generalizes notions of pathology so that all who choose a sacrificial life are reconstituted as victims, either of their own psychosexual longings or of an institution that placed its own interests beyond the interests of those in its service.

Charity is no longer the primary signifier of the love of God, but the primary signifier of a racialized frontier, and its recipients are not the worthy poor or the spiritually bereft, but unwilling victims to the violence of assimilation. By its very nature, the sisters' charity marks a moral divide between the superior, who accept sacrifice, and the inferior, who must be saved.

In the First Nations' perspective advanced by the Assembly of First Nations, the traumas of sexual abuse and colonial education are reconceptualized as "spirit wounding" and independently and jointly constitute spiritual abuse. Adapting the discourse of psychoanalysis that explains trauma as the rupture of consciousness and the body, First Nations' leaders construe colonial education generally, and residential schooling practices most particularly, as "spiritual violence," which they define as "any behaviour or situation which denies or undermines an individual's identity, values, and beliefs. This form of violence includes denying an individual the expression of their [sic] language, their way of praying, for example, as well as ridiculing or shaming their way of life." The spirit is wounded by defining it through an alien belief system and by introducing such alien concepts of morality as "sin, evil and the devil." In indigenous perspectives, a wounded spirit, or life source, may become lost through afflictions such as alcoholism, which may even result in death.[32]

Motherless daughters, in this narrative, are condemned to a pathological existence that can be remedied only by healing practices uniting psychology and spirituality. Lacking the teaching and wisdom of their own mothers and grandmothers, former female students emerge as incapable of parenting. Generations of residential school "victims" are represented as the cause of community dysfunction and social crises. Motherless daughters, both former students and the daughters of incapable mothers, are cast as the villains in a set social drama of betrayal. Without maternal development, they fail their sons, who turn to street gangs for kinship or to sexual violence to establish their identities on the margins of a hostile, postcolonial society.[33]

Representations of the subject as harmed and potentially, albeit unintentionally, a victimizer allow the mergence of psychological and legal discourses. For once harmed by actions that could have been avoided by church and the supportive state, the emergent subject is reconstituted in legal terms – that is, as a rights-bearing subject who can now claim redress. Spiritual subjects bearing the right to know God, and the sense of a God with rights to the soul, are repudiated. The legal subject refuses religious aspirations that violate legal protections and human rights. Redemption through tears and penitence is dismissed in favour of psychological healing and the restoration of the wounded spirit through legal action and political recognition.

Implications

Who were they (am I) really? In the process of "identifying" their former tormentors and teachers as subjects of psychosexual trauma and/or of heroic sacrifice, former school residents understand the "other" through the prism of their own motherless experience. In the discursive process, the motherless daughter is poised as an ambivalent symbol of im/morality; with her permeable subjectivity, she can be positioned as a metonym of the Aboriginal nation bereft of mother earth. With this discursive shift, "traditional" maternal principles are recuperated. The morality of the traditional collective is reclaimed and political possibilities are enunciated.

But this is not all. The psychological/legal Aboriginal subject who relationally emerges in juxtaposition to the sacrificed/sacrificial daughter of the church is now resituated in a discursive regime of rights as claims. Rights, as Wendy Brown asserts, are protean and irresolute signifiers, varying not only across time and culture, but also across the other vectors of power whose crossing, indeed, they are sometimes deployed to effect – class, race, ethnicity, gender, sexuality, age, wealth, education.[34]

Rights of redress from spiritual violence signify at one and the same time the right to inclusion, as a psychosexually harmed individual claiming compensation, and the right to difference, as a member of an Aboriginal collective that seeks some degree of autonomy from the state itself. To this end, the quest for redemption marked by narratives of maternal deprivation provides an equivocal bridge between the desire for membership within the secular Euronational state and the proclamation of a spiritual charter claimed by the celebration of ethnonationalism grounded in cosmological peculiarity.

Notes
1 Marc Augé, *Non-Places: Introduction to an Anthropology of Supermodernity* (London: Verso, 1995), 52.
2 Pierre Bourdieu, *Outline of a Theory of Practice* (Cambridge: Cambridge University Press, 1977).
3 Verne A. Dusenbery, "The Poetics and Politics of Recognition: Disaspora Sikhs in Pluralist Polities," *American Ethnologist* 24, 4 (1997): 739-62.
4 Veena Das, *Critical Events* (Delhi: Oxford University Press, 1995); Dusenbery, "Poetics and Politics of Recognition," 740.
5 Jean Comaroff and John Comaroff, *Of Revelation and Revolution: Christianity, Colonialism, and Consciousness in South Africa* (Chicago: University of Chicago Press, 1991).
6 Don Kulick, "Introduction," in *Taboo: Sex, Identity and Erotic Subjectivity in Anthropological Fieldwork*, ed. Don Kulick and Margaret Wilson, 1-28 (London: Routledge, 1995), 4.
7 Eleanor Brass, *I Walk in Two Worlds* (Calgary: Glenbow Museum, 1987); Jo-Anne Fiske, "And Then We Prayed Again: Carrier Women, Colonialism and Mission Schools" (MA thesis, University of British Columbia, 1981); Raymond Huel, *Proclaiming the Gospel to the Indians and the Métis* (Edmonton: University of Alberta Press, 1996), 126.
8 Huel, *Proclaiming the Gospel*, 135.
9 Ibid., 144, 158. Examples of similar fears abound in public conversations respecting sexual abuses on the part of the clergy. When Bishop Hubert O'Connor was convicted of sexual

assault and revealed to have lied about fathering a child with a young staff member (and former student), a man was prompted to complain to the newspaper that "there was never any talk about the sexual potency of a woman in her late teens, and the effect it might have on a middle-aged celibate male, especially if there was flirtation involved" (*Vancouver Sun*, 5 October 1996, D24).

10 Frantz Fanon, *The Wretched of the Earth* (New York: Grove Press, 1963), 250.

11 Kirsten Hastrup, *A Passage to Anthropology: Between Experience and Theory* (London: Routledge, 1995), 22.

12 Peter Goodrich, *Legal Discourse: Studies in Linguistics, Rhetoric and Legal Analysis* (London: Macmillan, 1987), 125.

13 Carol Smart, *Law, Crime and Sexuality: Essays in Feminism* (London and Thousand Oaks, CA: Sage, 1995), 8.

14 I first recorded former students' narratives of mother loss as explanation for sisters' behaviours in 1979 when conducting research for my MA thesis, and I have recorded similar narratives over the past twenty-five years. In conference papers and lectures I applied the term "motherless daughters" to refer to this narrative motif. In 1994 Hope Edelman published *Motherless Daughters: The Legacy of Loss* (New York: Addison Wesley), which has engendered a network of support groups and websites in the United States. It is difficult to determine the extent to which the current social emphasis on mother loss has influenced the narratives of residential school experiences. The two bodies of narratives share common motifs of lifelong trauma, the need for healing, and loss of maternal skills across generations, motifs that are also found in a range of narratives of child abuse and sexual abuse that are implicitly grounded in psychoanalytical theory. For the origins of psychoanalytical theory, see Sigmund Freud, *The Origin and Development of Psychoanalysis* (Chicago: Henry Regnery Company, 1965); for application of psychoanalysis to studies of motherhood and mother/daughter relations, see Ann Dally, *Inventing Motherhood: The Consequences of an Ideal* (London: Burnett Books, 1982); Nancy Chodorow, *The Reproduction of Mothering: Psychoanalysis and the Sociology of Gender* (Berkeley: University of California Press, 1978).

15 Agnes Sutherland, SGM, *Northerners Say: "Thank You Sisters"* (Ottawa: Tri-graphic Printing, 1996); Jo Anne Kay McNamara, *Sisters in Arms: Catholic Nuns through Two Millennia* (Cambridge, MA: Harvard University Press, 1996); Martha McCarthy, *From the Great River to the Ends of the Earth: Oblate Missions to the Dene, 1847-1921* (Edmonton: University of Alberta Press, 1995); Margaret McGovern, SP, "Perspectives on the Oblates: The Experiences of the Sisters of Providence," *Western Oblate Studies* 3 (1993): 91-108.

16 Kenneth L. Woodward, *Making Saints: How the Catholic Church Determines Who Becomes a Saint and Who Doesn't, and Why* (New York: Touchstone Press, 1996), 338, citing Margaret Miles, *Carnal Knowing: Female Nakedness and Religious Meaning* (Boston: Beacon Press, 1989), 67.

17 McNamara, *Sisters in Arms*, 1, 616.

18 Fiske, field notes 1979-80, 1993-97; Sutherland, *Northerners Say*. Between December 1979 and May 1980 I conducted interviews with former residents of the Lejac Residential School of central British Columbia. These interviews comprised open-ended questions regarding personal experiences at the school and life-long impact. From 1993-97, I conducted interviews at the Lejac site during annual celebrations held each summer. As well, I conducted a series of interviews in April 1995 with religious sisters who had served at residential schools. These sisters have requested that all identifying information be kept confidential, including names of their religious orders.

19 Woodward, *Making Saints*, 272-73.

20 Fiske, field notes 1995; Sutherland, *Northerners Say*, 8, 117.

21 In Roman Catholic doctrine, to be celibate means to forego marriage, while chastity refers to the absence of all sexual relations. Chastity is a gendered concept; for women it is represented as virginity.

22 Sutherland, *Northerners Say*, 163.

23 Fiske, field notes 1995.

24 Sutherland, *Northerners Say*, x.

25 Fiske, field notes, interviews with former students of Lejac Residential School, January 1979.
26 Fiske, field notes 1995.
27 Fiske, "And Then We Prayed Again," 37.
28 Fiske, field notes 1993.
29 Sutherland, *Northerners Say,* vii-xi.
30 These stories are pervasive; I have collected variations of these narratives for more than twenty years and have found them in virtually every collection of narratives regarding former mission stations and residential schools. See also Joan F. Burke, "These Catholic Sisters Are All Mamas! Celibacy and the Metaphor of Maternity,' in *Women and Missions: Past and Present,* ed. Fiona Bowie, Deborah Kirkwood, and Shirley Ardener, 251-63 (Providence, RI, and Oxford: Berg Publishers, 1993), 253; Isabelle Knockwood, *Out of the Depths: The Experiences of Mik'maw Children at the Indian Residential School at Shubenacadie* (Lockport, NS: Roseway Publishing, 1992).
31 Fiske, field notes 1995.
32 Assembly of First Nations, *Breaking the Silence: An Interpretive Study of Residential School Impact and Healing as Illustrated by the Stories of First Nations Individuals* (Ottawa: First Nations Health Commission, Assembly of First Nations, 1994), 190, 58.
33 Reasonably, stories of community dysfunction consequent upon rejection of colonial education as cultural/psychological trauma should offer sympathetic accounts of women and men who resided against their will in residential schools. But the pathological narrative endangers women who claim to lack parenting skills because either they, their mothers, or their foremothers suffered cultural loss and personal humiliation at the hands of foreign teachers. This representation of Aboriginal mothers, for example, has been linked to the dilemmas of youth gangs in Winnipeg. While it is meant to be sympathetic to the mothers and sons, it falls into many of the traps of Oscar Lewis' "culture of poverty" thesis in which matrifocal families and strong mothers are condemned for producing emasculated sons and a lifestyle that is self-perpetuating. Oscar Lewis, *La Vida: A Puerto Rican Family in the Culture of Poverty – San Juan and New York* (New York: Random, 1966). See also David Hertzer, "Family Breakdown Feeds Growth of Gangs," *Today's Native Father* 114 (March/April 2001): 3. CBC Radio reported on this issue giving attention to residential schooling as a causal factor to poor maternal discipline. Susan Lund, Report on Aboriginal Youth Gangs, 24-25 November 1999.
34 Wendy Brown, *States of Injury: Power and Freedom in Late Modernity* (Princeton, NJ: Princeton University Press, 1995), 97.

Part 2
Regulating the Body: Domesticity, Sexuality, and Transgression

5

Metropolitan Knowledge, Colonial Practice, and Indigenous Womanhood: Missions in Nineteenth-Century British Columbia

Adele Perry

The colonial encounter was an historical exercise in gender as well as in race. When Europeans met Aboriginals in nineteenth-century British Columbia, they did so as men and as women. Their meetings brought different ways of performing what it meant to be male and female into contact, sometimes conflict and sometimes coexistence. Yet the seductive language of "contact" and its various metonyms, including "encounter," implies a simplicity that belies the layered and fractured character of the meetings between Europe(s) and America(s) here and elsewhere. Ramón A. Gutiérrez is correct to note that "the conquest of America was not a monologue, but a dialogue between cultures, each of which had many voices that often spoke in unison, but just as often were diverse and divisive."[1] But, as Mary Louise Pratt has so eloquently insisted, the existence of polyphony does not mark the absence of power.[2] Gendered encounters in British Columbia were not simply two-sided, nor were they free contests between relative equals. They were complicated interactions that cannot be disaggregated from the asymmetrical power relations upon which Europe's colonizing project was premised, nourished, and maintained. Nor were they strictly local events. Colonization occurred in particular places with distinct histories, but it was read through metropolitan knowledges, including those of appropriate manliness and womanliness. And, as historians of Britain and other metropoles are increasingly if somewhat belatedly acknowledging, such knowledges would not emerge from the colonizing experience unscathed.[3]

This chapter explores these points through an examination of Christian missions in British Columbia between the 1840s and the 1890s. It joins work by historians like Susan Neylan and Jean Barman, who argue for the centrality of gender, class, and sexuality to British Columbia's missionary project, and a transnational scholarship that insists we treat empire and colony as a single and, more importantly, mutually constitutive project.[4] Missionary efforts to transform Aboriginal women, I want to suggest, were animated and guided by images of respectable, metropolitan, working-class womanhood. The difficulty of transporting this gendered model to indigenous North America and, ultimately, upholding its social universality, was revealed by the persistence with which missionaries felt compelled to turn to institutions – most notably the residential school – to foster the domestic, conjugal, and labour roles that they falsely touted as natural.

Missions, Gender, and Colonial Society in British Columbia, 1840s to 1890s

Missionaries were an integral if always ambivalent component of the colonial project in British Columbia during the last half of the nineteenth century. The extent and character of church involvement in state formation was up for debate in the years following the establishment of a British colony on Vancouver Island in 1849. In 1851 the governor explained that the region had attracted a handful of Roman Catholic clerics but had thus far eluded the attention of Britain's growing legions of protestant missionaries, one disgruntled Anglican schoolteacher notwithstanding.[5] It was only when a substantial settler population arrived in the 1850s and 1860s that the various missionary churches established a firm foothold in the colony. Oblate brothers and, after 1858, sisters from the Daughters of St. Ann's boosted the Roman Catholic presence. The Anglican Columbia mission was established in 1858 through the largesse of British philanthropist Angela Burdett-Coutts, and with it came clerics and projects sponsored by both the Church Missionary Society (CMS) and the Society for the Propagation of the Gospel in Foreign Parts (SPG). Methodists connected to the Canadian church arrived in 1859. By the 1870s, Roman Catholics operated missions at the Fraser River, Williams Lake, the Okanagan Valley, Stuart's Lake, Fort Rupert, Cowichan, and Victoria. Anglicans worked amongst Aboriginal people at Comox, Yale, Lytton, Nanaimo, Cowichan, Kincolith, Metlakatlah, and Lytton. The Methodists' scope was narrower: Nanaimo, Victoria, New Westminster, Port Simpson, and, at other times, Bella Bella and Clayoquot.[6]

The colonial state lauded the growth of this missionary project, but the state's commitment to tangibly supporting it was limited. The mainland colony of British Columbia was proclaimed in 1858 in an effort to shore up British control in the wake of the Fraser River gold rush, but the colonial state remained fragile, its settler population small, and the place of missionaries within it contested and insecure. This was settler colonialism on the cheap and at its most prosaic, and it was a disappointment to missionaries. Like the Baptists so ably studied by Catherine Hall, they had a "missionary dream" in which claims to human brotherhood jostled with beliefs in racial hierarchy, and a critique of the violence and exploitation of colonialism coexisted with a faith in the superiority of British culture.[7] In British Columbia, missionaries navigated the contradictions invoked by these

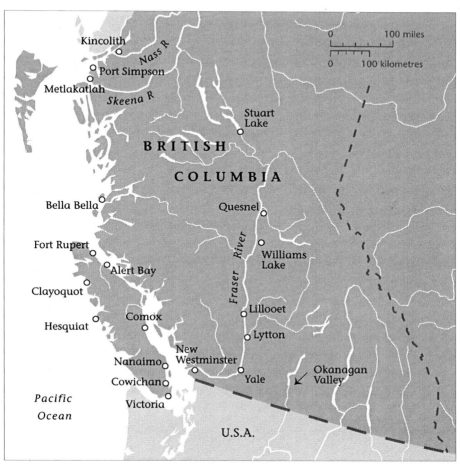

Map of colonial British Columbia
Cartographer: Eric Leinberger

competing beliefs by claiming what Jean Comaroff and John Comaroff call the "self-appointed role as the conscience of the colonizer."[8]

This missionary "conscience" served as the touchstone for an alternative model of imperialism rather than as a critique of it. Apostles of God despaired that the imperial state in British Columbia so clearly failed to embrace their vision of a guiding, superior role for European, and more particularly British, peoples. After being told that the colony would grant the CMS a bit of land for its mission at Kincolith but nothing more, missionary Robert Tomlinson explained that his was not simply the work of religion, but of empire in its full social and political sense: "The Church

Missionary Society sends forth its labourers to teach not only the distinctive doctrines of Christianity but also the practice of it, and to further in every way the civilization and moral improvement of the natives. To overthrow dark superstition and to plant instead Christian truth to change the natives from ignorant, bloodthirsty, cruel savages into quiet, useful, subjects of our gracious Queen is the object held out to those whom this Society sends as its agents."[9] Tomlinson articulated the tellingly uneven fit between the mission and state branches of this local colonial project and the vision of social transformation that lay at the heart of the missionary vision of empire in British Columbia.

Ideas and practices of womanhood were central to this and other missionary dreams. The written records of Roman Catholic, Anglican, and Methodist missionaries working in culturally, geographically, politically, and economically diverse areas of British Columbia speak to a common concern with the quotidian business of femininity. The missionary vision of womanhood was putatively dualistic, swinging between the heathen and degraded and the Christian and civilized. This apparent symmetry masked a more awkward intellectual heritage that drew selectively from Christian faith, the intellectual baggage of the European Enlightenment, and the social imperatives of industrializing Anglo-America, all read through the knowledges produced by Europe's colonization of the non-Western world. A belief in the hierarchical ordering of humanity along lines of race and culture existed alongside a profound investment in class structure, both of which could complement or challenge abiding beliefs in the liberal, individual subject and a Christian commitment to personal salvation and transformation. An investment in "separate spheres" for men and women was paired with a core belief in the transcendency of what was coyly called *the* family, or the domestic unit of man, wife, and children. Beliefs about the inherent morality of toil were enlivened by the idea that industry was progressive but haunted by fears of the larger workspaces and new power relations born of industrialization.

This shifting and sometimes conflicting set of precepts, assumptions, and practices developed not in the abstract or even in the metropole, but in daily dialogue with First Nations societies. There was, of course, no one First Nations society in nineteenth-century British Columbia, but a wide range of nations with a variety of social organizations – and systems of organizing gender – that ranged from the egalitarian, mobile, small societies of the southern Interior, which made their living foraging, hunting, and fishing, to the wealthy, stratified, large, and, by North American standards, densely populated societies of the Northwest Coast. All divided their communities along lines of gender, although they did so in different ways that reflected various modes of organizing work, prestige, and identity. Northwest Coast societies like the Haida and Tsimshian were matrilineages, where high-ranking women could exercise considerable institutionalized authority but where slave women possessed few resources and little power. Interior societies like the Carrier, as Jo-Anne Fiske notes, stressed gender equality and affirmed women's contributions to subsistence, social regulation, and social reproduction.[10] That First Nations conceptualized and practised womanhood in a variety of ways did not stop missionaries from returning, time and time again, to three overlapping components of women's lives: the domestic, the conjugal, and labour. Missionaries worked from the assumption that houses, marriages, and female duties were the necessary stuff of womanhood, but they found these ideas challenged, fractured, and eventually revised by the colonial experience.

Domesticity
The domestic was central to the construction of nineteenth-century, bourgeois femininity and its dissemination through the imperial world. The image of the domesticated European woman was animated by a set of overlapping corresponding images generated in and through Europe's encounter with its many "others": the harem, the African "tribal," the zenana, and, in North America, the "wandering" Indian. These images relied on essentially spatial imagery of too little (the harem and the zenana) or too much (the tribe and the wanderer) movement. In British Columbia, as in the Americas, the Antipodes, and parts of Africa and Asia, the problem was the latter one, and the central problem of colonialism became the creation of permanence where there had only been mobility, whether by importing sedentary peoples or by literally fixing migratory ones.[11] British Columbia's governor, James Douglas, explained to an approving Secretary of State for the colonies that the civilization of Aboriginal peoples would flow from permanent settlement. Once they were fixed, "civilization would at once begin" and "law and religion would become naturally introduced among them."[12]

Missionaries also thought that First Nations people would have to abandon mobility if they wished to be civilized. "It will I think be readily understood," explained an Anglican in 1870, "how very difficult it is to exercise an efficient oversight over a body of Indians so independent and nomadic as ours, divided up into so many small families or settlements, and so widely scattered throughout so extensive a range of country."[13] Missionaries would accordingly try to fix people by fixing them. Some worked to relocate mobile peoples to permanent villages that were, not incidentally, amenable to Christian teaching and control. Following Jesuit experience in Paraguay, the Roman Catholic Durieu system reorganized mobile, foraging, egalitarian peoples like the Secwepemc into strict, hierarchical villages from the late 1860s until the 1940s.[14] CMS missionaries established permanent villages at Metlakatlah and Kincolith, as did Methodists at Port Simpson, Bella Bella, and elsewhere.[15] The doctrinal differences between these missionaries were belied, or at the very least complicated, by the fact that they possessed, as Margaret Whitehead is correct to observe, a similar vision of the mission as a "city on a hill."[16] Such cities were permanent villages, made up of homes that were inspired by, but never strictly replicated, European fashion, ranging from log cabins to row houses laid out on a grid.[17] In these missions, the home itself was, as Nayan Shah has noted, "a key regulative norm of modernity."[18]

Domesticity was a regulative norm with particular resonance for women. Given the abiding connections between domesticity and womanhood in nineteenth-century Anglo-American culture, it could hardly be otherwise. This notion of domestic womanhood was in large part a bourgeois one that, as Leonore Davidoff and Catherine Hall have shown, was intimately connected with the rise and development of the middle class. But it was given shape and meaning by perceptions of plebeian peoples, most notably by the mid-nineteenth-century moral-reform discourse that connected domestic disorder with working-class women and ultimately with disease and immorality.[19] Patrick Wolfe argues that the anthropological "discovery" of mother-right in indigenous Australia was central to mid-nineteenth-century debates about married women's property in Britain.[20] Likewise, it is not coincidental that the "problem" of working-class women's domesticity – or, better, their lack of it – emerged when Europeans were busy cataloguing and observing the household arrangements and gendered structures of the non-Western world. The variety of ways people organized households gave the lie to the foundational assumption that there was a universal and transhistoric connection between womanhood, the home, and morality.

Missionaries in British Columbia worked hard to shore up this connection in the wake of its challenge. They encouraged people to build and live in houses and also worked to impress upon them the necessity of "keeping" their houses in the various meanings of the word. Efforts to shift Tsimshian people at Port Simpson from collective houses to a village constituted of individual homes were justified on the grounds that "'Christian streets' were needed for Christian homemaking."[21] Methodist missionary Charles Tate and his wife held various missionary postings throughout British Columbia. Wherever they went they promoted a domesticity premised on the virtue of cleanliness. They were gratified by what they saw as Clayoquot people's emulation of their clean, domestic ways.[22] Sometimes they turned to more direct intervention, as when Mrs. Tate went door to door, checking on the breadmaking efforts of women she considered "pupils."[23]

The attempted domestication of Aboriginal women revealed the strength of the connections between womanhood and domesticity, but it also suggests its profound vulnerability. Instructing Aboriginal women in the virtues of feminine domesticity led missionaries quite literally outside the domestic to the small institutions that would precede the more infamous residential schools of the late nineteenth and twentieth centuries. From the 1860s onward, missionaries opened small residential schools throughout British Columbia, usually beginning with female students alone. Messianic lay-missionary William Duncan began a boarding school for young women at Metlakatlah that aimed to explicitly recast Tsimshian women along the lines of respectable, working-class British womanhood. One observer commented approvingly that former schoolgirls were "quite domesticated," had clean homes, and exercised a "good influence throughout the village."[24] The convent near Cowichan was justified on similar grounds. A "great number of girls," explained the Roman Catholic bishop, "are being educated and trained in the habits of domestic life, *gratis*."[25] Another residential school at Alert Bay similarly sought to "teach the girls domestic economy" away from what the federal Department of Indian Affairs described as "the debasing influences of camp life."[26] Schools allowed missionaries to reformulate domesticity on their own grounds – they were "residential" in more ways than one.

Missionary efforts to domesticate Aboriginal women were premised on an obvious discomfort with the matrilineal family and clan organization of the Northwest Coast and the egalitarian band societies of the Interior and southern Vancouver Island. In trying to convince Aboriginal women to embrace the European home, missionaries were embracing a vision of respectable, working-class womanhood and, at the same time, working to create it. Their recourse to the institution suggests that this domestic mission was flawed, partial, and ultimately impractical. So too were their efforts to promote what we might call a Christian conjugality.

Conjugality

Christian conjugality – by which I mean lifelong, domestic, heterosexual unions sanctioned by colonial law and the Christian church – was a staple of the missionary program throughout nineteenth-century British Columbia. This too was a response to missionaries' disapproval of the variety of sexual and familial forms they found in British Columbia and an affirmation of their investment in a model of European femininity. This twinned rejection and embrace cannot be disaggregated from metropolitan anxieties. Missionaries to the British working class found that a disturbing number of people were "married but not churched," had "besom weddings" or "lived tally."[27] Followers of socialist Robert Owen and, in the United States, free-love advocate Frances Wright politicized the gap between plebeian practices and middle-class expectations around marriage.[28] Such sexual heterodoxy would come under sharp pressure in the middle of the nineteenth century as so-called domestic missionaries worked to regularize marital and domestic arrangements in metropolitan centres.

It is no coincidence that reformers "discovered" the free unions of the urban working class at the same time that missionaries "discovered" the plurality of marital forms practised throughout the imperial world. Missionaries to British Columbia offered consistent critiques of how indigenous peoples coupled. They did so because marriages, like households, were linchpins in the larger family and social structures that missionaries sought to alter. Duncan's aim, as Tsimshian anthropologist William Beynon argued in 1941, was "to destroy the intricate social structure of the Tsimshians," and displacing the matrilineal clan with the patrilineal family was central to this.[29] Missionaries everywhere focused on two of the customs that garnered negative attention in the imperial press the world over – bride-price and plural marriage.[30] Linking marriage to potlatches (a link, by the way, that has not been sufficiently investigated in the enormous literature on potlatches and colonial efforts to regulate them), one missionary argued that "Indian barter marriages" were one of the "greatest difficulties to be met in Christianizing and civilizing the Indian tribes of the coast."[31] Upon arriving in Port Simpson in 1858, Duncan remarked on bride-price, child marriage, and clan exogamy, but was particularly disturbed by plural marriage. "I am sorry to say," he intoned, "that polygamy is by no means uncommon here."[32]

Critiques of Aboriginal marriages were animated by a little global knowledge that circulated quite profitably about the colonial world, namely that "savagery" was both constituted and defined by a "low" estimation of women and that civilization was marked by a "high" status accorded to women.[33] Oblate missionary A.G. Morice explained the connection. Those working with the mobile, subarctic Dene people, he wrote, "had to do a great deal in order to lift up [women's] condition, not only from a religious and moral standpoint, but also as regards civilization as well, which second aspect is often the result of the first." He substantiated this by turning to the images of the Aboriginal "drudge" and her necessary counterpart, the European "queen of the home": "With most Indian tribes, and the Dénés of Northern British Columbia form no exception to the rule, woman is not the companion, or equal, of man, and the queen of the home as with us, but a servant, a drudge and almost a slave, who will never dare eat with her lord and master and who, when on the wing, is the perfect beast of burden of the whole family."[34] Missionaries – in this case a celibate Oblate priest – thus positioned themselves as saviours of Aboriginal women who would, as Gayatri Chakravorty Spivak so evocatively put it, save brown women from brown men.[35]

Spivak is right to note the way that gender and race collided in discussions of colonized women's apparent degradation and their appropriate "saviour." But the equation could also be more complicated. In nineteenth-century British Columbia, it was not any white men who could save brown women from brown men. Missionaries were persistent if not especially effective critics of settler-Aboriginal relationships, which had long been a feature of colonial life in British Columbia. Roman Catholics, who often hailed from French Canada or, in the case of Oblates, the margins of southern Europe (most often Corsica), operated with what seemed to be a more complicated set of cultural assumptions about hybridity. Protestant missionaries associated mixed-race relationships with female victimization and with the dangerous degradation of European men, especially working-class ones, in colonial contexts. Anglican missionary John Sheepshanks characteristically told a British audience that "the Indians have learned our vices, they have contracted habits of intoxication, and their poor women have been led away, by the ungodly white men, who are often what is called the 'pioneers of civilisation.'"[36]

Sheepshanks was not the first to draw this link, and he would not be the last. As occurred elsewhere in the Pacific, marriages, sexual relations, and domestic lives forged between European and Aboriginal became a potent symbol of the rough, abusive imperialism Protestants hoped to replace with a gentle, Christian, and distant administration.[37] In her study of missions to Hawaii, Patricia Grimshaw credits this to the missionaries' response to "the conjunction of the Western male's sexual predacity and the Hawaiian's easiness about sexuality."[38] Certainly Crosby saw the doubling of heathen sexuality and working-class white male depravity as especially dangerous. To him, they fed off each other and were, tellingly, part of a single phenomenon:

> Much of the old-time slavery was passing away when the missionary came, but a slavery in a new and more horrible form was being established. The advent of thousands of white men, miners, and lumbermen, many of whom were vicious and depraved, brought temptation to their doors. The Indian's love of display, and his ambitions to be considered of importance, which found expression in his giving of great feasts and potlatches, led him to seize any ready and easy means of gain.
>
> At one time among the Indians, as among all heathen people, the girls were counted of little value. If they grew up they were to become burden-bearers of their masters of the other sex. An Indian mother had been known to take her little baby girl out into the woods and stuff its mouth with grass and leaves and leave it to die. And when asked why she did so, she would say 'I did not want her to grow up and suffer as I have suffered.' But heathenism crushed out a mother's love and turns the heart to stone and changes a father into a foul, indifferent fiend. And so when the miners came the natives willingly sold their daughters, ranging from ten to eighteen years of age, for a few blankets or a little gold, into a slavery which was worse than death.[39]

For Crosby and his ilk, the "old-time slavery" and the new slavery were different in degree but not, at heart, in kind.

Where some missionaries saw the presence of undesirable marriages – whether plural, mixed-race, or sacramented with material exchange – others saw simple absence. Victoria bishop George Hills could sometimes see First Nations regulatory norms, but sometimes he could not see past the absence of European markers of marital commitment, as when he commented that "pure affection & sacredness of tie are unknown" among the Tsimshian.[40] Writing about the hierarchical Northwest Coast Haida nation, another missionary writer declared that "among these simple and primitive tribes marriage is unknown." This he deemed a profound absence that signalled the enormous gap between civilized and savage. "The beautiful attachment and heroic constancy of affection ending only in death" was something that existed only "amongst civilised or Christian nations."[41]

If First Nations people had no marriages, it would presumably be easy to encourage them to adopt the kind missionaries had in mind. But deeming Aboriginal marriages insufficient, both morally and religiously, made the missionary project an easy one only in rhetoric. Just as inculcating domesticity led to its revision, peddling Christian conjugality produced results that the missionaries never anticipated. This was not for lack of effort. Protestants promoted conjugality by literally modelling it. Unmarried male missionaries were seen as a problem, both because they might enter into relationships with local women and because they could not serve as conjugal exemplars.[42] Myra Rutherdale has shown how the ideal Protestant missionary worked as part of a married pair, lived in a mission house positioned at the literal and symbolic centre of the mission communities, and in doing so provided an example of Christian conjugality and domesticity for First Nations people.[43] Roman Catholics, who lived in gender-segregated, celibate communities, provided a different sort of example. Sisters and brothers departed from conjugal norms and, as Linda Gordon observes, believed that institutional life could be nurturing and complete.[44] Yet this did not, as Diane Langmore notes in her study of the South Pacific, stop them from promoting the nuclear family as the cornerstone of Christian practice.[45]

Missionaries worked to encourage conjugality in more direct ways as well. They targeted indigenous women who maintained free unions with settler men, suggesting, tellingly, that they viewed the former as better candidates for salvation than the latter. Anglican R.C. Lundin Brown preached on the meaning of marriage near Lillooet in the early 1860s. He argued that "concubinage of their women with the whites" was "a thing accursed" and that Nlaka'pamux women should demand Christian marriage from white men:

> If any white man wanted honestly to wed with an Indian girl, that, we said, was another thing; they should be married; "leplate" [priest] would make them join hands, and give them God's blessing; they should then be no longer two but one, and live together as man and wife for ever till they died. But, as for those temporary and unhallowed connexions, they were thoroughly bad. Indians must steer clear of them, or their canoes would be

smashed among the rocks; and if any girl there was already entangled in such a connexion, so degrading, so offensive to the Great Spirit, so deadly, – she must not hesitate, but do at once what God required of her, – she must break it off.[46]

Missionaries were pleased when followers heeded their marital advice. Hills wrote of an Aboriginal woman who, under missionary instruction at Metlakatlah, "learnt to see her sin" and separated from her white partner. Hills was convinced that this act had a beneficial impact on her spouse, who also "became impressed with a sense of shame" and agreed to a wedding. "She has steadily improved, and has made her husband a good wife," approved the bishop.[47]

Missionaries also worked to transform marriages between Aboriginal partners. In 1872, Tomlinson explained to his superiors in London why it mattered so much that he had married his first couple at the Kincolith mission. "One of the chief blemishes in these tribes is the demoralized state of their marriage laws," he explained. "Husbands have no confidence in their wives and the wives no confidence in their husbands they are continually separating and remarrying." In response, he made the union of man and wife as "solemn and binding as possible and certain." In performing his first marriage, Tomlinson was sure he had acted as an instrument of God. His fear that the bride was too young was outweighed by the conviction that the simple act of marriage had saved her "from the fearful Gulf of immorality" and put her under the jurisdiction "of a Xian husband to be cherished and guided by him until 'death them do part.'"[48]

Mass marriages made the point that this was a social as opposed to individual transformation. Methodist Thomas Crosby claimed to have married forty couples at once after a revival.[49] J.B. Good looked forward to holding a group wedding in 1879. Christian marriage, he explained, was not an end in itself but a literally spectacular symbol of a broader, deeper, and, for him, profoundly satisfying transformation. Marrying couples were to purchase a gold ring, and the women were to dress in white and the men in a "goodly array." This bodily attire, he hoped, would be "the first fruits opening the way for an entire change eventually in the domestic relationships," and the second step in a three-part process of conversion.[50] Oblate missionaries to the Stó:lō people similarly worked to encourage Christian marriage as a tangible symbol of refashioned families.[51] Between 1864 and 1887, 170 couples were married at Metlakatlah alone.[52]

Missionary sources, not surprisingly, give us only limited windows into Aboriginal responses, resistances, and reappropriations to this or to anything else. Yet even within the self-serving, self-promoting, and profoundly self-referential missionary archive, it is clear that First Nations people did not always welcome Christian conjugality, and that women could be especially immune to all its alleged charms. Duncan regularly complained that he had more Christian men than women he considered suitable mates for them. "I feel very troubled about what to do for wives of the young men of the settlement," he told his journal. "I could pick up not less than a dozen fine young men who are wanting wives & no suitable women are forthcoming."[53] "It is easier," agreed an observer, "for Mr. Duncan to keep his young men straight."[54] Roman Catholic priest Joseph Brabant found women and elders disruptive forces in his attempts to encourage Christian conjugality on Vancouver Island's west coast. After attempting a church marriage in 1882, Brabant "learned what was being said and the protestations that were uttered in public against my taking in their matrimonial affairs." He appealed to what he identified as men's support of Christian marriage and threatened women that men would look elsewhere for wives if they continued their opposition.[55] This brings us back to the old argument that, in effect, women had more to lose in rejecting cultural traditions of marriage and domesticity that offered them either formal authority or considerable latitude for individual expression.[56] There was not one, singular Aboriginal response, but many, and sometimes they were gendered.

Christian conjugality had to be enforced as well as sacramented and ritualized. Missionaries encouraged people to take their Christian vows seriously, to live out the promise of lifelong, Godly heterosexuality in tangible and, above all, daily ways. Missions nurtured a pervasive gender segregation and were sometimes willing to resort to brute force to keep men and women apart. In Durieu villages, boys and girls could not play together, women and girls were rarely alone, especially at night, and "any man or grown boy who entered the room of a woman when she was alone and engaged her in conversation had to be punished." In the 1880s Bishop Paul Durieu increasingly supported the use of physical punishments, most notably whipping, to curb these and other "sins."[57] Missions also targeted specific breaches of conjugality dubbed "adultery," a term that, not unlike "prostitution," could serve as a catch-all marker of all sexual expression deemed inappropriate or deviant. Catholic missionaries to Hesquiat in the 1870s were advised to take special care to instruct churchgoers about adultery.[58] Sexual practice outside of Christian conjugality could be grounds for eviction from mission communities. Duncan excommunicated three parishioners for "adultery" on one 1866 day alone.[59]

It was in this attempted enforcement that the artificiality of Christian conjugality became most clear. Vexing complications arose when missionaries encouraged or enforced notions of marital sovereignty that conflicted with existing relationships. Good found that "the question of dealing wisely and yet in strict accordance with the spirit and teaching of the New Dispensation with the custom of concubinage and polygamy as practised by the

Indian tribe had come to the front with us and caused us no small trouble and perplexity." His bishop insisted that those seeking baptism must "content themselves with one wife." But how could Good ask men to "dismiss" one partner and consign her to social marginality or, he feared, even a life of prostitution?[60]

Missionaries might trumpet Christian conjugality as universally desirable, but trying to simply "apply" it to Aboriginal lives revealed it as partial. Hills, the Anglican bishop, was troubled by the disjunctures between Christian doctrine and Tsimshian marital and familial practice. He explained that it was "too intricate a matter to unravel the tangled thread of their lives & reinstate each wife to her first husband & each husband to his first wife. " His solution – namely, that "a veil must be cast over the past, it must be viewed with regret & we must take the converts as we find them & fix them from henceforth in a right course of principle & duty" – did not solve the problem he identified, and that was the clash between Christian doctrine and the salience of indigenous relationships and obligations.[61] Twenty years later, the Canadian Department of Indian Affairs was similarly stumped. The department suspected this could become a messy legal problem and opted, ironically enough, to leave the matters to missionaries.[62]

That mission policy had serious and often damaging repercussions for Aboriginal peoples, especially Aboriginal women, was apparent to even the most dogged promoters of marriage as a tool of social transformation. Hills argued that missionaries should refuse to marry Christian men to "heathen" women, but was haunted by the fear that his position could increase rather than decrease the same sin he sought to vanquish.[63] As bishop, Hills rarely had to navigate such gaps, but his missionaries did. Brown described advising a woman, Kenadqua, about *how* to manage the apparent contradiction between her consensual, mixed-race relationship and her new faith in Christianity and the conjugality it demanded. He suggested that she should demand marriage within a few weeks. If her loutish white partner refused to appear before the priest, she should leave him. That she did, and Brown was clearly ambivalent about the results. Kenadqua's was a choice between degraded, mixed-race concubinage and savagery, here symbolized by an underground house and ultimately death.[64]

Missionary-run institutions emerged as a solution to this quandary, just as they did to the messy politics of domesticity. An Anglican considering how to reform mixed-race, consensual partnerships argued that only industrial or residential schools would allow them to offer women a choice that was not, in one way or another, more savagery. "I am longing for the day," he explained to his British audience, "when I can ask them to break such unholy bonds, and offer them maintenance in some industrial school. At present, if they were to leave their (all but) husbands, they must return to their native way of living, which will not do."[65] Only an institution would allow them an option that was neither indigenous savagery nor colonial degradation.

That it was so practically difficult to ask people to embrace Christian conjugality is a telling indication of the real frailties of the missionary project. Native peoples, as the scholarly literature on colonialism has so often shown, could selectively and syncretically incorporate Christian mores and ways into their own lives for their own purposes, and no doubt they did so here. Missionaries also used Christian conjugality to gain the approval of, and reap rewards from, settlers. Joseph, a Catholic Aboriginal man, showed a gold miner and future missionary named Henry Guillod his marriage certificate when he wanted to impress him as a reliable canoe man.[66] But some things were harder or simply less desirable to syncretize than others. Rejections and ruptures, as much as creative adaptation and appropriation, show us how colonialism was adaptive and improvisational. That Aboriginal people were so often unwilling to abandon local ideas of conjugality in exchange for Christian approval or a job, and so committed to fashioning their own hybrid traditions, helps us to question one of imperialism's own self-sustaining truths, namely, as Antoinette Burton writes, "that imperial power acted like the proverbial juggernaut, razing opposition and, more to the point, fixing with absolute authority the social and cultural conditions out of which citizens and subjects could make and remake their relationships to the state and civil society."[67] The puzzling and sometimes painful disjunctures that marked missionaries' efforts to foster Christian marriage and monogamy made clear the significance of European notions of appropriate womanhood, but also suggested how very fragile they could be.

Work

Labour, like marriages and households, bore enormous symbolic and obviously economic meaning in the nineteenth-century world. The necessity of industry and its necessarily gendered character became a hallmark of reform enterprises in both metropolitan and imperial contexts. Working-class people were to adopt the much-lauded "habits of industry" that they were thought to both lack and require. They also worked to re-gender, as it were, some forms of work, campaigning, for instance, to remove women from mining or from kinds of industrial work thought injurious to their reproductive and moral selves.[68]

Steady and appropriately female labour was part of the package of Christian transformation for indigenous women in nineteenth-century British Columbia. Missionaries expressed surprise about what was, in Aboriginal communities, considered women's work. One of Duncan's first experiences in British Columbia was watching First Nations women work on canoes. He found their apparent inequality and willingness to do physical work incongruous. "The women," he wrote in his journal, "though very passive took an equal share of the work."[69] Women's participation in physical labour, and most particularly in packing and other transportation, signalled their savagery and the need for salvation that went with it. The missionaries responded by working to reassociate certain tasks with certain genders. Father Léon Foucet established "a society of midwives" amongst Kutenai women "to assist in confinement cases" in the late 1880s. The "president" and her three assistants had nine duties, one of which was "to notify the chief of women with child carrying loads."[70]

If savagery was symbolized by women doing the wrong kind of work, civilization would be built and demonstrated by their socialization into appropriate labour. The governor told the Colonial Office that "the employment of Indians in any menial capacity produces an immediate change in their personal habits" and indeed "confirms the influence of civilisation, and prepares their mind for the reception of Christian Knowledge."[71] For Douglas, wage work was culturally transformative. It was certainly economically so: Aboriginal women's labour as domestic servants, agricultural labourers, and industrial, especially cannery, workers was critical to the development of capitalism in British Columbia.[72]

Missionaries agreed on the transformative potential of labour – Good considered "the formation of habits of steady industry, economy, and sobriety" to be key steps in Christian transformation.[73] Yet he, like others, was ambivalent about what happened to Aboriginal people who found waged work in the settler economy. "I will endeavour to prevent any of my people going to the new cannery at Alert Bay," explained one missionary to the Tsimshian, "as I think they have just enough of such temptations as arise in connection with this kind of work here at hand."[74] Waged work gave Aboriginal women the dangerous independence that went with having ready cash income and the means to support themselves outside of male authority and the family. The dangers of such independence were confirmed by the moral degradation that missionaries thought so often befell women who went to Victoria and succumbed to the appeal of the sex trade. "There are constantly in Victoria, on the average, about five hundred Indian women subsisting on prostitution," argued the popular press in 1867, "who from time to time return in many cases to distant tribes with the earnings of this traffic."[75] In order to harness the transformative potential of labour but disaggregate it from the dangers of its local practice, work, like domesticity and conjugality, had to be put under missionary control. By 1871 the Anglican missions alone operated some three hundred farms.[76] Duncan went further at Metlakatlah, where he developed a dazzling retinue of industries, including a sawmill, cannery, store, schooner, brickmaking shop, blacksmith shop, weaving shop, and soap factory.[77]

Women had a special role in these efforts to forge an indigenous, Christian capitalism. First Nations women, one missionary explained plainly, needed to be taught "to work."[78] The kind of work they needed to be taught was that performed by the respectable, working-class women of metropolitan centres. It usually had to do, in one way or another, with textiles. "The great need of this place is employment for the young women," explained Duncan, requesting that benefactors send him needles and wool, so that "the girls" might knit their own stockings, and braid for them to make aprons. He did not want finished articles, lest the lessons of dutiful, appropriate labour be lost on the young Tsimshian women.[79] A carding machine "for the use of the Indian Girls," who worked with the largely Québécois sisters of St. Anne at Cowichan, was described as "intended for the work of the civilization of these Indians" and thus exempted from taxes.[80] Women in Cowichan could also opt for Protestant textiles, since across town, Anglican Mrs. Reece taught women to sew and knit twice a week.[81] Mrs. Raybold, "a good lady from town," instructed First Nations women to sew under Methodist auspices in early 1860s Nanaimo.[82] The irony of middle-class women "teaching" such skills to Aboriginal women was not lost on the descendants of Alice Woods Tomlinson: "They always had girls in the house working for them, working with them so grandma could teach the girls how to do things. She had never done much sewing herself because they were pretty well protected. They came from Ireland and they belonged to the gentry in Ireland and moved over here. So she'd never done much housework and she'd never knitted in her life. But now she had to teach the Indians how to knit a sock."[83] Gendered, racialized, and classed meanings all clashed within the walls of the Anglican mission house at Kincolith.

The irony of a bourgeois Irish woman teaching "Indians how to knit a sock" reminds us that the missionary project was not to turn Aboriginal women into European women as much as it was to turn them into working-class ones. Textiles had enormous allegorical flexibility beyond their ability to sign plebeian respectability. Madeleine McIvor is correct to point out that the significance of textiles and clothing in understandings of appropriate indigenous women's work reflects ideas of the body and respectability as well as of labour.[84] The lowly socks and dresses produced by Aboriginal women stood for labour and bodily respectability, and their production signified transformation itself. Anglican missionaries described the completion of the first stocking in Victoria's Humbolt Street mission. It was, they explained, "a noteworthy achievement." They signalled the centrality of labour in the process of social transformation by signalling the "intelligence" of the stocking-maker, but depicted her as childlike. Her full humanity, like her work, is thus rendered *potential:*

Anda, an intelligent Tchimsean [sic] woman, married to an Anglo-American, was the first who attempted it. For a long time her work, even to herself, was questionable: often it was condemned and taken off; yet she plodded trustfully on. It never, they said, "grew like" a stocking, for all was "straight down," right enough for the leg, but how about the foot? Those most sanguine regarded it with a "klouass" (may-be), and "Mrs. Lenna" kept silence. But at last the heel was "turned," and the foot began "to come;" all, having laid their own work on their laps, waited the event in silence. When the work was at length given back, Anda helped the wonder up (it was to the length of one's hand), and the curious little sounds expressive of admiration were heard all round – a circle of brown faces seeming to say, "Saw ye ever the like o' this?"[85]

The indigenous women are, as Nicholas Thomas explains, constructed as childlike to signal the miraculousness of the missionary project – here represented by the stocking.[86]

The symbolic role of women's handicraft production was confirmed when missionaries displayed it as evidence of their successful conversion. At his "Annual Indian Industrial Exhibition," Vancouver Island Anglican missionary W.H. Lomas gave prominent place to women's needlework and knitting.[87] The superintendent of Indian Affairs heartily approved. Visiting the exhibition, he commented that he liked the crops displayed well enough, but was more taken with "the exhibition of needle, crochet, and knitted work, by the native women," which he deemed "both surprising and most credible." He took care to relate the women's work to their representation of bodily self, commenting that they were remarkably "clean and neat in appearance."[88] He did not remark that they lived in permanent houses or were married by Christian rite, but he might as well have.

Christian missionaries of all denominational stripes were interested in Aboriginal women and, more particularly, in reforming their relationships to domesticity, to conjugality, and to work. This triple program reflected missionaries' profound unease with the different ways that First Nations people experienced and understood manliness and womanliness. The collective, moveable, and matrilineal households; their plural, mixed-race, or consensual relationships; and their physical labour or apparent lethargy all signalled a world of irreparable and dangerous difference. The various reform efforts launched throughout nineteenth-century British Columbia were products of this meeting of imperial knowledge and indigenous lives. Like the Presbyterian missions in Vanuatu studied by Margaret Jolly, these were complex and multilayered interactions that were "dense with contradictions – contradictions between European and local models, between European ideals and the reality of European domestic life in the colonies, and between the aim of improvement and that of domestification which implied marginalization and devaluation relative to men."[89]

Such contradictions reveal much about the politics of colonialism and the politics of nineteenth-century womanhood from which they cannot be separated. Missionary attempts to encourage domesticity, conjugality, and suitable work roles suggest the reach of Western expectations of appropriate womanhood, but they also suggest how such expectations were reshaped – or in Dipesh Chakrabarty's suggestive lexicon, provincialized – by their experience in colonial contexts. The fact that missionaries so often turned to carceral institutions as the only feasible way of bringing their vision of Christian womanhood to Aboriginal British Columbia belied their claims, implicit or explicit, to social universality and to imperialism's famous monopoly on truth, identity, and knowledge about women and so much else.

Acknowledgments
This research has been supported by a Social Sciences and Humanities Research Council of Canada Doctoral Fellowship, a Social Sciences and Humanities Research Council of Canada Postdoctoral Fellowship, and the Canada Research Chairs Program. This chapter was originally prepared for a roundtable at the 2002 Berkshire Conference on the History of Women, and the members of that roundtable – Jean Barman, Robin Jarvis Brownlie, Tina Chen, Ann McGrath, and Kathryn McPherson – all deserve my thanks. Eric Leinberger made the map. Constance Backhouse and Antoinette Burton provided further suggestions and comments, for which I am also grateful.

Notes
1   Ramón A. Gutiérrez, *When Jesus Came, the Corn Mothers Went Away: Marriage, Sexuality, and Power in New Mexico, 1500-1846* (Stanford, CA: Stanford University Press, 1991), xvii.
2   Mary Louise Pratt, *Imperial Eyes: Travel Writing and Transculturation* (London: Routledge, 1992).
3   On this, see Antoinette Burton's essays, "Who Needs the Nation? Interrogating 'British' History," in *Cultures of Empire: A Reader,* ed. Catherine Hall, 137-56 (Manchester, UK: Manchester University Press, 2000) and "Rules of Thumb: British History and 'Imperial Culture' in Nineteenth- and Twentieth-Century Britain," *Women's History Review* 3, 4 (1994): 483-501; and Ann Laura Stoler and Frederick Cooper, "Between Metropole and Colony: Rethinking a Research Agenda," in *Tensions of Empire: Colonial Cultures in a Bourgeois World,* ed. Frederick Cooper and Ann Laura Stoler, 1-58 (Berkeley: University of California Press, 1997).
4   Susan Neylan, "Longhouses, Schoolrooms, and Workers' Cottages: Nineteenth-Century Protestant Missions to the Tsimshian and the Transformation of Class through Religion," *Journal of the Canadian Historical Association,* 11 (2000): 51-86; Jean Barman, "Taming Aboriginal Sexuality: Gender, Power, and Race in British Columbia, 1850-1900," *BC Studies* 115/116 (Autumn/Winter 1997-98): 237-66. For programmatic analyses of the need to consider colonies and metropoles simultaneously, see Antoinette Burton, "Introduction: The Unfinished Business of Colonial Modernities," in *Gender, Sexuality and Colonial Modernities,* ed. Antoinette Burton, 1-16 (London: Routledge, 1999); Patrick Wolfe, "History and Imperialism: A Century of Theory, from Marx to Postcolonialism," *American Historical Review* 102, 2 (April 1997): 388-420; Stoler and Cooper, "Between Metropole and Colony"; Catherine Hall, *Civilising Subjects: Metropole and Colony in the English Imagination, 1830-1867* (Chicago: University of Chicago Press, 2002); Susan Thorne, *Congregational Missions and the Making of an Imperial Culture in Nineteenth-Century England* (Stanford, CA: Stanford University Press, 1999).
5   James Douglas to Earl Grey, 31 October 1851, Colonial Office, Original Correspondence, Vancouver Island, CO 305/3 (hereafter cited as CO 305), mflm R288:1, University of British Columbia Library (UBCL).
6   *Report of the Superintendent of Indian Affairs for British Columbia for 1872 and 1873* (Ottawa: I.B. Taylor, 1873), 28-29.
7   See Hall's majestic *Civilising Subjects,* Chapter 1.

8 Jean Comaroff and John Comaroff, "Images of Empire, Contest of Conscience," in *Ethnography and the Historical Imagination,* 188-214 (Boulder, CO: Westview, 1992), 201.
9 Robert Tomlinson to Joseph Trutch, 25 January 1870, "Colonial Correspondence," GR 1372, reel B-1367, file 1708a, British Columbia Archives (BCA).
10 See Jo-Anne Fiske, "Carrier Women and the Politics of Mothering," in *Rethinking Canada: The Promise of Women's History,* 4th ed., ed. Veronica Strong-Boag, Mona Gleason, and Adele Perry, 235-48 (Toronto: Oxford University Press, 2001), 362-63.
11 See, for instance, Kate Brown, "Gridded Lives: Why Kazakhstan and Montana Are Nearly the Same Place," *American Historical Review* 106, 1 (February 2001): 17-48; John K. Noyes, "Nomadic Landscapes and the Colonial Frontier: The Problem of Nomadism in German South West Africa," in *Colonial Frontiers: Indigenous-European Encounters in Settler Societies,* ed. Lynette Russell, 198-215 (Manchester, UK: Manchester University Press, 2001).
12 James Douglas to Edward Bulwer Lytton, 14 March 1859, Colonial Office, Original Correspondence, British Columbia, CO 60/4, MG 11, mflm B-80, Library and Archives Canada (LAC).
13 J.R. Good in *Thirteenth Annual Report of the Missions of the Church of England in British Columbia for the Year 1871* (London: Rivingtons, 1872), 57.
14 Elizabeth Furniss, "Resistance, Coercion, and Revitalization: The Shuswap Encounter with Roman Catholic Missionaries, 1860-1900," *Ethnohistory* 42, 2 (Spring 1995): 231-263; see Bridget Moran, ed., *Stoney Creek Woman: The Story of Mary John* (Vancouver: Arsenal Pulp Press, 1988) for a memoir of growing up in a Durieu village.
15 See Peggy Brock, "Building Bridges: Politics and Religion in a First Nations Community," *Canadian Historical Review* 81, 1 (March 2000): 67-96; Peter Murray, *The Devil and Mr. Duncan: A History of Two Metlakatlas* (Victoria: Sono Nis, 1985); Jean Usher, *William Duncan of Metlakatla: A Victorian Missionary in British Columbia* (Ottawa: Museum of Man, 1974); Michael E. Harkin, *The Heiltsuks: Dialogues of Culture and History on the Northwest Coast* (Lincoln and London: University of Nebraska Press, 1997); Clarence Bolt, *Thomas Crosby and the Tsimshian: Small Shoes for Feet Too Large* (Vancouver: UBC Press, 1992); Susan Neylan, *The Heavens are Changing: Nineteenth-Century Protestant Missions and Tsimshian Christianity* (Montreal and Kingston: McGill-Queen's University Press, 2003); Carol Ann Cooper, "'To Be Free on Our Lands': Coast Tsimshian and Nisga'a Societies in Historical Perspective, 1820-1900" (PhD dissertation, University of Waterloo, 1993).
16 Margaret Whitehead, "Introduction," in *They Call Me Father: Memoirs of Father Nicolas Coccola,* ed. Margaret Whitehead, 1-73 (Vancouver: UBC Press, 1988), 14.
17 On housing more generally, see Adele Perry, "From 'the Hot-Bed of Vice' to the 'Good and Well-Ordered Christian Home': First Nations Housing and Reform in Nineteenth-Century British Columbia," *Ethnohistory* 50, 4 (Summer 2003): 587-610.
18 Nayan Shah, *Contagious Divides: Epidemics and Race in San Francisco's Chinatown* (Berkeley: University of California Press, 2001), 106.
19 Leonore Davidoff and Catherine Hall, *Family Fortunes: Men and Women of the English Middle Class, 1780-1850* (Chicago: University of Chicago Press, 1987). On working-class "domestic" reform, see Frank Mort, *Dangerous Sexualities: Medico-Moral Politics in England Since 1830* (London: Routledge, 1987), esp. Parts 1 and 2; Judith Walkowitz, *Prostitution and Victorian Society: Women, Class, and the State* (Cambridge: Cambridge University Press, 1980); Mariana Valverde, *The Age of Light, Soap and Water: Moral Reform in English Canada, 1885-1925* (Toronto: McClelland and Stewart, 1991); Christine Stansell, *City of Women: Sex and Class in New York, 1789-1860* (Chicago: University of Illinois Press, 1986).
20 Patrick Wolfe, *Settler Colonialism and the Transformation of Anthropology: The Politics and Poetics of an Ethnographic Event* (London: Cassell, 1999), Chapter 3.
21 Mrs. Frederick C. Stephenson, *Canadian Methodist Missions, 1824-1924,* vol. 1 (Toronto: The Missionary Society for the Methodist Church, 1925), 167. Thanks to Jean Barman for this citation.
22 "Life and Missionary Activities of Rev. Charles Montgomery Tate, 1852-1933," p. 28, transcript, Add Mss 303, BCA.
23 "Diary of Mrs. C.M. Tate, Victoria, 1897-98, 1906, 1908-11," p. 2, transcript, Add Mss E/C/T181A, BCA. Also see Harkin, *The Heiltsuks.*

24 Alfred J. Hall to Church Missionary Society, 6 March 1878, CMS, mflm Aw I R4796:32, UBCL. On women and residential schools in this period, see Rosemary R. Gagan, *A Sensitive Independence: Canadian Methodist Women Missionaries in Canada and the Orient, 1881-1925* (Montreal and Kingston: McGill-Queen's University Press, 1992); Jean Barman, "Separate and Unequal: Indian and White Girls at All Hallows School, 1884-1920," in *Children, Teachers and Schools in the History of British Columbia*, ed. J. Barman, N. Sutherland, and J.D. Wilson, 110-31 (Calgary: Detselig, 1995); Jo-Anne Fiske, "Pocahantas's Granddaughters: Spiritual Transition and Tradition of Carrier Women of British Columbia," *Ethnohistory* 43, 4 (Fall 1996): 663-81.

25 Modest Demers, *Letter from Mgr. Demers: Mission on Vancouver Island, Founded in 1846* (n.p.: 1866?), 8.

26 Canada, "Report of the Department of Indian Affairs for the Year Ended 31st December, 1881," *Sessional Papers 1881*, No. 6 (Ottawa: MacLean, Roger and Co., 1882), 141.

27 See John Gillis, *For Better, For Worse: British Marriages 1600 to the Present* (New York: Oxford University Press, 1985), 192-206.

28 See Barbara Taylor, *Eve and the New Jerusalem: Socialism and Feminism in the Nineteenth Century* (London: Virago, 1983), Chapter 6.

29 William Beynon, "The Tsimshians of Metlakatla, Alaska," *American Anthropologist* 43 (1941): 83-88. Also see H.G. Barnett, "Applied Anthropology in 1860," *Human Organization* 1 (June 1942): 19-32, at 26.

30 See, for instance, work on South Asia like Mrinalini Sinha's "The Lineage of the 'Indian' Modern: Rhetoric, Agency, and the Sarda Act in Late Colonial India," in *Gender, Sexuality and Colonial Modernity* (see note 4), 207-21; and Dipesh Chakrabarty's "The Difference-Deferral of a Colonial Modernity: Public Debates on Domesticity in British Bengal," reprinted in *Tensions of Empire* (see note 3), 373-405, and his *Provincializing Europe: Postcolonial Thought and Historical Difference* (Princeton, NJ: Princeton University Press, 2000).

31 Thomas Crosby, *Among the An-ko-me-nums of the Pacific Coast* (Toronto: William Briggs, 1907), 65-66. There is an extensive literature on the late-nineteenth-century and early-twentieth-century efforts to ban potlatches, but it makes little mention of the relationship between marriages and potlatches. See, most recently, Douglas Cole and Ira Chaikin, *An Iron Hand upon the People: The Law against the Potlatch on the Northwest Coast* (Vancouver: Douglas and McIntyre, 1990); Christopher Bracken, *The Potlatch Papers: A Colonial Case History* (Chicago: University of Chicago Press, 1997).

32 W. Duncan, "First Report, Fort Simpson," February 1858, CMS, mflm AW 1 R4796:31, UBCL.

33 See David D. Smits, "The 'Squaw Drudge': A Prime Index of Savagism," *Ethnohistory* 29, 4 (1982): 281-306; Ranya Green, "The Pocahontas Perplex: The Image of Indian Women in American Culture," in *Unequal Sisters: A Multicultural Reader in U.S. Women's History*, ed. Ellen Carol DuBois and Vicki L. Ruiz, 15-21 (New York: Routledge, 1990); Carroll Smith-Rosenberg, "Captured Subjects/Savage Others: Violently Engendering the New American," *Gender and History* 5, 2 (Summer 1993): 177-95.

34 D.L.S., *Fifty Years in Western Canada; Being the Abridged Memoirs of Rev. A.G. Morice, O.M.I* (Toronto: Ryerson Press, 1930), 57.

35 Gayatri Chakravorty Spivak, "Can the Subaltern Speak?" reprinted in *Colonial Discourse and Post-Colonial Theory*, ed. Patrick Williams and Laura Chrisman (New York: Columbia University Press, 1994), 66-111.

36 John Sheepshanks, "A Lecture on the Origin, Habits, Modes of Thought, Past and Present, and Future of the 'Red Indians of the West,'" in *Sixth Annual Report of the Columbia Mission for the Year 1864*, 39-50 (London: Rivingtons, 1865), 49. On this, see Adele Perry, *On the Edge of Empire: Gender, Race, and the Making of British Columbia, 1849-1871* (Toronto: University of Toronto Press, 2001), Chapters 2 and 5.

37 See Annette Hamilton, "Bond-Slaves of Satan: Aboriginal Women and the Missionary Dilemma," in *Family and Gender in the Pacific: Domestic Contradictions and the Colonial Impact*, ed. Margaret Jolly and Martha Mcintyre, 236-58 (Cambridge: Cambridge University Press, 1989).

38 Patricia Grimshaw, *Paths of Duty: American Missionary Wives in Nineteenth-Century Hawaii* (Honolulu: University of Hawaii Press, 1988), 63.

39 Crosby, *Among the An-ko-me-nums*, 62-63.

40 George Hills, "Hills Journal, 1866" (transcript), p. 64, Anglican Church of Canada, Archives of the Diocese of New Westminster/Ecclesiastical Province of British Columbia (ADNW/EPBC), Vancouver School of Theology, UBC.
41 J.J. Halcombe, *The Emigrant and the Heathen, or, Sketches of Missionary Life* (London: Society for Promoting Christian Knowledge, [1870?]), 238.
42 On this, see Adele Perry, "The Autocracy of Love and the Legitimacy of Empire: Intimacy, Power and Scandal in Nineteenth-Century Metlakahtlah," *Gender and History* 16, 2 (August 2004): 261-88.
43 Myra Rutherdale, "'I Wish the Men Were Half as Good': Gender Constructions in the Canadian North-Western Mission Field, 1860-1940," in *Telling Tales: Essays in Western Women's History*, ed. Catherine Cavanaugh and Randi R. Warne, 32-59 (Vancouver: UBC Press, 2000).
44 Linda Gordon, *The Great Arizona Orphan Abduction* (Cambridge, MA: Harvard University Press, 1999).
45 Diane Langmore, "The Object Lesson of a Civilised, Christian Home," in *Family and Gender in the Pacific* (see note 37), 84-94.
46 R.C. Lundin Brown, *Klatsassan, and Other Reminiscences of Missionary Life in British Columbia* (London: Society for Promoting Christian Knowledge, 1873), 151-52. This story is repeated from R.C. Lundin Brown, *British Columbia: The Indians and Settlers at Lillooet; Appeal for Missionaries* (London: R. Clay, Sons, and Taylor, 1870), 9-11. Translation mine.
47 *Eighth Annual Report of the Columbia Mission for the Year 1866* (London: Rivingtons, 1867), 27, 11-12.
48 Robert Tomlinson to unknown, 5 June 1872, CMS, mflm Aw I R4796:32, UBCL.
49 Thomas Crosby, *Up and Down the North Pacific Coast by Canoe and Mission Ship* (Toronto: Missionary Society of the Methodist Church, 1914), 73.
50 *Twentieth Annual Report of the Missions of the Church of England in British Columbia for the Year 1878* (London: Rivingtons, 1879), 40. Also see John Booth Good, "The Utmost Bounds of the West: Pioneer Jottings Forty Years Missionary Reminiscences of the Out West Pacific Coast A.D. 1861 – A.D. 1900" [transcript from original held at BCA] pages added, p. 83, PSA 52, file 9, ADNW/EPBC.
51 See Vincent J. McNally, *The Lord's Distant Vineyard: A History of the Oblates and the Catholic Community in British Columbia* (Edmonton: University of Alberta Press, 2000), 131-32.
52 Metlakatla, 1863-1924, Marriage and Baptism Records, Diocese of Caledonia, Parish Records, roll 6, mflm 77-4:22, ADNW/EPBC.
53 William Duncan, "Journal," 6 June 1865, mflm AW 1 R2547:12, UBCL.
54 Edmund Hope Verney to Harry Verney, 29 October 1863, in Allan Pritchard, ed., *Vancouver Island Letters of Edmund Hope Verney, 1862-1865* (Vancouver: UBC Press, 1996), 173.
55 Joseph Brabant, *Mission to Nootka, 1874-1900: Reminiscences of the West Coast of Vancouver Island*, ed. Charles Lillard (1900; Sidney, BC: Gray's Publishing, 1977), 92-93, 100.
56 See, for instance, Karen Anderson, *Chain Her by One Foot: The Subjugation of Native Women in Seventeenth-Century New France* (New York and London: Routledge, 1991); Carol Devens, "Separate Confrontations: Gender As a Factor in Indian Adaptation to European Colonization in New France," *American Quarterly* 38, 3 (1986): 460-80.
57 Margaret Whitehead, "Introduction," in *They Call Me Father* (see note 16), 1-86, at 16. Also see Duncan Duane Thomson, "A History of the Okanagan: Indians and Whites in the Settlement Era, 1860" (PhD dissertation, University of British Columbia, 1985), esp. 52-61.
58 "The Charter for the Establishment of the First Mission at Hesquiat, 1875, Given to the Rev. A.J. Brabant by the Rt. Rev. Chas. J. Seghers, Bishop of Victoria," in Rev. Chas. Moser, *Reminiscences of the West Coast of Vancouver Island* (Victoria: Acme Press, 1926), 6.
59 Duncan, "Journal," 9 December 1866, mflm AW 1 R2547:12, UBCL.
60 Good, "The Utmost Bounds of the West," 101-2. For Hills' version of this issue, see *Fourteenth Annual Report of the Missions of the Church of England in British Columbia for the Year 1872* (London: Rivingtons, 1873), 23.
61 Hills, "Hills Journal, 1866," 64-65, ADNW/EPBC. Missionaries in Hawaii faced similar issues. See Grimshaw, *Paths of Duty*.
62 Canada, "Annual Report of the Department of Indian Affairs for the Year Ended 31st December 1884," *Sessional Papers 1884*, No. 3 (Ottawa: MacLean, Roger and Co., 1885), lxi.

63 Bishop Hills to Rev. C. Knipe, 3 June 1861, "Bishop George Hills Correspondence In and Out," Text 57, 43-45, Anglican Church of Canada, Anglican Diocese of British Columbia Archives, Victoria BC.

64 Brown, *Klatsassan*, 152-53.

65 J. Reynard in *Ninth Annual Report of the Columbia Mission, for the Year 1867* (London: Rivingtons, 1868), 25.

66 Dorothy Blakey Smith, ed., "Henry Guillod's Journal of a Trip to Cariboo, 1862," in *British Columbia Historical Quarterly* 19 (July-October 1955): 187-232, at 231.

67 Burton, "Introduction," 2-3.

68 Angela V. John, *By the Sweat of Their Brow: Women Workers at Victorian Coal Mines* (London: Croom Helm, 1980); Constance Backhouse, *Petticoats and Prejudice: Women and Law in Nineteenth-Century Canada* (Toronto: Women's Press, for the Osgoode Society, 1991), Chapter 9.

69 Duncan, *Journal*, 13 January 1857, mflm AW 1 R2547:12, UBCL.

70 Whitehead, *They Call Me Father*, 118.

71 James Douglas to Sir Edward Bulwer Lytton, 25 May 1859, CO 305/10, mflm B-238, LAC.

72 Rolf Knight, *Indians at Work: An Informal History of Native Indian Labour in British Columbia, 1858-1930* (Vancouver: New Star, 1978); John Lutz, "After the Fur Trade: Aboriginal Wage Labour in Nineteenth-Century British Columbia," *Journal of the Canadian Historical Association* (1992): 69-94; Alicja Muszynski, *Cheap Wage Labour: Race and Gender in the Fisheries of British Columbia* (Montreal and Kingston: McGill-Queen's University Press, 1996).

73 *Tenth Annual Report of the Columbia Mission, for the Year 1868* (London: Rivingtons, 1869), 35.

74 W.H Collinson to William Duncan, 5 April 1881, "Correspondence Received, 1881," William Duncan Papers, reel AW 1 R2547:4, UBCL.

75 "Our Social Evil," *British Colonist*, 22 October 1867.

76 G. Columbia, "Enclosure," 27 May 1871, in Joseph Howe, "The Secretary of State for the Provinces to the Lieutenant-Governor," British Columbia, *Papers Connected With the Indian Land Question, 1850-1875* (Victoria: Richard Wolfenden, 1875), 97.

77 [William Duncan?], untitled notebook, William Duncan Papers, AW 1 R2547:16, UBCL. On economy at Metlakatlah, see Brian C. Hosmer, *American Indians in the Marketplace: Persistence and Innovation among the Menominees and Metlakatlans, 1870-1920* (Kansas: University of Kansas Press, 1999).

78 *Report of the Columbia Mission, with List of Contributions, 1860* (London: Rivingtons, [186?1]), 94-95.

79 Henry Schutt to the CMS, 5 November 1877, CMS, reel Aw I R4796:32, UBCL.

80 Sister Mary Providence to Governor, 26 May 1871, and P. Hankin to Sister Mary Providence, 29 May 1871, both in "Colonial Correspondence," GR 1372, reel B-1360, file 1545, BCA.

81 "Cowitchen. European and Indian Mission," in *Ninth Annual Report of the Columbia Mission*, 36.

82 Crosby, *Among the An-ko-me-nums*, 45.

83 Mrs. Robert Tomlinson, Jr., in Margaret Whitehead, ed., *Now You Are My Brother*, Sound Heritage Series 34 (Victoria: Provincial Archives of British Columbia, 1981), 11.

84 Madeleine McIvor, "Science and Technology Education in a Civilizing Mission" (MA thesis, University of British Columbia, 1993), 57. See also Malathi de Alwis, "'Respectability,' 'Modernity' and the Policing of 'Culture' in Colonial Ceylon," in *Gender, Sexuality and Colonial Modernities* (see note 4), 177-92.

85 *Ninth Annual Report of the Columbia Mission*, 23-24.

86 See Nicholas Thomas, *Colonialism's Culture: Anthropology, Travel, and Government* (Princeton, NJ: Princeton University Press, 1994), 133.

87 *Thirteenth Annual Report of the Missions of the Church of England*, 20.

88 *Report of the Superintendent of Indian Affairs*, 3, 4.

89 Margaret Jolly, "'To Save the Girls for Brighter and Better Lives': Presbyterian Missions and Women in the South of Vanuatu, 1848-1870," *The Journal of Pacific History* 26, 1 (1991): 27-48, at 31.

6
Creating "Semi-Widows" and "Supernumerary Wives": Prohibiting Polygamy in Prairie Canada's Aboriginal Communities to 1900
Sarah A. Carter

Historically and culturally specific meanings of masculinity and femininity, and grave concern about alternate meanings of these, profoundly shaped the policies that Canada's Department of Indian Affairs (DIA) devised to "civilize" Aboriginal people living on reserves in Western Canada in the post-1870 era. Legal, political, and missionary authorities shared the view that a particular marriage model – of lifelong monogamy in the tradition of the Christian religion and English common law – symbolized the proper differences between the sexes and set the foundation for the way both sexes were to behave. Sustained efforts were made to introduce and perpetuate this marriage model, and this endeavour is clearly illustrated in the 1890s resolve of the DIA to abolish polygamy.[1] Yet there were limitations and challenges to the authorities' ability to impose and enforce one marriage model. Aboriginal marriage law proved tenacious, because of the determination of Aboriginal people, but also because of the limited capacity of the state to control the domestic domain. While constrained and never fully accomplished, however, these interventions caused considerable turmoil and rupture in Aboriginal communities.

Prohibiting polygamy among the Aboriginal people of Western Canada was not an isolated, or unique development, and this study points to the concerns Canadian colonizers shared with the broader colonizing world about the "intimacies of empire."[2] In other colonial settings, polygamy was similarly condemned, but the nature, timing, purpose, and outcomes of programs of intervention varied widely. In Western Canada, as in other colonial contexts, ideologies of gender and sexuality were a foundation of the colonial regime, but this was an unstable foundation. As Antoinette Burton wrote in the introduction to *Gender, Sexuality and Colonial Modernities*, modern colonial regimes are "always in process, subject to disruption and contest, and [are] therefore never fully or finally accomplished, to such an extent that they must be conceived of as 'unfinished business.'"[3]

Plains Aboriginal marriages were varied and complex, and they were not well understood by newcomers to Western Canada.[4] The ceremonies and protocol involved differed from the Christian and English common-law model. In Plains societies, marriage was more of a process than a particular defining moment. Among the Blackfoot, marriages were family affairs – both sets of relatives had to give their consent. The relationship involved reciprocal obligations among the sets of relatives. The marriage was validated, and the reciprocal obligations of both parties established, through an exchange of gifts that could be initiated by either set of relatives. It became a matter of pride for the family receiving the first gifts to return gifts of greater value. Obligations were ongoing; they did not end with a defining wedding moment.

There were a variety of ideal types of conjugal union, not just one as in Euro-Canadian society. Lifelong, monogamous unions were common, but there were other kinds of marriages, seen not as a departure from a norm, but as a desirable family unit. Many of the leading men in Plains societies had more than one spouse. The term "polygamy" does not have a parallel in the Cree or Blackfoot languages, suggesting that it was not seen as a separate, distinct departure from a norm but as one of several possible forms of marriage. Often sisters were married to the same man. A man might also marry his deceased brother's widow, adopting the children and preserving the relationship with the grandparents and extended family. Only hard-working men of wealth could maintain these large households, so parents sought these marriages for their daughters.

Cree and Blackfoot sources indicate that subsequent wives were brought into a family generally after consultation with, and with the approval of, the first wife. These domestic arrangements provided economic assistance, companionship, and enhanced status for the senior wife. In 1891 Chief Red Crow of the Kainai (Blood) of southern Alberta described marriage practices to Indian agent R.N. Wilson, saying that the first wives seldom objected to the presence of other wives and that it was very often they who proposed that sisters or other relatives become second or third wives.[5]

Cree Chief Fine Day provided a detailed description of marriage practices in his 1934 sessions with anthropologist David Mandelbaum.[6] Fine Day's father had two wives, his mother being the second wife, and he said that the two got along well. Fine Day stressed that permission was required from the first wife, and that the acquisition of a second wife was a joint decision in recognition of the needs of the first wife. According to Fine Day, if a wife required assistance running her household, the husband would say, "How would you like to have a helper?" If she said yes, they then both would pick out some likely girl. He would ask her again, 'Would you be kind to her?' She would say, 'Yes, that's why I want her.' Then he would go and get the other woman. But the first wife was always the boss."[7] Fine Day stressed

Blackfoot women and their husband, late 1870s
Glenbow Archives, NA-1376-6

the authority of the wives to determine the size and nature of the family unit:

> It was not a man's abilities as a hunter that determined the number of wives he had, but upon the arrangements he made with his wife. Both a man and his wife paid for the second wife. Young girls would not want to be married to a man that was of no account. They wanted to marry a Worthy Man because they know that there would be no quarrelling – he would stop it.
>
> If a man wanted to take a third wife, his first would usually agree but his second would often say no. That usually would settle it.[8]

If the permission of the wives had not been obtained there were consequences. Fine Day noted that if a man married a third wife without the
permission of his first two, they would never be friendly toward her. According to Red Crow, if a husband brought home a second wife to the disgust of the first, she would "keep up a continual row until the newcomer
was sent away."[9]

Kainai historian Beverly Hungry Wolf wrote that women did a tremendous amount of work, and it was thought to be desirable for a young woman
to marry a prominent man with several wives as this eased the burden of
work.[10] Work was divided. A seventy-three-year-old Blackfoot woman, Middle
Woman No Coat, who was interviewed in 1939, recalled the division of
labour in her father's household with five wives. The first two wives "are
older and do all the tanning. Younger wives do the cooking. In winter, all
take turns getting wood; someone always present to take care of the fire."[11]
Other advantages for the co-wives were that women in polygamous marriages tended to have fewer children, and the mothers of the sister co-wives
were often part of the household.[12]

Maxidiwiac (born circa 1839), also known as Buffalo Bird Woman, of the
agricultural Hidatsa nation of present-day North Dakota, explained that
the sisters married to the same husband might not be sisters in the way
Europeans used this term, but relatives, sometimes adopted, who regarded
each other as sisters.[13] Maxidiwiac grew up in a household where her mother,
her mother's sisters, and a cousin regarded as a sister were all married to her
father. When she was six, her own mother and one of the other wives died
of smallpox. She called the two surviving wives her mothers. The mothers
of the surviving wives, who had been raised together although not related
by blood, also lived in the household, and she addressed both these women
as grandmother.

Among the Blackfoot the first and generally the oldest wife was known as
the "sits-beside-him" wife, and this was a position of honour. She was the
female head of the household and she had an important role in ceremonies
such as those involving sacred bundles. She accompanied her husband to
feasts and ceremonies, and she directed the other wives in their work. The
other wives did not have as high a standing in the community as the "sits-
beside-him" wife. These marriages were not always successful, but such incidents seem to have been the exception in an environment in which
cooperation and sharing was vital, and in a society where women did almost all of their work communally. Anthropologist Esther Goldfrank, who
did fieldwork among the Kainai in the 1930s, was told about a family in
which the three wives were always quarrelling.[14] The family was once out
on the prairie and found itself short of water. One wife had water but refused to share with the others, and they stopped speaking to each other at
all. One of the wives died, presumably as a result of the unwillingness to

share water. This story was related almost as a cautionary tale, and in such a way as to suggest that it represented a departure from the behaviour that normally had to prevail in a family of several wives. According to Beverly Hungry Wolf, there were occasions when a younger wife in a large household and with a much older husband suffered from loneliness and a desire to be loved. She noted that some older husbands sanctioned outside relationships as long as they were discreet and brought no public disgrace.[15]

In his study of the Cheyenne, anthropologist John H. Moore concluded that "from an American Indian standpoint, the institution of polygyny was seen to benefit both husbands and wives. For men, a larger household meant that they would have more children and more relatives, with a concomitant increase in wealth and status in the community. For women, polygyny usually meant that they could maintain co-residence with their sisters as co-wives, could get daily help with child care and other household chores, and have an increased probability of keeping their mother in the household."[16]

Church, government, political, and legal authorities severely censured what they understood as polygamy in Aboriginal societies. It was seen as deviant and morally depraved. Polygamy became a towering example of the shortcomings of Aboriginal societies, which were understood to subordinate women, in contrast to the ideal of monogamous marriage, cherished by Europeans as an institution that elevated women. Polygamy was viewed as a system that exploited and degraded women, depriving them of respect and influence. It was thought that jealousy and friction among the wives was inevitable. The husbands were seen as idle, debauched, and tyrannical. The sexual desires of the husband were seen as a main motivation for polygamy. (As John Moore has noted, this notion probably tells us more about the sexual fantasies of European male observers than about the culture and values of Aboriginal people.)[17] Missionaries were among the most outspoken critics. They were deeply concerned about the propriety of a host of customs involving sexuality, marriage, and divorce. Aboriginal marriage, even when monogamous, was misunderstood and condemned as a heartless business transaction without love, courtship, or ceremony – a commodity simply changed hands.[18] But polygamy topped the list of forces that allegedly degraded women. As Methodist missionary John Semmens wrote in his 1884 memoirs, multiple wives were "general slaves, subject to the behests of the most thoughtless and relentless of taskmasters."[19]

These views were common throughout the imperial world in the late nineteenth century. In a book entitled *Women of the Orient*, Rev. R.C. Houghton described his thoughts on polygamy: "Deceit, bickerings, strife, jealousies, intrigues, murder and licentiousness have followed in its train; true love has, in its presence, given place to sensual passion, and woman has become the slave, rather than the companion of man. The word home, as symbolical of confidence, sympathy, rest, happiness and true affection, is not found in the vocabulary of polygamous lands. Polygamy is subversive of God's order; and, beginning by poisoning the very sources of domestic and social prosperity, its blighting influences are felt and seen in every department of national life."[20]

In favourable contrast to the supposed domestic despotism under polygamy, the monogamous, lifelong model of marriage was held up as an institution that elevated rather than enslaved women, placing them on a pedestal while allowing them a high degree of liberty. As Inderpal Grewal has written about India, the discourse of the "caged" woman became the "necessary 'Other' for the construction of the English woman presumably free and happy in the home."[21] All of this served as a significant indication that the colonizers were introducing a superior civilization, at the core of which were the "proper" gender identities embedded in the cherished marriage model.

While missionaries and other reformers were ostensibly concerned with what they depicted as the despotism and degradation that Aboriginal women had to contend with from the men who were their "ruthless taskmasters," there was at the same time a contradictory and muted recognition that these women had some freedoms and privileges not enjoyed by non-Aboriginal women. Sexual freedom before marriage was tolerated. Divorce was relatively easy. People separated and divorced for reasons of incompatibility, physical abuse, laziness, or lack of support. Among the Blackfoot a marriage was dissolved when a wife left, returning to her parents or an older brother, taking her property, which included the tipi, with her. Children normally stayed with the mother following a divorce.[22]

In Plains societies it was also permissible to permanently or temporarily adopt role components of the opposite sex. Among the Blackfoot there were women who led and participated in war parties, earning respect and admiration. Trim Woman of the Kainai, for example, went on horse raids and once was the leader of a war party against the Crows. According to Blood informants who spoke to anthropologist Esther Goldfrank: "That kind of woman is always respected and everyone depends on them. They are admired for their bravery. They are 'lucky' on raids so the men respect them."[23] The "manly-hearted women" of the Blackfoot excelled at feminine occupations and were always married, but they also displayed characteristics classified as "masculine"; they were aggressive, independent, bold, and sexually active.[24] Often these women had been designated as the parents' favourite child early in life. Esther Goldfrank concluded that Blackfoot women had considerable power and influence, emphasizing also their central role in sacred ceremonies. Women "enjoyed a comparatively strong position ... a woman could lead a war party; she could own property, receive and exercise medicine power, and give names. She was a necessary part of every ceremonial transfer; she was the custodian of the bundles that her husband bought.

The pubic initiation of the Horn Society still dramatized the man's dependence. It is the wife who receives the power from the seller. Her husband can only gain possession from her."[25]

In contrast to widely held assumptions about their servitude and misfortunes, Aboriginal wives enjoyed more options and autonomy than Canadian women of the nineteenth century married under English common law. Legal historian Constance Backhouse has described this form of marriage as "very rigid, overbearing [and] patriarchal."[26] Husbands were expected to wield all the power, and wives were denied independence or autonomy. Under the "doctrine of marital unity," the very existence of the wife was legally absorbed by her husband. Her property became his property. Divorce was almost unknown; marriages were regarded as virtually indissoluble. Divorce was also expensive, and it carried a social stigma, attached strongly to the divorced woman regardless of the cause of marital breakdown. If a divorce did occur, the woman risked the loss of custody of children.

It was the missionaries in Western Canada who made the first efforts to discourage polygamy. Their methods, however, and the enticements at their disposal (refusal to baptize, excommunication) were not particularly compelling. Missionaries were also uncertain about how best to proceed, and there was concern especially for the "discarded" wives and their children. These perplexing issues were discussed at the highest church levels. Anglican missionaries of the Church Missionary Society (CMS) were instructed not to baptize any man who had more than one wife, but the wives, perceived as victims, could be baptized. This policy, embodied in Henry Venn's Memorandum of 1856, stated "that while the wives of a polygamist, if believed to be true converts, might be received to baptism, since they were usually the involuntary victims of the custom, no man could be admitted who retained more than one wife."[27] Although the policy was confirmed at the Lambeth Conference of 1888, it was not without considerable discussion of perplexing conundrums that might arise. While the bishops at the conference unanimously agreed that any baptized Christian taking more than one wife would be excommunicated, there was debate about other issues, with some arguing for greater liberty and tolerance, while others were strongly opposed to any concessions. The bishop of Exeter put forth the following questions: "But suppose a Heathen chief converted who has three wives already, all lawful wives according to the custom of the country. And suppose the 'first in order of time is old and childless, the second the mother of all his children, the third the last married and best beloved.' If he is to put away two of the three before baptism, which is he to keep? And what is the condition of the two put away? Are they to be counted as married or single? Can they marry other men? And what of the children?"[28]

John William Colenso, Anglican bishop of Natal, South Africa, shocked his contemporaries in the 1850s by publicly questioning the wisdom of his church's policies on polygamy. According to biographer Jeff Guy, Colenso believed that polygamous marriages were "uncivilized," but he "could not accept that it was compatible with the Christian message to demand that a man put away his wives and children before joining the Christian Church."[29] Colenso felt that the price of conversion to Christianity could never be the dissolution of family and perhaps the destitution of wives and children. He argued that "those who broke up families in the name of Christian abhorrence of polygamy denied the true message of Christianity."[30] Colenso sanctioned the baptism of polygamists without requiring them to divorce their second or subsequent wives.

While Colenso was an exception to the majority of missionaries, he was not alone in his doubts about the wisdom of casting off wives and children. Stationed on the Blood Reserve in 1887, Anglican missionary Samuel Trivett confided his doubts about the strict policy in his correspondence to his superiors. While he had recently refused to baptize two men who had polygamous marriages, he wrote: "I must confess that I have often thought it would be wrong for these Indians to put away their wives. They are old and have no homes." Trivett noted that in former days this was the custom and "they didn't think it was wrong or give a thought to the matter." Trivett was concerned, however, that any leniency might encourage young men to feel that they should be permitted more than one wife.[31] His Methodist missionary colleague, also on the Blood Reserve, may have shared some of these doubts, as he wrote in one of his books that the practice of polygamy ensured that there were no "old maids" in the community.[32]

Missionaries in Western Canada were not in agreement about how to proceed when dissolving polygamous marriages. Which wife should be retained? How should the "semi-widows" or "abandoned" wives and children be provided for? Methodist missionary E.R. Young regretted the fate of the abandoned ones, but claimed in his memoirs that he felt obliged to enforce the rule that the first wife must take precedence over a later one, even if the first was childless and the later wife had a larger family.[33] John Semmens, however, felt that while the rule favoured the claim of the senior wife, there were "many instances ... in which the right is waived voluntarily in favor of the younger women."[34] He felt the husband should care for the younger children, permitting the abandoned wives to earn a living. The Hudson's Bay Company, he noted, felt charitable toward these "semi-widows," allowing them job opportunities where others were refused. The children of a first wife, Semmens wrote, would be grown up and able to support their mother. In his memoirs of missionary life, Anglican John Hines wrote that he "followed no definite rule in deciding which wife should be retained, but that those with the greatest number of small children had the strongest claim."[35] Hines found that it was generally the eldest wife who left the marriage, moving to the homes of grown-up daughters.

There were some critics of the missionaries' efforts to abolish polygamy, with concern expressed about the fate of "supernumerary" women. Edwin Thompson Denig, an American fur trader, wrote three major manuscripts on the people of the Upper Missouri. He had two wives, according to Rudolph Friedrich Kurz, employed at Fort Union: an older and a younger wife. Kurz wrote that "for the sake of his kind feeling toward her [his first wife] and of keeping her here as companion for his younger wife ... he will not cast her off. Further more, he has a son and a daughter by her."[36] In his manuscript on the Assiniboine, Denig was sharply critical: "The first thing a missionary does is to abuse the Indian for having a plurality of wives. Would the good missionary be so charitable as to clothe, feed, and shelter the supernumerary woman; should all the Indians follow his advice and have but one wife? Will the Indian consent to separate his children from their mothers, or to turn both adrift to please the whim of any man? The advice is uncharitable, unjust, and can only be excused on the plea of ignorance of their customs and feeling."[37]

While missionaries sought to eradicate polygamy from the beginning of their work on Western Canadian Indian reserves after the 1870s era of treaties, federal government administrators were, until the 1890s, hesitant, even reluctant, to pursue any concerted efforts. The Indian agents, farm instructors, inspectors, school officials, teachers, and bureaucrats in Regina and Ottawa worked within the legal framework of the Indian Act and pursued a cluster of policies that together were to have the effect of imposing gender roles and identities drawn from the experiences of the colonizers. Men were to be yeoman farmers, and for a time the residential and industrial school system trained them for other trades such as shoemaking or blacksmithing. Women were to be farm homemakers, undertaking their tasks of butter-making, sewing, cleaning, and cooking individually in permanent (not mobile) homes. (Women were also to be mothers, but their capacity in this regard was viewed by authorities as suspect, necessitating the residential school system.) These homes were to house nuclear families, and there would be decent partitions allowing privacy.

As part of this program, administrators wanted to impose what they regarded as legal, permanent, and monogamous marriages. The Indian Act was of some assistance in imposing this model of marriage. Under this legislation a widow could inherit her husband's property only if she could prove she was of good moral character and had lived with her husband until he was deceased.[38] A DIA official, most likely the Indian agent, would decide whether the widow was "moral" and so qualified. Also helping to impose the patriarchal and monogamous model of marriage was a clause of the act which stipulated that annuities (annual payments promised under treaties) and any interest money (which might arise from the sale of reserve land) could be refused any Indian "who may be proved, to the satisfaction of the Superintendent-General, to have been guilty of deserting his or her family and the said Superintendent-General may apply the same towards the support of any family, woman or child so deserted." The superintendent-general could also "stop the payment of the annuity and interest money of any woman having no children, who deserts her husband and lives immorally with another man."[39] These laws, which reflected a range of stereotypes about Aboriginal women, particularly their potential for "immorality," were aimed at keeping women within monogamous, lifelong marriages.

Based on legal advice from the Department of Justice, however, DIA authorities found that it was not possible to simply impose their marriage model. Indian agents expressed grave concern about what they perceived as a tenuous, invalid, impermanent form of marriage, as divorce was permitted. Yet they could not abolish or prohibit Aboriginal marriage. Not to recognize these as marriages, to proclaim them all invalid, would mean that married persons would feel free to consider their relationships null and void. The children would be illegitimate. There was also no one to perform civil or Christian marriages in many regions of the West. The superintendent inspector for Manitoba, Ebenezer McColl, complained in 1893 that couples were "living illegally together, according to the unorthodox custom of their pagan ancestors," but he was forced to admit that people did not have the money to obtain licences, and that the visiting missionary seldom remained long enough to enable the banns to be published the requisite number of times to legalize a marriage. "Hence," wrote McColl, "they have either to postpone indefinitely the regular consummation of their nuptials or live unlawfully together without having any authorized wedding ceremony performed."[40]

The resistance of Aboriginal people, who showed a preference for their own marriage laws, also hampered any program of intervention. According to the Fort Macleod *Gazette,* the first marriage of an Aboriginal couple in southern Alberta to be solemnized through obtaining a marriage certificate took place in 1895.[41] Two years later on the Blackfoot reserve, the first marriage of a Siksika couple at that mission was performed according to the rites of the Catholic Church, over fifty years after the first Catholic missionaries arrived on the prairies, and after twenty years of reserve life.[42] The DIA could do little to impose a new regime, although officials were instructed to work to end "tribal customs and pagan views," and to facilitate an understanding of the "true nature and obligations of the marriage tie."[43]

An 1888 Department of Justice opinion on Indian marriage and divorce established the policy that the DIA would pursue well into the twentieth century. "[Marriages of] Pagan Indians which have been contracted in accordance with tribal customs should be treated by your Department as *prima facie* valid and the issue of such marriage as legitimate," wrote a law clerk in 1888. "If, however, an Indian so married deserts the woman who is recog-

Wedding group at the Anglican mission on the Siksika Reserve, ca. 1900,
Jim Abikoki and family
Glenbow Archives, NC-5-8

nized or is entitled to recognition as his wife, and during her life time lives
with and has children by another woman, the Minister does not think that
such cohabitation should in any case be recognized as marriage, unless there
has been an actual divorce from the first wife. The resulting issue should
therefore be treated as illegitimate and as having no right to share in the
annuities of the band."[44]

By about 1900 a complicated situation had emerged in which Aboriginal
marriage law was recognized as valid if both parties were of that ancestry,
and if the marriage conformed to the ideal of a monogamous, lifelong bond.
Aboriginal divorce law was not regarded as valid. This policy, and the way
in which it was interpreted by many reserve administrators, caused upheaval
and instability in a society that had easily permitted remarriage in the event
of marriage breakdown. Those who were divorced or deserted by their
spouses were without their former option of forming a new family. "Legal" divorce was a virtual impossibility for reserve residents, and it was
rare at this time for all Canadians.[45] Indian agents had tremendous power
to decide which couples were legally married, which were living together
"immorally," in their view, and which children were legitimate. For the
purposes of annuity payments, the agents decided what constituted a valid
family unit. Agents gave and denied permission for couples to marry, and
they also refused permission for people to remarry in the event of divorce
according to Aboriginal law. At times agents, the North-West Mounted

Police, and school principals took concerted action to break up what they saw as illegal marriages.[46]

DIA officials took few steps to abolish polygamous marriages until the early 1890s, and even then no action was taken against those who had entered into treaty in these circumstances. Annuity paylists indicate that leading men had two, three, or four adult women in the household. It was hoped that the practice would die naturally under the influence of missionaries and under the new conditions of reserve life. Officials did take steps to discourage any new polygamous marriages. An 1882 departmental circular established a policy that was intended to achieve this goal. Indian superintendent J.F. Graham wrote: "There is no valid reason for perpetuating polygamy by encouraging its continuance in admitting any further accessions to the number already existing, and I [illegible] to instruct you not to recognize any additional transgressions by allowing more husbands to draw annuities for more than their legal wives."[47] There is no indication that Indian Affairs officials were aware that until 1890 no statute existed that explicitly asserted that polygamy was illegal in Canada; a comprehensive antipolygamy bill was only introduced in 1890 in response to the arrival of Mormons in Alberta.

Why did the DIA decide that more active intervention was necessary by the early 1890s? In other colonial settings, programs of intervention were motivated by economic factors and the desire for indigenous labour. In Natal and southern Rhodesia, for example, colonial authorities argued that married men would not be compelled to work while they were permitted to live "idly" at home with their wives doing all the work for them. Thus polygamy was understood to deprive the settler colony of African male labour, undermining the economic progress of the region. Men would have to seek wage labour if they could no longer accumulate many wives.[48] In the US West, punishing polygamists was a means of undermining the authority of many of the leading Native American men. The Court of Indian Offenses, established in 1883, took aim at polygamy. Judges were to be selected from among the leading men of the reservations, but a polygamist could not serve as a judge. Polygamists were to be fined or to serve time with hard labour. As historian John D. Pulsipher has written, the Court of Indian Offenses was designed to strike at the heart of the power of Native American male leaders: "As with Mormons, polygamists in Native groups were usually the leading men of their tribes. By barring polygamists from judicial service – monogamy being the only qualification for serving on the bench – and actively prosecuting anyone who tried to take multiple wives, the Bureau could hope to subvert the existing tribal power structures and replace them with structures which were properly subsumed under federal authority."[49]

In Western Canada there was little demand for the labour of Aboriginal males, so this factor can be ruled out. By the late nineteenth century in

Canada, however, there was a widespread fear that the nuclear family and the home, the central institutions of the social order, were disintegrating in the wake of industrialization, rural depopulation, and urbanization. Reformers and leaders in Canada took steps to reinforce the institution of marriage. As historian James G. Snell has written, "in particular, Canadian leaders pressed for a stronger role by the state in defending marriage and in punishing any deviations from the moral code and social order associated with marriage."[50] The forces of industrialization, rural depopulation, and urbanization were somewhat remote from Western Canada in the 1890s, when policymakers remained desperate to attract agriculturalists. But in this new region of the Dominion, the imperative to reinforce the institution of lifelong monogamous marriage took on added dimensions and urgency. The nuclear family, centring on a husband and wife, was to be the basic building block of the West. This goal was embedded in the Dominion Lands Act and the homestead system that established the economic and social foundation of the prairie West. Yet there were challenges to this marriage and family model, not only from Aboriginal residents, but also from recent immigrants. In the late 1880s, missionaries had publicly voiced concern about the morality of some of the white men of the West who had a sequence of Aboriginal wives and were not supporting their children.[51] Some prominent men had cast aside women married according to Aboriginal law and had remarried newly arrived white women. Immigrants had marriage customs and domestic units that departed from the cherished single model. These multiple definitions posed a threat, endangering convictions about the naturalness or common sense of the European family formation. The arrival of the Mormons in southern Alberta in the late 1880s, however, combined with the Blackfoot's open resistance to and defiance of interference in their domestic arrangements, altered the situation. Charges of polygamy also in some cases permitted DIA authorities to depose, or threaten to depose, chiefs who challenged government authority.

Beginning in 1887, Mormons from Utah, fleeing antipolygamy laws in the United States, settled next door to the Blood Reserve, where polygamy was common. They established prosperous farms around present-day Cardston (known to the Blackfoot as "Many Wives"). The Mormons believed that they had a "mandate to engage in polygamy, a revelation given by God commanding faithful Mormon men to marry more than one wife."[52] They believed that they were following the practice of the Old Testament prophets and that this was part of God's law. In the 1880s there was a wave of antipolygamy sentiment in the United States directed at the Mormons. As historian Sarah Barringer Gordon has written, "antipolygamy sentiments were common coin among politicians, clergymen, newspaper editors, novelists and temperance activists."[53] Antipolygamists claimed that polygamy meant unmitigated lives of slavery, bondage, and horror for the wives.[54]

They were often critics of divorce as well; polygamy and divorce were seen as a coherent whole, as "two sides of the same corrupt coin."[55] Utah had the most permissive of all divorce statutes.

The Supreme Court of the United States ruled against polygamy in an 1879 court case, and Congress then moved to abolish the practice, passing the Edmunds Act in 1882. This act disenfranchised all those who either practised or believed in polygamy. An 1887 act repealed suffrage for Mormon women in Utah, who had been granted the vote in that territory in 1870. There were heavy fines and prison sentences for those convicted of polygamy. The children of these marriages were declared illegitimate, 1,300 Mormons were sent to jail, and the church was dissolved as a corporate entity. As a result of these measures, and also, according to historian Richard White, because of the damage to the free market in Utah, the president of the Mormon church announced in 1887 that the practice of polygamy would end.[56]

Charles Ora Card, the founder of Cardston, was one of the Mormons arrested in the United States, but he escaped custody and headed north to

Cardston, Alberta women, ca. 1900. *Back row, left to right:* Elizabeth Hammer, Zina Y. Card, Lydia J. Brown. *Middle row, left to right:* Catherine Rilling, Rhoda C. Hinman, Mary L. Woolf, Jane Hinman, Sara Daines. *Front row, left to right:* Mary L. Ibey, Jane Elizabeth Bates.
Glenbow Archives, NA-147-4

Canada with a small party of colonizers.[57] Card was a community and church leader who had three wives and was divorced from his first wife. In 1888 three Mormon leaders, including Card, travelled to Ottawa and met with officials including the prime minister. They asked permission to bring their wives and families to Canada and promised that no new polygamous marriages would be contracted. Sir John A. Macdonald informed them that "two wives of one man could not live in Canada."[58] At this time, however, as mentioned earlier, there was no statute making polygamy illegal. Bigamy was illegal, but plural marriages among Mormons, solemnized in private ceremonies, were technically outside the reach of Canadian law.[59] An antipolygamy bill was introduced in the House of Commons on 4 February 1890.

The presence of the Mormons in Canada caused fear and anxiety. They also had supporters, as they were viewed as excellent dry land farmers, but support fell away after their request to continue in their polygamous marriages.[60] There was concern that Canadian men might be tempted to join up, and these fears seemed to be realized in 1889 when Anthony Maitland Stenhouse, a member of the British Columbia legislative assembly, tendered his resignation, renounced his own faith, and joined the Mormons in southern Alberta. He vocally and vigorously defended polygamy in the press (although he himself remained unmarried).[61] It was Stenhouse who read the Canadian statutes and discovered a loophole: marrying two wives at the same time did not violate existing laws.[62] Other concerns were that the Mormons would proselytize, dragging young non-Mormon girls into lives of degradation. But polygamy was seen as a deeper threat to the very fabric of the young nation. As one Ontario Liberal parliamentarian declared in the House of Commons during the 1890 debate on "An Act respecting Offences relating to the Law of Marriage," polygamy was "a serious moral and national ulcer."[63]

Amendments to Canadian law, passed in 1890, imposed a five-year prison sentence and a fine of $500 on any person guilty of entering into any form of polygamy, any kind of conjugal union with more than one person at the same time, or what the "persons commonly called Mormons" knew as "spiritual or plural marriage." Any kind of ceremony, rite, or form practised by any society, sect, or denomination, religious or secular, or mere mutual consent could qualify – a binding form of marriage recognized by law did not have to have taken place.[64]

That the Mormons had settled next to a community where polygamy was relatively common was not an issue that was raised either in the House or in the public debate in the press. There were those who were acutely aware, however, that Canadian officials were not on strong ground when they declared that polygamy was not tolerated in this country. In the summer of 1890, Bishop Vital Grandin of St. Albert travelled to Ottawa to make representations to the government "regarding the probable bad moral effect which the presence of the Mormons will necessarily have on the Blood Indians whose reserve is close to the Mormon colony."[65] Grandin pointed out that his church had been labouring to convert the Bloods from polygamy, and he feared for this work if "the Mormons are to be allowed to teach contrary doctrine by both precept and example close by." Card chose land near the Blood Reserve for economic reasons, but also because the Mormons hoped to do missionary work among their neighbours. Indian agents in the United States who were located on reservations near Mormon settlements claimed that Native Americans were converting to the Mormon faith, "not because they have any profound religious convictions, but because the polygamy of the Mormons suits their tastes."[66] There was likely also concern in government circles that the Bloods would be teaching the Mormons, by both precept and example, that polygamy was in fact permitted in Canada.

Given the public attention to the issue of polygamy, the widespread anxiety about the disintegration of the nuclear family, the proximity of the Mormons to a reserve community where polygamy was practised, and the new legislation that specifically prohibited polygamy, the time had come for the DIA to act. Also motivating action was evidence that new polygamous marriages were being contracted. A final factor to be considered is that in the early 1890s in Western Canada, the land on fertile Indian reserves was being subdivided at great expense into forty-acre lots that were to be the small-scale farms and homes of nuclear families.[67] This plan was inspired in part by the US Dawes Severalty Act, as well as by Canada's Dominion Lands Act, but it was not precisely the same as either. It was similar, however, in that the ideal of a self-sufficient, independent family in which the male was the breadwinner and the farm wife his helpmate served as a rationale for the scheme. Large extended families of several wives, grandmothers, and many children could simply not survive on these miniature farms. In the United States, the implementation of the Dawes Act became an effective method of undermining polygamous households.

Yet measures aimed at eradicating polygamy remained reluctant and hesitant. In 1892 Indian Commissioner Hayter Reed asked his Ottawa superior for an opinion from the Department of Justice on questions that could guide a possible criminal prosecution "to suppress polygamy among our Indians," as cases still continued to occur "and the question arises whether some more stringent measures than heretofore resorted to should not now be adopted."[68] Not receiving a reply, Reed wrote in a similar vein the next year, saying that "their pernicious practices" were "far from showing sign of the gradual eradication which was expected," and asking for an opinion on questions including: "Is an Indian liable to criminal prosecution, if, in accordance with the customs of his Band, he lives with more than one wife?"[69]

In a December 1893 circular letter, each of the Indian agents in Western Canada was asked to report on the state of polygamy in their agencies by ascertaining the numbers, and recording the names, of husbands and wives and recording the number of years of marriage. Agents were also to fully explain the law on the subject. In preparing the lists, Assistant Commissioner Amedée Forget emphasized "the necessity for the utmost carefulness, in order that injustice may not be inadvertently done to anyone named therein."[70] What Forget may have meant was that there was great potential for misunderstanding in drawing up these lists; not all of the households with more than one adult woman were necessarily polygamous. Some of the Indian agents were aware that such distinctions were necessary but could not always be made. The Indian agent on the Blackfoot reserve reported that "some of the women reckoned as wives are really female relations; it is difficult to prove if they are living with them as wives or not."[71] From the Crooked Lake agency, agent Allan McDonald reported that there were four cases, but in two of these the parties were elderly, and he would "look on the man more in the light of a protector than a husband."[72] On many agencies no cases were reported, and on others there were very few. Not all agents viewed this as a pressing issue. The Indian agent for the Duck Lake agency, for example, said that there was one case in his agency, but "they appear to live happily together and give no trouble, and with regard to other Indians there is no inclination on their part to follow his example and break Department rules."[73]

The initial lists of polygamous families were submitted to Ottawa in September 1894, but any action was delayed as bureaucrats there asked that further information be supplied as to the "ages of the Indians shown to have added to the number of their wives since entering into Treaty."[74] M. McGirr explained to Forget that knowing the ages was necessary "in order to learn whether the individuals concerned had reached an age prior to Treaty at which expectation might justly have been entertained of contact with civilization affecting a change in their sentiments and practice regarding such matters, and whether any of the comparatively younger men have continued the custom of having a plurality of wives, despite the improving influences brought to bear upon them." The results so far gave "satisfaction that those in Treaty the longest had made progress in the right direction."

The people of southern Alberta's Treaty 7, however, stood out from the others in the persistence of polygamy. There were seventy-six polygamous families on the Blood Reserve, and forty-nine on the Blackfoot Reserve.[75] The list of polygamous marriages entered into since the treaty were twenty-three Blood, forty-one Blackfoot, and forty-nine Peigan.[76] Armed with this evidence, and now occupying the position of deputy superintendent general of Indian Affairs, Hayter Reed once again sought the advice of the Department of Justice on the question of prosecution. E.J. Newcombe, deputy minister of Justice and solicitor of Indian Affairs, delivered the following complicated and cautious opinion in January 1895:

> If such an Indian is validly married to one of the women with whom he lives and has gone through a form of marriage with the other or others which would make her or them his wife or wives but for the fact that he was already married, there can be no question that he is guilty of bigamy and liable to the Penalties for that crime (Criminal Code, Sec. 276). Even if there has been no valid marriage, but the Indian intended by complying with the customs of the band relating to marriage to make both or all the women his wives, or if, even without such intention he has complied in the case of two or more of the women with the requirements of the tribal customs, I am inclined to think that he may be successfully prosecuted under Sec. 278 of the Criminal Code, the maximum Penalty under which is imprisonment for five years, and a fine of five hundred dollars.[77]

Newcombe was referring to the 1890 Criminal Code amendment that was intended to address Mormon polygamy.

Resolve to take legal action was strengthened when new cases of polygamous marriages continued in the Blood agency, despite the fact that in the summer of 1894 the people had been notified that no plural marriages would be permitted for the future.[78] Indian agent James Wilson reported that marriages were defiantly continuing.[79] Two young men had taken second wives and "upon [Wilson's] ordering them to obey instructions of the Department they refused." Wilson had warned them they were liable to be sent to prison, and he was refusing the families rations until they obeyed. He wanted to send them up before a judge and felt that "a little coercion" was necessary now to "put a stop to what is probably one of the greatest hindrances to their advancement." Threats of legal action and withholding rations worked in two cases, but a man named Plaited Hair refused to give up his second wife. Wilson sought permission to place the second wife in a residential school, and Forget agreed with this course of action.[80] Forget stated that threats of prosecution had been made for years, that regard for the "prestige of the law" would be lessened if they did not proceed, and that their wards might be emboldened by what would seem to them to be evidence of weakness if no action was taken.[81]

In all the correspondence concerning the eradication of polygamy, DIA officials expressed almost no concern about the fate of the "semi-widows" who would be the result of a successful policy or prosecution. There is no indication of the kind of discussion of the conundrums that bedevilled the missionaries, such as which wife would be regarded as legitimate and which would have to go, and were they able to remarry. The records also contain almost no indication of the thoughts or reactions of the wives. Concern that women were treated within their own society as chattels, to be moved about at will, seems hollow when officials were prepared to remove them from their homes and place them in residential schools without any apparent consultation or permission. A central rationale for eradicating polygamy was that women were to be saved from lives of slavery, yet if the initiatives were successful, the "semi-widows" or "supernumerary wives" and children were to be abandoned.

In 1895, Deputy Superintendent General Hayter Reed remained uncertain about the ability to successfully prosecute. He reasoned that while Section 278 of the Criminal Code appeared broad enough to cover the case, it might be necessary to prove that there was some form of contract of marriage, and this was not clear in the case of Plaited Hair. "As you know," Reed wrote to Forget, "it would be better not to take action at all than to fail after having taken proceedings. And, moreover, it would be necessary to go very cautiously lest any general feeling should be worked up among the Indians on the subject."[82] Reed left it up to Forget to decide whether "sufficient evidence could be procured to give us a moral certainty of convicting." He also recommended that the second wife of Plaited Hair be removed and placed in a residential school.

Casting about for options and precedent in May 1896, Reed wrote to the commissioner of Indian Affairs in Washington, DC, inquiring about what he understood to be an important legal decision given in the United States in the case of an Indian tried for polygamy. The answer he received would not have been encouraging. Reed was informed that there was no such judicial decision, that in the summer of 1895 prosecutions were begun in South Dakota against a man named American Horse and some others charged with bigamy, but that these prosecutions were stopped by order of the Department of Justice.[83] In the United States, the Court of Indian Offences approach to abolishing polygamy produced few results. The Dawes Severalty Act of 1887 divided reservation land into individual plots and distributed them to each Native American man, woman, and child, except for plural wives, who were not entitled to allotments.[84] This policy was regarded by many reformers as a means of encouraging monogamous families, and according to John Pulsipher it did succeed in driving polygamy from the reservations, at least officially.[85] But in the summer of 1895 the prominent Lakota chief American Horse from Pine Ridge, South Dakota, was charged with bigamy under the Edmunds Act. Historian Robert Utley describes American Horse as "a man of great dignity and oratorical distinction, [who] had visited the Great Father and travelled with Buffalo Bill" and as one of the "progressive" leaders at Pine Ridge who believed it was necessary to cooperate with the new regime.[86] Utley clearly overlooked the refusal of American Horse to cooperate with the new regime if it meant giving up his wives.

According to the *Rapid City Daily Journal,* American Horse, who had four wives, bore "the distinction of being the first Indian arrested for bigamy," and it was "proposed to make an example of him and if possible break up the practice of polygamy among the Indians."[87] American Horse was released on bail pending trial. Several days later some other leading men were brought into custody on the same charge. It was reported that the proceedings against the men were based on a recent federal court decision in which it was held that an Indian could have only one valid wife, and that the "surplus" could be subpoenaed to testify against the husband.[88] It was further reported that the arrests were causing much dissatisfaction at Pine Ridge, as they were regarded as "an unwarranted innovation upon their ancient rights and customs and a violation of their treaty with the government which ... expressly states that their tribal and domestic relations shall not be interfered with." Residents of the Pine Ridge agency had decided to "resist to the last extremity these innovations upon their rights, and trouble is feared if the proceedings are not stopped." The Indian agent at Pine Ridge asked that steps be taken to stop the proceedings, claiming that all the other chiefs had "several wives for forty years and no one has dreamed of interfering before."[89] The proceedings were halted, and the attorney general indicated that the Edmunds Act had no possible application to Indians living in tribal relations. It was also pointed out that such interference could cause serious trouble.[90]

It is unclear if Hayter Reed ever learned any more details about these unsuccessful efforts in South Dakota, but if he had, they would have added to a list of concerns about the potential for resistance and turmoil, as well as the possibility of losing the case and losing face. In criminal court a case must be proven beyond the shadow of a doubt, and in this case there were potential shadows of doubt. For a conviction, it would be necessary to show that there was a form of contract, recognized as binding by all parties. No offence was committed between the parties where there was no form of contract. A recent decision in the Supreme Court of the North-West Territories, similar to the one that had apparently motivated the arrests in South Dakota, was of dubious assistance. In the 1889 case of *Regina v. Nan-e-quis-a-ka,* a man who had two wives was charged with assault. The court dismissed the first wife, who was found to be a wife in law and therefore could not be compelled, and was not competent, to testify against her husband. The second wife, however, was admitted as a witness as she was not regarded as a legally valid wife.[91] This case, however, also upheld the validity of Aboriginal customary marriage when such a marriage was monogamous. The court found that "marriage between Indians and by mutual consent and according to Indian custom since 15 July 1870 is a valid marriage, providing neither party had a husband or wife as the case may be, living at the time."[92]

DIA administrators became ever more determined to take stringent measures as new cases of polygamy arose. It was also reported that girls were being promised in marriage as a means of preventing them from being sent to residential schools.[93] Before proceeding with the uncertain criminal prosecution, consideration was given to the tactic of placing girls in residential schools under the compulsory education clauses of the Indian Act. In 1895 Forget was wondering whether this might be more successful, causing "less friction than by proceeding to prosecute for bigamy under the Criminal Code." The linking of the residential school program with the campaign to abolish polygamy further inflamed protests on reserve communities of southern Alberta.

On the Blackfoot Reserve early in 1895, zealous Indian agent Magnus Begg decided to pursue the repression of polygamy according to his own interpretation of the law. His actions generated controversy and were protested by both his superiors and the people under his supervision. There were new cases of polygamy in his agency; two girls, who Begg thought were no more than twelve, were promised by their fathers to men who already had wives. At a meeting held on the North Blackfoot Reserve in February, Begg declared that no man could marry a girl under the age of eighteen. He also stated that no man could marry a young woman graduate of an industrial or boarding school unless he had built a house with two rooms and had cows and a stable.[94] Begg further said that all children were to remain in schools unless their discharge was sanctioned by the department, and that all school-age children were to be sent to residential schools, as day schools were to be done away with as much as possible. According to Begg's account of this meeting, White Pup, spokesman for the chiefs, said that if the regulation was carried out about the age of marriage for girls, Begg "might expect blood."[95] Begg told them that they were "talking foolish" about shedding blood, and that all instructions must be carried out. Begg was severely reprimanded, by his superior Forget, for his statements at that meeting. Forget said that the agent had misinformed people, as a girl was marriageable at the age of twelve.[96] Begg was told to correct this false impression, as nothing would be gained by deceiving the Blackfoot.

Agent Begg did little to defuse the situation, however. At his next meeting, held in March, he informed the chiefs and headmen that if the betrothed girls were not sent to a school, it would be necessary to take them by force or to arrest the men who married them.[97] The chiefs replied that they were willing to have new regulations apply to the girls already in the schools, but that these should not be applied to other girls of the community. Begg suspected that their tactic was to promise all the young girls in marriage so that "there would be none for the schools." He sought Forget's permission to take the girls to the school with the assistance of the police and warned that arrests might cause trouble as "all the older Indians are strongly against any interference in the matter." Once again Forget reprimanded Begg for his actions – for not obtaining the permission of the parents of the girls to place them in school and for threatening the chiefs about the use of force and arrests.[98] Forget advised that, having committed himself to such a course, Begg ought to proceed to enforce the school regulations in the two cases mentioned "if the prestige of the Department and its Agent is to be maintained." Begg was to act prudently, cautiously, and with great tact, exhausting every peaceful means before considering a resort to any other. The agent soon reported that the two cases of early betrothal had been rescinded.[99]

By the late 1890s, DIA officials were worried about the determination of the Blackfoot to resist interference in their domestic relations. Chief Red Crow of the Kainai continued to live with his four wives despite the fact that in 1896 he was baptized into the Roman Catholic Church and was married in a Catholic ceremony to his youngest wife, Singing Before. Father Emil Legal performed both the baptism and the marriage.[100] This was a distinct departure from the priests' firm rule not to perform a marriage ceremony for a polygamous husband until he had cast aside his other wives. Agent James Wilson was astonished at this course of action, writing that "the Rev. Father Legal put Red Crow and one of his wives through a form of marriage, but as he has *three* other wives living with him, each of whom has been his wife for a longer period than the married (?) one, I fail to see what good this ceremony has done. The Indians on the other hand say it has been done so that his wife may claim all the old man's property to the exclusion of others."[101] According to historian Hugh Dempsey, these speculations were true. Red Crow was wealthy in cattle and horses, and this marriage ensured that his baptized Catholic son Frank, a student in an industrial school, would gain the inheritance.[102]

As evidence of new cases of polygamy accumulated in 1898, Indian Commissioner Forget wrote the new Deputy Superintendent General of Indian Affairs, James Smart, requesting "a definite and unqualified authorization to take measures of repression. Department's sanction of proceedings in such cases having hitherto been so qualified as to practically nullify same."[103] J.D. McLean, acting secretary, replied that the department was willing to leave the matter in his hands. Newcombe's 1895 opinion was quoted, and Forget was told that if he felt it was in the best interests of the Indians, and of public morality, he could take the necessary proceedings.[104] Forget was determined to take action, as he was convinced that "unless severe measures are taken it will be many years before the evil is eradicated."[105] In 1898 Indian agent James Wilson reported that notwithstanding all his efforts on the Blood reserve, six or seven young men had taken second wives, and he felt others would follow this example.[106]

In the Treaty 4 district, Cree Chief Star Blanket was reported in the fall of 1898 to have taken another wife.[107] The File Hills Indian agent informed the chief that more was expected of him as he had only recently been reinstated as chief. According to the agent, Star Blanket said that "he would rather give up the Chiefship [sic] than give the woman up."[108] After several months, Star Blanket complied with DIA policy to some extent by giving up his first wife, who appealed to the department for assistance as she was in a state of destitution.[109] Star Blanket was regarded as "difficult" to handle as he was opposed to policies on schools. It was recommended that he be deposed.

Forget decided to focus on the Blood Reserve after first giving the parties reasonable notice that they would be prosecuted unless they abandoned polygamy. He hoped that with firmness and the "hearty co-operation" of the police, the law would be enforced. In August 1898 Forget instructed agent Wilson to collect and submit information regarding all the new cases of polygamy to the Crown prosecutor, C.F. Conybeare of Lethbridge.[110] If Conybeare thought that criminal proceedings could be brought against any of these men, the agent was to call a meeting of the chiefs, bring the young men before them, and explain the law on the subject. Forget instructed Wilson to emphasize that the DIA had no desire to be harsh with them, "and that while it would see with pleasure the old men abandoning the practice, yet no prosecution is intended regarding them as they commenced the practice before they knew of the existence of the law." As for the others, the greatest leniency was to be extended, as the desire was not to punish but to prevent wrongdoing. The parties were to be informed that they had one month to abandon polygamy, or criminal proceedings would begin.

The Kainai were determined to resist. By November 1898 Wilson could report no changes, despite numerous meetings on the subject. He tried another tactic by refusing to pay the wives their annuities.[111] Wilson explained to Forget that the Indian Act "gave power to refuse payment to women who deserted their families and lived immorally with another man, and that as these women knew what they were doing they were equally guilty with the men." Wilson told Red Crow that the paylist books would be kept open for ten days, and that during that time the chief was to hold a meeting with the women to persuade them to give up their marriages. A meeting was held, but it was reported that Red Crow's position was that the new rules about marriage should apply only to the graduates of the schools.[112] Wilson declared that the young people were bound to obey and that Red Crow should insist they obey. The chief refused to do this. Once again the young men were given one month to withdraw from the position they had taken. Wilson reported that the tactic of holding back annuities worked with a number of the wives, but three refused to comply or to give up their marriages. Wilson sought permission to continue to withhold annuities. In his view, these women were "living immorally" as they had "undoubtedly" left their families to reside with another married man. Two of the women were widows with children when they remarried. Forget permitted Wilson to withhold the annuities of the women who "still persist to live immorally."[113]

By December 1898 Wilson was determined that legal proceedings should be taken to "enforce the law as those young men still refuse to obey."[114] In consultation with Coneybeare, he decided to proceed against Bear's Shin Bone, a scout for the North West Mounted Police and the man who had most recently entered into a polygamous marriage. Bear's Shin Bone was brought before Judge C. Rouleau at Fort Macleod on 10 March 1899 on a charge of practising polygamy with two women, an offence under Section 278 of the Criminal Code.[115] His wives were Free Cutter Woman and Killed Herself, and there is no indication that any evidence was taken from them during the trial. To do so would have raised the question of whether they were competent to, or could be compelled to, testify against their husband. If, as in *Regina v. Nan-e-quis-a-ka*, the second wife was found not to be a valid wife, the case for the prosecution for polygamy would be weakened. Coneybeare had to prove that there was a form of contract between the parties, which they all regarded was binding upon them. M. McKenzie for the defence argued that this section of the statute was never intended to apply to Indians (as discussed earlier, it was originally designed to address Mormon polygamy).[116] The court held that the law "applied to Indians as well as whites," and that the marriage customs of the Bloods came within the provisions of the statute and were a form of contract, recognized as valid by the case of *Regina v. Nan-e-quis-a-ka*. Both marriages had to be recognized as valid in order to invalidate the second marriage. This anomaly was recognized in the local newspaper's coverage of the case, in which it was noted that "Bare-Shin-Bone, the Blood Indian charged with polygamy, was convicted and allowed to go on suspended sentence, being instructed to annul his latest marriage (?) and cleave to his first spouse and none other."[117] If he did not, he would be brought up at any time for sentencing.[118]

The DIA regarded this as a test case, with the goal being not to punish, but to make the prisoner and the others obey the law. The DIA agreed to pay for the defence barrister, even though the Kainai had raised a sum of money for that purpose. Wilson also sought and received permission to pay arrears for the 1898 annuities withheld from the women who refused to give up their marriages. Wilson further sought permission to have the children listed as legitimate, allowing them to draw rations and annuities. These measures would, in Wilson's view, "help to allay the feeling of soreness which one or two of them feel at having to give up their second wives."[119] Permission was granted, and newly appointed Indian commissioner David Laird was advised from Ottawa that the offspring of these marriages would be considered legitimate and not only rationed, but also placed on the paylist.[120] DIA accountant Duncan Campbell Scott endorsed these measures, writing in a memorandum that "the right of the women themselves to payment of annuity is not impugned by the relation referred to, and if we were to consider the offspring of such unions illegitimate it would hardly be possible to advance just grounds for our decision, as a great number of adult Indians and children throughout Manitoba and the North West are the fruit of such marriages. The effect of leniency in these cases will assist in furthering an easy transition to civilized ways of matrimony."[121]

The 1890s flurry of activity aimed at prohibiting polygamy, which culminated in the Bear's Shin Bone case, did not entirely result in the desired goal. There was much "unfinished business." The 1901 census for the Blood Reserve indicated over thirty polygamous families.[122] Not all of these would have been marriages contracted before or at the time of Treaty 7, as some involved younger men and women. Indian agents continued to report polygamous marriages, although concerns about divorce and cases of bigamy became the more frequent complaints.[123] The 1890s prohibition campaign was one chapter in a lengthy saga of efforts, using diverse tactics, rewards, and punishments, which were aimed at imposing monogamous morality and "proper" gender roles. The concerted resistance and defiance demonstrated by the Kaina did not continue after Bear's Shin Bone, but Aboriginal people continued to challenge and contest interference in the domestic domain. Although unfinished and not always successful, however, these interventions continued well into the twentieth century.

Notes

1 The term "polygamy" embraces both "polygyny" (one husband taking multiple wives) and "polyandry" (one wife taking multiple husbands). Plains Aboriginal societies practised polygyny (as did the Mormons), but non-Aboriginal people at the time and since have referred to this as polygamy. In Blackfoot and Cree there are no words for polygamy, polygyny, or polyandry.

2 For an overview of recent "intimacies of empire" studies see Ann Laura Stoler, "Tense and Tender Ties: The Politics of North American History and (Post) Colonial Studies," *The Journal of American History* 88, 3 (December 2001): 829-65. I am grateful to Joan Sangster and Bryan Palmer for providing me with a copy of their commentary on this article, which notes that Canadian history does not fall within the rubric of "North American" history in this article.

3 Antoinette Burton, "Introduction," in *Gender, Sexuality and Colonial Modernities*, ed. Antoinette Burton (London: Routledge, 1999), 1-16.

4 Jane Fishburne Collier, *Marriage and Inequality in Classless Societies* (Stanford, CA: Stanford University Press, 1988).

5 R.N. Wilson Papers, vol. 1, edited and annotated by Philip Godsell, p. 118, Glenbow Archives.

6 David G. Mandelbaum field notes, Fine Day # 1B, 6 August 1934, pp. 4-5, Canadian Plains Research Centre.

7 Ibid., 4.

8 Ibid., 5.

9 Glenbow Archives, Wilson Papers, 118.

10 Beverly Hungry Wolf, *The Ways of My Grandmothers* (New York: Quill, 1982), 201.

11   Sue Sommers Dietrich typescript of 1939 interviews on the Blackfoot Reservation, Montana, p. 4, Marquette University Archives. Thanks to Alice Kehoe for this reference.
12   John H. Moore, "The Developmental Cycle of Cheyenne Polygyny," *American Indian Quarterly* (Summer 1991): 311-28, at 311.
13   Gilbert L. Wilson, *Buffalo Bird Woman's Garden: Agriculture of the Hidatsa Indians* (St. Paul: Minnesota Historical Society Press, 1987), 9.
14   Esther Goldfrank field notes, 172, Glenbow Archives.
15   Hungry Wolf, *Ways of My Grandmothers,* 27.
16   Moore, "The Developmental Cycle," 311.
17   Ibid.
18   I discuss non-Aboriginal views of Plains societies' marriages in *Capturing Women: The Manipulation of Cultural Imagery in Canada's Prairie West* (Montreal and Kingston: McGill-Queen's University Press, 1997), 163-66.
19   John Semmens, *The Field and the Work: Sketches of Missionary Work in the Far North* (Toronto: Methodist Mission Rooms, 1884), 163.
20   Rev. Ross C. Houghton, *Women of the Orient: An Account of the Religious, Intellectual and Social Condition of Women* (Cincinnati: Hitchcock and Walden, 1877), 190-91.
21   Inderpal Grewal, *Home and Harem: Nation, Gender, Empire and the Cultures of Travel* (Durham, NC, and London: Duke University Press, 1996), 54.
22   L.M. Hanks Jr. and Jane Richardson, *Observations of Northern Blackfoot Kinship,* Monographs of the American Ethnological Society, no. 9, ed. A. Irving Hallowell (Seattle: University of Washington Press, 1944), 23.
23   Esther Goldfrank field notes, 412, Glenbow Archives.
24   Oscar Lewis, "Manly-Hearted Women Among the Northern Piegan," *American Anthropologiste* 43, 2 (1941): 173-87. See also Sabine Lang, *Men As Women, Women As Men: Changing Gender in Native American Cultures* (Austin: University of Texas Press, 1998), 305-6.
25   Esther Goldfrank, *Changing Configurations in the Social Organization of a Blackfoot Tribe during the Reserve Period,* Monographs of the American Ethnological Society, no. 8, ed. A. Irving Hallowell (Seattle: University of Washington Press, 1944), 47.
26   Constance Backhouse, *Petticoats and Prejudice: Women and Law in Nineteenth-Century Canada* (Toronto: Women's Press, for the Osgoode Society, 1991), 176.
27   Eugene Stock, *The History of the Church Missionary Society: Its Environment, Its Men and Its Work,* vol. 2 (London: Church Missionary Society, 1899), 111.
28   Ibid., vol. 3, 646.
29   Jeff Guy, *The Heretic: A Study of the Life of John William Colenso, 1814-1883* (Pietermartizburg, South Africa: The University of Natal Press, 1983), 49.
30   Ibid., 78.
31   Samuel Trivett letter, 22 March 1887, Church Missionary Society Collection (microfilm), no. 979, reel A114, Provincial Archives of Manitoba.
32   John Maclean, *Canadian Savage Folk: The Native Tribes of Canada* (Toronto: William Briggs, 1896), 62.
33   John Webster Grant, *Moon of Wintertime: Missionaries and the Indians of Canada* (Toronto: University of Toronto Press, 1984), 235.
34   Semmens, *The Field and the Work,* 166.
35   John Hines, *The Red Indians of the Plains: Thirty Years' Missionary Experience in the Saskatchewan* (Toronto: McClelland, Goodchild and Stewart Ltd., 1916), 158-59.
36   Edwin Thompson Denig, quoted in David R. Miller, "Introduction," *The Assiniboine,* ed. J.N.B. Hewitt (Regina: Canadian Plains Research Centre, 1998), xix n. 10.
37   Ibid., 74.
38   Sharon H. Venne, ed., *Indian Acts and Amendments, 1868-1975: An Indexed Collection* (Saskatoon: University of Saskatchewan Native Law Centre), 94.
39   Ibid., 139-140, Sections 72 and 73.
40   Canada, "Ebenezer McColl's report on the Manitoba Superintendency, 18 October 1893," in "Department of Indian Affairs report for 1893," *Sessional Papers,* no. 14, vol. 27, 45.
41   *Macleod Gazette,* 25 January 1895.

42 M.B. Venini Byrne, *From the Buffalo to the Cross: A History of the Roman Catholic Diocese of Calgary* (Calgary: D.W. Friesen and Sons, 1973), 50.

43 Canada, "Annual Report of the Superintendent-General of Indian Affairs," in "Department of Indian Affairs Report for 1898," *Sessional Papers,* no. 14, vol. 33, xxv.

44 "Questions on Indian Marriage," pp. 3-4, Records of the Department of Justice, Record Group (RG) 13, vol. 2406, file 1299-1914, Library and Archives Canada (LAC).

45 James G. Snell, *In the Shadow of the Law: Divorce in Canada, 1900-1939* (Toronto: University of Toronto Press, 1991).

46 See Records of the Department of Indian Affairs, RG 10, vol. 3559, file 74, pt. 4, LAC.

47 Circular letter of J.F. Graham, 24 July 1882, Records of the Department of Indian Affairs, RG 10, vol. 3602, file 1760, LAC.

48 Diana Jeater, *Marriage, Perversion and Power: The Construction of Moral Discourse in Southern Rhodesia, 1894-1930* (Oxford: Clarendon Press, 1993), 78.

49 John D. Pulsipher, "The Americanization of Monogamy: Mormons, Native Americans and the Nineteenth-Century Perception that Polygamy Was a Threat to Democracy" (PhD dissertation, University of Minnesota, 1999), 162.

50 James G. Snell, "'The White Life for Two': The Defence of Marriage and Sexual Morality in Canada, 1890-1914," in *Canadian Family History: Selected Readings,* ed. Bettina Bradbury, 381-400 (Toronto: Copp Clark Pitman Ltd., 1992), 381.

51 Sarah Carter, "Categories and Terrains of Exclusion: Constructing the 'Indian Woman' in the Early Settlement Era in Western Canada," *Great Plains Quarterly* 13 (Summer 1993): 147-61, at 150.

52 Sarah Barringer Gordon, "'The Liberty of Self-Degradation': Polygamy, Woman Suffrage, and Consent in Nineteenth-Century America," *Journal of American History* 83, 3 (December 1996): 815-47, at 820-21.

53 Ibid., 816.

54 Ibid., 815.

55 Ibid., 835.

56 Richard White, *"It's Your Misfortune and None of My Own": A New History of the American West* (Norman: University of Oklahoma Press, 1991), 174.

57 Dan Erickson, "Alberta Polygamists? The Canadian Climate and Response to the Introduction of Mormonism's Peculiar Institution," *Pacific Northwest Quarterly* 86, 4 (Fall 1995): 155-64, 155.

58 This is what Francis Lyman (Mormon church apostle on the mission to Ottawa) reported about the meeting with Prime Minister Sir John A. Macdonald. See Erickson, "Alberta Polygamists?" 159.

59 Ibid., 159-60.

60 Ibid.

61 Robert J. McCue, "Anthony Maitland Stenhouse, Bachelor Polygamist," in *American History and Life* 23, 1 (1990): 108-25.

62 Erickson, "Alberta Polygamists?" 160.

63 Quoted in Brian Champion, "Mormon Polygamy: Parliamentary Comments, 1889-90," *Alberta History* 35, 1 (Spring 1987): 10-17, at 13.

64 Ibid., 16.

65 *Edmonton Bulletin,* 23 August 1890.

66 Quoted in Pulsipher, "The Americanization of Monogamy," 137.

67 Sarah Carter, *Lost Harvests: Prairie Indian Reserve Farmers and Government Policy* (Montreal and Kingston: McGill-Queen's University Press, 1990), 193-236.

68 Hayter Reed to Deputy Superintendent General of Indian Affairs (DSGIA), 8 September 1892, Records of DIA, RG 10, vol. 3881, file 94-189, LAC.

69 Reed to DSGIA, 25 September 1893, ibid.

70 Circular letter, Assistant Commissioner Amedée Forget to Indian Agents, 19 December 1893, ibid.

71 Forget to DSGIA, 30 January 1895, "Statement showing ages of Indians who have entered into polygamous relations since taking treaty," 5, ibid.

72 A. McDonald to Assistant Commissioner Forget (copy, n.d.), ibid.
73 R.S. McKenzie to Assistant Commissioner Forget (copy, n.d.), ibid.
74 M. McGirr to A. Forget, 26 September 1894, ibid.
75 These figures are from the copies of the 1893 agents' reports prepared by A. Forget. The statements for the Peigan are incomplete and unclear (ibid.).
76 These figures are from the "Statement showing ages of Indians who have entered into polygamous relations since taking treaty," ibid.
77 E.J. Newcombe to Hayter Reed, 4 January 1895, ibid.
78 J. Wilson to A. Forget, 21 January 1895, ibid.
79 Ibid.
80 Wilson to Forget, 20 February 1895, ibid.
81 Forget memo, n.d., ibid.
82 Reed to Forget, 4 March 1895, ibid.
83 D.M. Browning to Reed, 13 June 1896, ibid.
84 Pulsipher, "The Americanization of Monogamy," 169-70.
85 Ibid., 170.
86 Robert M. Utley, *The Indian Frontier of the American West, 1846-1890* (Albuquerque: University of New Mexico Press, 1984), 234-36.
87 *Rapid City Daily Journal*, 4 May 1895.
88 Ibid., 16 May 1895.
89 Ibid.
90 Ibid., 26 May 1895.
91 Brian Slattery, ed., *Canadian Native Law Cases*, vol. 2, 1870-1890 (Saskatoon: University of Saskatchewan Native Law Centre, 1981), 368-72.
92 Ibid., 372.
93 Magnus Begg to Forget, 23 March 1895, Records of DIA, RG 10, vol. 3881, file 934, 189, LAC.
94 Begg to Forget, 23 February 1895, ibid.
95 Ibid.
96 The federal government of Canada has not established a minimum age for marriage, which has resulted in the adoption of the minimum ages under English common law: fourteen years for males, twelve years for females. Provinces and territories have legislation requiring a higher minimum age. See Dwight L. Gibson and Terry G. Murphy, *All About Law: Exploring the Canadian Legal System,* 4th ed. (Toronto: Nelson Canada, 1996), 355.
97 Begg to Forget, 9 March 1895, Records of DIA, RG 10, vol. 3881, file 934, 189, LAC.
98 Forget to Begg, 11 March 1895, ibid.
99 Begg to Forget, 16 March 1895, ibid.
100 Hugh Dempsey, *Red Crow: Warrior Chief* (Saskatoon: Western Producer Prairie Books, 1980), 197.
101 Quoted in ibid.
102 Ibid., 217.
103 Forget to J. Smart, 15 April 1898, Records of DIA, RG 10, vol. 3881, file 934, 189, LAC.
104 J.D. McLean to Forget, 22 April 1898, Records of DIA, RG 10, vol. 3559, file 74, pt. 3, LAC.
105 Forget to McLean, 8 August 1898, Records of DIA, RG 10, vol. 3881, file 934, 189, LAC.
106 Wilson to McLean, 23 July 1898, ibid.
107 Forget to the Secretary, DIA, 13 September 1890, Records of DIA, RG 10, vol. 3559, file 74, pt. 6, LAC.
108 Ibid.
109 Forget to Indian agent, File Hills agency, 20 January 1899, ibid.
110 Forget to Wilson, 18 August 1898, Records of DIA, RG 10, vol. 3559, file 74, pt. 3, LAC.
111 Wilson to Forget, 4 November 1898, ibid., file 74, pt. 19.
112 Ibid.
113 Forget to Wilson, 10 December 1898, ibid.
114 Wilson to Forget, 6 December 1898, ibid.
115 Slattery, *Canadian Native Law Cases*, 513. See also Backhouse, *Petticoats and Prejudice*, 26.
116 Wilson to Forget, 13 March 1899, Records of DIA, RG 10, vol. 3559, file 74, pt. 19, LAC.

117 *Macleod Gazette,* 11 March 1899.
118 Wilson to Forget, 13 March 1899, Records of DIA, RG 10, vol. 3559, file 74, pt. 19, LAC.
119 Ibid.
120 S. Stewart, Secretary, to Indian Commissioner David Laird, 1 April 1899, ibid.
121 Duncan Campbell Scott, memorandum, 29 March 1899, ibid.
122 1901 Census Data, Canada Census Records, Glenbow Archives.
123 Records of the Department of Indian Affairs, RG 10, vol. 3559, file 74, part 3-30, LAC.

7
Intimate Surveillance: Indian Affairs, Colonization, and the Regulation of Aboriginal Women's Sexuality
Robin Jarvis Brownlie

In 1924 Duncan Campbell Scott, head bureaucrat of Canada's Department of Indian Affairs, wrote a personal letter to a woman on the Chippewas of Nawash Indian Reserve in Ontario.[1] This powerful civil servant, who wielded extraordinarily broad powers over Aboriginal people's lives, had taken time out of his busy day to counsel a woman he did not know personally on her marital difficulties. At the request of the woman's local Indian agent, Scott provided some fairly standard Euro-Canadian prescriptions for Mrs. A. to improve her marriage through a proper performance of her "duty as a wife and a mother." He urged her to spend less time "running around to the neighbours" and more time in her home, making the place attractive, so that her husband would be interested in staying there. This was supposed to deal with the problem of her husband paying attentions to other women. If the woman failed to mend her ways and her marriage, Scott threatened that the department would have to cancel the loan on her husband's farm.[2] Although the Indian agent had asked that a second letter be sent to the husband, ordering him to attend to his farm work and leave other women alone, it appears that only the wife received the written warning.[3] Mrs. A. was thus held responsible both for the state of her marriage and for the survival of the family farm.

Such a direct intervention in marital relations by a top-ranking civil servant is a striking instance of the intensely personalized colonial regulation to which First Nations people were subjected. This chapter explores the discourse and practice of the Department of Indian Affairs (DIA) with respect to the regulation of Aboriginal women's gender and sexuality between 1918 and 1939. It also considers the racialized understandings officials brought to bear on their work. DIA officials took considerable interest in the marital and sexual habits of both men and women. Their positions of authority provided a range of measures by which they could punish both parties involved in extramarital liaisons. Women, however, were more likely than men to be in positions of economic need that facilitated closer surveillance and control. Aboriginal women were closely scrutinized when they were believed to be violating Euro-Canadian sexual prescriptions, and they could be disciplined in a variety of ways for their presumed transgressions. Officials were particularly concerned to deter the open exercise of non-marital sexuality, but were also involved in the era's campaign to enforce Aboriginal conformity to Christian forms of monogamous, lifelong marriage.

These preoccupations, of course, reflect the same moralism that was applied to Euro-Canadian women in the period, particularly to the socially marginalized who came within the purview of social service agencies. For example, single mothers awarded the newly established mothers' allowance were subject to similar kinds of surveillance and regulation.[4] In fact, when mothers' allowances were approved for Aboriginal women, authorities cooperated to ensure that the funds were placed under the control of the Indian agent or local missionary.[5] Yet as several scholars have persuasively demonstrated, Canadian racial discourses had long constructed Aboriginal women as *particularly* likely to be promiscuous and immoral.[6] Moreover, the extensive powers and multiple roles of the Indian agent permitted a level of intimate surveillance and interference that even social workers implementing the mothers' allowance program could not match. Through the extensive body of correspondence they created, DIA officials produced a colonial knowledge of Aboriginal people that assessed and categorized them by their degree of conformity to white middle-class normative sexuality and foregrounded race as a determinant of sexual transgression. They also acted on the premises of this colonial knowledge, exercising economic and social power to regulate sexual and gender behaviour and to discipline the transgressive.

This chapter is based primarily on the records of Indian agents around Georgian Bay, particularly those of two agents of the 1920s and 1930s: Robert J. Lewis on Manitoulin Island and John M. Daly in Parry Sound. In their work and correspondence, these two men revealed understandings of proper gender and sexual behaviour that conformed to those of their own class and community. Both agents were middle-class Euro-Canadians – Lewis a Canadian-born Protestant of Irish descent; Daly a Protestant, Scottish-born immigrant. They differed in personality, however. While Daly was a confirmed paternalist, Lewis showed considerable reluctance to intervene in personal and even political affairs. Daly probably made more prompt and decisive interventions when required, but ironically it was Lewis who was involved in the most punitive measures. These differences apparently arose from the divergent conditions in the agencies they administered. Lewis managed a larger agency, which was also policed by the morally vigilant Jesuits based at their Wikwemikong mission on Manitoulin Island. The Jesuits pressured Lewis to enforce Christian morality by means of his economic and political power, and in some cases he was compelled to act. In

Daly's agency, by contrast, there was no resident missionary during his tenure, and moral regulation of First Nations people was left largely to his discretion.

In the first half of the twentieth century, DIA officials remained firmly entrenched in a well-established department tradition of promoting and supporting colonialism. In pursuit of the primary goal of assimilating First Nations people, they attempted to reshape Aboriginal societies in the Euro-Canadian image. As one of the key axes of identity construction and behaviour prescriptions, gender was a crucial area in which officials evaluated Aboriginal societies and intervened to alter older patterns. At the same time, the actions and rhetoric of these officials reveal the intersection of gender with notions about race and class. As "Indians," First Nations people were expected to be integrated into mainstream society at the level of the unskilled or semi-skilled working class. Constructions of Aboriginal gender within Indian Affairs, then, were premised on ideas about gender roles and behaviours assigned to the working class and to a racialized "Indian" minority. For women, the agents' regulation of femininity focused particularly on sexual behaviour. In working to advance the process of Europeanization and assimilation that was intended to lead to the absorption of Native people into mainstream society, the DIA hoped to eliminate the "Indian problem," along with the troubling resistance offered by some Aboriginal people to Euro-Canadian social and sexual norms.

Gender and Race in DIA Discourse and Practice

The discourses embedded in DIA correspondence of the interwar period reveal a number of patterns. Not surprisingly, the records do not betray an overt adherence to the more malicious stereotypes that circulated in other sectors of Canadian society. Instead, they reveal considerable care in the use of language, as indicated, for instance, by the avoidance of the sexualized images of Aboriginal women commonly enunciated by other Euro-Canadians.[7] Significantly, DIA employees assiduously avoided use of the derogatory term "squaw," in spite of the fact that it was widely used until at least the 1960s, even by nominally sympathetic Euro-Canadians.[8] Terms like "heathen" and "savage," as well as "papoose," were also carefully elided from Indian Affairs discourse. For the most part, officials referred to women either by name or with the phrase "Indian woman." Both Lewis and Daly occasionally spoke of "ladies," sometimes "Indian ladies," when discussing the women for whom they had the most respect – in practice, these were always elderly women. Men, by contrast, were described simply as "Indians," never as "Indian men" or "Indian gentlemen." The term "Indian" was male unless specifically feminized by a female gender term. Although other writers of the time commonly spoke of Aboriginal people in the singular, as "the Indian," federal officials seldom employed this convention. A final noteworthy characteristic of these records is the conspicuous absence of the concept of "halfbreed." While Lewis and Daly constantly made decisions about people's racial status as "Indian" or non-Indian, they did not do so with reference to parentage or the idea of "blood quantum." Rather, lifestyle and place of residence were the key considerations, although undoubtedly appearance played a role as well.

The absence of overtly racist terminology does not indicate a rejection of gendered and racialized discourses about sexuality. Rather, the department had its own more subtly nuanced language that embodied such discourses. Within the Indian Affairs system, it was axiomatic that Aboriginal people were capable of improvement and "civilization," and department officials were required to pay lip service to this premise. But it was equally taken for granted that such improvement continued to be necessary, that the civilization process was not yet complete. First Nations people, in the DIA's view, were still inferior to Euro-Canadians in important areas such as their work ethic and their ability to take responsibility for their lives. In spite of the significant economic adaptations the people had undertaken in the southern parts of Ontario, they were still considered to be too firmly attached to the ways of their ancestors, especially to hunting, idleness, and mobility. Another area in which they remained suspect was in their sexuality, and here it was the women, primarily, who came under scrutiny.

It was principally the agents' role as regulators of Aboriginal women's sexuality that gave rise to the expression and enactment of gendered notions about Aboriginal women. An obvious mode of colonialism in DIA practice and discourse lay in agents' assumption of the right to regulate Aboriginal women's sexuality and enforce obedience to Euro-Canadian models of correct gender expression. Indian agents had a unique ability to enforce these codes against women, especially through the use of financial control. For example, they could deny women their right to treaty and interest payments on the grounds of sexual transgressions; they could take away their children; and they could grant or refuse relief in time of need. Indian agents' roles in controlling Aboriginal people's money and dispensing social welfare greatly magnified their ability to discipline Aboriginal women, especially given their poverty in the 1920s and 1930s. Moreover, a series of DIA policies and Indian Act provisions had the effect of limiting Aboriginal women's access to money and resources.[9] Federal policy was designed to impose a European patriarchal model of gender relations on Aboriginal people, enforcing female dependence on men. Although women continued to be active in a number of ways as family providers, economic changes had resulted in reduced opportunities for them to contribute to family support.

The records reveal a number of characteristic attitudes and practices among Indian agents in relation to women and their sexuality. In the first place, the agents distinguished among women according to their age. Older women frequently received particular respect when they were mentioned in correspondence. Only older women merited the designation "ladies," and both Lewis and Daly tended to speak of them in tones of respect and even affection. Lewis cited one, for example, as "a splendid type of her race."[10] Both men emphasized the importance of seeing to their welfare, part of a paternalistic responsibility to those who could not care for themselves. There was no official concern about the sexual behaviour of older women – only their economic affairs, their ability to feed and shelter themselves, were relevant to the DIA. It is unlikely that these women gave occasion for moral concern, but it is still worth noting that in Euro-Canadian culture, older women were considered to be out of the realm of sexuality.

References to younger women, on the other hand, suggest that the "squaw" image, though unnamed, exercised its influence on the agents. This image has been easily manipulated since the beginnings of colonialism in North America, and it was very much in circulation in the interwar period (as it still is today). Although colonial constructs of Aboriginal women initially included the notion that they were overworked drudges in their own societies, the image was later reversed and First Nations women were reimagined as symbols of idleness and related traits, such as gossiping.[11] The letter from Duncan C. Scott to Mrs. A., quoted at the beginning of this chapter, bears visible traces of this belief. Over time, the sexual aspect of the squaw construct arguably became its most prominent feature. First Nations women were portrayed as depraved figures who embodied indiscriminate sexual contact and immorality. Especially in the United States, there was also an opposing stereotype, the "Indian Princess," typifying the white fantasy of a woman who was receptive to European colonization and even helped further it. In practice, most First Nations women did not comply with this fantasy of the willingly subjugated colonial subject. Instead they pursued their own interests and those of their people. The most negative images, then, can be seen partly as a reaction to Aboriginal women's refusal to follow the convenient script of legends such as that of Pocahontas.[12] Indian agents of the 1920s and 1930s were clearly influenced by demeaning constructs of Aboriginal women, particularly the entrenched notion that Aboriginal women were likelier than Euro-Canadian women to engage in sexually immoral activities.

Negative images of Aboriginal women emphasized not only sexual immorality, but also a failure to conform to Euro-Canadian ideals of feminine domesticity. There was a preconception that domesticity did not come "naturally" to First Nations women, associated as it was with the settled habits and steady labour that were held to be "white" virtues. The common Euro-Canadian belief that First Nations people had an innate predisposition to "wander" or "roam" was reflected in officials' observations about excessive mobility among some Aboriginal women. It is also evident in the correspondence relating to Mrs. A. This correspondence included, for example, her local Indian agent's claim that "every time I go near the home I find the woman away and can always see her on the roads and not paying any attention to her home, which is always like a pig sty and dirty."[13] When officials described Mrs. A. as being "out on the roads" or "running around to the neighbours," these phrases alluded to a variety of discouraged practices (visiting and gossiping, for example) that were related to racialized notions about idleness and work avoidance.

But Mrs. A.'s reprimand was also fundamentally about maintaining her marriage and restoring its monogamous character – something the officials were suggesting could be achieved through more diligent attention to her domestic role. In objecting to the woman's physical mobility, the officials were also alluding to her incursions out of the domestic realm into public space. Mrs. A. was warned back into the domestic space, which was gendered female and functioned in part as a means of physically and symbolically containing women's sexuality. The spectre of women uncontained, roaming around in public, was associated in European patriarchal discourse with immorality, and especially with sexual transgression. Although the Victorian ideology that associated female respectability exclusively with domesticity had waned by the interwar period, DIA officials still showed a marked tendency to link housework with morality, and mobility with immorality.

Indian agents' constructions of Aboriginal gender, and their personal evaluations of individual gender conformity, had material consequences for the people they administered. Aboriginal women were granted or refused certain kinds of aid partly in accordance with the agents' judgments about their gender-role conformity. For example, outspoken or sexually transgressive women who received relief rations from the DIA could face withdrawal of this aid as punishment for their actions. Women who left their husbands, even if the relationship was abusive, might apply in vain for DIA aid to help support their children. In theory, an agent could also continue to pay an erring wife's share of interest and annuity money to her husband, or he could withhold her own and/or her children's payments. Lewis, for instance, withheld these payments from two "immoral" women who he argued spent too much time travelling (both also cohabited outside marriage with Euro-Canadian men).[14]

Agents showed particular objection to two kinds of behaviour in women: becoming politically active in some way, usually in the form of fighting for an improvement in living conditions; and pursuing extramarital or unchurched relationships. Although political activism is not an apparently sexual activity, women who challenged the DIA ran the risk of being labelled sexual transgressors, or of being punished more harshly for perceived sexual transgressions than women who were less outspoken. Although agents objected to male challengers as well, women who spoke out were violating the Euro-Canadian feminine ideals of passivity and submission. This meant that their actions brought them into the realm of gender regulation.

Regulation of Political Activity

Aboriginal women had limited avenues for political expression in the 1920s and 1930s. Status Indian women living on reserves did not enjoy the franchise federally, provincially, or for band council elections. In fact, there was no place for them in formal politics. Efforts to mount organized protests against federal policies were spearheaded by men and seem to have been aimed exclusively at men. But questions of daily survival are also political issues, and here women were active in the period. This is not surprising, given that this is still an important sphere of Aboriginal women's political activity.[15] Some women agitated for improved economic support, especially during the Great Depression when the DIA was the sole source of relief for First Nations people. Relief was provided at extremely low levels, well below the rates at which nearby non-Aboriginal people received aid from municipalities. Women wrote to their agents to protest the insufficiency of relief, and some fought repeatedly to improve their financial position by inducing the department to provide more adequate assistance.

One such woman was Julia K., who lived on Parry Island Reserve. Mrs. K. had a hard lot in many ways: she suffered from rheumatism, all of her children had tuberculosis, and the family had been abandoned by her husband. Until the Depression of the 1930s, she nevertheless apparently managed to feed her family, in part by selling crafts to the local tourist market. By 1932 these means were insufficient, and she began to seek relief from agent Daly. In spite of her obvious need and the national economic crisis, Daly refused several requests before finally approaching the DIA to place the question before his superiors. She was granted five dollars per month in July 1932, but soon began to importune various officials to raise this entirely inadequate amount.[16]

Mrs. K. was known to the agents for her outspokenness (Daly remarked, "This woman has a 'tongue'"[17]), and she was thus a thorn in their sides. In 1933 Indian agent H.J. Eade wrote to Daly about Mrs. K.'s agitation for improved relief issues. Eade insisted that she was "getting more than her share" relative to other First Nations women. He added, "Further I hear she is doing some running around with other men." He advised Daly to "watch her very closely," and if she were involved in sexual relationships, to cut off her relief.[18] The element of surveillance is obvious here. At the same time, the concern about her sexual behaviour had an instrumental quality as well. If Eade could link this agitator with sexual immorality, he could impose a serious financial consequence. Eade wrote that he was "getting tired of this woman's constant complaints," and he clearly wanted to teach her a lesson about the risks of doing battle with the Indian department. The association of this woman's assertiveness with sexual transgression appears to have been Eade's way of discrediting her as a political actor (Daly made no reference to immorality in his correspondence about Mrs. K.). In fact, this agent's accusations about "running around" appear to represent a kind of sexualization of dissent. At the same time, his insinuations can be related to the larger sexualizing discourse with which whites responded to Aboriginal women's refusal to cooperate in their own oppression and marginalization.

Clearly, punitive actions of various sorts were readily available for agents wishing either to discipline political opponents or to regulate women's sexuality. It is likely that far more women were cut off or denied relief for these sorts of reasons than the Indian department's correspondence ever documented. Decisions about relief requests belonged to the large repertoire of issues in which the agents exercised broad discretionary powers. They could grant or deny relief without committing the interaction to paper at all – especially if the answer was no. Another tactic was to delay relief payments in order to "show the Indians which way the wind was blowing," as activist Harold Cardinal has described it.[19] The exercise of moral authority could be a reflection of a genuinely held belief, or it could serve other purposes such as political intimidation. Either way, the agents' arbitrary power over First Nations people permitted them to give moral regulation a concrete material form.

Controlling Extramarital Sexuality

The second form of behaviour to which Indian agents objected was Aboriginal women's involvement in extramarital relationships. During the interwar period, the DIA pursued a campaign to confine Aboriginal women's sexuality within European-style patriarchal marriage. This campaign had a major impact on Aboriginal women and men, even though it was not completely successful in eradicating older Aboriginal practices such as divorce and remarriage. Some agents were quite ardent in chasing down unchurched couples. In this period, in fact, Aboriginal women and men could face charges of immorality under the Indian Act for cohabiting, and an undetermined number were actually jailed.[20] By the Second World War, the Indian department had been forced to abandon this draconian approach. Agent Edwards of Kenora wrote in 1941 that the agents had ceased to jail people for living common-law because they "found [they] did not have the right to imprison treaty Indians for things that others could legally do."[21] But this recognition came too late for those charged in the 1920s and 1930s.

Echoes of the campaign can be heard in Daly's and Lewis' records, although apparently neither of them actually jailed anyone for simple cohabitation outside marriage. This was another area in which agents enjoyed wide discretionary latitude, and neither Daly nor Lewis was prepared to take drastic steps in defence of church marriage. In fact, Lewis seems to have done as little as possible much of the time, resisting pressure to adopt a more activist position. The Jesuits at Wikwemikong made repeated efforts to engage Lewis in their own drive to prevent separation, divorce, and non-marital cohabitation. Some chiefs and councils joined in these efforts, perhaps at the behest of their missionaries. When informal social pressure and church-based regulatory forms failed to part a determined couple, attempts were made to call in the Indian agent, who had much more effective forms of power at his disposal. While Daly and Lewis both clearly believed that they were responsible for discouraging immorality, they also preferred to avoid interference in personal matters.

Older Anishinabe[22] marital practices had permitted divorce and/or remarriage when a conjugal relationship broke down completely.[23] Although Christianity had had a significant impact on Aboriginal social systems, some individuals continued to leave unhappy relationships and form new ones, to the dismay of the missionaries. In a study of his order's Aboriginal missions, Jesuit historian Julien Paquin asserted that this pattern was widespread among the Anishinabek around Georgian Bay: "Separated wives and husbands living in concubinage [common-law relationships] were a common feature in the parish."[24] If those concerned were typically married to others, as the term "separated" suggests, their choice to cohabit would not represent an outright rejection of Christian marriage. Rather, they had married their first partners by Christian rites, but when they decided to end these relationships and start new ones, the church's refusal of divorce forced them to flout its precepts.

The persistence of this practice highlights First Nations people's ongoing resistance to assimilative efforts and to the interventions of missionaries and government officials. Both women and men sometimes left their marriages for new partners, and they often withstood considerable pressure in doing so. Many such couples refused to separate in spite of numerous efforts to break them up. Daly, characteristically, took a more activist tack than Lewis: he expelled at least one couple from his agency for living together out of wedlock, and he compelled two other couples to get married, apparently because the two women were pregnant.[25] He also moved to *prevent* one couple from marrying formally in order to prevent bigamy, since the woman had a husband who was still alive.[26]

Lewis clearly disapproved of extramarital sexuality, especially when it took the form of adultery, and he was particularly censorious when women were unfaithful to their husbands. On the other hand, he was also reluctant to intervene directly in such cases. In one instance, in fact, he left an unmarried couple alone, despite community pressure to separate them. The agent knew that this man and woman had been together for many years and would have liked to marry, but the man had a wife who was still alive. Since they had children and were pursuing a long-term, monogamous relationship that conformed to the characteristics of Christian conjugal relationships, Lewis saw no good reason to force them apart.[27]

There are also many instances in this agent's records of adulterous couples evading his rather half-hearted efforts to make them separate. Often couples simply ignored pressure to end their relationships or moved somewhere else to evade it. If both belonged to the same band and lived on that band's reserve, there was little the agent could do, besides refusing them any kind of assistance and possibly withholding treaty and annuity payments. Similarly, off-reserve residence probably removed them from the risk of DIA discipline. But if either lived on a reserve where they were not a band member, they could be expelled by the agent. Lewis threatened a number of couples with expulsion, but seems to have stopped short at threats.[28] In September 1923 he promised the chief of the Whitefish River band that he was sending a provincial constable to the reserve to deal with "the different Indians living in adultery," but there is no record of the outcome in this case.[29] Since there was further correspondence about unmarried couples cohabiting, this measure obviously failed to have the desired effect. For the most part, those living on relatively isolated reserves could easily escape policing by disappearing whenever any authorities entered the community.

There is only one example in this agent's records of punishment meted out for extramarital cohabitation. Lewis did not frame this action as a punishment, even though the woman concerned may well have perceived it as such. In this instance, Lewis reacted negatively when he discovered a woman of his agency "living an immoral life with a Whiteman." He had visited the woman's home to take her daughters back to residential school, and he took away the youngest daughter too, claiming that she "could not be left with the mother under such undesirable living conditions."[30] This woman did not wish her children to be returned to the residential school, and now she was being punished by the loss of the last remaining daughter. The removal may have been unfortunate indeed for the young girl, given the conditions of the residential schools, and it was probably painful for the mother. While the agent's explanation of his action did not cite the goal of ending the "immoral" relationship, the effect remained disciplinary.[31] Not only did the mother lose her children, but the girls were subjected to the moral surveillance and discipline of the residential school. Underlying Lewis' actions was the assumption that the school would produce chaste, assimilated young women who had internalized the Euro-Canadian Christian moral code.

Ironically, the Indian Act itself, thanks to its patriarchal provisions, provided First Nations women with a strong incentive to avoid formal marriage with men who lacked Indian status. If a woman with Indian status married a white man or a non-status Aboriginal man, she lost her own status, and with it a number of important benefits such as the right to live on an Indian reserve. Any children from the marriage also lost status. Aboriginal leaders in Ontario had complained about the impact of this provision as early as 1878, pointing out that First Nations women who married white men were struck off the paylist, but if they lived common-law with the same man, they continued to draw their annuity and interest payments.[32] Even marrying a status Indian from another band involved losses, since wives became members of their husbands' bands and lost membership in their own. For women, then, it sometimes made more social and economic sense to live common-law than to marry, at least for those who were aware of the liability of marrying non-treaty men or those from other bands.

Although First Nations people were generally not well-informed about the provisions of the very lengthy Indian Act, apparently some women *were* aware of this particular issue. Aboriginal scholar Kim Anderson recounts an incident related by a woman she interviewed, whose mother had advised her at the age of twelve about the disabilities the Indian Act imposed on women. As Gertie Beaucage told the story, her mother gave her a copy of the Indian Act and discussed its implications with her: "She said it would probably not be a good idea to get married ... And she said, 'Look in there further, and realize that if you marry somebody from another reserve, then you have to go over there. You lose your right even to be buried here amongst your own family.' That's how much the *Indian Act* affected us."[33]

In some cases, then, the Indian Act actually fostered a practice of avoiding legal marriage in order to escape the consequences imposed for marrying outside one's own community. This means that for some women, cohabiting outside marriage was an act of economic and social self-interest. It may also have been an act of resistance to Euro-Canadian patriarchal gender relations as imposed by the Indian Act, particularly its insistence that women assume the status of their husbands.

Liaisons with White Men

The DIA did not have a discernible policy on interracial relationships, and the issue undoubtedly caused some unease. As government officials living in local communities, Indian agents were located within two related but competing discourses about First Nations people. On the one hand, they were socialized into the long-standing DIA discourse that constructed Aboriginal people as culturally inferior to Euro-Canadians but capable of "civilization." This ideology prescribed a future of total assimilation into the mainstream population, despite many quiet doubts about the feasibility of this project. At the same time, the agents lived in Euro-Canadian communities that nurtured their own notions about First Nations people. The local discourses of these particular communities have not been closely studied as yet, but it can be assumed that, as in many other Canadian towns and small cities, ideas about Aboriginal difference played an important role in the symbolic ordering of social relations and the construction of a local Euro-Canadian identity.[34] Since Lewis and Daly lived in different communities – Lewis in Manitowaning on Manitoulin Island, and Daly in Parry Sound on the eastern shore of Georgian Bay – they may have been located within slightly different, historically and geographically specific, forms of racism. Nonetheless, it is likely that in both towns, Aboriginal people were perceived as irrevocably different from and inferior to Euro-Canadians, and that assimilation through intermarriage was considered undesirable. These local discourses were thus significantly at odds with the constructs and goals of the DIA, particularly in their rejection of racial integration. In their correspondence, the agents were careful to underline their commitment to the DIA's goals, but as members of Euro-Canadian communities they cannot have been immune to the views of their peers.

Agents faced a certain dilemma, then, in handling the question of relationships between First Nations women and white men. Their own local societies would disapprove of these liaisons and perhaps even pressure the agent to police racial boundaries. But the department's policy of assimilation would be furthered by lasting interracial relationships. In keeping with racial ideology, white men were also supposed to be better husbands and breadwinners. Daly conspired on one occasion to prevent a marriage between a favourite young woman and an Aboriginal man, on the premise that the latter would be a poor provider and would lower her status. A white man, by contrast, would confer higher status, perhaps even something close to "white" status. This young Cree woman, Emily Donald, was an orphan who had been raised in the St. John's Indian residential school in Chapleau. When she graduated, the principal sent her to Daly as a schoolteacher. Daly took a close interest in her, treating her in many ways like his own daughter. This personal relationship explains the particular interest Daly took in her marriage plans. Nevertheless, his words on this subject convey a clear sense of his beliefs about the relative merits of white and Aboriginal husbands. Daly wrote that he saw in Emily Donald "the possibilities of rising above the status that she has come from," and he regretted the thought that, by marrying an Aboriginal man, "she would be dragged down again."[35]

Committed interracial relationships crossed racial boundaries that most Euro-Canadians wished to see rigorously maintained. The agents must have been aware of the general social disapproval of such relationships, but they apparently did not consider it part of their duty to regulate them – as Emily Donald's case illustrates, the agents may have been in favour of white husbands for at least some Aboriginal women. Moreover, these relationships advanced the most important objectives of Indian policy. When a First Nations woman entered into legal marriage with a white man, she ceased to be an Indian within the meaning of the Indian Act. The avowed goal of DIA policy was to reduce the "Indian" population continually, through enfranchisement and intermarriage, until there were no status Indians left. Thus the trickle of women who took white husbands served DIA purposes, especially when they moved into white communities and joined the cultural mainstream.

This consideration may explain an otherwise remarkable fact: no DIA record examined for this study makes any direct reference to the impact of the Indian Act on women who married outside their own communities. Officials never discussed the economic and other disadvantages the act imposed on women who married white men, particularly the permanent exile from their home communities that it created. Possibly they did not always enforce this exile – Daly, for example, wrote of one widow that she could "claim membership in the Mud Lake Band" if the other members would accept her back.[36] The one question they did discuss in correspondence was the compensation provided under the act for the loss of treaty and interest payments. Women who lost their status through marriage were supposed to receive "commutation" of their treaty and interest payments. That means they would receive a lump sum of money representing their per capita share of the band funds and ten years' worth of treaty annuity payments (for bands that had treaties and annuities). It is not clear if this practice was always followed, but some women in Lewis' agency requested and received it. In some cases, Lewis first inquired into the character of the woman's husband, and at least once he refused to grant the commutation on the grounds that the husband would spend all the money.[37] Instead, the woman apparently continued to receive the payments annually – something normally accorded only to band members with status.

This example once again demonstrates the fundamentally problematic operation of the DIA system in this period. The Indian Act prescribed that band membership would be lost, along with Indian status, but in practice the Indian agents retained the discretionary power to alter that dispensation. Although the long-term outcome may be considered positive for the woman concerned (or for her descendants), it is worth noting that she did not receive what she had asked for at the time, namely the lump-sum commutation to which she was entitled by the Indian Act upon her loss of status.

Promiscuity and Prostitution

Promiscuity and prostitution represented the most egregious offences against Euro-Canadian Christian morality. There is more evidence of such allegations in Lewis' records than in Daly's. There are two possible reasons for this disparity, both of which are probably relevant. One is the fact that the surviving record base for Daly's agency consists of what I call the Franz Koennecke Collection, an extensive but incomplete set of photocopies, made in the early 1980s by researcher Franz Koennecke from the original collection of agency records held by the DIA. The original records apparently no longer exist (at least, the DIA is unable to locate them, and they have not been transferred to the National Archives), so it is impossible to know exactly what is missing.

The second important factor is that Lewis' agency contained a large mission station of the Jesuits, who were highly vigilant about matters of morality and sexuality, and who communicated relatively frequently with the agent about these issues. In Daly's agency, by contrast, the missionary presence was intermittent rather than constant. Even when women were accused of these scandalous forms of sexual disorder, Lewis was reluctant to intervene. Again, he sent some threatening letters warning women to mend their ways, and on one occasion he sent a provincial constable to investigate the circumstances of a woman accused of prostitution. But when the constable left without taking any action, the agent apparently let the matter drop.[38] He also wrote to one band secretary that a woman could not be convicted "on public gossip of the village," but that evidence had to be provided of her wrongdoing.[39] This agent was clearly cautious about such accusations and perhaps aware of internal dissension among some communities. On the other hand, he promised to lay criminal charges against the woman if there was actual evidence. It does not appear that any was provided.

Despite their task of regulating sexuality, agents' correspondence placed greater emphasis on their role in providing social services and their responsibility to prevent actual destitution. For example, Lewis' correspondence with a young, unmarried woman who had three children reveals a combination of moral reproof and financial aid. This young woman had apparently been left to make her own way until the Depression, and she must have had a hard time, surviving mainly by taking in other people's laundry. Lewis' words suggest that he had scolded her before: "She will not take warning and still at times harbours white men around her house."[40] In the economic crisis of the 1930s, the laundry business could no longer supply enough to feed the family, and the young mother's appeal for help did bring her some minimal relief from the agent. Lewis took the opportunity to chastise her again, in terms that combined disapproval with some level of sympathy: "It seems lamentable for a girl to become in a position that you are in, unmarried with a large family of children without any means of support, and now I think it is time that you should try and make a better success of life."[41] But Lewis sent an initial supply of food and undoubtedly secured for her the DIA's standard, very low relief ration for the remainder of the economic crisis. The DIA's patriarchal ideology of protecting women and children could ward off punishment for such women and gain them minimal levels of financial support, especially in the Depression. Indeed, in the tough times of the 1930s, agents were heavily occupied with providing relief and dealing with the economic crisis, and sexual regulation seems to have taken a back seat.

On one occasion, this agent did resort to exceedingly harsh measures. In the most severe case that appears in his records, Lewis apparently laid vagrancy charges against a young woman, who was sent to jail for six months.[42] After her release, the agent attempted to have her committed to a poorhouse, preferably one nearby. When he could not locate an appropriate local institution, he had her committed to the Hospital for the Insane in Toronto, far from her home.[43] His rather extreme actions in this case appear to have been shaped by his perception that the girl was disabled (she was mute) and therefore not fully responsible for her actions. It was necessary to put a stop to the immoral life he claimed she was leading, and his solution was incarceration, probably for a lengthy period. Here disability, as well as race, seems to have conditioned the agent's response to the challenge this young woman posed to the existing gender and sexual order. Although Lewis' letters suggest that he viewed his actions as a means of protecting the young woman from herself, they could only appear highly punitive to her.

Clearly, then, women could face tough punishment for perceived sexual transgressions. Yet as a rule, Lewis' handling of promiscuity was relatively mild and non-interventionist compared with that of other agents, who were less hesitant to send women to prison.[44] And like many other authorities, Lewis always favoured a first line of defence in which women's sexuality was contained within the family, either by ensuring legal marriage or by engaging families to discipline young women. For the mute girl who was institutionalized, for instance, Lewis would have preferred the solution of returning the offender to her grandfather's home. Only when he was certain that the grandfather could not exercise the necessary control did he resort to institutional incarceration.

Marriage also remained an important form of containment, even when women were mistreated by their husbands. One woman, for example, appealed to Lewis for financial aid to help raise her children in the Depression. Lewis responded that she should be living with her husband, even though the latter had served a term in jail for assaulting her. The agent refused financial aid on the grounds that the woman should repair her marriage and live with her husband: "As [this man] and his wife are both enjoying good health and [are] well able to work I cannot see any reason why they cannot support the other two children [two were in residential school] if they would only live and work together as man and wife should."[45] These views were consonant with Euro-Canadian views on gender and marital relations at the time, but they probably did not match Anishinabe values, especially the right of the woman to end a relationship without moral sanction.

Conclusion

Indian agents took their role in regulating gender and sexuality seriously and adhered to the DIA ideology that assumed inferior morality among First Nations people. On the other hand, their paternalistic, custodial role prescribed a protective approach that often tempered their use of the most coercive provisions available in the Indian Act. Undoubtedly their own writings do not document many of the informal disciplinary measures they applied to Aboriginal women and men. In addition, these records provide no information about the kinds of illicit relationships the agents themselves may have pursued with First Nations women. Inevitably, some of these men must have become involved with Aboriginal women – one Ontario agent in the 1920s is known to have run off with a young woman of his agency, and others may have engaged in shorter-term affairs.[46] These matters are important, and their likelihood must be acknowledged here, but one would have to conduct oral history to obtain more concrete evidence of sexual relationships between agents and First Nations women.

In the 1920s and 1930s, women of all races and ethnicities were objects of scrutiny regarding their sexual behaviour. For First Nations women, there were two factors that made their experience distinctive. First, they were subject to racial stereotyping that constructed them as generally sexually immoral and debased. Second, they were exposed to significantly intensified levels of surveillance by the Indian agents. In the agents, First Nations women encountered a designated authority whose job was to oversee their lives and promote their transformation into imitations of the ideal middle-class Euro-Canadian woman. Thanks to the multiplicity of the agents' roles in the Indian Affairs system, these men had an exceptional capacity to regulate and discipline First Nations women. To a limited extent, Aboriginal women could insulate themselves from the dominant society and thus from that society's negative opinions of them. But most had to reckon with the Indian agent and with the very real economic and social power he could wield over them.

Acknowledgments
I would like to thank the Social Sciences and Humanities Research Council of Canada for its financial support during the research on which this chapter is based. In addition, I am grateful to the women who gave comments on various versions of this chapter that I gave as conference presentations, particularly those at the Twelfth Berkshire Conference on the History of Women held at the University of Connecticut at Storrs in 2002.

Notes
1 This reserve is also called Cape Croker and is now known as the Chippewas of Nawash First Nation.
2 Duncan Campbell Scott to Mrs. A., 15 October 1924, Record Group (RG) 10, vol. 7490, file 25008-4, pt. 1, Library and Archives Canada (LAC). The husband, a veteran of the First World War, had received a Soldier Settlement loan to start a farm on the reserve. The program involved the DIA in more direct control of reserve lands, at least those owned by

soldier settlers, because it could foreclose the loan and sell the farm and equipment, though the land could be sold only to fellow band members. For more on this program, see Robin Brownlie, "Work Hard and Be Grateful: Native Soldier Settlers in Ontario after the First World War," in *On the Case: Explorations in Social History,* ed. Franca Iacovetta and Wendy Mitchinson, 183-203 (Toronto: University of Toronto Press, 1998).

3 The letter to Mrs. A. was in a case file kept to track the husband's Soldier Settlement loan from the DIA, but there was no similar letter to him in the file. Since all DIA correspondence with this man was supposed to be in his case file, it appears that no letter was sent to him on this subject. The Indian agent, who had asked the department to warn the woman *and* her husband, blamed both spouses equally for their marital troubles.

4 Margaret Hillyard Little, "'A Fit and Proper Person': The Moral Regulation of Single Mothers in Ontario, 1920-1940," in *Gendered Pasts: Historical Essays in Femininity and Masculinity in Canada,* ed. N.M. Forestell, K. McPherson, and C. Morgan, 123-38 (Don Mills, ON: Oxford University Press, 1999), 130-33.

5 See, for example, R.J. Lewis to Mothers' Allowance Commission, 7 March 1924, and Lewis to Rev. T.A. Desautels, SJ, 29 May 1924, RG 10, vol. 10601, LAC.

6 See, for example, Jean Barman, "Taming Aboriginal Sexuality: Gender, Power, and Race in British Columbia, 1850-1900," *BC Studies* 115/116 (Autumn/Winter 1997-98): 237-66; Sarah Carter, *Capturing Women: The Manipulation of Cultural Imagery in Canada's Prairie West* (Montreal and Kingston: McGill-Queen's University Press, 1997); Joan Sangster, *Regulating Girls and Women: Sexuality, Family, and the Law in Ontario, 1920-1960* (Toronto: Oxford University Press, 2001), Chapter 6; Adele Perry, *On the Edge of Empire: Gender, Race, and the Making of British Columbia, 1849-1871* (Toronto: University of Toronto Press, 2001); as well as several other chapters in this volume.

7 For excellent analyses of these stereotypes and their political uses, see Sarah Carter, *Capturing Women: The Manipulation of Cultural Imagery in Canada's Prairie West* (Montreal and Kingston: McGill-Queen's University Press, 1997); and Sherene H. Razack, "Gendered Racial Violence and Spatialized Justice: The Murder of Pamela George," in *Race, Space and the Law: Unmapping a White Settler Society,* ed. Sherene H. Razack, 121-56 (Toronto: Between the Lines, 2002).

8 For example, in his book *The Canadian Indian,* published in 1969, journalist Fraser Symington uses "squaw" habitually to refer to Aboriginal women. Although the book is riddled with stereotyped images and notions, Symington clearly did not intend to deride First Nations people in general.

9 Many examples could be cited, but a few will suffice to make the point. Annuity and interest payments were paid to the male head of the family, who received his wife's share as well as those of the couple's children. Loans from band funds or federal coffers were made only to men. Decisions about the use of band-owned resources such as timber and minerals were made by the band council, which was exclusively male and elected by the male band members.

10 R.J. Lewis to DIA, 9 December 1921, RG 10, vol. 10593, LAC.

11 See David D. Smits, "The 'Squaw Drudge': A Prime Index of Savagism," *Ethnohistory* 29, 4 (1982): 281-306. For images in the late-nineteenth-century prairie West, see Carter, *Capturing Women.*

12 See Rayna Green's much-cited article, "The Pocahontas Perplex: The Image of Indian Women in American Culture," in *Unequal Sisters: A Multicultural Reader in U.S. Women's History,* ed. Ellen Carol DuBois and Vicki L. Ruiz, 15-21 (New York: Routledge, 1990). For the Canadian context, there are useful discussions in Janice Acoose/Misko-Kìsikàwihkwè (Red Sky Woman), *Iskwewak – Kah' Ki Yaw Ni Wahkomakanak: Neither Indian Princesses nor Easy Squaws* (Toronto: The Women's Press, 1995); and in Kim Anderson, *A Recognition of Being: Reconstructing Native Womanhood* (Toronto: Second Story Press, 2000).

13 A.D. Moore to DIA, 9 October 1924, RG 10, vol. 7490, file. 25008-4, pt. 1, LAC.

14 Lewis to Rev. B.P. Fuller, Shingwauk Home, Sault Ste. Marie, 20 June 1921, RG 10, vol. 10591, LAC.

15 See Jo-Anne Fiske, "Carrier Women and the Politics of Mothering," in *Rethinking Canada: The Promise of Women's History,* 4th ed., ed. Veronica Strong-Boag, Mona Gleason, and Adele Perry, 235-48 (Don Mills: Oxford University Press, 2002).

16 Daly to DIA, 19 July 1932; Daly to DIA, 14 November 1932, Franz Koennecke Collection (henceforth FKC), Wasauksing First Nation. The Franz Koennecke Collection is an extensive set of photocopies from the old Shannon Files of the Department of Indian Affairs, representing the correspondence and other papers of Indian agent John M. Daly, as well as of other agents from the Parry Sound agency. They were gathered by the late Franz Koennecke in the course of preparing his master's thesis on the history of the Parry Island (Wasauksing) Reserve. Most of them relate to Parry Island itself, but some relate to other reserves in the area.

17 Daly to DIA, 14 November 1932, FKC.

18 H.J. Eade to Daly, 14 September 1933, FKC.

19 Harold Cardinal, "Hat in Hand: The Long Fight to Organize," in *The Unjust Society: the Tragedy of Canada's Indians*, 96-106 (Edmonton: MG Hurtig, 1969), 98-99.

20 Sangster, *Regulating Girls and Women*, 178-79.

21 Ibid., 179. Aboriginal people in the interwar period, then, had been much more harshly regulated than non-Natives, who could not be jailed for extramarital cohabitation.

22 By *Anishinabe*, I mean the cultures of the Ojibway, Odawa, and Potawatomi people who constituted almost all the people in Lewis' agency and the large majority of Daly's (the only major exception was the Gibson Band in the Parry Sound agency, which consisted of Mohawks who had moved to the Georgian Bay area from Kanehsatake in the 1880s). The term *Anishinabek* is the plural, meaning "people," and can be used to refer either to First Nations people in general, or to the Ojibway, Odawa, and Potawatomi in particular.

23 See, for example, Ruth Landes, *The Ojibwa Woman* (New York: W.W. Norton and Co., 1971), 51-123.

24 Father Julien Paquin, SJ, "Modern Jesuit Indian Missions in Ontario," p. 134, unpublished manuscript, n.p., n.d., Jesuit Province of Upper Canada Archives, Regis College (Toronto).

25 Daly to H.J. Eade, 14 October 1933; Daly to DIA, 21 April 1933, FKC.

26 Daly's action to prevent the wedding was recorded in his correspondence with the Indian agent at Rama Reserve, A.S. Anderson. Daly told Anderson that he had notified the town clerk not to issue a marriage licence and was trying to contact the United Church minister to prevent him from marrying them, at least until Daly had a chance to object. He also promised to get the Parry Island constable and "root them out of there." Daly to A.S. Anderson, 5 August 1933, FKC.

27 Lewis to DIA, 15 January 1933, RG 10, vol. 10627, LAC.

28 See, for example, Lewis to Mary Jane E., 9 August 1922, RG 10, vol. 10595, LAC; Lewis to Mr. James N., 15 May 1923, RG 10, vol. 10599, LAC; Lewis to Mr. Joseph A., 12 August 1924, vol. 10601, LAC.

29 Lewis to Mr. Gregor McGregor, 10 September 1923, RG 10, vol. 10599, LAC.

30 Lewis to DIA, 14 October 1924, RG 10, vol. 10603, LAC.

31 The fact that the relationship was interracial may have been an additional factor incurring Lewis' disapproval. But this woman appears elsewhere in the records accused of immoral or suspect behaviour (including excessive mobility), and it was probably her reputation with the agent which determined his view that the home was immoral.

32 Peter S. Schmalz, *The Ojibwa of Southern Ontario* (Toronto: University of Toronto Press, 1991), 200. Schmalz is summarizing comments made at a meeting of the Grand General Indian Council of Ontario in 1878.

33 Anderson, *A Recognition of Being*, 122.

34 For an excellent discussion of these processes in a contemporary rural Canadian community, see Elizabeth Furniss, *The Burden of History: Colonialism and the Frontier Myth in a Rural Canadian Community* (Vancouver: UBC Press, 1999), esp. Chapter 5, "Indians, Whites, and Common-Sense Racism."

35 Daly to Rev. Vale, principal of St. John's Indian Residential School (Chapleau), 15 March 1933, FKC.

36 Daly to V.M. Eastwood, 24 January 1935, FKC. This woman had been married to a non-treaty Aboriginal man and thus, under the Indian Act, would have lost her status. Daly's comment suggests that the band may have been given the informal authority to reinstate her membership. Presumably this could occur only if the local agent chose not to challenge the reinstatement.

37 R.J. Lewis to DIA, 17 December 1921, RG 10, vol. 10593, LAC.
38 Lewis to Rev. G.A. Artus, Wikwemikong, 18 March 1922, ibid.
39 Lewis to William Kinoshameg, secretary of the Manitoulin Island Unceded Band, 6 April 1922, RG 10, vol. 10595, LAC.
40 Lewis to Miss Annie K., 28 September 1932, RG 10, vol. 10627, LAC.
41 Ibid.
42 Lewis to DIA, 4 March 1933, RG 10, vol. 10629, LAC. The vagrancy provisions of the Criminal Code were used to punish women involved in prostitution, since prostitution itself was not against the law.
43 Lewis to DIA, 15 May 1933, ibid.
44 See Sangster, *Regulating Girls and Women*, 168-94.
45 Lewis to DIA, 3 August 1933, RG 10, vol. 10629, LAC.
46 For the Indian agent who quit his position and went off with a young woman from his agency, see RG 10, file 25008-13, pt. 1, LAC.

8
Domesticating Girls: The Sexual Regulation of Aboriginal and Working-Class Girls in Twentieth-Century Canada
Joan Sangster

Creating "proper" and moral families was an integral part of early-twentieth-century Canadian nation building, a project that appeared to link social reformers' efforts to domesticate and "civilize" both the working class and Native peoples. Christian missionaries consciously linked these goals, claiming that "the Indian ... like the German or Irish immigrant" was "a human with the same right to live a decent, honest, industrious life, to become a good citizen, with a clean, moral character." Like white ethnics, the Indian was to be assimilated and civilized through charity, uplift, "manual training and character building," with boys becoming "self-independent" and girls directed toward marriage.[1] Colonial rule directed at First Nations peoples through residential schools, domestic science teachers on reserves, and coercive legal attempts to remake the Indian family parallelled attempts to "Canadianize" non-Anglo immigrants by changing their language and culture, and also efforts to alter the lazy and immoral character of working-class delinquents in industrial schools. A minority of more biologically determinist reformers trained their sights on more drastic solutions such as sterilization, with the latter used in the Canadian West disproportionately on immigrant, working-class, and Aboriginal children.[2]

The dominant themes of early-twentieth-century social reform thus appeared to sweep up both working-class and Native families in a common project of regeneration,[3] the goal of which was to create "heteronorms"[4] characterized by marriage and monogamy, male breadwinning/female domesticity, and premarital female sexual purity. This chapter attempts to question both colonial and classed dimensions of sexual regulation in mid-twentieth-century Canada by examining how Native and working-class girls were targeted as sexual problems by the law, the state, social reformers, even their own families and, as a result, found themselves incarcerated in training schools. What were the overlapping reasons for labelling white and Native girls "delinquent," and which strategies were used to reshape their behaviour? Did different rationales and tactics, shaped by the politics of racism, characterize the treatment of Native girls? Drawing on both anti-colonial and materialist-feminist theory stressing the "intersectionality" of gender, race, and class,[5] I use three keywords – domesticity, femininity/purity, and honest labour – to exemplify the reform agenda of one Ontario training school dedicated to transforming both the visible behaviour and interior sensibilities of girls deemed incorrigible. While attention to the specificity, complexities, and contradictions of gender oppression, class exploitation, and colonialism is essential, we also need to reflect on the training school project as a whole, explaining the visible and not-so-visible connections between cultural definitions of "proper" sexuality and the material conditions of their possibility, between the discursive practices of sexual regulation and the distorting social structures of Canadian society.

Putting Sex in Context

Recent historical writing has shown that attempts to regulate sexuality were never a one-way street of class or state control; sexual regulation assumed a multitude of medical, legal, and social forms that crossed the boundaries of state and civil society, and was shaped by changing relations of race, class, and gender, including relations of resistance. However, scholarship has often concentrated *either* on colonialism, especially in the period of contact during the eighteenth and nineteenth centuries, *or* on working-class sexuality in the twentieth century,[6] in part because of the discrete projects of historical excavation involved, in part because, by the time postcolonialism became a preoccupation, class was increasingly marginalized in intellectual inquiry. Even recent works claiming to link class and colonialism often explore the *languages,* not the structures, of class.[7] Indeed, the trajectory of scholarly writing on sexuality since the 1960s reflects the initial theoretical/political embrace of feminism, historical materialism, and structuralism, followed by a decided movement toward Foucauldian, poststructuralist, and postcolonial approaches by the 1990s. Feminists, as Rosemary Hennessy notes, are now concerned more with cultural articulations of sexual identity than with the connections between "capitalist profit and sexual pleasure."[8]

A renewed interest in exploring the sexual frontiers of empire has been stimulated by the anti-racist challenges of whiteness studies, by demands that historians interrogate "race" more critically, by "third world" critiques of white Western feminists' inability to truly "hear" subaltern voices, and, finally, by the theoretical linkages proposed between poststructuralist views of sexuality and colonial studies, with Ann Laura Stoler's insightful evaluation of Foucault an exemplar of this trend.[9] Although some colonial studies argue white women created distinct, even less exploitative, intimate relations with indigenous peoples, more often they "divest [white women] of this innocence,"[10] arguing they occupied, at best, an "ambiguous"[11] or, at worst, a collaborative role in the cruelties of colonialism. White women buttressed and brokered European expansion and internal settler colonialism; the construction of their respectability/superiority was inseparable from the negative sexual "othering" of indigenous women, and they were used both to stave off miscegenation and "tame" men in danger of going "Native."[12]

Yet a binary perspective can emerge from the "current moralistic strain in feminist criticism" of white women's complicity in colonialism, argues Amy Kaplan.[13] Trying to avoid a polarized view of white versus colonized womanhood, some authors have explored the contradictory politics of white women dedicated to anti-colonial struggles,[14] or they have stressed the need to situate colonialism within wider, complex "relations of power and ruling," including social relations of class. Himani Bannerji's critical commentary on the prevailing "binary" bias of postcolonial studies, juxtaposing the "colonizing self vs colonial other, subsuming social relations under linguistic signs," urges us to avoid an "undifferentiated category of colonized/ colonizer," which ignores the larger canvas of social relations, "relegating gender and class to a black hole"[15] Some materialist critics of postcolonial "culturalism" go even further: imperialism, they remind us, has a *history*, which was, and is, inextricably connected to exploitative global relations of capital, labour regimes, and the state, whether colonial or neocolonial. If we are to understand sexual and familial regulation, we must also interrogate these patterns of power, showing their close imbrication.[16] At the same time, we need to avoid a transhistorical "globalization" of postcolonial theory, locating the distinct patterns of North American colonialism and racism in historical time and place.[17] Similar cautions are pertinent to some studies of working-class sexuality, which also run the risk of severing questions of identity from the lived, material realities framing identity, assuming, as some critics charge, that social transformation can be "simply cultural."[18]

One way to examine the patterns of sexual regulation shaped by gender, class, and colonialism is to examine anti-delinquency work in a correctional institution in which a majority group of white, working-class girls was slowly augmented, over two decades, by Native girls. Understanding the political, social, and economic context, the "wider relations of ruling," framing these changes is crucial. First, one reason that Native girls were increasingly enmeshed in this correctional system, their fate intertwined with that of white, working-class and poor girls, was the historically specific impact of advanced mid-twentieth-century colonialism, designated a dark period of "displacement and assimilation" by the Royal Commission on Aboriginal Peoples. Although the roots of the problem lay in the earlier dislocations of the white settler economy and later crises such as the Great Depression, economic shifts in the post-Second World War period put especially severe stresses on Native peoples, leading to a period of "economic and welfare dependency."[19] Economic marginalization intensified with the "renewed capitalization, mechanization, and the de-casualization of labour that was associated with resource development, especially in northern Ontario in the 1950s and 1960s."[20] Reserve economies struggled, traditional subsistence was imperilled, and an already precarious relationship to the market economy deteriorated, especially for the burgeoning number of Native migrants moving from rural to urban contexts, unable to find work. The situation was worsened by the fixed resource base of reserves and a rapidly growing Native population in the post-Second World War years, not to mention the government's long indifference to reserve economic development – which sometimes included acquiescence to the theft of reserve resources by the private sector.

In response, governments offered a program of "guilt management"[21] that reinforced patterns of dependence; moreover, Native political organization on reserves, influenced by the state's historic search for acquiescent local leaders, sometimes only accentuated internal class and power differentials. These underlying social problems did place some children at risk, which reinforced professionals' tenaciously racist perceptions (already apparent in the residential school project) that Native parents were bad parents and that Native children were better served by removal from their communities. Government and social welfare intervention in Native families accelerated, and though many well-intentioned liberals saw the extension of child welfare practices to Native peoples as a sign of inclusive citizenship, this carried with it intrinsically assimilative, culturally destructive implications, causing untold "pain and humiliation" as children were taken away from families.[22] The state was thus most concerned, on one hand, with capitalist development and efficient labour power, and on the other, with "managing" Native civil society through a myriad of social controls involving everything from liquor to political organization, and including assimilative schooling and the creation of a "stable" Native family.

Working-class and poor girls were also the focus of a project of moral regeneration shaped by mid-twentieth-century optimism concerning economic possibility, coupled with increasing child welfare and state intervention in the family. While the Ontario Training School for Girls (OTSG) was founded in the Depression, the state expanded the institution in subsequent years, encouraged initially by women's charitable/reform groups such as Big Sisters, which endorsed the OTSG as an enterprise of medical treatment, education, and moral redirection for less affluent girls caught up in a cycle of neglect, poverty, and immorality. While Ontario during the Second World War and after has been portrayed as an increasingly affluent society, pockets of abject poverty still existed, and both governments and social welfare experts were even more determined to remove poor, abused, and neglected children to a new institutional environment, breaking the "culture of poverty," creating new moral values, and imparting work skills that could remake the family over time. As one OTSG superintendent noted, the aim was to raise up girls from the "sordid slums" to be "respectable"[23] working-class mothers, workers and citizens.

To suggest overlapping regulatory regimes for Native and white girls is not a simple invocation of hybridity between the colonial and the colonized.[24] It is important to locate the historically specific nature of Canadian colonialism in this period. In contrast to earlier nineteenth-century projects of dispossession in which lands were appropriated – anxieties also related to the lust for land and resources[25] – Ontario governing elites in the mid-twentieth century undoubtedly felt that *this conquest* was "over" and that development could proceed with little opposition. The neocolonial project of managing (read "assimilating") Native peoples now meant completing their "integration" into advanced capitalist society, teaching them the values and skills needed to create proper families and useful work habits. As the urbanization of Native peoples rapidly increased, the much-decried, publicized "crisis" by the 1960s was the "Native person in the city."[26] More attention was focused on Métis, non-status, and status Indians who supposedly occupied "skid row," a perception that homogenized Aboriginal peoples as a perceived underclass in need of reform. Native women were a target of particular scorn, in part because of long-standing racist perceptions of their loose sexuality, and also because they were increasingly "intruding" on "white" space in cities and towns and, as such, needed to be monitored and controlled.[27] It is not surprising, therefore, that the Canadian correctional system increasingly targeted Native girls and women – supposedly to prevent them from "falling into skid row" – who had previously been designated a federal "problem" or been insulated in communities that regulated their own affairs.

A component of this correctional system was the Ontario Training School for Girls, established in 1933 as a secular, state-supported reform school designed to resocialize neglected and delinquent girls, sixteen and under, who were perceived to be on the path to potential adult criminality.[28] Although the majority of girls in conflict with the law were dealt with through probation or suspended sentences, a minority deemed intractable were incarcerated in the OTSG. Their misdeeds included incorrigibility, theft, truancy, and sexual promiscuity, with incorrigibility often connoting running away and libidinal "looseness," supposedly leading to sexual endangerment. As in other juvenile justice regimes across North America, delinquency was defined with immense latitude, and sexual promiscuity (perhaps better termed "sexual nonconformity") was often the precipitating anxiety causing incarceration, even if theft, truancy, or running away were also involved.[29] Girls were sentenced under the federal Juvenile Delinquents Act (JDA, 1908), which forbade infractions of the Criminal Code and local laws, but also defined a delinquent as one *"liable* ... to be committed to an industrial school" (emphasis added) or, in a 1924 amendment, one guilty of "sexual immorality or any similar form of vice." Girls could also be incarcerated under the provincial Training School Act (TSA, 1931, 1939) for simply being "incorrigible and unmanageable,"[30] and this could transpire without a court appearance, merely on the recommendation of a child welfare agency or pressure from relatives, foster parents, or guardians. Native girls' families were also subject to the extra layer of legal control through the Indian Act, with its wide powers of moral surveillance and immense latitude for Indian agents to arrest, judge, and even incarcerate reserve inhabitants.

Though it was premised on a rhetoric of treating problem girls, the juvenile justice regime was paternalistic, if not authoritarian and arbitrary, and resulted in intense surveillance of many working-class and poor children and their families, though some parents welcomed the use of the law as a means of imposing family discipline upon sexually wayward daughters. Once in the OTSG, inmates as young as eleven, but usually fourteen or fifteen on arrival, were offered a "cure" of academic education, vocational training, and character transformation for about twelve to eighteen months, followed by placements (much like parole) as fostered or boarded-out students, or, far more often, as early wage earners, until they finally escaped the scrutiny of the institution when they were twenty-one (later eighteen).[31] Most OTSG girls came from impoverished or working-class backgrounds, and many had witnessed family crises related to violence, mental health, addiction, or family dissolution. The majority were white and Canadian-born, but the number of Native girls – both Aboriginal and Métis – increased steadily after the 1940s,[32] mirroring the growing overincarceration of all Native peoples, as well as the state's increasingly interventionist approach to Native child welfare.[33]

Domesticity
An ideal of domesticity was fundamental to the initial prognosis designating which girls had to be sent to training school and what shape their re-education would take. Even if this ideal no longer embraced a nineteenth-century notion of separate spheres and the spiritual benefits of domesticity, it still embodied the belief that many women would likely be mothers, manage homes, or work as domestics and that they needed to be properly prepared for such work. The ideal also implicitly constituted sexual and familial norms: a nuclear, heterosexual family, female monogamy, and male breadwinning/female homemaking. Domesticity thus signified both the problem *and* the solution, the representation *and* containment of the "cultural and bodily spaces" occupied by delinquent girls.[34]

Sentencing reports for both Native and white girls, usually penned by male and female child welfare and court workers from white, middle-class or middling backgrounds, detailed the degenerate physical and moral conditions of their families as rationales for incarceration. Family morality was considered a key indicator of the girl's future, so much so that girls were sometimes removed so they would not "inherit" parents' morals or "imitate" siblings' behaviour. In the most tragic cases, girls who were sexually abused were removed in order to "reshape" their moral character while male perpetrators were left within the family.

A typical sentencing report detailed the various family members, their conflicts with the law, their failure to hold down jobs, and, most important, their lack of moral fibre. Child welfare and court workers assessing girls' families relied on gossip drawn from various sources, even commenting on the dead: one girl's deceased mother, it was claimed, "was rumoured to be a bad housekeeper and of low mentality ... while her step sister was reported to be a prostitute."[35] Another assessment of a Native girl noted that her family's "church affiliation was not known, however other members of the family have reputation for poor moral standards."[36] Parents were criticized for homes that were too crowded, that allowed children to sleep together, that took in "strange" (non-family) boarders, and especially for domestic dirt: "The house is filthy, deplorable ... mouldy wine glasses everywhere."[37]

In 90 percent of all girls' delinquency, declared one OTSG superintendent, "bad home training" was at fault; it was "parents [who] needed training" to suppress their "physical appetites and vices."[38] Very real problems of domestic poverty and/or neglect quickly became intertwined with judgments about sexual morality. One case condemned an "immoral" mother who was cut off her mother's allowance when she had an illegitimate child with her boyfriend, even though court authorities acknowledged her concern for her children. However, domestic life was characterized by her poverty and absences from the house; her children supposedly "ran wild" in the streets, "playing cowboys and indians to all hours," making noise, begging in public places, and, in the daughters' case, taking money in exchange for sex. Not only was domestic discipline absent, but so too was cleanliness, as the girl had arrived at a charity camp one year "without even a toothbrush" to her name.[39] Similarly, in the case of a Native girl whose reform was deemed a success, the OTSG superintendent noted that her home was "deplorable and immoral," but that the girl now realized she could not return to such "bad people."[40]

Sentencing reports for Native girls did indicate some different designations of domesticity. Reserve homes that were judged clean and respectable were deemed unusual. These families were singled out for praise, but reserve life was more often equated with backwardness, poverty, and alcoholism. Families still engaged in subsistence hunting and fishing were especially problematic because they did not have the proper domestic abode, instead resorting to a "primitive" tent part of the year. The transience of some Native

parents – such as those working on tobacco farms or going hunting season-
ally – was held up as evidence of their failure to create a proper settled
domestic environment for children. Discipline was perceived to be a particular problem, as direct and corporal punishment was usually anathema
to Native parents. This was the consequence of cultural notions of "non-
interference" and "learning by example" in most Native cultures in relation
to child rearing.[41] Native parents who admitted to such "lax" disciplinary
standards, however, were labelled inadequate by white observers. One Native father told a juvenile court judge that his daughter "did not go to school,"
but added, "I can't do anything else than tell her to go to school, if she
doesn't want to listen to me, what can I do?" The Indian agent on this
reserve, however, with decidedly Anglo and middle-class notions of family
discipline, testified against the girl, helping to clinch her incarceration.[42]

The positivist, optimistic view of delinquency reformation that prevailed,
however, maintained that training schools could create a more *competent*
version of domesticity. Girls initially lived in "cottages" modelled on a household, with kitchens and dining rooms so that inmates could practise their
domestic skills on a daily basis. Vocational training in the early years was
often limited to domestic training. Even as options were added, and additional time was spent in academic schooling in the 1950s, domestic training occupied more of a girl's time than any other institutional activity. This
intense program of domesticity was implemented in the OTSG by female
matrons and a superintendent whose own lives usually encompassed a "career," not just domesticity, for the superintendent usually had either social
service training or, later, a university education.

Seen as entirely appropriate for their class and gender background, domestic training was to replace what inmates lacked in their own family
background, to prepare them for motherhood and housekeeping, and to
train them for wage labour. Many girls articulated their desire for other
occupations, such as secretarial or other white-collar work, but were chan-
nelled into the domestic stream. One unhappy inmate's reaction was recorded by the psychiatrist: "She does not want to be a domestic and feels
doomed to this if she stays here."[43] When sent out on "placement" as domestics, girls were to learn the value of wage labour, saving, and budgeting,
but they were also to learn how a "normal, happy family group" (read
"middle-class family") lived.[44] The truth, of course, was that girls working as
domestics were unlikely to be integrated into the family in affective ways.
This was true for both Native and non-Native girls, though the school admitted the former were more difficult to place with non-Native families. It
was often hoped that Native girls would return to their families and reserves
and impart their newly acquired domestic skills to their own children.

Domesticity was always more than a kind of work. The aim was *to domesticate* these girls, a project encoding power and subordination, superiority

and inferiority. Since the early 1900s, domesticity had been central to the education of working-class girls, taming and assimilating indigenous and "foreign" families. Domesticity also had a "direct relation to imperialism and nationalism,"[45] providing a justification for the dispossession and segregation of Native peoples in the nineteenth century, with their "primitive" families and customs. Just as in Africa, a colonial discourse on domesticity relied on images of the wild, the foreign, the untamed, not only within the family, but also as a means of establishing new geographical borders (such as reserves) between citizen and "savage."[46]

Although the context was different in twentieth-century Canada, with the reserve system well-established, domesticity, with its emphasis on a woman's responsibility for family life and her commitment to monogamy, marriage, and motherhood, remained very important. This was promoted as a project of older, educated, moral women helping younger, marginalized women adjust to future work roles, but it was, in fact, a project that reinforced both class and race hierarchies among women, and it never confronted difficult questions of violence *within* the domestic realm, taking for granted a hierarchical distribution of power separating men, women, and girls.

Femininity and Purity

Domesticating girls was also linked to civilizing them, in character and morality, in body and demeanour, which was a second aim of the training school. Welfare, court, and medical assessors who examined delinquent girls looked for their embrace or rejection of feminine manners of politeness, passivity, and cleanliness. Girls who were considered problems were often designated rambunctious, loud, and boisterous, characteristics seen as more masculine than feminine. Their loud and aggressive behaviour, combined with disobedience, was an indication that they would not develop into respectable and respectful adult female citizens, and this persona would certainly inhibit their ability to hold down a job.

Even after a full training-school sentence, penal workers worried that girls would revert to their former selves. One white girl, who was initially cast as too "brash boisterous, [and] does not realize she is rude until checked," was still a concern after her long training-school sentence. "She has developed a veneer of manners," noted a follow-up report, but with too much independence on the outside, "it might crack."[47] Similar fears were articulated about Native girls, who, it was assumed, had special trouble internalizing the moral lessons of the OTSG. "She makes little progress, goes along creating no trouble but absorbs little from the environment," was the pessimistic prognosis for one Native girl,[48] while in another case a Native inmate on placement was dismissed as "a typical Indian who does not understand our moral standards ... although in a supervised home and treated like one of the family, she [still] ... became pregnant."[49]

A belief in deep cultural impoverishment shaped the reform agenda. Poor and Native families were perceived to be *poor in character* as well as poverty-stricken, which resulted in a failure to socialize their daughters to appropriate feminine manners and mores. Workers often made critical comments about appearance and demeanour, an added consideration in the girl's need for retraining. Some welfare and court workers understood the problems of maintaining middle-class standards of cleanliness in working-class, rural, and impoverished households, but many did not. Assessing one unkempt girl, who was stealing from the local market by the time she was nine, just to help feed the family, the intake psychologist described her, with revulsion, as "slovenly and with slow speech ... in keeping with her low mentality."[50] Like adults assessed in forensic psychiatric courts, these girls were judged by "patriarchal and class" assumptions concerning speech, dress, weight, demeanour, and language, which were held by white, middle-class professionals.[51]

Girls were also criticized for being self-pitying, self-centred, duplicitous, and, especially, saucy and rude. Native girls, however, were more likely to be seen as *too* quiet, withdrawn, and "unreachable," the latter a standard characterization of both Métis and Aboriginal girls by many court and penal workers. Employing racist stereotypes, Native girls were also described as "cunning, sneaky, deceitful,"[52] supposedly hiding their true agendas from others. It is true that, once they were in the OTSG, more Native girls used the strategy one Mohawk psychiatrist has called "conservation withdrawal": retreating from hostile surroundings and the alien culture of the school with silent observation and noncommunication.[53] At its worst, this cultural tactic of self-preservation was interpreted by white medical experts as simply low intelligence, and some of these Native girls were transferred to institutions for the mentally retarded. Racist stereotypes thus created different designations for white and Native girls: the former had to quiet down, but the latter were *too* quiet, a sign of cultural inferiority.

Not all Native girls retreated into silence; a few rebelled, as did their white counterparts, by talking back, disobeying orders, running away, or even resorting to violence.[54] Understanding full well the middle-class makeover expected of her, and its dissonance with her life on a reserve, one Native girl retorted to penal workers intent on changing her manners, "I'm no lady!"[55] Despite some inmates' rejection of the training school agenda, penal workers retained a fairly strong belief in the positivist possibilities of actually creating a more feminine character in their charges. The OTSG program of informal activities such as healthy recreation, team sports, games, crafts, music, church going, even military drill was used to create more polite, cooperative, and unaggressive girls. They were also given health, hygiene, and sex education (the latter stressing abstinence), and some received beauty care instruction so they could become better groomed, socially presentable teens. Some community activities with the YWCA or middle-class women's clubs were allowed if they presented appropriate "role models" on display, but along with all these carrots came the stick. Girls were reprimanded or punished for bad behaviour. Failing to obey the smallest rules; using "vile" language, including sex talk; being loud and rambunctious; or, occasionally, meting out violence to their enemies, usually matrons or other inmates, would all bring punitive sanctions.

The attempt to reshape femininity embodied a key part of the reform agenda: changing girls' sexual behaviour. Indeed, boisterousness and aggressiveness also spelled sexual danger. One girl brought to the attention of the court authorities by her own parents was a potential problem because of her aggressive sexual nature: "Her attitudes towards men are very bad, she hangs around beverage rooms, throwing her arms around older men ... behaving in a fashion so as to invite serious sexual difficulties."[56] Moreover, the more contrite a girl was about her sexual misdeeds, the better her chances of release. If she failed to express guilt and remorse about sexual experience, and especially if she bragged about these exploits or claimed she intended to continue them, she was seen as a more serious problem.

Sexual immorality was also closely tied to domesticity. In those inadequate families where licentiousness reigned, girls supposedly never imbibed lessons of purity and self-control. One girl from a deplorable home, noted the court file, never learned proper sexual behaviour from her "low intelligence" father. Rather, says the report in the file, "she admits ... she has been promiscuous with different boys ... and was apprehended for having intercourse with men behind the dance hall, being out all night ... she can hardly be blamed for taking sex intercourse as a matter of indifference other than gratifying her own pleasure and that of her companions ... she was apparently initiated at a young age by her brother."[57] As in other cases, incest was assumed to be *her* moral problem.

In the interwar period, female delinquency was almost synonymous with "sex delinquency," and even after the Second World War, when sexual mores had altered slightly, sexual endangerment, perceived promiscuity, venereal disease, and pregnancies remained key markers of girls' delinquency. Class and race also shaped the treatment of the female delinquent at every stage of her conflict with the law,[58] so much so that these categories were inextricably linked with sexuality, but there is no doubt that sexual nonconformity was one guiding thread in this history. This was apparent, first, in the definitions of delinquency created by experts in the social sciences, social work, and medical/psychological fields, and, second, in the actual implementation of the law through police, courts, probation work, and the training school. "The predominant expression of female delinquency in our society is promiscuous sexual activity,"[59] concluded one such expert, and this view echoed throughout the courts and training schools. Sexual anxieties were often key to incarceration: when a fourteen-year-old Native girl at a residential school was accused of theft, the fact that "she had been found overnight in a cabin" with a man was an important consideration in the judge's sentencing.[60] Some girls were subject to gynecological exams to ascertain their virginity, an invasive practice that continued in the OTSG with regular VD tests – both of these a reminder that attempts to remake girls' femininity/purity were forcefully imprinted on their bodies. OTSG officials were deeply relieved when girls (still under surveillance) married, even at the young age of seventeen; domesticity would "contain" their sexuality as well as provide a vocation and male protection.

Dominant images of sexuality were not simply under control of the experts; they were also embedded in language and everyday experience, articulated in ideology, influencing the way families judged their own daughters. The fact that some families participated in policing daughters, initiating complaints with the police and the courts, emerged from their own embrace of the dominant sexual norms concerning heterosexual monogamy and premarital female purity. Parents who turned in exasperation to state intervention sometimes initiated the court process as a discussion or warning, but quickly found it moving out of their control into the hands of middle-class professionals who commanded more social and moral authority. Others never fully understood the indefinite sentences in training schools that resulted, making their children wards of the state. When parents, white or Native, wrote trying to secure their child's release from the OTSG, their own "deplorable" domestic lives, or presumed lack of intelligence, were then used as reasons not to let the girl return home.

While most studies have explored how working-class parents used the courts to deal with delinquent daughters, some Native parents also used the local Indian agent, police, or Anglo-Canadian courts to try and correct sexually wayward or disobedient daughters. As some First Nations scholars have argued, by the mid-twentieth century, patriarchal values had "worked their way into the fissures and cracks" in Native communities, "exploiting existing divisions" and also reproducing colonial relations of "domination and exclusion" within those communities.[61] When Native parents and guardians residing on reserves (still the majority in this period) used the agent, police, or courts to control daughters, however, they found themselves disadvantaged by the formal and informal paternalism of the Indian Act. Indian agents, for example, might well favour those relatives – like one Christian Native grandmother who took her rebellious granddaughter to juvenile court – who shared *their* moral values.[62]

This latter dynamic speaks to the complications of class and colonialism noted earlier by Bannerji. First, the training school project was not simply one of middle-class control over working-class girls, or white colonialism directed at subjugating Native girls. Power was also articulated by working-class and Native families (and sometimes the girls themselves) through their practical use of the juvenile justice system to control daughters (or their resistance to this system of control). Second, just as working-class families were divided by experts into the "respectable" and the "unworthy," with the latter seen as more hopeless, so too were Native families judged by their proximity to "white," which meant middle-class, norms of behaviour. Native families deemed more "primitive" were treated as if they were just as problematic as those poor white families seen to be inherently depraved, but some "respectable" Native parents, who embraced a work ethic, went to church, and, especially, did not drink, were assumed to provide exemplary moral guidance to their daughters. The social "classification" of Native behaviour and identity, long "central to the process of colonization,"[63] took on more multifarious dimensions than a colonized/colonizer binary. Finally, although Native families were often seen as part of "culturally backward" communities, their perceived cultural "differentness" sometimes became an avenue for their independence or resistance; for example, penal and court workers occasionally let Native families look after their own daughters using "traditional" family and community controls, or they simply gave up on (and left alone) Native girls who went back to their communities.

Descriptions of white girls could also be complicated by perceived ethnic differences. The delinquency of both white and Native girls supposedly emerged from their immersion in a "culture of poverty," a backwardness linked not to biology but to environment. As such, both groups were salvageable through assimilation to new cultural codes. There were common symbols of familial respectability – sobriety, dedication to the work ethic, intact nuclear families, sexual morality – and if Native, non-Anglo, or Anglo families appeared to embrace these norms, the girls were seen as more likely candidates for reform. However, just as Native girls were considered more "unreachable," white girls with southern and eastern European parents were sometimes designated difficult "cultural" problems, as their parents supposedly lacked crucial social skills necessary for good parenting. Ethnocentrism thus reared its head precisely when non-Anglo white parents failed to conform to the desired stereotype of the "hard-working immigrant"; the latter supposedly best approximated anglo and *white* norms necessary to make good citizens. It is also possible that the strong disgust directed at some very poor white families, even their designation as racialized "white trash," betrayed lingering eugenic prejudices (at least until the 1940s) – after all, such eugenic concerns preoccupied North American professionals up until the Second World War.[64] Perhaps poor whites' fall from moral grace was particularly reprehensible because they *were* white, while racist prejudices of the time led authorities to assume that Native families would more likely be less than adequate.

Honest Labour

The complicated, layered designation of delinquents according to ethnicity, race, and class background could be juxtaposed to a recurring concern in each and every case: the fear that girls were not embracing the work ethic. Because of the emphasis in the historical archive left by court and penal workers, as well as by experts and reformers, on the need to control girls' sexuality, historians have stressed this as the raison d'être of training schools. Perhaps, however, this has led us to underestimate the importance of honest labour as a coinciding cure for delinquency. These young girls' bodies were not simply signifiers of errant sexuality; they also became labouring bodies in a correctional system designed to correct profligacy with the work ethic.

Designating one girl as training school material because she "cannot hold a job, will not obey, is out all night"[65] nicely captured the integration of a number of anxieties concerning work, sexuality, and respect for authority. Alarm over girls' propensity to "follow their own rules" often encapsulated linked signs of delinquency: "lazy, saucey and does not want to work."[66] "Shiftless, useless" parents who supposedly would not work[67] were used as a rationale for committing a girl to training school, and learning skills for future work was a reason that other, more "respectable" parents accepted the courts' decisions to send their girls away to training school. One such father declared that he "wanted [his daughter] to be [sent to the Ontario Training School for Girls] and trained for work."[68]

The rejection of honest labour was often linked to concerns about truancy; girls (and boys too) who skipped school would not learn respect for authority, work discipline, and the three Rs – resulting in their becoming unemployables on the welfare rolls rather than good "worker-citizens." Declaring that one white working-class girl was a "regular gypsy" when it came to school attendance (an interesting racialization of her behaviour as well), the court assessment came down in favour of a training school sentence, though certainly her "late nights" out, and one late-night run-in with the police, were important factors as well. This girl's case highlighted juvenile court officers' confused views of wage labour. The mother of this struggling working-class family was condemned for working for wages, not "appreciating how important it is to have a stable home life with the mother at home," while at the same time the court declared the importance of inculcating the work ethic into her daughter.[69] In another sentencing report written by an Indian agent, the claims that the children from one family lived in one or two filthy rooms, did not work, "ran wild ... [and] were not going to school" were contributing factors in the thirteen year old's incarceration after facing petty theft charges.[70]

There were certainly cases where sexual misbehaviour trumped girls' willingness to work. In one case before the Toronto family court, a fourteen year old, already working in a factory during the Second World War, believed that her new wage work also allowed her adult hours and freedom at night. Both her mother and the judge believed that her sexual endangerment was the more important issue, resulting in a training school sentence.[71] A girl's refusal to attend school or hold down a job was often an *added* reason for a training school sentence, revealing fears that her sexual nonconformity would eventually lead to life on the streets and "dishonest" labour in prostitution.

The training school regime also revealed the importance of honest labour to the reform agenda. Referring to a girl sentenced for "incorrigibility," the superintendent concluded that "the best we can do is give her good work habits for later life."[72] Girls provided unpaid labour – everything from scrubbing floors to gardening – to help run the institution itself; this labour was also meant to keep idle hands busy, distract girls from their self-preoccupied teenage ways, and, of course, provide skills for future wage labour. It was understood that these girls might not have the luxury of living a life of domesticity, untouched by paid work. In fact, the class position of most of the girls at the OTSG was made clear by the government's expectation that early wage work *should* be their lot in life. In the interwar years, a high-placed government bureaucrat refused the superintendent funds to continue one or two girls in high school, noting that by the time they were sixteen, they "should be out earning their keep, not on [the] taxpayers bill."[73] Even after the Second World War, when more hours were spent in the academic classroom and a wider range of jobs was available, inmates spent more time at the OTSG in domestic training than any other activity, and their early entry into blue-collar work, domestic labour, and service sector positions was simply taken for granted. Those daring inmates who entertained ideas of becoming lawyers or writers were usually discouraged, if not regarded as wild and fanciful.

Labour was to be valued not only in terms of the skills acquired, but also, crucially, because of the new values embraced as one's own – a commitment to do a job properly, and a willingness to follow a schedule and rules: in short, a *desire* to work. This new work discipline, inscribed upon the body of the delinquent, would help rescue her from a dismal, criminalized future, particularly one in the sex trade. As a superintendent argued in the 1950s, OTSG girls had to learn that "to be constructively busy is *satisfying,* and to finish a difficult task brings a sense of *accomplishment.*" These were part and parcel of a program to "develop a mature and socially acceptable behaviour pattern as a result of this positive training, orderly environment and improved work habits."[74] Ironically, the intense concern about girls' ability to internalize the *pleasure* of honest labour (perhaps replacing the pleasure of sexual encounters)[75] was counterposed to the reality that many came from families where early wage labour was common, and some girls had already shouldered immense work responsibilities, caring for siblings and helping in the home. Some, understandably, wanted to avoid the drudgery of work, extending their youth as long as possible.

Girls in the OTSG worked toward their ultimate release by progressing through a hierarchy of tasks, both academic and vocational, earning bows of different colours, which culminated in their placement in the community. While some of the younger girls were boarded out or went back to school, the majority performed some kind of wage labour, either part or full time. Thus graduation from the training school and girls' partial freedom were equated with their ability to take on honest labour; exhibit obedience, politeness, and deference to employers; and act with some feminine comportment. Teaching girls how to groom their bodies was also linked to wage work, as an unkempt or inappropriately dressed girl would not last long as a live-in domestic. Taming the sexual body, therefore, was not completely distinct from creating good work habits. When one "difficult" inmate was sent out to work in a candy store, her employer complained that she was lazy, but also "slatternly," entertaining fellow workers with ribald sex talk that was simply unacceptable. She lost her job and was returned to the OTSG.[76]

Both sexual purity and holding down a job were important parts of the regular assessments done by placement officers who monitored the girls after they were released. Officers wanted to see whether the ex-inmate was working steadily at one job and how she spent her wages; if flashy clothes and questionable outings (involving men and drink) were purchased, their reports were negative. Girls had to show that their wages were used to create a new sexual and feminine respectability. Responsible consumption was thus a litmus test of the effectiveness of the OTSG. Girls who saved money or bought practical winter coats with their wages were commended, while those who spent time in penny arcades or dance halls were watched more carefully. Placement officers also expressed particular concern about whether Native women were internalizing the work ethic, replaying common racist stereotypes about "lazy" Natives. "As with the custom of the Indian, M works for a few days or weeks, then takes a holiday until she needs the money, or is ready to return to work," wrote one placement officer, almost declaring her apathy at even attempting to alter this "backward" cultural custom.[77]

Honest labour was thus preventative and formative. It would help prevent a girl from becoming a vagrant or prostitute; indeed, the image of the "old, worn out hag" was used as a direct threat by the superintendent when trying to persuade the girls to alter their ways.[78] The remaking of girls' physical, mental, and sexual bodies was intricately tied together, but there were also differences between the colonized and the working class. An assumption that environmental cultural values had to be exorcised and counteracted operated for both sets of girls, but for poor whites the values were more often seen as a familial inheritance, while Native girls were assumed to imitate collective cultural patterns leading to poverty and indolence. Even if a "culture of poverty" approach was the overall explanation, the more specific understandings of honest labour still took on racialized and racist connotations.

Conclusion

Loss of subsistence, dependence on the state, the beginnings of a diaspora to the cities, and intensified racist interventions into Native families were all crucial factors shaping Native girls' increased incarceration in training schools, already well-established as a means to tame immoral and inadequate working-class and underclass white girls. Assimilative aims to domesticate overly sexual girls, to create an idealized, middle-class family form, and to mould future worker-citizens shaped the training school project as a whole, although perceived racial differences between Native and white, *and* the divisions between the respectable and unreformable – for both white and Native – differentiated the girls' experiences as well. It is thus difficult to isolate one rationale for sexual regulation that trumps all others, because colonialism, gender, and class were closely intertwined, though they sometimes worked themselves out in contradictory ways.

The broader theoretical insights of anti-colonialists and Marxist-feminists remind us that class and capitalism do not operate separately from advanced colonialism, and that capitalism in turn draws on internal social hierarchies of race and gender produced by colonialism. The cultural-ideological construction of patriarchal "heteronorms" concerning sex and family – the labelling of "bad" girls so central to the sexual regulation of delinquents – is connected to patriarchal power, familial divisions of labour, the reproduction of labour power, and accumulation associated with capitalism. Moreover, colonialism is a historical process that alters its tactics and targets over time; by the mid-twentieth century, government policies directed at controlling Indian civil society overlapped with those bent on "re-educating" the problematic working class. For the unfortunate girls caught in this web of regulation, their bodies were "sites of power relations" encoding sexuality, but also shaped by relations of production and reproduction as well.

The political economy of both advanced capitalism and colonialism, and the need to consolidate a stable working-class family bereft of indolence and shiftlessness, thus created a hospitable climate for the training school project. For girls, this endeavour was inseparable from the regulation of their sexuality because of the continuing importance placed on premarital purity, the monogamous married couple, and the patriarchal nuclear family. The sexual morality of Native girls was sometimes seen as more precarious because of racist perceptions of their weak willpower and cultural "unreachability." But it was particularly those Native girls who came from "primitive" reserves, with transient, underemployed, or "unrespectable" parents, who were of most concern. In contrast, the racial and cultural background of an urban Indian girl (who had official Indian status), from a fairly "stable" blue-collar family, was barely mentioned as a factor in her delinquency. To those overseeing the inculcation of domesticity, femininity, and honest labour, this urban, working-class, Native girl was already closer to the white *and* middle-class ideal that they thought would save delinquent girls from becoming criminal women.

Asking what girls themselves thought about their incarceration is not the intent of this chapter, but it is revealing that girls' patterns of accommodation and resistance in the OTSG also both overlapped and differed. While racial tensions between girls existed, the records suggest that they more often built alliances based on hostility to their correctional keepers. In one case, a Native girl led a group of her (non-Native) friends on a long escape as far as Detroit in search of her father; another older Native girl, out on placement and arrested for theft, demanded she be sent to Mercer to "be with her friends."[79] In a complicated escape plot uncovered by the matron, a very young Native girl from the North, already in detention (solitary), wrote in secret to a friend: "Oh my love, now that I'm doing correspondence courses, I have pencil and paper [before she was writing on toilet paper] ask Mrs B to do your two months up here it will be long and boring but at least you will be with me ... in the Mercer, I used to kite this girl from Windsor and [now she can] get money and clothes [for us] ... then we could go up north to a cabin, dye our hair, you could change your name ... We could be sisters, as well as blood sisters."[80] Even though it was foiled, her escape plan indicated that poor white and Native girls sometimes understood that, however different their pasts, their hope for the future might lie in solidarity and common cause.

Notes
1 Rev. Thompson Ferrier, *Our Indians and Their Training for Citizenship* (Toronto: Methodist Mission Room, [1913?]), 18.
2 *The Sterilization of Leilani Muir,* video, directed by Glynis Whiting (Montreal: National Film Board of Canada, 1996).
3 As in nineteenth-century Britain, endeavours to remake British working-class and African native homes according to a dominant middle-class, white, and capitalist ideology of domesticity were connected projects of nation building. See Jean Comaroff and John Comaroff, "Homemade Hegemony," in *Ethnography and the Historical Imagination* (Boulder, CO: Westview Press, 1992), 265-95. For some works on Canada see Pamela White, "Re-structuring the Domestic Sphere – Prairie Indian Women on Reserves: Image, Ideology and State Policy, 1880-1930" (PhD dissertation, McGill University, 1987); Sarah Carter, "First Nations Women of Prairie Canada in the Early Reserve Years, the 1870s to the 1920s: A Preliminary Inquiry," in *Women of the First Nations: Power, Wisdom, Strength,* ed. Christine Miller and Patricia Chuckryk (Winnipeg: University of Manitoba Press, 1996), 51-76; Carolyn Strange, *Toronto's Girl Problem: The Perils and Pleasures of the City, 1890-1930* (Toronto: University of Toronto Press, 1995); J.R. Miller, *Shingwauk's Vision: A History of Native Residential Schools* (Toronto: University of Toronto Press, 1996); Jo-Anne Fiske, "Gender and the Paradox of

Residential Education in Carrier Society," in *Women of the First Nations,* 167-82; J.S. Woodsworth, *Strangers within Our Gates* (Toronto: University of Toronto Press, 1974).

4 Rosemary Hennessy, *Profit and Pleasure: Sexual Identities in Late Capitalism* (New York: Routledge, 2000), 105.

5 For some examples see Kimberle Crenshaw, "Intersectionality and Identity Politics: Learning from Violence against Women of Colour," in *Reconstructing Political Theory: Feminist Perspectives,* ed. Mary Shanley and Uma Narayan, 178-93 (University Park: Pennsylvania State University Press, 1997); Joanna Brenner, *Women and the Politics of Class* (New York: Monthly Review, 2001); Patricia Hill Collins, *Fighting Words: Black Women and the Search for Justice* (Minneapolis: University of Minnesota, 1998); Eileen Boris and Angelique Janssens, "Complicating Categories," *International Review of Social History* 44 (1999): 1-13.

6 Some works exploring early contact, eighteenth- and nineteenth-century Native history, and sexual regulation include Sylvia Van Kirk, *Many Tender Ties: Women in Fur-Trade Society in Western Canada, 1670-1870* (Winnipeg: Watson and Dwyer, 1980); Karen Anderson, *Chain Her by One Foot: The Subjugation of Native Women in Seventeenth-Century New France* (New York and London: Routledge, 1991); Adele Perry, *On the Edge of Empire: Gender, Race, and the Making of British Columbia, 1849-1871* (Toronto: University of Toronto Press, 2001); Jean Barman, "Taming Aboriginal Sexuality: Gender, Power, and Race in British Columbia, 1850-1900," *BC Studies* 115/116 (Autumn/Winter 1997-98): 237-66; Jo-Anne Fiske, "Colonization and the Decline of Women's Status: The Tsimshian Case," *Feminist Studies* 17, 3 (Fall 1991): 509-35; Carol Devens, *Countering Colonization: Native American Women and Great Lakes Missions, 1630-1900* (Berkeley: University of California Press, 1992). Twentieth-century regulation is discussed in Joan Sangster, *Regulating Girls and Women: Sexuality, Family, and the Law in Ontario, 1920-1960* (Toronto: Oxford University Press, 2001). On sexual violence, see Sherene Razack, "Gendered Racial Violence and Spatialized Justice: The Murder of Pamela George," in *Race, Space and the Law: Unmapping a White Settler Society,* ed. S. Razack, 121-56 (Toronto: Between the Lines, 2002); Theresa Nahanee, "Sexual Assault of Inuit Females: A Comment on 'Cultural Bias,'" in *Confronting Sexual Assault: A Decade of Legal and Social Change,* ed. Julian Roberts and Renate Mohr, 192-204 (Toronto: University of Toronto Press, 1994).

7 For example, Susan Thorne, "The Conversion of English Men and the Conversion of the World Inseparable," in *Tensions of Empire: Colonial Cultures in a Bourgeois World,* ed. Frederick Cooper and Ann Laura Stoler, 238-62 (Berkeley: University of California Press, 1997), 241. This emphasis on the language of class did not characterize the Comaroffs' pathbreaking essay on this topic. Thorne's claim that the idea "imperialism mattered" to the course of "British industrialization" has been "ignored and resisted" seems to erase a whole body of earlier writing in Marxist and materialist veins, which linked imperialism to capitalism and/or to class relations.

8 Hennessy, *Profit and Pleasure,* Chapter 2.

9 Ann Laura Stoler, *Race and the Education of Desire: Foucault's History of Sexuality and the Colonial Order of Things* (Durham, NC: Duke University Press, 1995). For an earlier, key work in a more feminist-materialist vein, see Anna Davin, "Imperialism and Motherhood," *History Workshop Journal* 5 (Spring 1978): 9-66. On whiteness, see David Roediger, *The Wages of Whiteness: Race and the Making of the American Working Class* (London: Verso, 1991). On "subaltern" voices, see Chandra Mohanty "Under Western Eyes: Feminist Scholarship and Colonial Discourse," *Feminist Review* 30 (Autumn 1988): 61-88; and G. Spivak, "Can the Subaltern Speak?" in *Marxism and the Interpretation of Culture,* ed. Cary Nelson and Larry Grossberg, 271-316 (Urbana: University of Illinois Press, 1988). A few key discussions of sexuality and colonialism include Vron Ware, *Beyond the Pale: White Women, Racism and History* (London: Verso, 1992); Antoinette Burton, ed., *Gender, Sexuality and Colonial Modernities* (London: Routledge, 1999); Clare Midgley, ed., *Gender and Imperialism* (Manchester, UK: Manchester University Press, 1998); Anne McClintock, *Imperial Leather: Race, Gender and Sexuality in the Colonial Contest* (London and New York: Routledge, 1995); and Ann Laura Stoler, *Race and the Education of Desire.*

10 Ruth Roach Pierson, "Introduction," in *Nation, Empire, Colony: Historicizing Gender and Race,* ed. Ruth Roach Pierson and Nupur Chaudhuri, 1-20 (Bloomington, IN: Indiana University Press, 1998), 4. See also Jane Haggis, "Gendering Colonialism or Colonising Gender?

Recent Women's Studies Approaches to White Women and the History of British Colonialism," *Women's Studies International Forum* 13, 1 (1990): 105-15.

11 Ann Laura Stoler and Frederick Cooper, "Between Metropole and Colony," in *Tensions of Empire* (see note 7), 1-56, at 4-5.

12 Perry, *On the Edge of Empire*; Sarah Carter, *Capturing Women: The Manipulation of Cultural Imagery in Canada's Prairie West* (Montreal and Kingston: McGill-Queen's University Press, 1997).

13 Amy Kaplan, "Manifest Domesticity," *American Literature* 70, 3 (September 1998): 581-605, at 583.

14 Dolores Janiewski, "Gendered Colonialism and the Woman Question," in *Nation, Empire, Colony* (see note 10), 57-76; and Marilyn Lake, "Citizenship As Non-Discrimination: Acceptance or Assimilationism? Political Logic and Emotional Investment in Campaigns for Aboriginal Rights in Australia, 1940-70," *Gender and History* 13, 3 (November 2001): 566-92.

15 Himani Bannerji, Shahrzad Mojab, and Judith Whitehead, "Introduction," in *Of Property and Propriety: The Role of Gender and Class in Imperialism and Nationalism*, ed. Himani Bannerji, Shahrzad Mojab, and Judith Whitehead, 3-33 (Toronto: University of Toronto Press, 2001), 6; and Bannerji, "Politics and the Writing of History," in *Nation, Empire, Colony* (see note 10), 287-302, at 294.

16 Arif Dirlik, "The Postcolonial Aura: Third World Criticism in the Age of Global Capitalism," *Critical Inquiry* 20 (Winter 1994): 328-56; Ella Shohat, "Notes on the Post-Colonial," *Social Text* 31/32 (1992): 99-113; and Aijaz Ahmad, *In Theory: Nations, Classes, Literatures* (London: Verso, 1992). Even Stoler and Cooper admit that "current academic fashions risk privileging ... cultural and representational features of colonial authority" over political economy, diverting our gaze from "relations of production and exchange," which also constituted colonialism. Stoler and Cooper, "Between Metropole and Colony," 18.

17 Ruth Frankenberg and Lata Mani, "Crosscurrents, Crosstalk: Race, 'Postcoloniality' and the Politics of Location," *Cultural Studies* 7, 2 (1993): 292-310. On the specificity of white settler societies and the need to take structures into account, see Patrick Wolfe, "History and Imperialism: A Century of Theory, from Marx to Postcolonialism," *American Historical Review* 102, 2 (April 1997): 388-420.

18 Judith Butler, "Merely Cultural," *New Left Review* 227 (1998): 33-44, and especially the critical response by Nancy Fraser, "Heterosexism: Misrecognition and Capitalism: A Response to Judith Butler," *New Left Review* 228 (March/April 1998): 140-50; see also critical response to Butler by Rosemary Hennessy in *Profit and Pleasure*, 115-21.

19 My debts here to political economy. In contrast to explanations that give priority to "cultural" – and thus, by implication, to "racial" – explanations for the increased social marginalization of Native peoples, political economists argue that changing material circumstances and Native peoples' active struggles for subsistence and survival provide a framework for their increased criminalization. Native peoples certainly attempted to navigate these difficult changes, their choices shaped by culture, gender, and identity, though they were somewhat limited in their responses by the political straitjacket of continued colonialism, symbolized by the Indian Act. See Vic Satzewich and Terry Wotherspoon, *First Nations: Race, Class, and Gender Relations* (Toronto: Nelson, 1993); and Anthony Boldt, *Surviving As Indians: The Challenge of Self Government* (Toronto: University of Toronto Press, 1993). For quote, see Canada, Royal Commission on Aboriginal Peoples, *Report of the Royal Commission on Aboriginal Peoples (RCAP)*, vol. 2, *Restructuring the Relationship* (Ottawa: Canada Communication Group Publishing, 1996), 788.

20 Satzewich and Wotherspoon, *First Nations*, 49.

21 Boldt, *Surviving As Indians*, 19 and 226.

22 *RCAP*, vol. 3, *Gathering Strength*, 28.

23 OTSG Superintendent to Deputy Minister, 18 November 1953, Record Group (RG) 20 16-2, Container J15, Galt File, Archives of Ontario (AO).

24 For one critical perspective on postcolonial hybridity, see Ella Shoat, "The Struggle over Representation: Casting, Coalitions and the Politics of Identification," in *Late Imperial Culture*, eds. Roman de la Campa, E. Ann Kaplan, and Michael Sprinket (London: Verso, 1995), 174-75. Native scholars also remain divided on hybridity, and on postcolonialism more

generally, especially in the United States, where postcolonialism has not been as readily embraced by scholars of colour, including Native Americans. For some discussion see Bonita Lawrence, "'Real' Indians and Others: Mixed-Race Urban Native People, the Indian Act, and the Rebuilding of Indigenous Nations" (PhD dissertation, Ontario Institute for Studies in Education, 1999), 25.

25   Renisa Mawani, "In Between and out of Place: Mixed-Race Identity, Liquor, and the Law in British Columbia, 1850-1913," in *Race, Space and the Law* (see note 6), 47-70.

26   Walter Currie, "The Indian in the City" (address to Indian-Eskimo Association, Winnipeg, 1966); Mark Nagler, *Indians in the City* (Toronto: University of Toronto Press, 1970). For the dominant views on Aboriginal women in this period, see Barbara Freeman, *The Satellite Sex: The Media and Women's Issues in English Canada, 1966-71* (Waterloo, ON: Wilfrid Laurier University Press, 2001).

27   For an important discussion of racialized space, see Sherene Razack, "When Place Becomes Race," in *Race, Space and the Law* (see note 6), 1-20.

28   Note on sources: As well as the government's records for training schools, I examined forty-seven individual case files of First Nations girls who spent time in training schools, almost all of them at OTSG. These were compared to my larger study of 350 OTSG case files, as well as files on girls' delinquency on reserves in the Department of Indian Affairs (DIA) papers. OTSG records offer sentencing reports; court transcripts; educational, medical, and social work commentaries on the girls; as well as the girls' and their families' recorded responses, but these are highly mediated sources, articulated through the eyes of those with authority, and must be interpreted as such.

29   Despite their smaller numbers in the system, in contrast to boys, girls were consistently more likely to be incarcerated in reform schools. Similar conclusions have been drawn by most North American historians of female delinquency: Mary Odem, *Delinquent Daughters: Protecting and Policing Adolescent Female Sexuality in the United States, 1885-1920* (Chapel Hill: University of North Carolina Press, 1995); Ruth Alexander, *The "Girl Problem": Female Sexual Delinquency in New York, 1900-30* (Ithaca, NY: Cornell University Press, 1995); Joan Sangster, "Girls in Conflict with the Law: The Construction of Female Delinquency, 1940-60," *Canadian Journal of Women and the Law* 12, 1 (2000): 1-31; and Joan Sangster, *Girl Trouble: Female Delinquency in English Canada* (Toronto: Between the Lines, 2002); Tamara Myers, "The Voluntary Delinquent: Parents, Daughters, and the Montreal Juvenile Delinquents' Court in 1918," *Canadian Historical Review* 80, 2 (June 1999): 242-68.

30   Native girls could also be charged under the Indian Act, which prohibited such things as the consumption of alcohol and "profligacy." However, the other statutes provided all the latitude that judges needed. *Juvenile Delinquents Act,* Government of Canada, 1908, c. 40, 7-8; *Training School Act,* Statutes of Ontario 1939, c. 51. On the Juvenile Delinquents Act, see Canadian Welfare Council, *The Juvenile Court in Law* (Ottawa: Canadian Welfare Council, 1941); Neil Sutherland, *Children in English-Canadian Society: Framing the Twentieth-Century Consensus* (Toronto: University of Toronto Press, 1978); Marge Reitsma-Street, "More Control than Care: A Critique of Historical and Contemporary Laws for Delinquency and the Neglect of Children in Ontario," *Canadian Journal of Women and the Law* 3, 1 (1989-90): 510-30; Jean Trepanier, "Origins of the Juvenile Delinquents Act of 1908," in *Dimensions of Childhood: Essays on the History of Children and Youth in Canada,* ed. Russell Smandych, Gordon Dodds, and Alvin Esau, 205-32 (Winnipeg: Legal Research Institute, 1991). On the 1924 amendment adding sexual immorality, see Bruno Theorêt, "Regulation juridique pénale des mineur-es et discrimination à l'égard des filles: La clause de 1924 amendant *La Loi sur les jeunes delinquants,*" *Canadian Journal of Women and the Law* 4 (1990-91): 539-55.

31   Although they were usually released by age seventeen, girls could be under the supervision of OTSG until they were twenty-one. In 1949 this was changed to eighteen.

32   In the 1930s, one or two Native girls were admitted every year; this climbed to fourteen girls, or 9 percent of admissions, in 1958. The average number of admissions for the period 1950-59 was 7 percent, when the Census of Canada listed Indians as 0.8 percent of the Ontario population. These statistics, of course, are not definitive, as they rely on who the school designated "Indian." See Government of Ontario, "Annual Report of the Minister

of Public Welfare," until 1938, and after "Annual Report of Industrial Schools and Training Schools"; Government of Canada, *Census of Canada, 1951,* vol. 2, table 32.

33 On the overincarceration of adult women, see Joan Sangster, "Criminalizing the Colonized: Ontario Native Women Confront the Criminal Justice System, 1920-1960," *Canadian Historical Review* 80, 1 (March 1999): 32-60. On child welfare, see Patricia Monture, "A Vicious Circle: Child Welfare and the First Nations," *Canadian Journal of Women and the Law* 3, 1 (1989): 1-17; Emily Carasco, "Canadian Native Children: Have Child Welfare Laws Broken the Circle?" *Canadian Journal of Family Law* 5, 1 (1986): 111-21; Marlee Kline, "Complicating the Ideology of Motherhood: Child Welfare Law and First Nations Women," in *Mothers in Law: Feminist Theory and the Legal Regulation of Motherhood,* ed. Martha Albertson Fineman and Isabel Karpin, 118-41 (New York: Columbia University Press, 1995). H.B. Hawthorne's *A Survey of Indians of Canada* (Ottawa: Indian Affairs Branch, 1967), Part 1, recognized these trends in child welfare, but made little criticism.

34 Vicente L. Rafael, "Colonial Domesticity: White Women and United States Rule in the Philippines," *American Literature* 67, 4 (December 1995): 639-66, at 640.

35 OTSG [ward file] 131, AO.

36 OTSG, 15162, AO.

37 OTSG, 2127, AO.

38 *Annual Report of Ontario Training Schools,* 1946, AO.

39 OTSG, 430, AO.

40 OTSG, 1428, AO.

41 Clare Brant, *Collection of Chapters, Lectures, Workshops and Thoughts* (Trent University Archives [TUA]), especially his "Native Ethics and Rules of Behaviour," from *Canadian Journal of Psychiatry* 35 (1990): 534-39. This was also commented on critically by many social workers of the time; see Mary Woodward, "Juvenile Delinquency among Indian Girls" (MA thesis, University of British Columbia, 1949).

42 OTSG, 2353, AO.

43 OTSG, 165, AO.

44 *Annual Report of Ontario Training Schools,* 1942, AO.

45 Kaplan, "Manifest Domesticity," 582.

46 Domesticity was similarly crucial to British imperialism in Africa; "The routines and rituals of everyday life, especially household activity and sexuality," were turned into "political" matters as colonizers attempted to remake – with varying degrees of success and certainly some resistance – notions of property, labour, pride, and morality. See Karen Hansen, "Introduction," in *African Encounters with Domesticity,* ed. Karen Hansen, 1-33 (New Brunswick, NJ: Rutgers University Press, 1992), 1, 5.

47 OTSG, 235, AO.

48 OTSG, 1666, AO.

49 OTSG, 1353, AO.

50 OTSG, 365, AO.

51 Dorothy Chunn and Robert Menzies, "Gender, Madness and Crime: The Reproduction of Patriarchal and Class Relations in a Psychiatric Court Clinic," *Journal of Human Justice* 1, 2 (1990): 33-54.

52 OTSG, 1519, AO.

53 Brant, *Collection,* TUA, especially Clare Brant and P.G.R. Patterson, "Native Child Rearing Practices: Their Role in Mental Health," typescript, and Brant, "Native Ethics and Rules of Behaviour."

54 Tamara Myers and Joan Sangster, "Retorts, Runaways and Riots: Resistance in Canadian Reform Schools for Girls, 1930-60," *Journal of Social History* 34, 3 (Spring 2001): 669-97.

55 OTSG, 2328, AO.

56 OTSG, 210, AO.

57 OTSG, G135, AO.

58 Joan Sangster, "Girls in Conflict with the Law."

59 Herbert Herskotz, "A Psychodynamic View of Sexual Promiscuity," in *Family Dynamics and Female Sexual Delinquency,* ed. Otto Pollack and A. Friedman, 89-98 (Palo Alto, CA: Science and Behavior Books, 1969), 89.

60 OTSG, 1647, AO.
61 Lawrence, "'Real' Indians and Others," 445, 31.
62 It is important to make a historical distinction between the *current* emphasis in legal stud-ies on differences between "white" and "Native" value systems, and some past practices in which patterns of social control overlapped. For the latter, see Tina Loo, "Tonto's Due: Law, Culture and Colonization in British Columbia," in *Essays in the History of Canadian Law: British Columbia and the Yukon,* vol. 6, ed. H. Foster and J. McLaren, 128-70 (Toronto: Uni-versity of Toronto Press, 1995).
63 Lawrence, "'Real' Indians and Others," 115.
64 On such preoccupations in the United States, see Nicole Hann Rafter, *White Trash: The Eugenic Family Studies, 1877-1919* (Boston: Northeastern University Press, 1988); on desig-nations of some poor whites as "racially degenerate," see Lee Polansky, "I Certainly Hope That You Will Be Able to Train Her: Reformers and the Georgia Training School for Girls," in *Before the New Deal: Social Welfare in the South, 1830-1930,* ed. Elna Green, 138-57 (Ath-ens: University of Georgia Press, 1999), 146. On Canada, Angus McLaren, *Our Own Master Race: Eugenics in Canada, 1885-1945* (Toronto: McClelland and Stewart, 1990).
65 OTSG, 2210, AO.
66 OTSG, G150, AO.
67 OTSG, G 220 and 409, AO.
68 OTSG, G197, AO.
69 OTSG, 2080, AO.
70 OTSG, 875, AO. The term "running wild" was also applied to white girls.
71 York County Family Court Files, Box 1607, anonymous file, AO.
72 OTSG, G270, AO.
73 OTSG, G60, AO.
74 *Annual Report of Ontario Training Schools,* 1955, AO.
75 I recognize my reversion to a Reichan explanation here. See Reimut Reich, *Sexuality and Class Struggle* (Frankfurt am Main: Verlag Neue Kritik, 1968); and Juliet Mitchell, *Psycho-analysis and Feminism* (London: Penguin, 1974), 197-218.
76 OTSG, T75, AO.
77 OTSG, 1555, AO.
78 Memo on Detention by Superintendent, RG 20-16-2 (Dept. of Reform Institutions), Con-tainer J21, AO.
79 OTSG, 875, AO. Having seen this whole file, I do not believe that the "friends" she was referring to were simply Native friends, but a group of women whose records had landed them in the Mercer.
80 OTSG, 1572, AO.

Part 3
Bodies in Everyday Space: Colonized and Colonizing Women in Canadian Contact Zones

9

Aboriginal Women on the Streets of Victoria: Rethinking Transgressive Sexuality during the Colonial Encounter

Jean Barman

"Mary went to Victoria w[ith] Beans," William Hughes wrote on 27 July 1859, and the next day, "Mary A[rrived] from Victoria."[1] As his diary makes clear, Irishman William Hughes, his Cowichan Indian wife Mary Salslawit, and their children were engaged in a collaborative enterprise. He managed the day-to-day work on their small holding just outside the coal-mining village of Nanaimo on south-central Vancouver Island, and she took charge of the commercial end. She sold not just beans but potatoes as well, in the colonial capital of Victoria and also in Nanaimo, to get the cash needed to support their young family at a mostly subsistence level.

All was not, however, quite so straightforward as Hughes' diary entries suggest. Each time Mary Salslawit made the trip to the capital of the British colony of Vancouver Island, she was transformed into something quite different than what she was in her everyday life. Aboriginal women on the streets of Victoria were, almost by definition, either "prostitutes" or "crones." It was the presence or absence of physical desire in newcomer men that determined their identities. In the first instance, appearance, manner of dress, the way they behaved – all of the differences that separated them from the women these men knew back home – shouted out that they were willing and waiting for the first male who came along and might show them the least interest.

By repeatedly putting this image into words, newcomers gave it an authority that has survived remarkably intact to the present day. The Victoria press referred, often almost in passing, to "prostitution, so common with Northern [Indian] women"; to "women have[ing] rendered the whole outskirts of the town a perfect brothel"; and to how "the squaws might all be considered as prostitutes."[2] Exemplary is a lead editorial in the *British Colonist* newspaper, run by political activist Amor de Cosmos, that asserted early in 1861 how "[all the Indian] men to-day are a horde of thieves and cutthroats, and the women a community of prostitutes."[3] In a much-cited guide to British Columbia published in London in 1865, Congregational minister

Matthew MacFie, following five years' residence in Victoria, evoked "scenes after sunset calculated to shock even the bluntest sensibilities," "crowds of the more debased miners strewed in vicious concert with squaws on the public highway," and "hundreds of dissipated white men [who] live in open concubinage with these wretched creatures."[4] Some recent descriptions are not dissimilar, as with British Columbia historian Robin Fisher's seminal *Contact and Conflict:* "Some settlers did form temporary liaisons with Indian women, but more commonly they provided merely a temporary satisfaction of desires ... Large numbers of Indian women from the north came to Victoria annually to earn money by prostitution ... So-called 'squaw dance houses,' brothels, and Indian women 'dressed up as fine as "White Soiled Doves" do in California' were all features of certain streets in Victoria in the early 1860's." In Fisher's view, "prostitution was [just] another problem" among the various "social ills" besetting newcomers to Victoria.[5]

Such a perspective is far too neat and tidy to be left unexamined. Not only does it assume a single, generic definition of something called "prostitution" from a wholly newcomer perspective; it also trivializes and essentializes Aboriginal women. They are, in effect, given agency, but only to do wrong. I am not so much doubting contemporary observations as I am wanting to understand what newcomers saw, why they saw what they saw, and what were the consequences for Aboriginal women.[6]

My argument has two parts. The first is consistent with the findings of a new generation of scholars.[7] In Victoria, as in other colonial outposts around the world, indigenous women had to be portrayed as sexually transgressive in order for men away from home and home life to be able to seduce them with impunity, without accountability. All behaviour unlike that of women whence newcomers came was equated with prostitution, with a willingness to provide sexual favours if remunerated. Women who claimed space on the streets, who dared to occupy their own homes independent of men, or who socialized in dance halls were particularly suspect.

The second part of my argument has not, so far as I am aware, been extensively examined by other scholars. Just as women were not alike, not all men were alike. The gratification newcomer men sought from Aboriginal women differed considerably. For one set of stakeholders it was physical gratification; for another, economic gain; for a third, political advantage; and for a fourth, a kind of moral rape. The women themselves were not pawns. They acted and they resisted. They often did so in settings where their options were far narrower than they themselves might have considered them to be.

The events themselves are not much in dispute.[8] The northwest corner of North America comprising the present-day Canadian province of British Columbia was a fur-trade outpost, loosely under British oversight, until gold was discovered on the mainland adjacent to Vancouver Island, some nine years after the California rush of 1849. News of the finds transformed Victoria, near which lived the Songhees people, from a very small company town servicing the fur trade into a way station for thousands of newcomers hoping to get rich quick and be on their way. Esquimalt, the British naval port about three miles away, became the entryway for boatloads of men arriving in waves from California and elsewhere over some seven or eight years of gold fever. Hundreds of entrepreneurs, many of whom self-identified as Jewish, brought supplies north with them to open shops. By the end of 1858, two British colonies, Vancouver Island and British Columbia on the mainland, existed side by side. Other newcomers, most often from England or British North America, serviced the two colonies as government officials, newspaper editors (such as Amor de Cosmos), and clerics (like Matthew MacFie). Victoria quickly became a bustling emporium that not only provisioned men on the way to the goldfields, but also housed many of them over the winter when bad weather prevented mining, particularly as the gold rush moved north into the Cariboo region. Several thousand North Coast peoples – Tsimshian, Haida, and others – were already travelling to Victoria each year to sell furs, carved goods, and their labour.[9] They continued to camp around its edges, wherever they could haul their large canoes ashore, on a seasonal basis during the gold-rush years.

Such a mix of peoples gave a variety of opportunities for contact between Aboriginal women and newcomers. As a close reading of newspaper accounts, government records, and other contemporary sources makes clear, Aboriginal women walked the streets of Victoria and engaged in a far greater variety of activities than what newcomers reduced to prostitution. A considerable number lived there as the wives of fur traders, both officers and labourers, or as part of Aboriginal families.[10] An arrival of 1862 encountered, "scattered over the town, groups of dirty and stolid Indians, in many-colored blankets, with their squaws and little red-skins."[11] Many women, like Mary Salslawit, came to trade. Yet others, as one observer put it, were "employed as servants in our dwellings and in the culinary departments of our restaurants and hotels."[12] A poem of 1862 included a sidebar testifying to Aboriginal women's workaday world on the streets of Victoria:

Next morn the sun has risen
Higher o'er Victoria Town,
Whiskey shops are opening
And shutters going down.
Along the streets with turned-in feet,
The squaws are kloc-kloc crying out their wares for sale.[13]

Another rhyme evoked women "sinking under loads of berries ... loudly crying 'klosh olilly,' fiercely shouting k-k-clams."[14] Aboriginal women, in other words, had every reason to be on the streets of Victoria.

All the same, it was the word "prostitution" that won out, a term as revealing of newcomers' assumptions as it was of the women themselves. The societies from which most men came considered sex acts as acceptable only within the confines of legal marriage, and then for the purposes of procreation. Intimations of sexuality, or activities perceived as encouraging sexual desire, indicated a tendency toward promiscuity wholly out of tune with proper behaviour. Female sexual independence was the ultimate threat to the patriarchal family of the nineteenth century. As succinctly summed up by George Stocking, for Victorian England, "if the ideal wife and mother was 'so pure-hearted as to be utterly ignorant of and averse to any sensual indulgence,' the alternate cultural image of the 'fallen woman' conveys a hint of an underlying preoccupation with the threat of uncontrolled female sexuality."[15] Gail Hawkes, among others, describes how "prostitution provided a forum within which to express, covertly, anxieties about, and fascination with, the characteristics of women's sexuality."[16] Merely by virtue of being on the streets of Victoria, Aboriginal women misbehaved and thereby need not be treated with the same proprieties as their newcomer counterparts. These women were made, so to speak, the authors of their own destiny.

Victoria during the gold rush shared in the distinctive circumstances of colonial frontiers.[17] If unspoken, and for the most part unwritten, it was generally accepted in the societies whence men came that, so long as women of their own kind were absent, indigenous women could be used to satisfy what were perceived as men's natural needs. Differences in everyday behaviour, appearance, and skin tone conveniently confirmed that indigenous women were not just sexually transgressive, but also racially inferior.[18] As Adele Perry has described in *On the Edge of Empire,* newcomer women not already taken as wives were few and far between during the British Columbia gold rush. Given such circumstances, few scruples existed over what Philip Mason, a pioneering scholar on race, has termed "the casual use of a social inferior for sexual pleasure."[19] Aboriginal women's transformation into prostitutes eliminated any sense of guilt even as it enabled satisfaction. Anne McClintock perceptively observes how "prostitutes flagrantly demanded money for services middle-class men expected for free."[20] Newcomer men did not want to need Aboriginal women, but if they were prostitutes it was possible to use and abuse them with impunity.

The social contexts of Aboriginal women's sexual contacts with newcomers varied. Some of the Songhees, Tsimshian, Haida, and other Aboriginal women on the streets of Victoria had some experience with newcomers growing out of the fur trade. Its patterns of expected behaviour were, however, more predictable and less unsettling than the assumptions that arrived with the gold rush.[21] Aboriginal women, moreover, came from a variety of cultural backgrounds, with distinctive notions of sexuality. In her doctoral thesis on the Tsimshian, Carol Cooper contends that "within their own societies there was little censure of Native women who engaged in sexual activity for payment."[22] Sexual relations were, Cooper explains, part of gift giving, a means to impart luck and power, and a way to cement alliances between different tribes.

Without doubt, many Aboriginal women, and also some non-Aboriginal women, did engage in sexual relations with newcomers outside of "marriage," in the newcomer sense of the word. The post journal from Fort Simpson noted in 1862 that "a larger number than usual of females are going to prostitute themselves."[23] A mining engineer exploring the Queen Charlotte Islands at about the same time recalled how "some Queen Charlotte women went to spend the Winter in Victoria, hoping to 'earn blankets,' and came back loaded with blankets, trinkets, tobacco, whiskey, and other presents, which they proceeded to distribute among their peoples."[24] Some likely did very well, as indicated by the report of a Haida man arrested in Victoria in December 1862 for stealing $210 in gold coin from an Aboriginal woman, described in the press as a "prostitute."[25] There was, of course, a tremendous downside. Long-time Victoria physician John Sebastian Helmcken wrote in his memoir about how "Hyder women and men came in flocks, to go away ruined forever – Indians from the North West coast met with the same fate, from which they have never and never will recover."[26] In 1867 the *British Colonist* raised the "taboo" subject of venereal disease, lamenting "the absence of any provision" for its "relief amongst the aborigines."[27] As Cooper acknowledges, "it is hard to estimate the number of Nisga'a and Coast Tsimshian [and other Aboriginal] women who engaged in prostitution, and it is impossible to know the full circumstances of their entry into this activity."[28]

Three settings were particularly scrutinized for indications of sexual transgression. The first were the streets themselves. Victoria was sited around James Bay. Government buildings were located on the south side, from where a bridge ran across the bay into Government Street. The Hudson's Bay post lay just across the bridge on the north side, set back from Humboldt Street, known familiarly as Kanaka Road because of the many indigenous Hawaiian, or Kanaka, fur-trade labourers who lived there. West along the water was Wharf Street, which farther north turned into Store Street. At the junction between the two streets, another bridge ran west from Victoria to the Songhees village, or reserve, located at the tip of the Esquimalt peninsula. Running inland from the trading post was Fort Street, parallelled a couple of blocks to the north by Yates, where most shops were located.

Liquor often was the impetus for labelling Aboriginal women on the streets of Victoria. It was illegal to sell or give spirits to Indians.[29] Charges against men caught doing so, or otherwise abusing Aboriginal women, were commonplace. In August 1861 "a colored man, beat a squaw on Kanaka road."

The report on his arrest commented that every night in that area along the waterfront, "a number of whites and blacks, who consider themselves civilized beings, delight in getting squaws drunk" and seeing them misbehave.[30] Reports tended to belittle men's victims. In February 1862 "a respectable looking man, formerly attached to the police force" of Victoria, was charged with "assaulting a miserable, sickly-looking squaw, at the old bridge, on Sunday night last." The woman claimed he "had attempted to ravish her person" after giving her a blow on her head with his fist. The police officer making the arrest stated that "beating squaws was quite a common occurrence in the neighborhood of the bridge." The judge was unusually sympathetic, remarking that "the cowardly habit indulged in by certain men of beating squaws, was becoming quite as common as it was disgraceful."[31] Women might be enticed indoors, as was the case when a watchmaker was discovered on an autumnal night in his apartment, "*en dishabíle,* giving a squaw a drink" of liquor.[32] A magistrate observed as late as November 1866 that "it was an every day occurrence for white men to rob klootchmen," the word in the Chinook trading jargon for Aboriginal women.[33]

While women could be targeted anywhere, they were especially suspect on the road running from Victoria, across the bridge, and through the Songhees reserve to the harbour at Esquimalt. In September 1860 a self-styled "new settler in this Colony" lamented: "On last Sunday afternoon I walked to Esquimalt and was more deeply pained than I can find words to express, to see the road lined for a considerable distance with troops of young Indian females evidently there for the purposes of prostitution."[34] A grand jury recommended a month later "that energetic measures be taken to suppress the Indian prostitution daily going on upon the Esquimalt Road."[35] Two years later came a report that "about 30 Indian women were observed sitting by the side of Esquimalt road, ready to entrap the unwary strangers who came on the steamer Brother Jonathan."[36]

A second set of accusations were levelled against women who occupied their own "cabins" or "shanties," or resided with other women, and sometimes also men, in what were termed "squaw dens" or "brothels."[37] Some of the activity so easily condemned served multiple purposes for a kind of demi-world along the waterfront that crossed racial lines in search of everyday survival and sociability. A report of July 1860 referred to "the Indian brothels on Store street and its vicinity, and in other parts of the town, used as they are for the still worse purpose of selling liquor to the Indians."[38] Many accounts are tentative, as with a report the next September that "late on Monday night a quantity of clothing was stolen from a squaw ranch on or near Broad street," just north of the fur-trade post. The items "belonged to a white man, who professes to believe that one of his dusky friends took them."[39] A year later the *British Colonist* editorialized about "the state of moral degradation into which a number of the *habitues* and residents of

Kanaka road have fallen." The account described how "a continual howling nightly is maintained by the drunken wretches who occupy or visit the miserable huts that have been erected along the bank of James Bay." As to the remedy: "The Indian women should be sent to the [Songhees] Reserve to live, and the white and black men who glory in keeping them proceeded against under the Vagrancy Act – for we hazard nothing in saying that very few, if any, of their number can show an honest means of obtaining a living."[40] A report to Victoria city council in September 1862 described "a number of houses of ill-fame on Humboldt street, with Indian women."[41]

Such women were almost inherently suspect at a time when females were expected to live visibly subservient to their fathers, husbands, or sons. Indicative is the court case of May 1860 against a Hawaiian named Na'hor, who lived with his daughters by an Aboriginal woman in a house on the waterfront on Humboldt Street.[42] The police officer who instigated the charge testified: "Every time I pass the house I see five or six half breed women and Indian women and there are some half breed boys and kanakas in the same room together. I have seen both the squaws and kanakas drunk and disorderly on several occasions." A newcomer father and son testified that a young woman at Na'hor's house had, when they passed, called out to them in Chinook, "Cla-hoy-a," or "hello." The restaurant keeper for whom Na'hor worked testified on his behalf that Na'hor had told him he could not control his daughters.[43] Na'hor was convicted and imprisoned for two weeks.[44]

A warning in a Victoria newspaper followed two years later suggesting that "the gentlemen ... in the habit of going around at a very late hour knocking at the doors of private residences in search of squaws had better be a little more careful," or they would end up in the police court.[45] The next spring the principal of the public school, located on Fort Street, made a charge of assault against his next-door neighbour, who he considered to be "the keeper of a squaw den." The principal did so in the hopes of having "the disreputable squaw harem which the prisoner kept cleared away from the neighborhood."[46] Over time, "Indian shanties" became concentrated along Humboldt Street, and also on Cormorant and Fisgard streets just north of Yates.[47] The superintendent of police claimed in August 1865: "There are no less than 200 Indian Prostitutes living ... in filthy shacks."[48]

Agitation over Aboriginal women on the streets of Victoria or in their own accommodations was minor in comparison to the uproar over a third form of activity. Dance halls were a form of sociability brought north from the California gold rush. The difference between the halls in San Francisco and those that sprang up in Victoria, in the mainland capital of New Westminster, and across the goldfields was, one account noted scornfully, that in California "the females were at least civilized."[49] Many believed, as did one letter writer, that "a dance hall is only a hell hole where the females are white: but it is many times worse where the females are squaws," as they were in the colonies of Vancouver Island and British Columbia.[50]

Dance halls operated in remarkably similar fashion, whatever their location. As one participant recalled: "25 cents (about a shilling) was the entrance fee, and there was a kind of master of ceremonies who called out the figures – 'first gent to the left with the left hand round, back again and turn' – 'balance in a line' – it was really wonderful what a good time they all kept and how serious they all were about it."[51] Among the dances led by "the dulcet strains of a fiddle," "a violin, bass violi, and a brass instrument," or perhaps only by a "fifer," were cotillions, waltzes, and the "Lancers" and "Julien's Quadrilles."[52] New Westminster novelist Frances Herring described how "each man paid fifty cents for a dance, and had to 'stand drinks' at the bar for himself and his dusky partner after each."[53] This was how dance halls made their money. "When the Quadrille was finished 'Waltz up to the bar' was shouted out in a very loud voice – when every one did so at once, and we all had a drink and our partners generally took lemonade, or ginger ale. 50 cents was charged for each drink whatever it might be so one can easily understand what a good profit was made. Sometimes champagne was ordered. I should be sorry to say what it was made of but it always cost $10 a bottle."[54] At a Victoria dance hall, "a buff of conversation and a rush to the bar" was quickly followed by "the poppings of soda-water corks and the munchings of apples."[55] As for communication, one attendee recalled that Aboriginal women "had learned a little English and all the men could speak Chinook more or less, which was the lingua franca of British Columbia and Vancouver Island."[56]

Dance halls followed the miners, operating on a seasonal basis. Contemporary newspaper accounts make it possible to pinpoint their locations around Victoria. A dance hall existed from the fall of 1860 to at least early 1862 on Humboldt Street.[57] Others opened in the autumn of 1861 in the former "market building" and in at least two other locations along Fort Street.[58] In the autumn of 1863, dance halls appeared on the corner of Government and Johnson streets, the latter parallelling Yates a block to the north, and also a bit farther away from the centre "on the flats between Fisgard street and the Gas Works ... in the immediate vicinity ... of the Esquimalt road."[59] In autumn 1864 they turned up on Johnson and Store streets, in January and again in October 1865 on Cormorant Street, and so on.[60]

The association of dance halls with prostitution rested more on supposition than on hard evidence. The *British Colonist* asserted in December 1861: "They are sinks of iniquity and pollution. Prostitution and kindred vices, in all their hideous deformity, and disease in every form lurk there."[61] Another account ran: "Squaws reel home drunk at the dead hour of the night, in company with boisterous and scarcely less graceless white companions ...

We will not say anything about the notions of refinement and taste, which these Dancing Dervishes will inculcate amongst the patrons of such halls of gaiety."[62]

The repeated condemnations of Aboriginal women as sexual transgressors, be it on the streets of Victoria, in their houses, or in dance halls, gave enormous benefit to four groups of male stakeholders. Each was enabled to make use of them for their own purposes. In each case a form of gratification was sought – physical, economic, political, or moral.

Physical gratification was the most straightforward. The arrival of many thousands of men had its consequences, hence an American miner's description of that heady summer of 1858. "There were over ten thousand miners in Victoria, and the Indians from up north in their large war canoes, some of which held from 75 to 100 men, were trading with the Hudson's Bay Company's stores, and the squaws got badly demoralized, and the miners had plenty of money to spend with them, and they gave them whiskey and there was an awful time among them, and they dressed up as fine as 'White Soiled Dove' do in California."[63] A minority of contemporaries condemned this first group of stakeholders, as in descriptions of "the lust, vice, and brutality of the deprived white men" seeking "to gratify their basest passions."[64] More often there was some attempt at justification, as in this "Plea for the Dance-Houses" from the *British Colonist:* "I think you will allow that in a town containing a large predominance of *men,* and men who, by their mode of life (even suppose them to be so inclined), are precluded from marriage, it is almost, if not totally impossible, to prevent prostitution. There is a great evil there can be no doubt; but under the circumstances I fear it is a necessary evil."[65] As late as 1865, by which time the gold rush was moderating, there were still over four times as many newcomer men as women in Victoria.[66] Everywhere else the proportions were far more skewed.

For miners, would-be miners, former fur traders and their sons, and just plain adventurers who passed through Victoria during these years, Aboriginal women offered pleasure for the moment and sometimes for longer periods of time. Their appeal is evident in the description of the "lady friend" of a man charged in court in April 1862 with "giving wine to Indians, and for haunting a house of ill-fame." She "made quite a neat little Chinook speech in his favour, and with her forensic eloquence, brilliant sallies of wit, and sparkling black eyes, exerted so profound an influence in favor of the accused, that the charge of whisky giving was dismissed."[67]

Then there was William Giles, described as "a native of one of the Western States of America," "a Caribooite, commonly known as 'Jack of Clubs,'" and "half-miner, half-sporting man."[68] Giles was fined £1 in February 1862 for being drunk "and assaulting an [Haida] Indian woman named Jenny," who was in turn fined five shillings for being drunk and disorderly.[69] Just a week later rumours began to circulate, after he had some "difficulty with Jenny," of young Giles' murder. Wintering in Victoria, he had been visiting Jenny regularly in the Haida encampment, and it was mooted her family had taken their revenge. About a hundred of Giles' social set "armed themselves with revolvers and proceeded to the encampment, where they had commenced to examine the huts, when a *posse* of Police arrived and conducted the search." When she was located, Jenny said "she was drunk all night and [did] not remember having seen Jack at all."[70] The next morning the sporting Jack of Clubs turned up alive and well, being shaved in a barber's chair, about the same time Jenny was once again charged with being "drunk and disorderly."[71] Giles arrived to retrieve her just as the case ended, and the "next morning was seen a drinking tea with his Jenny by his side."[72] Some of these relationships made it through the winter, if not longer. Two months after the Jack-of-Clubs incident, the steamer *Otter* departed for New Westminster with a load of men headed to the goldfields, an event, a Victoria newspaper reported, "much enhanced by the howling of four forlorn *clootchmen,* whose 'husbands' were aboard the steamer bound for Cariboo."[73]

A second group of stakeholders sought economic gratification from Aboriginal women. Helmcken put the argument squarely: "Miners used to come to Victoria with lots of gold and exchange it for U.S. coin – this they absolutely squandered – chiefly in brothels or gin shops – so these places flourished and so did dance houses."[74] It was not just that miners patronized Aboriginal women, but rather that the women's presence caused miners to be in Victoria in the first place. The London *Times* correspondent observed in November 1859 that many of the miners "would winter in Victoria did the place afford attractions which would relieve the monotony of life ... but at present we have no places of amusement – no theaters nor 'dance houses,' which afford the miners so much pleasure and recreation."[75] A newspaper editorial acknowledged some time later: "Without amusements Victoria is a dull place. Miners complain that they can enjoy themselves just as well at the Fraser River towns [on the British Columbia mainland] as here. Many will leave, we fear, on the next steamer for San Francisco, and money that might just as well have been spent here, will go to further enrich our American neighbours, who already enjoy the lion's share of the products of our mines."[76]

Dance halls gave the answer. The police magistrate acknowledged in December 1861 that he had been "induced to allow the Dance house to be opened to afford amusement to the miners."[77] As one observer soothed Victorians, "there are public dance-houses in San Francisco as well as in most any sea town of importance," and "this does not hurt their reputation."[78] A letter to the editor a few months later paraded dance halls' economic advantages: "As long as they are kept open more or less of them [miners] will frequent such places, for the very reason that they have no place else to go to while away an hour or two. Miners, as a general rule, are used to an active life; but when they come down here to pass away the winter they soon become tired – having nothing to occupy their minds, and consequently they wander around and through the town in quest of excitement, and naturally hop into every hole and corner whence a little fun is to be had."[79] It is hardly surprising that a poem written to celebrate Jack of Clubs' supposed murder talked about how "the town was filled with mourning ... and few they were that did repair to the squaw dance-house."[80]

Two economic interests fed off Aboriginal women. The first was a handful of Victoria businessmen and government officials who invested in dance halls. The most persistent rumours pointed to Vancouver Island attorney general George Hunter Carey, real estate agent John J. Cochrane, and other unnamed "dignitaries" as having "a high stake in the dancing house building on Fort street," constructed in the fall of 1861.[81] As each new dance hall opened, the press speculated as to who might be financing and then profiting from it.

The second group comprised small businessmen, some of them Jewish merchants who had operated along bustling Yates Street since arriving from San Francisco early in the gold rush.[82] Represented among seventy-seven "inhabitants of the City of Victoria," who in November 1862 requested that a dance hall be permitted to open over the winter, was virtually every Yates Street occupation – tobacconist, newsman, grocer, clothier, bootmaker, dry goods merchant, hotelier, saloon keeper.[83] "We think it will be a benefit to the City to retaining the miners here, as they all bespeak of some such place of entertainment," they wrote.[84] That autumn had, according to a contemporary's recollection, "witnessed the return from Cariboo of a large number of miners with heavy swags of gold dust [who] seemed to find difficulty in getting rid of their money."[85] The signatories were determined to capture that wealth by keeping the men in Victoria over the winter. For both investors and shopkeepers, Aboriginal women were incidental but essential.

Aboriginal women were also used by a third group of stakeholders for political advantage. These years saw a plethora of attempts to regulate and deregulate their presence on the streets of Victoria.[86] As of 1860 a law prohibited Aboriginal people from remaining in Victoria after dusk, and repeated efforts were made, as indicated by the police magistrate's charge book, "to enforce it against the women" and thereby have the streets "cleared from a nuisance which has long infested them."[87] In April 1861 "orders were given to the officers of the police force, to prohibit squaws from promenading our streets after 7 o'clock, P.M., and to prevent their entering till after 6 A.M."[88] Another spate of arrests followed, but, as with most nuisance bylaws, enforcement was spasmodic.[89]

Political power became more concentrated with the incorporation of the city of Victoria on 2 August 1862, which brought into existence a mayor and council distinct from the colonial officials who had formerly been in charge.[90] A petition requesting that dance halls be permitted to operate another season hit the new council early in its mandate. The previous autumn, the police magistrate had sanctioned their opening; now it was council's decision.[91] Politics had a class dimension, one observer pointed out: "Be it remembered that citizens may have their private halls, but these assuredly are not for those miners who are unacquainted in town and who moreover might not be thought refined enough to partake in them."[92] As well, dance halls served to get Aboriginal women off the streets of Victoria, for which politicians could then take credit. "Yesterday [Christmas day] when no theatre nor dance-houses were open, more inebriate men were parading the streets than in preceding days," a *Colonist* writer reported, then queried: "Is dancing worse than to get beastly drunk!"[93] According to another commentator, "the falling off [of] the Indian whiskey trade is imputed to the establishment of the Dance Houses."[94]

Press reports of the council meeting in November 1862 that considered the businessmen's request for dance halls indicate general opposition among the councillors, who occupied such mid-range white-collar occupations as architect, commission merchant, clerk, and druggist.[95] "The Council generally spoke in condemnatory terms of the application, with the exception of Mr. [Richard] Lewis [architect], who thought that if conducted in a proper way, the existence of such an establishment as that petitioned for, might be of benefit to the town."[96]

In the end the matter was too hot for the council to handle. It voted unanimously to refer it to Mayor Thomas Harris, a butcher by trade, who appears to have given tacit consent to construction on the condition the buildings would be located farther away from the town centre than they had been the previous year.[97] Very soon rumours were flying that "a dance-house is being built in the hollow near the gas-works, under the sanction of his Worship the Mayor, who our informant says, believes that the 'boys' should have an opportunity to enjoy themselves during the long winter evenings."[98] Despite opposition petitions, the first dance hall of the season opened, its licence apparently signed by the mayor.[99] Council could no longer duck the issue. After a contentious, unresolved debate on "prohibiting persons from harboring squaws within the city limits," council in late December 1862 passed a more moderate motion "that squaw dancing houses within the city limits are a nuisance and the parties keeping such are amenable to the same penalties as are competent to be levied in the case of any other nuisance under the ordinance on nuisances."[100] In the interests of conciliating their bases of support, politicians had come full circle from the earlier nuisance bylaw whereby Aboriginal women were able to be harassed merely for being on the streets of Victoria.

The fourth group of stakeholders sought moral gratification. If individuals were sometimes ham-handed, economic groups not that intrusive, and politicians unable to act decisively, the virtuous had no hesitation in using Aboriginal women for their own purposes. The quest for moral gratification was the most significant in its consequences over the long run. Aboriginal women had to be seduced – no, raped. They had to be overpowered, stripped of their agency and their dignity, in order for missionaries, clerics, and other self-styled reformers to fulfill the purposes for which many of them came to Victoria in the first place. These men's ambition knew no bounds, being grounded in a racism more strident and unforgiving than that expressed by any other stakeholder group in gold-rush Victoria.

From the outset, race mattered, as evidenced in Amor de Cosmos' fiery editorials in his *British Colonist* newspaper. The absolute assurance with which he pontificated in early 1861 that Aboriginal women were "a community of prostitutes" lay in his conviction that they belonged to "an *inferior* race." Aboriginal peoples' "indolent habits, dishonest disposition and intellectual degradation" meant that they must give way to "a race more enlightened, and by nature and habits better fitted to perform the task of converting what is now a wilderness into productive fields and happy homes."[101]

Clerics and missionaries built on this moral fervour, often heightening the rhetoric. Indicative was a letter to the editor from Methodist minister Ephraim Evans at a time when the dance halls were causing much public debate. In his view, the only persons who could possibly support them were those "who for the sake of the paltry fees of admittance and other unavowed sources of emolument, are ready to pander to the lowest passions of their victims, regardless of the wide-spread destruction of health, morality, and public order to which they are contributing." The dance halls' clientele, he asserted, consisted of "tangle wood manufacturers, illicit traders in small wares from the Indians, receivers of goods from parties whose possessory rights are not too strictly scrutinized, light-fingered gentry who are not scrupulous as the means of acquisition; and kindred characters [who] are not to be confounded with an honest and industrial population," in which he included most miners. As for the women, "the only female participants in these 'Terpsichorean exercises' are the lowest order of the pagan community around us, degraded by vices unknown among them before the advent of their present white associates, and diffusing abroad disease and wretchedness." Like most clerics, Evans sought Aboriginal peoples' complete separation from newcomers in order to give reformers like himself the best possible opportunity to carry out their "civilizing" work, so he wrote bitterly about how "crowds of depraved women" were "harboured in the dance houses until half the night is spent and then turned out to roam at large in their drunken excitement." For Evans, "the whole system of permitting them to frequent the town, or to live in its vicinity, is radically wrong."[102]

It was the smallpox epidemic of 1862-63, more than any other factor, that did the moral reformers' work for them. Demographer Robert Boyd has estimated that the Aboriginal population along the North Coast was halved to fourteen thousand, with the heaviest losses in areas of sustained contact with newcomers. According to Boyd, death claimed seven out of ten Songhees, leaving fewer than five hundred alive.[103] The morally virtuous were quick to depict smallpox as just punishment for past wickedness, "a fit successor to the moral ulcer that has festered in our doors throughout the last four years."[104] Unanimity quickly developed that, to quote de Cosmos' *British Colonist,* "the entire Indian population should be removed ... to a place remote from communication with the whites." The interests of economic stakeholders were dismissed. "No half-way measures can be tolerated with safety; nor no whining about Indian trade can be allowed to interfere."[105] Shortly thereafter all Indians were evicted from the city of Victoria, excepting women living with newcomers, who could apply for a permit to remain.[106] Like all regulations, this one too proved imperfect. When a Spanish sailor died in January 1863 from smallpox, the press took great pleasure in asserting that "there are strong grounds for believing that the unfortunate man caught the infection when mingling amongst Indian women at the squaw dance house."[107]

For the morally virtuous, the dance halls became the symbol of the struggle between the forces of good and evil. They continued to operate, but the moral tide had turned, led not unexpectedly by clergymen. Stakeholders seeking political gain from using Aboriginal women now also lost out. The nuisance bylaw was already being used against "squaw dance-houses" or "squaw halls," as well as against individual women,[108] but never quite so determinedly as in the campaign the Reverend Evans led in the autumn of 1864. Debating the issue a couple of years earlier, one of the more moderate city councillors had argued that if "prostitution" were to be the grounds for action, "the law must be equally enforced without respect to race or nationality."[109] The righteous had no such compunctions about using race to serve their cause. As soon as a dance hall opened on Johnson Street, Evans, who lived nearby, persuaded a couple of neighbours to join him in a nuisance suit intended to shut it down.[110] The proceedings made abundantly clear how race and moral fervour had become joined, as in a witness's claim that, while he would not mind having a dance "in a genteel manner," he "would not dance with a squaw as she is not a lady."[111] A newspaper editorial supporting the suit asserted that "it was useless for it to be contended that white men frequent squaw dance houses for the purpose of innocent recreation and enjoyment. Everyone knew that their objects were fornication and prostitution."[112] The indicting jury's verdict was telling: "We find that the house in question has been conducted as well as possible for one of its character, but that this, or any other assemblage of squaws within the city limits, is a nuisance." At the sentencing hearing, the defence lawyer pointed out the verdict's absurdity in declaring, by definition, "an assemblage of squaws a nuisance."[113]

The press coverage of this and subsequent prosecutions of dance halls became increasingly shrill. No longer did Aboriginal women have to be portrayed as sexually transgressive in order to be labelled prostitutes. They were assumed to be prostitutes by virtue of being racially inferior.[114] So it is not surprising that the Victoria police noted on 18 June 1866 how "all was quiet in town last night," excepting that "Constable Hough reports that Mr. [Amor] De Cosmos came on to his beat this morning at 1 a.m. drunk, and wanted the officer to shew him where he could get a squaw."[115] Aboriginal women had become so wholly sexualized that even this most fervent moral reformer now found nothing wrong with using and abusing them.

Aboriginal women did not, however, know the end of the story, however inevitable it might appear in retrospect. Unaware that their fate was, in the larger scheme of things, sealed, they employed a variety of means to assert their autonomy on the streets of Victoria. Numerous ethnographic studies have described gender relations along the coast as more equitable than in the societies from which newcomers came.[116] As a descendant explained to me about Mary Salslawit's husband William Hughes, "the Indian society his wife came from was matrilineal" and "she did what she would do regardless of who she was married to."[117]

So it is not surprising that Aboriginal women repeatedly fought back. In January 1862 a woman turned up at the Victoria police barracks with a white "man by the throat," having "actually dragged him [there], to be locked up as a witness." As to the reason, "the squaw had been assaulted by a friend of the captive," who had then run away.[118] A couple of weeks later a Tsimshian women named Jenny charged an Irishman with assault. "Jenny stated that she was very nearly killed last night by the prisoner, who came to her house and wanted her company. She refused, and he went away but came back in a little time with a knife and said he would kill her. He beat her and kicked her on the arm."[119] Even when women acquiesced, they were in no way passive. In August 1860 a Portuguese man charged that "a Hydah squaw," who he had admitted to his house "for improper purposes," had "stolen $5 from his pantaloons pocket during the night."[120]

Dance halls and other forms of socialization gave Aboriginal women very real opportunities in a world that, for many of them, had turned upside down. Faced with the disruption of traditional ways of everyday life, they saw the dance halls as a means, not only to make a bit of money, but also to learn to dress and behave as their newcomer counterparts did and thereby, they hoped, to secure a measure of acceptance and even respectability. A press description of seven mostly North Coast women, arrested in May 1860 for loitering, took particular pleasure in noting how "some of their hoops [were] so large that they could scarcely get inside the railing" at the prisoners' dock.[121] Anglican bishop George Hills noted, at an encampment of North Coast peoples, "a woman making up a dress" for the dance house that night.[122] An evocation of a dance hall described its participants as being "well and in some instances tastefully dressed," wearing "the silk dress and the dainty garter, with the air of a Parisian dame."[123]

Aboriginal women's mimicry became cause for scorn, but they themselves were unaware of it, at least for a time. Bishop Hills ridiculed "the young women decked out in every sort of vulgar finery – even to the wearing of crinoline & hoops."[124] A newspaper reported in February 1861 how "a Fort Rupert and a Stekeen squaw, each wearing immense hoops and a black silk dress," had got in a fight, much to a crowd's amusement.[125] A poem penned in 1862 and intended to be satirical was in its way quite flattering in evoking the fundamental shift instigated by the gold rush:

Only three years since, in blankets,
  Slovenly they rolled along,
Like old-fashioned Dutch-built vessels
  Lurching surging, in a storm.

Now Aboriginal women had a very different appearance on the streets of Victoria:

Sound the voice of exultation,
  Let it everywhere be known,
That the Indians round Victoria
  Almost civilized have grown.
That the squaws in radiant colors,
  Dress'd in ample crinoline,
And with graceful tread of turkeys,
  And with proud and stately mien,
Down the streets like gay gondolas
  Gliding o'er Venetian stream
Every day and in all seasons,
  May thus constantly be seen.

The reason for the change was attributed directly to the dance halls.

Now they trip the gay cotillion,
  With an elephantine prance,

In the Market Company building,
    Glide they through the mazy dance.

The rhyme emphasized Aboriginal women's agency, making clear that they themselves played a role in how the dance halls should operate:

Without form of introduction,
    They will not allow their forms
To be clasped in waltzing graces
    Or in polkas flighty charms.
Not without a Caribooite
    On himself the task doth take,
To present a brother miner
    Will a foot the klootchman shake.[126]

An attendee at a goldfield dance house made a similar observation: "I recollect asking one of the Kitty's in Chinook to dance with me and she drew herself up in a very dignified manner and said 'Halo introduce' which signified I had not been introduced to her! And I couldn't help laughing which made her very angry."[127] It was much the same in New Westminster. "A strange miner going in one night, went to one of these 'maids of the forest' and intimated his desire for the pleasure of a dance with her. She eyed him with scorn and remarked, 'Halo introduce.' Accordingly he had to hunt up some one who would do him the favor."[128]

Not just in the dance halls, but more generally, Aboriginal women sought to behave in a manner consistent with the clothing they could now afford. A Victoria newspaper complained in November 1861 about the poor quality of the theatre, which "answers very well nowadays as a place of assignation for squaws and their paramours."[129] A fight in the theatre a year later revealed that the occupant of the adjoining store had been given "permission to introduce favorite squaws," who he described as his "particular friends," into the "boxes situated beneath the dress circle."[130] A visitor to Victoria in the fall of 1863 saw "a sort of San Francisco melodrama" with a "nigger melody," but was even more entranced by the audience, consisting "mostly of miners & rowdies with a gully set apart for the squaws (all prostitutes ... some very pretty)."[131] In retrospect, of course, all the women's efforts were in vain and served only to complete the equation, as one account put it, that "they wear hoops and are prostitutes!"[132]

It is difficult to know whether the various interest groups actually had anything to fear from permitting Aboriginal women to exercise agency, as opposed to using the women for their own purposes. The concluding lines of the 1862 poem suggest – albeit with tongue in cheek – that for at least a brief moment in time the dance halls, in particular, might have been playing a greater role in transforming traditional ways of life than were the morally virtuous or any of the other stakeholder groups.

> What a sad and sober moral,
>   Are we thus compelled to draw,
> From the missionary teachings –
>   From the Christian's moral law.
> Years and years of good men's efforts
>   Seem thus exercised in vain,
> Fiddle and the toe fantastic
>   Is the way we're to reclaim
> All the Indian tribes around us,
>   From their wild and savage life,
> And we'll teach them all the fashions,
>   All the voices that are rife.
> And to ... those who have an interest
>   In the Market Company [dance hall]
> Will we sing our loudest paeans
>   Will we chant the greatest praise,
> For their calm and Christian efforts
>   Teaching squaws the Christian's ways.[133]

In the event, Aboriginal women were given little opportunity to adapt to changing circumstances, being subordinated to stakeholders' goals. In Victoria, as elsewhere during the colonial encounter, most indigenous women didn't stand a chance. It is clear that many Aboriginal women living around Victoria did engage in sexual activity with newcomers. It is also clear that many others put themselves in situations where, so far as newcomers were concerned, it didn't much matter whether or not they actually did so. They were sexually transgressive merely by virtue of the differences that marked them out from newcomer women. This larger set of attitudes enabled the four interest groups to make use of them with impunity. Aboriginal women's identification as prostitutes, alternately as crones, obscured their many other reasons for being on the streets of Victoria, be it selling beans, as with Mary Salslawit, hawking clams, going about their everyday lives as the wives of Aboriginal or non-Aboriginal men, working for wages as servants or washerwomen, or perhaps also getting a bit of cash from evenings in the dance halls. Whatever their reasons for being there, Aboriginal women were harassed to the margins, for the most part off the streets of Victoria, just as they have been in most accounts of the colonial encounter.

Acknowledgments
I am grateful to the Social Sciences and Humanities Research Council of Canada for supporting the research from which this chapter draws. My special thanks go to Chris Hanna for his research into Victoria newspapers.

Notes

1 27 and 28 July 1859 entries in William Hughes, "Diary Kept by William Hughes of the Parish of St. Paul's, City of Dublin, Commenced Jan 1, 1857," Campbell River and District Museum and Archives.

2 "The Northern Indians," *British Colonist*, 7 September 1861; "Editorial," *British Colonist*, 18 April 1861; "City Council," *British Colonist*, 23 December 1862.

3 "Indian vs. White Labor," *British Colonist*, 19 February 1861.

4 Matthew MacFie, *Vancouver Island and British Columbia: Their History, Resources, and Prospects* (London: Longman, Green, Longman, Roberts, and Green, 1865; repr. Toronto: Coles, 1972), 471.

5 Robin Fisher, *Contact and Conflict: Indian-European Relations in British Columbia, 1774-1890* (Vancouver: UBC Press, 1977), 113.

6 In this sense this chapter is a prequel to Jean Barman, "Taming Aboriginal Sexuality: Gender, Power, and Race in British Columbia, 1850-1900," *BC Studies* 115/116 (Autumn/Winter 1997-98): 237-66.

7 Adele Perry makes a similar point in *On the Edge of Empire: Gender, Race, and the Making of British Columbia, 1849-1871* (Toronto: University of Toronto Press, 2001), esp. 54. Among the more perceptive recent examinations of aspects of the topic are Margaret Jolly and Martha MacIntyre, ed., *Family and Gender in the Pacific: Domestic Contradictions and the Colonial Impact* (Cambridge: Cambridge University Press, 1989); Margaret Strobel, *Gender, Sex, and Empire* (Washington: American Historical Association, 1993); Robert Young, *Colonial Desire: Hybridity in Theory, Culture and Race* (London: Routledge, 1995); Ann Laura Stoler, *Race and the Education of Desire: Foucault's History of Sexuality and the Colonial Order of Things* (Durham, NC: Duke University Press, 1995); Frederick Cooper and Ann Laura Stoler, ed., *Tensions of Empire: Colonial Cultures in a Bourgeois World* (Berkeley: University of California Press, 1997); Philippa Levine, ed., *Gender and Empire* (New York: Oxford University Press, 2004); and Tony Ballantyne and Antoinette Burton, eds., *Bodies in Contact: Rethinking Colonial Encounters in World History* (Durham, NC: Duke University Press, 2005). For a popular rendition, see Anton Gill, *Ruling Passions: Sex, Race and Empire* (London: BBC Books, 1995). Some earlier, more popular accounts of prostitution ignore the role of indigenous women, as with James H. Gray, *Red Lights on the Prairies* (Toronto: Macmillan, 1971); Anne Seagraves, *Soiled Doves: Prostitution in the Early West* (Hayden, ID: Wesanne, 1994); and Jacqueline Baker Barnhart, *The Fair but Frail: Prostitution in San Francisco, 1849-1900* (Reno: University of Nevada Press, 1986).

8 For more detail, see Jean Barman, *The West beyond the West: A History of British Columbia*, rev. ed. (Toronto: University of Toronto Press, 1996).

9 See John Lutz, "After the Fur Trade: The Aboriginal Labouring Class of British Columbia 1849-1890," *Journal of the Canadian Historical Association* 3 (1992): 71-75.

10 For British Columbia more generally, see Jean Barman, "Invisible Women: Aboriginal Mothers and Mixed-Race Daughters in Rural British Columbia," in *Beyond the City Limits: Rural History in British Columbia*, ed. R.W. Sandwell, 159-79 (Vancouver: UBC Press, 1999); and Jean Barman, "What a Difference a Border Makes: Aboriginal Racial Intermixture in the Pacific Northwest," *Journal of the West* 38, 3 (July 1999): 14-20.

11 R. Byron Johnson, *Very Far West Indeed: A Few Rough Experiences on the North-West Pacific Coast* (London: Sampson Low, Marston, Low, and Searle, 1872; repr. 1985), 49.

12 "The Small-Pox among the Indians," *British Colonist*, 28 April 1862.

13 "The Murder of 'Jack of Clubs,'" *Press*, 4 March 1862.

14 Prince Albertiana, "A Civilized Song of the Solomons," *Daily Press*, 10 March 1862.

15 George W. Stocking, Jr., *Victorian Anthropology* (New York: Free Press, 1987), 199-200, 202.

16 Gail Hawkes, *A Sociology of Sex and Sexuality* (Buckingham, UK, and Philadelphia: Open University Press, 1996), 14-15, 42. The literature on the emergence of the concept of prostitution and the subsequent attempts at suppression in the interests of some higher morality intended to contain women's sexuality within marriage is extensive, including, among other sources for Britain alone, Judith Walkowitz, *Prostitution and Victorian Society: Women, Class, and the State* (Cambridge: Cambridge University Press, 1980); her *City of Dreadful Delight: Narratives of Sexual Danger in Late-Victorian London* (Chicago: University of Chicago Press, 1992); Linda Mahood, *The Magdalenes: Prostitution in the Nineteenth Century* (London: Routledge, 1990); and Paula Bartley, *Prostitution: Prevention and Reform in England, 1860-1914* (London: Routledge, 2000).

17 On the general character of prostitution on the frontier, see Anne M. Butler, *Daughters of Joy, Sisters of Misery: Prostitutes in the American West, 1865-90* (Urbana: University of Illinois Press, 1985). California shared many characteristics with British Columbia, as described in Albert Hurtado, *Intimate Frontiers: Sex, Gender, and Culture in Old California* (Albuquerque: University of New Mexico Press, 1999); Albert Hurtado, *Roaring Camp: The Social World of the California Gold Rush* (New York: W.W. Norton, 2000); and Susan Lee Johnson, "'My Own Private Life': Toward a History of Desire in Gold Rush California," in *Rooted in Barbarous Soil: People, Culture, and Community in Gold Rush California*, ed. Kevin Starr and Richard J. Orsi, 316-46 (Berkeley: University of California Press, 2000).

18 One of the most revealing comparisons to gold-rush Victoria is found in Eileen J. Suárez Findlay, *Imposing Decency: The Politics of Sexuality and Race in Puerto Rico, 1870-1920* (Durham, NC: Duke University Press, 1999). Findlay describes "the sexual and often racial demonization of particular marginalized groups – those who refuse to fit within the prescribed limits of morality and 'decency'" (10). She explains how, "in Puerto Rico from 1870 to 1920, such repressive episodes consistently centered on racially charged excoriation of unruly plebian women, who were labelled 'prostitutes'" (10, elaborated on 81).

19 Philip Mason, *Patterns of Dominance* (London: Oxford University Press, for the Institute of Race Relations, 1970), 88.

20 Anne McClintock, *Imperial Leather: Race, Gender and Sexuality in the Colonial Contest* (New York: Routledge, 1995), 56. Comparable demand for prostitutes existed in diverse locations in the nineteenth and early twentieth centuries, including the Canadian prairies and rapidly expanding Singapore and San Francisco, described respectively in Sarah Carter, *Capturing Women: The Manipulation of Cultural Imagery in Canada's Prairie West* (Montreal and Kingston: McGill-Queen's University Press, 1997); Gray, *Red Lights on the Prairies;* James Francis Warren, *Ah Ku and Karayuki-san: Prostitution in Singapore, 1870-1940* (Singapore: Oxford University Press, 1993); and Benson Tong, *Unsubmissive Women: Chinese Prostitutes in Nineteenth-Century San Francisco* (Norman: University of Oklahoma Press, 1994).

21 See Jean Barman, "Family Life at Fort Langley," *British Columbia Historical News* 32, 4 (Fall 1999): 16-23; Jean Barman and Bruce Watson, "Fort Colville's Fur Trade Families and the Dynamics of Aboriginal Racial Intermixture in the Pacific Northwest," *Pacific Northwest Quarterly* 90, 3 (Summer 1999): 140-53.

22 Carol Ann Cooper, "'To Be Free on Our Lands': Coast Tsimshian and Nisga'a Societies in Historical Perspective, 1820-1900" (PhD dissertation, University of Waterloo, 1993), 184.

23 Hamilton Moffatt and William H. McNeill, entry for 2 February 1862, Journal, Fort Simpson, Hudson's Bay Company Archives, Winnipeg.

24 Francis Poole, *Queen Charlotte Islands: A Narrative of Discovery and Adventure in the North Pacific* (London: Hurst and Blackett, 1872), 313.

25 "Haida Joe," *Victoria Daily Chronicle*, 27 December 1862.

26 Dorothy Blakey Smith, ed., *The Reminiscences of Doctor John Sebastian Helmcken* (Vancouver: UBC Press, 1975), 186-87.

27 "Our Social Evil," *British Colonist*, 22 October 1867.

28 Cooper, "'To be Free on Our Lands,'" 182.

29 *British Columbian and Victoria Directory, 1863*, published by Howard and Barnett (Victoria: Searby and Moore, 1863), 90, refers to the Indian Liquor Act, passed on 24 November 1860, which prohibited the sale or gift of spirits to Indians, but prosecutions occurred earlier, as reported in "Whiskey Cases," *British Colonist*, 24 July 1860, and "An Interesting Whiskey Affair," *British Colonist*, 22 September 1860.

30 "Beating a Squaw," *British Colonist,* 24 August 1861. Charles Mitchel was sentenced to pay costs and be on good behaviour for six months.
31 "Assaulting a Squaw," *British Colonist,* 25 February 1862. Charles Steine was fined £2.
32 "An Interesting Whiskey Affair," *British Colonist,* 22 September 1860. Antoine Fassovier was fined $50.
33 "Dismissed," *British Colonist,* 27 November 1866.
34 "To the Editor," *Victoria Gazette,* 22 September 1860.
35 "Grand Jury Report," *British Colonist,* 6 October 1860.
36 "Indian Prostitutes," *British Colonist,* 13 July 1862.
37 "Serious Charge against a Policeman," *British Colonist,* 28 June 1860; "Police Court," *British Colonist,* 8 November 1862; "Assault," *Evening Express,* 21 January 1863; Smith, *Reminiscences of Doctor John Sebastian Helmcken,* 186-87.
38 "Grand Jury Report," *British Colonist,* 5 July 1860.
39 "Robbery of Clothes," *British Colonist,* 24 September 1860.
40 "A Disorderly Neighborhood," *British Colonist,* 14 October 1861.
41 "Town Council," *British Colonist,* 5 September 1862.
42 "A Brothel," *British Colonist,* 29 May 1860.
43 28 May 1860 session, court records, Victoria, GR419, box 1, file 1860/69, in British Columbia Archives (BCA).
44 Entries in Magistrate's Charge Book, Victoria, GR848, BCA. Two years later Na'hor was charged with "keeping house of ill-fame."
45 "Caution!" *British Colonist,* 29 December 1862.
46 "Ruffianly Assault," *Evening Express,* 25 June 1863. The man, named Jackson, was ordered to pay $5 or spend fourteen days in jail, but nothing else seems to have happened.
47 "Licensing Court," *Evening Express,* 6 October 1864.
48 Philip Hankin, superintendent of police, to Colonial Secretary, 25 August 1865, in Colonial Correspondence, reel 118/1992, BCA.
49 "The Dance Houses," *Daily Press,* 22 December 1861.
50 "Dance House," *British Colonist,* 29 November 1862.
51 Philip J. Hankin, "Reminiscences," microfilm, BCA. The admission fee in Victoria in 1864 was also a "twenty five cent piece" according to "The Squaw Dance House," *Evening Express,* 20 January 1864.
52 "Dance-Houses," *British Colonist,* 29 December 1861; "The Squaw Dance House," *Evening Express,* 20 January 1864; "Police Court," *Daily Press,* 22 July 1862; "A Relapse into Barbarism," *Evening Express,* 15 October 1863; "Fire Department," *Press,* 15 January 1862.
53 Francis E. Herring, *In the Pathless West with Soldiers, Pioneers, Miners, and Savages* (London: T. Fisher Unwin, 1904), 173.
54 Hankin, "Reminiscences."
55 "The Squaw Dance House," *Evening Express,* 20 January 1864.
56 Hankin, "Reminiscences."
57 "Fight at the Dance House – A Man Stabbed," *British Colonist,* 7 April 1860; "Nearly a Row," *Press,* 7 January 1862. This was the area known as Kanaka Road.
58 "The Dance House," *British Colonist,* 20 December 1861; "Rev. Dr. Evans on the Dance Houses," *British Colonist,* 25 December 1861.
59 "The Projected Dance House," *Victoria Daily Chronicle,* 30 November 1862; "The Dance House," *British Colonist,* 1 December 1862.
60 "Squaw Dance Houses," *Evening Express,* 7 November 1864; "Squaw Dance Houses," *Evening Express,* 25 November 1864; "The 'Hall of Miscegenation,'" *Victoria Daily Chronicle,* 16 January 1865; "Squaw Dance House," *Victoria Daily Chronicle,* 7 October 1865.
61 "The Dance House," *British Colonist,* 20 December 1861.
62 "The Dance Houses," *Daily Press,* 22 December 1861.
63 Herman Francis Reinhart, *The Golden Frontier: The Recollections of Herman Francis Reinhart, 1851-1869,* ed. Doyce B. Nunn Jr. (Austin: University of Texas Press, 1962), 143.
64 "City Morals," *Weekly Gazette,* 29 September 1860.
65 "A Plea for the Dance-Houses," *British Colonist,* 23 December 1861.
66 Philip Hankin, "Population of Victoria," 20 January 1865, in Police Department (Victoria), Colonial Correspondence, file 1392, BCA.

67   "Police Court," *British Colonist,* 17 April 1862.

68   "Possible Murder of a Well Known Caribooite," *British Colonist,* 26 February 1862.

69   "Assault," *Press,* 17 February 1862. Jenny was also ordered to enter £5 into security for good behaviour for two months, or suffer ten days' imprisonment.

70   "Possible Murder of a Well Known Caribooite," *British Colonist,* 26 February 1862.

71   "Drunk," *Press,* 26 February 1862.

72   "The Murder of 'Jack of Clubs,'" *Press,* 4 March 1862.

73   "Departure of the 'Otter,'" *British Colonist,* 24 April 1862.

74   Smith, *Reminiscences of Doctor John Sebastian Helmcken,* 186-87.

75   Donald Fraser, Victoria, 10 November 1859, in *Times,* 28 December 1859, E/B/F86, BCA.

76   "Theatricals," *British Colonist,* 8 November 1861.

77   "Brawl in the Dance House," *Press,* 16 December 1861.

78   "The Dance-Houses," *British Colonist,* 23 December 1861.

79   "Dance Houses – Miners not to Blame," *British Colonist,* 24 December 1861.

80   "The Murder of 'Jack of Clubs,'" *Press,* 4 March 1862.

81   Prince Albertiana, "A Civilized Song of the Solomons," *Daily Press,* 10 March 1862; "Sale of the Market Company's Property," *British Colonist,* 13 November 1861; "Theatrical Change," *Press,* 3 January 1862.

82   See Cyril Edel Leonoff, *Pioneers, Pedlars, and Prayer Shawls: The Jewish Communities in British Columbia and the Yukon* (Victoria: Sono Nis, 1978), 27.

83   "City Council," *British Colonist,* 8 November 1862. The names were checked in Edward Mallandaine, *First Victoria Directory* (Victoria: Edward Mallandaine and Co., March 1860), and in *British Columbian and Victoria Directory, 1863.*

84   "City Council," *British Colonist,* 8 November 1862.

85   D.W. Higgins, *The Mystic Spring and Other Tales of Western Life* (Toronto: William Briggs, 1904), 227.

86   Perry, *On the Edge of Empire,* esp. 110-19. Among the secondary literature on nineteenth-century efforts to regulate prostitution, a source with some comparability to Victoria and British Columbia is Joel Best, *Controlling Vice: Regulating Brothel Prostitution in St. Paul, 1865-1883* (Columbus: Ohio State University Press, 1998).

87   "Squaws Arrested," *Victoria Gazette,* 9 May 1860. For examples of enforcement, see entries in Magistrate's Charge Book, Victoria, GR848, BCA.

88   "A Move in the Right Direction," *Press,* 19 April 1861.

89   See, for instance, "Loitering," *British Colonist,* 21 August 1863; "A Move in the Right Direction," *Press,* 19 April 1861; "Loitering," *Evening Express,* 18 September 1863; "A Female Delinquent," *Evening Express,* 2 December 1863; "Malicious Mischief," *Evening Express,* 2 December 1863; and entries in Magistrate's Charge Book, Victoria, GR848, BCA.

90   See *British Columbian and Victoria Directory, 1863,* 93.

91   "City Council," *British Colonist,* 8 November 1862.

92   "The Dance-Houses," *British Colonist,* 23 December 1861.

93   "Dance-Houses Again!" *British Colonist,* 27 December 1861.

94   "Whiskey Seller," *Press,* 20 January 1862.

95   The councillors' names were checked in Mallandaine, *First Victoria Directory* and *British Columbian and Victoria Directory, 1863.*

96   "City Council," *British Colonist,* 8 November 1862.

97   "Got a License," *Victoria Daily Chronicle,* 3 December 1862.

98   "Can Such Things Be?" *Victoria Daily Chronicle,* 16 November 1862.

99   "Judge Pemberton," *Victoria Daily Chronicle,* 23 November 1862; "Got a License," *Victoria Daily Chronicle,* 3 December 1862.

100   "City Council," *British Colonist,* 23 December 1862; Minutes, City of Victoria, Council, 22 December 1862 meeting, Victoria City Archives.

101   "Indian vs. White Labor," *British Colonist,* 19 February 1861.

102   "Rev. Dr. Evans on the Dance Houses," *British Colonist,* 25 December 1861.

103   Robert Boyd, *The Coming of the Spirit of Pestilence: Introduced Infectious Diseases and Population Decline among Northwest Coast Indians, 1774-1874* (Vancouver: UBC Press, 1999), esp. 229.

104 "The Small-Pox among the Indians," *British Colonist,* 28 April 1862.
105 Ibid.
106 "Prostitution Recognized by Government," *British Colonist,* 2 June 1862.
107 "Small Pox," *British Colonist,* 21 January 1863.
108 "A Relapse into Barbarism," *Evening Express,* 15 October 1863; "Go In! – The More the Merrier!" *British Colonist,* 13 February 1862; "Police Court," *Daily Press,* 22 July 1862; "Nymphs of the Pave[ment]," *Evening Express,* 20 September 1864; "Another Nuisance," *Vancouver Times,* 8 December 1864; "A Caution," *Vancouver Times,* 2 July 1865; "Police Court," *Vancouver Daily Post,* 2 January 1866.
109 "City Council," *British Colonist,* 23 December 1862.
110 "Squaw Dance Houses," *Evening Express,* 7 November 1864.
111 "The Squaw Dance House Nuisance," *British Colonist,* 8 November 1864.
112 "Autumn Assizes," *Evening Express,* 17 November 1864.
113 "Court of Assize," *Vancouver Times,* 21 November 1864.
114 See "Squaw Dance House," *Evening Express,* 8 December 1864; "The Squaw Dance House," *British Colonist,* 10 December 1864; "The Squaw Dance House," *British Colonist,* 17 December 1864; "Prosecution," *British Colonist,* 16 January 1865; "Failed," *Evening Express,* 18 January 1865.
115 Police Sergeant's Report Book, Victoria, 18 June 1866 entry, GR308, BCA.
116 A useful introduction to this literature is William Sturtevant, ed., *Handbook of North American Indians* (Washington, DC: Smithsonian), esp. v. 7: *Northwest Coast.*
117 Conversation with Danny Joyce, Campbell River, 28 July 1992.
118 "A Squaw Arrests a White Man," *British Colonist,* 17 January 1862. The woman demanded that the man "be locked up as a witness," and "the man appeared much frightened and asked the protection of the police, which was granted until the woman had left."
119 "Assault Case," *Press,* 24 February 1862. Patrick Finnegan had resources far beyond Jenny's words, hiring an attorney, who "claimed that Finnegan belonged to a country the men of which were noted for their defence of the fair sex, and that he had only entered the house for the purpose of protecting the squaw from the fury of the Indians when he was set upon by them." The magistrate responded somewhat dryly that Finnegan was not a policeman and should not have played that role, and that "the woman had marks of violence on her person." To his credit, the magistrate ordered that Finnegan pay a fine of £3 or be imprisoned for two months.
120 "Promptly Dismissed," *British Colonist,* 24 August 1860. The case brought by Gregory Fernandez was dismissed.
121 "Arrest of Street-Walkers," *British Colonist,* 9 May 1860.
122 Bishop George Hills, Diary, 1 February 1862 entry, in Anglican Church, Ecclesiastical Province of British Columbia, Archives.
123 "The Squaw Dance House," *Evening Express,* 20 January 1864.
124 Bishop George Hills, Diary, 12 August 1860 entry.
125 "Squaw Fight," *British Colonist,* 15 February 1861.
126 Prince Albertiana, "A Civilized Song of the Solomons," *Daily Press,* 10 March 1862.
127 Hankin, "Reminiscences."
128 Herring, *In the Pathless West,* 173.
129 "Theatricals," *British Colonist,* 8 November 1861.
130 "The Fight in the Theatre," *British Colonist,* 22 November 1862.
131 Robert Brown, "Vol. 2: Journal of British Columbia Botanical Expedition – From Nov. 24th 1863 to Jan. 29, 1864," 25 November 1863 entry, Ms. 794, BCA.
132 "Prostitution Recognized by Government," *British Colonist,* 2 June 1862.
133 Prince Albertiana, "A Civilized Song of the Solomons," *Daily Press,* 10 March 1862.

10

"She Was a Ragged Little Thing": Missionaries, Embodiment, and Refashioning Aboriginal Womanhood in Northern Canada

Myra Rutherdale

External bodily appearance, including comportment, attire, and fashion, has attracted scholarly attention because it tells us much about perceptions of class, race, ethnicity, gender, time, and place. Susan Bordo has argued that the body can be read as a cultural text upon which trends are acted out and desires are expressed.[1] Decisions about how the body is clothed, decorated, and cared for are not incidental and often reveal how individuals wish to construct their cultural and social identity. In her consideration of class hierarchies in Upper Canada, for example, Jean Brunet noted how important one's fashion sense was for the preservation of rigid class differentiation. Brunet illustrated her point by mentioning how Susanna Moodie observed the Upper Canadian obsession with fashion: "They dress well and expensively, and are very particular to have their clothes cut in the newest fashion. In England, a lady may please herself in the choice of colours, and in adopting as much of a fashion as suits her style of person and taste, but in Canada they carry this imitation of the fashions of the day to extremes."[2] Moodie was surprised at how anxious Upper Canadians were to keep up to date with the "latest fashions." In this case, fashion was critical for defining membership in the upper middle class.

Besides influencing perceptions of social differentiation, one's outward appearance could become imbued with morality and be commented upon in racialized terms. Around the same time that Moodie was noting middle-class dress, another Upper Canadian observer of the social scene, William Lyon Mackenzie, after visiting a school for Mississauga children along the Credit River, noted the material aspect of the schoolhouse by commenting: "The walls of the school are adorned with good moral maxims; and I perceived that one of the rules was rather novel, though doubtless in place here. – It was, *NO blankets to be worn in school*."[3] Rules about what Mississauga children were to wear or, more importantly in this case, not wear were displayed with the moral maxims and became infused with morality. Good students, especially Aboriginal Christian students, would not dress in blankets.

Moodie and Mackenzie expressed the ways in which clothing became a marker for perceptions of class, race, and even morality. Moodie was struck by Upper Canadians' choices in fashion, whereas Mackenzie found it "rather novel" but necessary that Aboriginal children's dress be reformed. However, clothing was only one aspect of Aboriginal embodiment that concerned newcomers. Hygiene and health also attracted comment and became the target for reform.

The desire to reform or "colonize" bodies has recently received attention from scholars who investigate the nexus between colonization and Western medicine. Informed by Michel Foucault's analysis of power and surveillance, and influenced by postcolonial critiques, we now understand how, as Mary-Ellen Kelm argues, "the drama of colonization" was acted out on Aboriginal bodies.[4] Those involved in colonizing Aboriginal bodies, from Euro-Canadian doctors to field matrons, missionaries, and Indian agents, generally believed that in order to "capture" the minds of Aboriginal peoples, they had to "capture" their bodies first.[5] This link between colonization and the reformation of colonial bodies is also made by Anne McClintock, who argues that many attitudes expressed about Aboriginal cultures were similar to those displayed toward the underclass in Britain. As McClintock observes, soap and cleanliness were fetishes for colonizers, as was clothing: the "Victorian fascination with clean, white bodies and clean, white clothing stemmed not only from the rampant profiteering of the imperial economy but also from rituals and fetish. Soap offered the promise of spiritual salvation and regeneration through commodity consumption, a regime of domestic hygiene that could restore the threatened potency of the imperial body politic and the race."[6] Medical and sanitary matters were central to the modern colonial project in settings all around the world.[7] The introduction of Western products that would change both the appearance and, in some cases, the customs of indigenous populations was inextricably linked to colonization.

While international literature on colonization is critical to our understanding of the missionary enterprise in Canada, so too is a recognition that public hygiene and anxieties over social purity were an important part of Canadian social discourse in the years between 1880 and 1920. The public health and social purity movements examined by Neil Sutherland and Mariana Valverde had far-reaching and powerful implications in terms of how they attempted to reorganize gender, class, and race relations by introducing hegemonic discourses of morality and hygiene.[8] The ideas shared by school inspectors, public health nurses, and clergy reformers were not exclusive to southern towns and cities. This chapter considers how Anglican missionaries in northern British Columbia, the Yukon, and the Northwest Territories from 1870 to 1940 wrote about the bodies of Aboriginal women and children. Their attention to the ways in which bodies were cleaned, clothed, and medicated allows us to understand how they saw themselves and how they perceived Aboriginal peoples. Missionaries not only wanted to introduce regimes of hygiene and new medical practices, but they also wanted to ensure that Aboriginal peoples dressed in new ways.[9] This was important because clothing and comportment became markers of "civilization." Sometimes missionaries even imagined they represented Aboriginal people's conversion to Christianity, and Aboriginal women's transition to more "Westernized" practices was seen as a hopeful sign of change and success. Aboriginal hygiene, medicine, and clothing were all carefully scrutinized by the northern missionaries discussed here, who portrayed them in their diaries and the letters they sent home or to their sponsoring mission societies (the British Church Missionary Society or the Missionary Society for the Church of England in Canada). The Anglican Church had a particularly strong mission presence in northern communities. The Church Missionary Society, based in London, England, began to send missionaries to northern Canada during the 1850s, and both British and Canadian-born women became increasingly active in this mission endeavour, first as mission wives and later as career missionaries.

"No Native Doctor"

In his memoirs of life at Eskimo Point (Arviat) between 1926 and 1944, the Reverend Donald Marsh (consecrated bishop of the Diocese of the Arctic in 1950) discussed his hygiene program. Once Marsh had been in the community long enough to learn some Inuktitut, he began to hold school at his house. Like others before him, he complained immediately about the smell: "Soon the aroma of ancient caribou skin, putrid seal oil and unwashed bodies persuaded me to let the fire out and open wide the window. Despite a thirty-below temperature outside and a fair wind, there was no appreciable change made in either problem. At least part of the solution had to lie in soap and water. Therefore, I put out a basin of water, a towel, and a comb, ready for use before each session. This became a highlight of 'school,' with grandmothers and children alike assisting each other to delouse themselves."[10]

Marsh's goal was to change the relationship that the Padlimiut had with soap. He noticed that at the Hudson's Bay Company store there were always cartons upon cartons full of soap, an item that had not sold very well. And he was absolutely convinced that as the students became cleaner, they also "became much more studious." In his sermons he placed a strong emphasis on hygiene, informing his congregation about how influenza and tuberculosis were spread, and warning them not to spit on the floor. "School lessons," Marsh concluded, "like church sermons, were as much about hygiene and health as about religion and the three Rs."[11] These sentiments were echoed by another missionary, Ruth Latham, a schoolteacher at Shingle Point, who in 1932 reported progress in the Inuvialuit children's hygiene: "We have thirty-three in residence now ... the children are making good progress in school. We had a 'Neatness Contest' this winter in an effort to tidy up the Eskimo race of the future, and the results were gratifying – it was a big event – their receiving their prizes."[12]

Hygiene and health were at the centre of the mission project. Marsh, Latham, and other missionaries believed that if they could change the behaviour and appearance of Aboriginal peoples, they could claim success. In their view, if the children were clean, they were actually better scholars. Cleanliness was next to godliness because cleanliness was visible and belief in Christianity was certainly much less tangible. Appearance and perception became integral to missionaries' self-scrutiny. They judged their success on superficial and external changes because they were not necessarily convinced that absolute conversion was possible.

Almost every Aboriginal autobiography, biography, or oral history on residential schools inevitably turns to a discussion of bodily matters from cleanliness and clothing to hair and health.[13] Inspections of Aboriginal bodies by teachers, missionaries, doctors, and nurses were routine practice at residential schools across Canada. Alice French, a student at the Anglican All Saint's Residential School in Aklavik during the late 1930s, described in her memoir a typical initiation ritual for new students at most church-run residential schools:

I was in the youngest girls' dormitory for ages six to eight. The dormitories were joined by a big common washroom. There were towel hooks along bath walls, wash basins, and jugs of water on a long table. Little brushes and tins of powder were on a shelf built into the middle of the table. I had to wait to see what the other girls would use the little brushes for, so I watched what they did with them as we got ready for bed.

So that was what it was – to brush your teeth with. I wondered what that was supposed to do for you. Somebody told me that it was to keep you from having holes in your teeth. They certainly did have a lot of strange ideas. Another idea was combing your hair with coal oil when you first came to the school. That was to kill the head lice. I didn't have any but we all had to suffer through the coal-oil treatment whether we had lice or not.[14]

Along with coal oil and toothpaste, Alice was also introduced to cod-liver oil. She and her friends enjoyed dashing "to the toilet to spit it out" after it had been scooped into their mouths. Their pleasure soon ended when the supervisor caught word of the cod-liver oil's final destination.[15]

It is important to note that it was not just Aboriginal children in residential schools who were exposed to these lessons in hygiene. Men and women in Aboriginal communities also came under fairly close scrutiny by missionaries. From her mission station at Fort Selkirk, Yukon, Kathleen Martin wrote to the bishop about the women in the community whom she had

Aklavik schoolgirls all dressed up in Western-style clothing, 1940s
Fleming/NWT Archives, N-1979-050-0954

befriended: "There are five old squaws here who might need me anytime. I go to see them nearly every day, or they come to see me. They are dear old people, if I could only get them on better terms with soap and water."[16] Soap, toothpaste, coal oil, and cod-liver oil were only a few of the products used to colonize Aboriginal bodies. Efforts to "convert" hygienic practices parallelled attitudes toward the superiority of Western medicine.

The idea that missionaries had to compete with traditional medicine in order to assert their power was shared by Sarah (Sadie) Stringer, a nurse and missionary who worked at Herschel Island with the Inuvialuit from 1896 to 1901. In November 1897 she wrote of the sadness she felt after visiting a sick child in a snow house, where she witnessed the practice of traditional medicine: "When the child lies still and they think it is not breathing the doctor breathes life into it (so they say) and sings some Eskimo song. It is sad to see the hold superstition has on them." She went back to visit this child again before it died, but refrained from going into the house because "the doctor was there making a wild noise and all was darkness within."[17] Stringer wrote of other times when members of the community came to the mission house seeking medicine, apparently out of desperation. One boy was brought to the mission house only after the parents sought the help of five different medicine makers. Initially Sadie Stringer was reluctant and insisted that "no native doctor or in fact anyone else have anything else to do with the treatment of him." Within a few months the boy recovered. Stringer noted: "[His parents] feel very grateful for our care of their son, and it certainly will have its influence." She hoped that in return for the success-ful medical care, the people of the community would be encouraged to "give up their evil and superstitious ways" and abandon the traditional medicine.[18]

Mission narratives about defeating or competing with medicine makers in settlements across the north are remarkably similar. Reverend Donald Marsh recalled how his wife, Winifred, employed her skills as a midwife to help the Padlimiut women deliver children in a new way. Marsh describes the "dangers" of the traditional birthing practices of Padlimiut women: "At the first signs of labour, usually before the end of full term, a rope was placed around the pregnant woman just below the breasts and knotted tightly. Then, with her kneeling with legs apart, her upstretched arms held by two women (often female angakoks [medicine makers]), the rope was forced downwards until the child was expelled."[19] Children delivered using traditional methods, according to Marsh, were at risk of being premature, underweight, and born with broken ribs.

The moment of transformation for Padlimiut women came when Caroline Gibbons, a Christian Aivilingmiut who apparently rejected traditional methods for delivering her baby, sent for Winifred Marsh to help her. In Donald Marsh's retelling of the story, Winifred's first job upon arriving at Caroline's tent was to establish herself as the one in charge: "Inside were Caroline and her mother-in-law (also a Christian Aivilingmiut), all the camp midwives and angakoks. Win stopped, looked around, and asked Caroline, 'Do you want to have your baby this way?' The answer was a quick 'No!' Win politely asked the angakoks and midwives to leave and then rolled down the tent flaps, restoring privacy. Quickly and smoothly (and without ropes) the newborn baby appeared, a beautiful boy of 7 1/2 pounds. Caroline's mother-in-law carried out the entire procedure."[20] In his narrative of this "turning point" for women at Eskimo Point (Arviat), Marsh emphasized the desire that women had to mimic Caroline's birthing experience, claiming that "the cruel ways of the past began to change for the good of the people."[21] The comfort of delivering a child "naturally" could offer considerable advantage, but far greater importance was placed on the new and modern methods, only possible when the angakoks and midwives were removed from the scene.

The combative discourse against the medicine makers and midwives leaves one with the impression that there was no slippage between usage. The implication is that once the Inuit decided to take advantage of the services provided by the missionaries or nurses and doctors, they transcended a boundary and would not return to their "old ways." This was certainly the goal, but in reality northern Aboriginals were unlikely to give in to the "new ways" so readily.

Annie Okalik remembered when all the women in her community had children with Inuit midwives. When she was a young girl, before she and her family moved in to the settlement at Pangnirtung, she lived what she called a "traditional life." Okalik was a midwife herself and talked about the traditional knowledge that was passed down from one generation to the next:

> Pregnant women were advised to try to stay active as long as they weren't ill, to continue with tasks as long as they were not too heavy to handle, and not to stay in bed too long after waking up. This advice, I know, was told to pregnant women in all northern regions, because it was passed by word of mouth and by songs. We were told not to stay in bed too long after waking so the embryo could grow at a normal rate, and to move around so the fetus would not make an imprint in the pelvic area. This would make labour and giving birth easier and shorter. In Pangnirtung, we did not think to go to the nursing station when we were about to give birth.[22]

Even though she had the opportunity to use the hospital in Pangnirtung, Okalik initially resisted and gave birth to her first few children aided by Inuit midwives. When she later chose hospital delivery, she did not hesitate to state that she preferred having her children delivered with midwives in attendance because at the hospital she felt forced to "wait too long," and she found pregnant women were "treated like they're made of glass."[23] Okalik lamented the fact that most young women she knew would never know the comparative pleasure of delivering a child accompanied by Inuit midwives. She was certainly not convinced that the modern way was more civilized.

A more striking example of resistance is offered by Jane Willis, who remembered as a young girl being visited at her grandmother's house by a nurse who offered a needle in the backside and a bottle full of pills for her ailments. After the nurse's departure, Jane's grandmother told her that the nurse was really a "horrible person" and proceeded to mix her own remedies, which included a good dose of goose grease. Willis reflected on just how many such remedies her grandmother had at her fingertips: "My grandmother had a cure for everything – sips of warm goose-grease for coughs; goose or bear grease, sometimes rancid, rubbed on the chest and back for colds; weak tea or mother's milk for snow blindness; black bear bile for liniment; beaver castors for poultices; the oil from boiled and strained beaver castors to prevent hemorrhaging after childbirth; and brews from certain plants for various aches and pains."[24] Annie Okalik and Jane Willis' grandmother both looked upon the introduction of Western medicine and caregivers with a certain amount of skepticism. It is not surprising they placed more faith in their ways of healing and birthing. Although their comments suggest that they were willing to try out the nurses and missionaries, they were unwilling to substitute one form of medicine for the other. This was equally true for other bodily practices, like dressing.

Missionary Women's Fashion Sense of Self and "Other"

As in other colonial settings, including early-nineteenth-century Upper Canada, newcomers in late-nineteenth-century Dawson, Yukon, were especially aware of class differentiation. They participated in rituals associated with maintaining their newly acquired status. According to Charlene Porsild, Dawson residents moved quickly to distinguish themselves as belonging to the "upper crust" or "inner circle" by holding "at homes" or joining mission societies and fraternal associations.[25] Attire was associated with status, and Dawson women were so determined to "keep up appearances" that they made it a priority to order "the 'latest' fashions from Toronto, New York, and Paris for the many society functions they attended in Dawson."[26]

This does not seem to be the case for missionary women in the north. They were not quite so concerned about how they dressed. In some cases the practical realities of mission life were responsible for their relationship to clothing. Susan Bowen, a schoolteacher from Ireland and later a missionary in Dawson, recalled just how practical she had to be during the gold rush: "One Easter ... I wanted a new hat, and the milliner brought out one at $100. I said: 'Too dear!' In turn she brought one at $50, another at $25, and finally a common little sailor hat you could buy outside for 50 cents, 'very cheap at $15.' I said: 'The hat I have is only seven years old. I will wear it.'"[27] Bowen's approach to shopping in Dawson was practical. She was most certainly not going to be outwitted by the milliner and her inflated prices, no matter how much she may have wanted a new hat.

This practical, or casual, attitude toward apparel was especially evident after women missionaries had been in the north for a while and were on their way home for furlough. These transitional moments of crossing the border between north and south, in terms of fashion, at least, were remarked upon as a return to "civilization." For example, when Charlotte Canham, stationed at Rampart House, went on furlough in the spring of 1896, she was awestruck on arrival at San Francisco. "I cannot attempt to describe our feelings," she wrote to her friend in England, "at finding ourselves once more in civilization, it felt like coming into a new world and made us feel very much behind the times in everything."[28]

Sarah Stringer concurred with Canham's response. She too had been in the north, in her case on Herschel Island for five years, and was at the beginning of her furlough when she set foot in San Francisco: "It was November when we reached San Francisco and as I walked down the gangplank I could feel stares of the women on the dockside boring clean through me. It was a little while before I divined the reason: I had left Toronto five years ago when big sleeves and wide skirts were in fashion. Now all the dresses went straight up and down and I looked like a quaint creature from the past, which, in many ways I suppose I was. For the first time I realized how long we had been away from civilization!"[29] Suddenly concerned about their appearance, Stringer and Canham saw changed clothing fashions as the marker of their hiatus. Yet they were not so worried about their appearances when they were in the north. As female missionaries they rarely commented on their appearance or clothing. If they did mention "fashion," it was often in a lighthearted tone, as when Adelaide Butler at Shingle Point in the mid-1930s boasted about her freedom from changing tastes in fashion: "One doesn't have to worry about fashions up here."[30] Rather than being concerned about recent styles, they flaunted their disregard for clothing as a form of liberation.

Monica Storrs, in the Peace River area of northern British Columbia, seemed to have endless fun with various wardrobes. Storrs admitted that she and her Peace River companions hardly looked like religious women as they went about their work in the late 1920s: "I'm afraid we look more like Cossacks than holy Spinsters, but that can't very well be avoided and anyway we are all three practically identical as church Cossacks. We wear fur caps with ear flaps (mine is cyprus lamb), short brown canvas coats lined with sheepskin, two pairs of mitts – the inside wool and outside horse or moose hide, brown corduroy breeches, two pairs of woolen stockings fastened with thongs of the same undressed hide which fastens round and round the ankles and twists in anywhere – rather like the shepherds in a mystery play at home."[31] Storrs delighted in describing what may have seemed to home audiences to be slightly outrageous. During the early years of the Great Depression, she and the other Anglican women workers in the Peace River started wearing uniforms. Clothes had become too expensive and uniforms were certainly more functional. Like other missionary women, Storrs enjoyed not conforming to fashion constraints.

Sometimes women played with their identities by consciously dressing in what may have been considered men's clothes. While Monica Storrs and her close companion Adeline Harmer were supervising the building of their home, they helped out with some of the physical labour. "On Sunday," Harmer quipped in their diary, "we became perfect ladies shaking off the chrysalis of filthy dark blue overalls."[32] Harmer was aware of the difference between how they were supposed to appear – as "perfect ladies," especially on Sunday – and the manly but certainly practical dark blue overalls.

Not only did women enjoy their freedom from current styles, but they also did not feel compelled to shop. From Pangnirtung in the early 1930s, nurse Prue Hockin claimed that she did not miss shopping: "It doesn't look much like Xmas but I guess it is because there are no Xmas shop windows. It is sort of a relief not to have to shop."[33]

While they felt relieved not to have to shop or dress according to the most recent trends, they were keenly aware that winter necessitated a new wardrobe. Life in the north took on new meaning in the winter. They had to make preparations in advance for both the storage of food and the acquisition of clothing. Yukon missionary Selina Bompas urged that women be adaptable and willing to learn from Aboriginal peoples. She warned that one should listen and not be resentful "when your Indian girls offer to fill your moccasins with straw when suffering from cold feet, because it is a fact which many have found out for themselves that a little hay in the shoes is warmer than knitted socks or corked soles."[34] She also cautioned women to be aware that the hands and feet were the most important parts of the body to keep warm in very cold weather. To avoid potentially deadly frostbite, both had to be carefully protected: "For your hands nothing but mittens will do for you in winter, no gloves would keep your fingers from freezing, but any Indian woman would turn you out a pair of mittens, as neatly made as any white man can accomplish, beaded most tastefully and edged with fur."[35]

Bompas learned about adaptability the hard way. On her first trip to northern Canada, she had been told to dress warmly while travelling: "I had come provided with the thickest of serge dresses as none of my friends had realized the possibility of anything but frost and cold in these northern regions."[36] Instead she found the summer heat rather oppressive and enjoyed taking dips in rivers or lakes at any opportunity. She learned, however, that this behaviour was not well received. "The weather has been and still is oppressive 91 in the shade some days," she wrote to her sister-in-law. "Miss M & I only keep ourselves by frequent bathes in the Lake the water is so delicious – but the dear Indians are somewhat shocked and scandalized – they never would dream of such a thing as washing all over! & it is whispered that our bathing has driven away the fish."[37] Bompas found herself overdressed for the summer, but then had to adjust to yet another new climate and sought the advice of Aboriginal women for her winter wardrobe. Clothing, in the context of winter, became an area for negotiation between Aboriginal peoples and missionaries. As Bompas suggested, newcomers to the north would be wise to ask for help to design the most efficient winter clothing. Warmth was the main consideration.

For Bessie Quirt, an Ontario-born schoolteacher and later a missionary, the approach of her first Arctic winter was a mixed blessing, as she recorded in the fall of 1929: "We're rather dreading the period of darkness and the coldness of the winter, but even at that we're almost anxious to see what it will be like."[38] She was well prepared because Susie, wife of the Inuit catechist Thomas Umaok, had prepared an "ategee," or outdoor coat, for the cold winter days. At first Quirt was uncomfortable: "It feels so dreadfully long and sloppy – I feel precisely as though I were out in my bed-room slippers and night dress – I suppose I'll get used to it like everything else."[39] Her ambivalence eventually did give way to acceptance.

Winifred Petchey Marsh also relied on local Inuit knowledge. In 1937, after the birth of her first child, she realized that he would need a pair of winter boots: "An Eskimo woman, Nellie, kindly made him finely sewn, waterproof, white sealskin boots, which I kept clean by washing in soapy water and hanging up to dry. But they always became stiff. So Nellie taught me how to chew the shoes to soften and reshape them."[40] Like Marsh, Sarah Stringer also had a woman sew outdoor apparel: "I have my dressmaker engaged for the week (a Husky woman making a new fur suit for me and my baby also)."[41]

Photographs of white women wearing Aboriginal-made clothing were often sent home and were regularly used for recruiting purposes. When the Canhams were in England on furlough in 1898 they posed for a London photographer in full winter parkas with snowshoes in hand.[42] Similarly, when Stringer visited England on a promotional tour in 1929 she modelled an Inuit parka, and missionaries often sent locally made clothing, including parkas, back to England as gifts to friends and relatives.

While women missionaries delighted in their freedom from the latest fashions and felt liberated in their northern setting from shopping and keeping up appearances, this freedom was apparently not to be shared by Aboriginal women. What is quite evident instead is that missionary women made repeated attempts to re-dress Aboriginal women, even though they often relied heavily upon those women to provide them with winter clothing, teach them the utility of moss, show them how to soften sealskin boots, and prepare them and their children for winter. At the same time, missionary women could be quite critical of Aboriginal women's attire and somewhat forceful in their program to change it.

An article from the Anglican newspaper, the *North British Columbia News* reflects this attitude: "The average Indian woman is ignorant, hardworking, phlegmatic, unselfish, fond of gay colours in dress, dirty ... What an Indian calls fine clothes are clothes of many colours. Orange, purple, green, red, blue, pink and various other shades of each all put on at one time. A little girl in school the other day had on one pink stocking and one black, a yellow dress, and a red handkerchief on her head; another an orange and dark blue handkerchief, a gray coat, a pink hair ribbon, a green dress, a light blue bow at her neck and yellow stockings."[43] It was clear to the missionaries that Native girls and women would need advice about how to coordinate their clothing and clean their bodies. They were too "dirty" and "fond of gay colours."

Special occasions like Christmas and weddings provided poignant opportunities to re-dress Aboriginal women. Missionary women became very excited at the prospect of introducing Western rituals centred on "dressing up." One Tagish-Tlingit elder, Angela Sidney, remembered how an Anglican missionary, Mrs. Watson, who taught school in Carcross, Yukon, responded to the opportunity to prepare a wedding. In 1916, Angela and George were married in a traditional ceremony, but Mrs. Watson wanted a church wedding and quickly produced a "proper" wedding outfit for Angela. She brought her a cream-coloured linen suit, white shoes, a hat, and a string of pearls. "She told me everything I should wear," Angela recalled, but without bitterness. In fact, she said of Mrs. Watson: "Oh, she was so kind, she loved me up and everything." Mrs. Watson's efforts to re-dress Angela for her second wedding were seen as maternal and no doubt were meant in a kind-hearted manner.[44]

However, it was not only on special occasions that missionary women became enthusiastic about reforming Aboriginal bodies. Even on a day-to-day basis they expressed concerns about attire, appearance, and comportment. The need to re-dress Aboriginal women and children was especially apparent to E. Prudence Hockin, who recorded her impressions in a series of letters home to her parents. Hockin was born in Oak Lake, Manitoba, in 1903 to British immigrant parents, and as she recollected when she was growing up she was "never considered Canadian by her friends."[45] In 1931 she was appointed the first head nurse at the Anglican Pangnirtung Hospital, which was opened by Bishop Archibald Fleming after he encouraged private donors to supply funds for more health facilities in the north. In his memoir, Bishop Fleming remembered his impressions of the interview for the nursing position that Hockin would ultimately occupy for over thirty years: "When I had first interviewed Nurse Hockin for this responsible position I had not been favorably impressed. She had been shy and difficult to approach, peering over her steel-rimmed spectacles. However at the end of our interview I accepted her because her nursing qualifications were excellent and she was willing to commit herself to a four year term." Bishop Fleming went on to add that he had appointed her with "misgivings," and for that he was sorry, because she had proven him wrong.

During her first two years at Pangnirtung, Prudence Hockin and her nursing partner at the hospital, Carol Sausier, saw patients whose illnesses included fever, tonsillitis, tuberculosis, snow blindness, and thrush. One patient had to have his leg amputated, and there were a few babies born at the hospital. In the first few years, at least, there were probably no more than four patients in the hospital at any given time. Hockin never hesitated to give her opinions on the suitability of her patients: "Killabuck was admitted on the 21st with a pain in his tummy and just went out today. We thought we were going to have an operation for appendix but he disappointed us by recovering without. He was quite sick for a couple of days but quite a model patient."[46] A few months later she described another patient in similar terms: "Today our old Agatooga was admitted again ... His feet are very bad again, he is a very good patient and not sick otherwise."[47] Hockin appeared to respect her patients and to treat all of their illnesses in a professional manner.

Yet what is most striking and significant about Hockin's correspondence is not the catalogue of symptoms and cures, but rather her abiding obsession with clothing and cleanliness. Hockin's commentary on the physical appearance of the Inuit in Pangnirtung is more extensive than any of her descriptions of illnesses or disease outbreaks. For Hockin, Western clothes worn by Inuit women became an important marker of change and progress.

Hockin's first efforts at reform were bestowed upon a fourteen-year-old girl named Rhoda who was apparently orphaned. She was hired to help Hockin and Sausier with domestic chores, but she also gave her employees an opportunity to start refashioning women's style in Pangnirtung: "She comes to wash dishes, sweep, dust & generally run around. She comes at 9 & is off all afternoon returning at 5 for supper. We started her by putting her in the bath & rigging up new clothes. The only decent garment she had was a dress which when we had her wash & iron it turned out to belong to someone else."[48]

Rhoda was the recipient of many old dresses from Hockin and Sausier. However, as Hockin noted, it was not quite as easy to dress Rhoda as she initially imagined: "She has gone through all her winter dresses and has not enough out of her large salary for more just now so with an old one of Carol's and mine she will go through to spring we hope. It is a business to keep her covered on $3.00 per month, she is such a ruffian."[49]

Rhoda was not the only girl in Pangnirtung to receive old or new clothes from the Anglicans. Christmas especially became a time to encourage everyone to dress up and to celebrate the holiday's gift-giving traditions. According to Hockin, most of the families in Pangnirtung over the holidays would receive gifts from the mission bales or from the nurses: "Carol made a couple of dress [sic] for two little girls who needed them, one was our Illissipi, she was a ragged little thing, I gave her the rest of the blanket my skirt was made out of for a kooletang and with that and a decent dress she looked respectable for Xmas."[50]

Hockin was not alone in her efforts to re-dress Inuit women. She had plenty of support from the mission staff, whose goals were similar. In the minds of the missionaries and nurses, gift giving was no doubt benevolent, but it appears to have come at a cost. For example, in one letter Hockin described how the missionary wife, Mrs. Turner, helped to dress the baby of her domestic servant: "Mrs. T got rid of her Martha at last and now has Eto, she likes Eto and is having her bring up her baby according to rule. It is a pretty baby and dressed by Mrs. T looks sweet."[51] We are not told why Martha left or, more likely, why she was fired. What we do learn, however, is that Mrs. Turner is much more favourably disposed to Eto, at least in part because Eto allows Turner to dress her child and because Eto is willing to raise the child "according to rule," or according to Hockin's and Turner's standard of approval. Martha may not have been willing to agree to the *quid pro quo*.

Mary Kendi, child, and nurse Prudence Hockin at All Saints Hospital, Aklavik, early 1940s
Fleming/NWT Archives, N-1979-050-1368

In describing a family who worked for the hospital, Hockin used the same language. If the mother of the family was willing to change her ways, Hockin claimed she would be prepared to help out with offerings of soap, clothing, and the financial remuneration that came with the job. If the mother was unwilling to change, little could be done: "Did I tell you the Mike's have three small children two girls and a boy. They are ragged, oily little things but we hope to be able to help them along, if Mrs. Mike or Atchina is her name will spruce up a bit we will give them a start with clothes and give her a try at washing floors for us but if she won't then we can't do much."[52]

To Hockin's delight, Atchina was able to meet her expectations. As she reported a few months later: "She has certainly improved herself and the family since Mike got a job and a ration of soap."[53] Hockin sincerely wanted to help Mike's family and to show Atchina how to be "clean." Her intention was to be helpful, not harmful. But she imposed a rigorous standard that undoubtedly had change and conformity as its motivation. She was unwilling to give out the extra perquisites that came with the mission hospital if the Inuit were unwilling to conform or "spruce up a bit."

This is not to underestimate the important work of dispensing medicine, inoculating, and caring for patients, but we must also recognize that the new hospital at Pangnirtung, at least during its first years, gave more than medicinal remedies and treatments for fever; the staff was also involved in a program of public hygiene and dress reform. Sealskin pants would be augmented, if not replaced, by dresses in "sky blue material with red roses all over it."[54]

Conclusion

During this period of transformation from a traditional mode of living to permanent settlement, some Inuit chose to take advantage of the new ways and to accept, at least in part, the new clothes, hygienic practices, and remuneration for the work offered by hospitals and missions. But we should not confuse, as the missionaries often did, acceptance with adherence. Nor is it clear that acceptance meant the creation of a new desire for things Western. No doubt Inuit women responded in myriad ways to the clothes offered at the mission or acquired through the Hudson's Bay Company. Minnie Aodla Feeman, an Inuk woman from Cape Horn Island on James Bay, recalled that her grandmother was not thrilled with the new cotton clothes: "My grandmother ... upon first being sold a cotton jacket down on the beach at her settlement, tried it on and took it off as fast as she put it on and said 'How useless, the wind goes right through this.'"[55]

While the practicality of the new clothing and modern medicine could be debated, it is apparent that change did take place. Not only were hospitals introduced and traditional medical practices questioned by newcomers, so too were new methods of hygiene insisted upon and new clothing styles encouraged. By the late 1950s, Margery Hinds, a schoolteacher in the Arctic, found herself in a conversation about women's attire with Inuk elder and artist Johnny Inukpuk. He was amused by the way Hinds dressed, commenting that her attire reminded him of the way Inuit women once appeared: "Our women used to dress something like that," Inukpuk remarked, "only their clothes were made of caribou skin. There were lots more caribou here then than there are now. But after the missionaries came they taught our women to cover up their trousers with skirts. Then, after a time they didn't wear trousers any more, only bloomers that they bought at the store."[56] Hinds concluded that if she wore the "print dresses" and "fleece-lined bloomers" then in style, she would "freeze in such clothing."[57]

What seems clear is that missionary efforts to convert Aboriginals to Christianity were infused with ideas about hygiene, the supremacy of Western medicine, and the practicality of Western clothing that prevailed in their home societies. The mission enterprise was just as much about clean bodies, medicine, and Westernized clothing as it was about telling the old story of Jesus. Missionaries believed that if Aboriginals could be bathed and "rigged up" in "white man's" clothes, they might also stop seeking the help of their medicine makers and stop attending Aboriginal ceremonies. If the missionaries could appear to be doing their jobs by presenting photographic evidence of "civilized looking" Aboriginals, then they could be seen as successful by supporters at home. It was often a question of the visibility of the body over the invisibility of the spirit.

Missionaries elevated their sense of accomplishment by discussing the changes they thought they made, but their elation may not have been shared by all Aboriginals. Women like Annie Okalik, Caroline Gibbons, Angela Sidney, or Rhoda, and families like the "Mikes," took advantage of mission offerings at their convenience and for their own purposes. Sometimes their interactions were based on strategies of mutual benefit, and at other times they were prompted by curiosity. Mission bounty may have been welcome and seen in a positive light, or it may have been seen as intrusive. Either way, once the threshold of the colonial relationship was crossed, Aboriginal peoples were exposed to a new regime of bodily relationships.

Notes

1 Susan Bordo, "The Body and the Reproduction of Feminity," in *Writing on the Body: Female Embodiment and Feminist Theory,* ed. Katie Conboy, Nadia Medina, and Sarah Stanbury, 90-93 (New York: Columbia University Press, 1997).

2 Cited in Jean Brunet, "Occupational Differences and Class Structure," in *Readings in Canadian History Pre-Confederation,* 2nd ed., ed. R. Douglas Francis and Donald B. Smith, 257-69 (Toronto: Holt, Rinehart and Winston, 1986), 259. See also Andrew Holman, "Cultivation and the Middle-Class Self: Manners and Morals in Victorian Ontario," in *Ontario Since Confederation: A Reader,* ed. Edgar André Montigny and Lori Chambers, 105-25 (Toronto: University of Toronto Press, 2000). The most recent contribution to the history of fashion in Canada is Alexandra Palmer, *Couture and Commerce: The Transatlantic Fashion Trade in the 1950s* (Vancouver: UBC Press, 2001).

3 Cited in John Steckley, *Beyond Their Years: Five Native Women's Stories* (Toronto: Canadian Scholar's Press, 1999), 155.

4 Mary-Ellen Kelm, *Colonizing Bodies: Aboriginal Health and Healing in British Columbia, 1900-50* (Vancouver: UBC Press, 1998), 57.

5 Ibid., 59.

6 Anne McClintock, *Imperial Leather: Race, Gender and Sexuality in the Colonial Contest* (New York and London: Routledge, 1995), 211.

7 Philippa Levine, "Modernity, Medicine and Colonialism: The Contagious Diseases Ordinances in Hong Kong and the Straits Settlements," in *Gender, Sexuality and Colonial Modernities,* ed. Antoinette Burton, 35-48 (London: Routledge, 1999). See also in the same volume, Nayan Shah, "Cleansing Motherhood: Hygiene and the Culture of Domesticity in San Francisco's Chinatown, 1875-1900," 19-34. Other studies in this genre include Timothy Burke, *Lifebuoy Men, Lux Women: Commodification, Consumption, and Cleanliness in Modern Zimbabwe* (Durham, NC, and London: Duke University Press, 1996); Radhika Mohanram, *Black Body: Women, Colonialism, and Space* (Minneapolis: University of Minnesota Press, 1999).

8 Neil Sutherland, *Children in English-Canadian Society: Framing the Twentieth-Century Consensus* (Toronto: University of Toronto Press, 1978); Mariana Valverde, *The Age of Light, Soap and Water: Moral Reform in English Canada, 1885-1925* (Toronto: McClelland and Stewart, 1991).

9 Not everyone wanted to see Aboriginal people in western clothing. Karen Dubinsky offers a fascinating account of the Euro-American desire during the 1870s and 1880s to see Aboriginal peoples, in this case the Tuscarora, who lived close to Niagara Falls, as exotic. This led to staged spectacles of Wild West shows. See Karen Dubinsky, *The Second Greatest Disappointment: Honeymooning and Tourism at Niagara Falls* (Toronto: Between The Lines, 1999), 62-63.

10 Donald B. Marsh, *Echoes from a Frozen Land Donald B. Marsh,* Winifred Marsh, ed. (Edmonton: Hurtig, 1987), 29.
11 Ibid., 30.
12 Ruth Latham, "The Arctic," *The Living Message,* October 1932, 340.
13 See, for example, Shirley Sterling, *My Name is Seepeetza* (Vancouver: Douglas and McIntyre, 1992); Mary Lawrence, *My People, Myself* (Prince George, BC: Caitlin, 1996); Lee Maracle, *I Am Woman: A Native Perspective on Sociology and Feminism* (Vancouver: Press Gang, 1996); Nancy Wachowich, ed., in collaboration with Appha Agalakti Awa, Rhoda Kaukjak Katsak, and Sandra Pikujak Katsak, *Saqiyuq: Stories from the Lives of Three Inuit Women* (Montreal and Kingston: McGill-Queen's University Press, 1999). This theme is also prevalent in the secondary literature. See Celia Haig-Brown, *Resistance and Renewal: Surviving the Indian Residential School* (Vancouver: Tillicum, 1988); J.R. Miller, *Shingwauk's Vision: A History of Native Residential Schools* (Toronto: University of Toronto Press, 1996).
14 Alice French, *My Name Is Masak* (Winnipeg: Peguis Publishing, 1977), 26.
15 Ibid., 29.
16 Kathleen Martin to Bishop Issac Stringer, 26 July 1918, Stringer Martin-Cowaret Correspondence, Stringer Papers, Series 1 1-A-5, Anglican Church of Canada: General Synod Archives (ACC:GSA).
17 Sarah Ann Stringer, Diaries 1-17, 15-22 November 1897, Stringer Papers, Series 2 2-C (ACC:GSA).
18 Ibid., February 1900.
19 Marsh, *Echoes from a Frozen Land,* 117-18. This description stands in contradiction to the stereotypical image, which portrayed Aboriginal women as having very easy childbirth. On images of Inuit women in childbirth, see Patricia Jasen's very effective "Race, Culture and the Colonization of Childbirth in Northern Canada," *Social History of Medicine* 10, 3 (December 1997): 383-400.
20 Marsh, 118.
21 Ibid.
22 Annie Okalik, "A Good Life," in *Gossip: A Spoken History of Women in the North,* ed. Mary Crnkovich, 3-9 (Ottawa: Canadian Arctic Resources Committee, 1990), 6-7.
23 Ibid.
24 Jane Willis, *Geniesh: An Indian Girlhood* (Toronto: New Press, 1973), 9.
25 Charlene Porsild, *Gamblers and Dreamers: Women, Men and Community in the Klondike* (Vancouver: UBC Press, 1998), 196-97.
26 Ibid., 197.
27 "Clergy Widow Recalls Early Days in the Yukon," *London Free Press,* June 1960, 9. Although this article did not have a byline, it was written by Yukon resident Flo Whyard. A similar rendition of the story appears in Yukon Diocesan Board, Woman's Auxiliary, *Five Pioneer Women of the Anglican Church of the Yukon* (Whitehorse: Yukon Diocesan Board Women's Auxiliary, 1964), 3.
28 Mrs. Canham to Miss Large at Southsea, September 1896, Personnel File, Yukon Territorial Archives (YTA).
29 Yukon Diocesan Board, Women's Auxiliary, *Five Pioneer Women,* 36.
30 Adelaide Butler to Dollie Butler, 27 April 1935, Butler Papers, General Synod Archives.
31 Monica Storrs, Diary, week ending 2 January 1932, page 41, Diocese of Caledonia Synod Archives.
32 W.L. Morton, ed., *God's Galloping Girl: The Peace River Diaries of Monica Storrs, 1929-1931* (Vancouver: UBC Press, 1979), 229.
33 E.P Hockin correspondence files, 8 December 1931, M4745, Files 24 and 25, Glenbow Museum.
34 Charlotte Selina Bompas, "Mission Work on the Upper Yukon," Pamphlet Collection, 737, YTA.
35 Ibid.
36 Charlotte Selina Bompas to her sister-in-law Selina Anne Bompas, 13 August 1882, Bompas Papers, M89-3 N4, ACC:GSA.
37 Ibid.

38 Bessie Quirt Diary, 26 October 1929, Bessie Quirt Papers, ACC:GSA.
39 Ibid.
40 Winifred Petchey Marsh, *People of the Willow: The Padlimiut Tribe of Cariboo Eskimo Portrayed in Watercolours* (Toronto: Oxford University Press, 1976), 16.
41 Sarah Ann Stringer, Diary, 7 May-14 June 1897, Stringer Papers, Series 2 2-A, M74-3, GSA.
42 Charles Middleton, "A Voice from the Yukon Gold District," *Sunday Magazine* 27 (1898): 184-85.
43 "Indian Girls and Women," *North British Columbia News*, October 1912, 38-39.
44 Cited in Julie Cruikshank, *Life Lived Like a Story: Life Stories of Three Yukon Elders* (Vancouver: UBC Press, 1990), 113-14.
45 E.P. Hockin to parents, 3 September 1932, E.P. Hockin Correspondence Files, M4745 Files 24 and 25, Glenbow Museum.
46 Ibid., 28 September 1932.
47 Ibid., 18 December 1932.
48 Ibid., 8 November 1931.
49 Ibid., 30 January 1933.
50 Ibid., 4 January 1933.
51 Ibid., 24 May 1933.
52 Ibid.
53 Ibid., 15 July 1933.
54 Ibid., 4 January 1933.
55 Penny Petrone, ed., *Northern Voices: Inuit Writing in English* (Toronto: University of Toronto Press, 1988), 237.
56 Margery Hinds, *School-House in the Arctic* (London: Geoffrey Bles, 1958), 146.
57 Ibid., 147.

11
Belonging – Out of Place: Women's Travelling Stories from the Western Edge
Dianne Newell

Since the late eighteenth century, Europeans have employed the term Northwest Coast to describe the essential North Pacific coast of North America.[1] Viewed by Europeans from the settlement and development angle, this was also, significantly, the end of the western settlement line. It was the western edge of the Western world, a late, last European colonial frontier. Mary Louise Pratt's recent re-envisioning of the colonial frontier as a "contact zone," that is, "a space of colonial encounters," has important implications for historical investigations of the Northwest Coast and of Western women's movement within it. The "contact zone," writes Pratt in *Imperial Eyes,* is a dynamic, fluid social space "where different cultures encounter, interact, and conflict in an on-going power-charged set of exchanges."[2] A "contact" perspective emphasizes how subjects are constituted in and by their relations to each other, treating their relations "in terms of co-presence, interaction, interlocking understandings and practices, often with radically asymmetrical relations of power."[3] While Pratt's work has received remarkable play in gender and colonialism scholarship over the years, there is, I feel, more to be accomplished with her particular sense of the embodied privilege of Westerners as they moved through colonial spaces. The degrees of Westerners' engagement would have varied with mobility, and mobility is of course, as Pratt, Karen Lawrence, and others remind us, rife with gender possibilities and limits.[4]

Canada's Pacific coastal contact zone was the spectacular setting for Western women's travelling stories. Examined here are three stories. First is the published travel narrative of an 1890 steamboat excursion through the Inside Passage by Mrs. Maria Septima Collis, a well-connected New Yorker. Following that is the semi-fictional autobiographical story (based on her attempts to "word" her 1920s North Coast field experiences as a painter) by the "ever-single" British Columbia artist-writer Emily Carr. Although Carr is a well-worn topic in Canadian history and feminist scholarship, this treatment offers a novel and complex dimension. The final story concerns the local coverage of the murder of a young, single schoolteacher, Miss Loretta Chisholm, who was walking alone on the edge of a northern, coastal salmon-canning centre. The coverage is local in the double sense of both the local newspaper stories of the girl's murder and a young Aboriginal man's conviction for it, and the later local history produced by a true frontierswoman, Phylis Bowman, who reconstructs Chisholm's story and in so doing reveals something of her own. I ask about the range of meanings of Pratt's "dynamic, fluid social space" as it relates to these women. How did they position themselves in the environment (the point of view), acknowledge boundaries, and project a voice?

The Western Edge

The pioneer settler sense of the North Pacific coast as the literal and figurative western edge of the Western world is equally familiar on both sides of the Canada-US border, but it seems always to have played out differently in Canada, especially in the contentious immigrant project of simultaneously identifying Canadian culture and building a Canadian nation. Canada's formidable literary theorist Northrop Frye captured a sense of this difference in his celebrated 1960s nationalist-era discussion of the Canadian imagination, *The Bush Garden*.[5] Margaret Atwood's contemporary work of criticism, *Survival,* extended Frye's project by sketching an actual thematic map of the Canadian literary landscape.[6] The historical struggle with the unknown, dangerous wilderness was in both instances the dominant thematic concern.

In the Canadian historical imagination, Frye argued, the Pacific forms Canada's only actual ocean coastline: "[Unlike the United States] Canada has, for all practical purposes, no Atlantic Seaboard. The traveller from Europe edges into it like a tiny Jonah entering an inconceivably large whale ... then he goes up the St. Lawrence and the inhabited country comes into view ... The experience initiates one into that gigantic east-to-west thrust which historians regard as the axis of Canadian development, the 'Laurentian' movement that makes the growth of Canada geographically credible. This drive to the west has attracted to itself nearly everything that is heroic and romantic in Canadian tradition."[7]

If it is true, however, as the historians Vicki Ruiz and Janice Monk have suggested, that "the land, often imagined as a woman, and particularly as a virgin, has been an important actor in men's histories of the American West," then Frye's emphasis on the east-to-west thrust of settlement in Canada stems less from heroic and romantic sensibilities than from androcentric ones.[8]

In Canada, the natural climax of the great European journey was the "West Coast." By heading north along the coast, however, the journey would continue. This spatial-intellectual connection between the west and the north was central to Frye's idea of Canadian identity. Frye characterized the

Pacific coast as a wild north-south axis territory of empty spaces, "unknown," Frye suggested, except to the explorers and the "explorer-painters" who followed them "with their eyes continually straining [northward] into the depths of nature."[9] The explorer-painter that Frye had in mind was the celebrated Pacific coast artist, writer, and self-styled interpreter of West Coast Native culture, Emily Carr. Carr built her artistic reputation and became an "icon of Canadian culture" travelling in the high-profile reaches of the contact zone, exploring Aboriginal places of deep attachment thousands of years in the making.[10] When Carr began her documentary project of painting Native artifacts in 1907, she travelled by coastal steamer along the same popular tourist route Maria Collis had followed a few decades earlier, the beaten path to the north where moving and seeing were inextricably linked.

Bruce Braun's elegant exploration of "BC seeing/seeing BC" makes the crucial point that we should not forget the "very conditions that enabled and shaped the possibilities of seeing for white settlers and travelers in BC at the beginning of the twentieth century."[11] Braun argues, and demonstrates, the importance of bringing "the body of the observer into view, because vision must always be anchored in material practices." He extends to the BC coast at the end of the nineteenth century Jonathan Crary's study of the disciplining of modern observers in that era and Crary's key insight: "Seeing is an effect of heterogeneous relations."[12] Transportation routes and technologies also play crucial roles in the act of seeing, for, "crucially, any account of seeing in BC in this period must take on the question of *movement*" (emphasis added). Thus new systems of transportation and communication "ushered in new spaces of identity, culture, and politics" that, according to Braun, "helped to produce the 'west coast' as a distinct region both in terms of a set of material relations, and also in terms of emerging identities and imaginative geographies."[13] New ways of seeing and moving also placed a new emphasis on the visual relation of the traveller to the landscape, which the novel visual technologies available to most travellers in the late nineteenth century (binoculars, cameras, sunglasses) served to accentuate.

An important second look at the Northwest Coast in the late nineteenth and early twentieth centuries, then, reveals a landscape filled not only with Frye's empty spaces, but also with motion and industrial technological meaning that transformed the way Europeans looked at landscape. The coast was in reality a "technoscape," to borrow Rob Wilson's revisionist idea of Hawaii, where the locals came to associate Hawaiian pineapples with summer jobs, forklifts, and canning lines rather than the usual outsider's idea of a tropical paradise.[14] Present on the British Columbia coast by 1890, when Collis travelled north, was an expanding, dispersed network of industrial salmon-canning villages and associated industrial fisheries and transport systems. By the late 1920s, when Carr and Chisholm arrived on the North Coast, the industry had expanded to its maximum geographical range and reached its peak of productivity. Salmon canneries, the first factories on the BC coast, were labour-intensive, racialized, and gendered industrial settings that, although located in isolated and remote spots, were intimately linked with urban and international supply centres and markets.[15] In the BC coastal contact zone, canneries were both at home (belonged) and out of place, not unlike the travelling women whose stories I explore here.

Bird on a Wire

Mrs. (General C.H.T.) Septima Maria Collis (1842-1917) was a middle-aged, upper-middle-class, Alaska-bound, New York excursionist-writer in the summer of 1890. She travelled atop an industrial-age steamboat, outfitted in a Russian folk costume, recalling Old World monuments as she drank in the scene of coastal British Columbia. Of the dozen or so canneries operating along the route, she appeared oblivious.

Collis had travelled west by rail from New York City to Seattle, where she transferred to the steamship *Queen* and headed north following the Canadian coast. She perched on the *Queen* with her new Kodak camera, capturing images that would soon appear in her published account of the voyage, *A Woman's Trip to Alaska*.[16] The sweep of romantic sensibility to be found in Collis' travel writing typifies the collaboration between authors of travel-related writings and metropolitan reading publics engaged with expansionist enterprises, which Pratt points to in *Imperial Eyes*.[17] The immediate publication of Collis' book in New York speaks to the general popularity of the travel genre and the particular appeal of western wilderness destinations. Patricia Jasen's insight into the distinction between settlers' and excursionists' perceptions of "wilderness" is important to note. She writes in her Canadian study, *Wild Things,* that, unlike settlers (but much like the early explorers), tourists "moved through the landscape and carried their centre of gravity with them, secure in the distinction between self and other, consuming images of landscape and people, moving on when the romance began to fade."[18]

Late-twentieth-century scholarship, *Wild Things* and *Imperial Eyes* included, indicates that it was significant that the traveller-writer in this instance was female. Karen Lawrence argues in *Penelope Voyages* that the term "travel" "retains its historical associations with a Western, white, middle class and with a generally male, privileged ease of movement."[19] She suggests that women travellers tended to "map" their travels in a broad spectrum of genres, in "narratives that appropriated literary traditions developed by male writers to trace the itineraries of men." Along the way, however, women's narratives often reworked ideologies of domesticity, in effect producing "alternative myths or models for women's place in society."[20]

Collis' published travel account is a buried treasure, a veritable midden of information about the mental world and material environment of tourists.[21] It also supports Braun's sharp observation that coastal steamship service "remade the BC coast as a succession of sites/sights."[22] For the British Columbia leg of Collis' journey, coastal Aboriginal societies that were heavily involved in cannery labour would form only an implied presence (Native canoes are mentioned, but not Natives) in the "landscape" of the Inside Passage. Nature was understood from the vantage point of the upper deck of an industrial-age steamboat – Braun suggests we might call them "scenery machines"[23] – as it steered the excursionist-writer through, and separated her from, the (fixed, timeless) wildness on her way north to Alaska, several years before the Klondike gold rush along this very same tourist path:

> We pushed through these wonderful islands, twisting and turning as the necessities of navigation required, I suppose, each change of our course opening up some new sense of enchantment and the next one closing it to view, leaving nothing behind but the hope that another turn would bring it back, and then quite suddenly experiencing a realization of our wish. Making myself comfortable on the very uppermost deck, clad in an ordinary cloth walking-dress, with a little astrakhan jacket over my shoulders, I just sat and reveled in this monotony of constant change and let my fancy wander through a score of delicious flights of imagery.[24]

Collis, winding her way north to the Bering Sea that summer, her body warmed by the little Russian folk jacket, her person secured by the fortress her travel account refers to as "the floating home," the *Queen,* encountered the "sublime," which Nancy Paug suggests is a word with "a history on this coast."[25] The sublime refers to a dramatic encounter with natural phenomena – overwhelming, awe-inspiring, dangerous, a human transcendence, a Victorian craze. Collis' account goes on to recall the ancient Grecian and Roman wonders of empire. A glimpse of a glacier reminds her of home, of "our own Niagara Falls" – the latter being for Victorians what Elizabeth McKinsey calls the very icon of "the New World sublime."[26] Linked to McKinsey's notion is Victoria Dickenson's suggestion in *Drawn from Life* that Niagara Falls became for Europeans and transplanted Europeans in North America "a symbol of the strangeness of the Canadian landscape, and a metaphor for its vast expanse."[27] But Collis is now on the actual far side of that vast expanse, heading north along its depth and, given that particular direction, its gathering strangeness.

The visceral response of Collis' fellow passengers to the strange scene adds to the fleeting entertainment of the traveller-author, Mrs. Collis. The travellers below her embody a nervous excitement; the world-weary Collis keeps her distance:

Maria Levy Septima Collis, 1842-1917
Documenting the American South (http://docsouth.unc.edu), The University of North Carolina at Chapel Hill Libraries. Photo taken from Maria Levy Septima Collis, A Woman's War Record, 1861-1865 *(New York and London: G.P. Putnam's Sons, 1889).*

I observed on my Alaska excursion a nervous impulse produced by the excitement of the voyage which took the form of running around the ship and calling your fellow-passenger's attention to something that could only be seen at that particular spot. "There's a whale," says somebody as a spout of water is suddenly thrown ten feet in the air and is repeated at regular intervals; and instantly the little crowd disperses itself wildly all over the ship, shouting, "come and see the whale ..." And thus you are kept informed of water-falls, seals, porpoises, salmon, eagles and Indian canoes, till the day slips by with nothing specially to mark it, but with the mind saturated with the wonders of nature just as it is with those of art after a day spent at Versailles or the Vatican.[28]

The sort of "density in meaning" that Collis reads into her Pacific coast journey – gazing at wilderness and recalling visits to European seats of empire, thinking of Niagara Falls and Versailles – is typical of European travel writing, according to Pratt, and it conveys political weight as "the verbal painter must render momentously significant what is, especially from a narrative point of view, practically a non-event ... Crudely, then, discovery in this context consisted of a gesture of converting local knowledges (discourses) into European national and continental knowledges associated with European forms and relations of power."[29] Above all, Collis' description of her coastal excursion, her ease of movement (mobility), her dress (northern European folk costume), and her very travel perch, in particular, fall into Pratt's "monarch-of-all-I-survey" scenario. For Pratt, the perch for travel writers is any kind of promontory: a balcony, railcar, or, as here, the upper deck of a steamship. But note in this list how Western industrial technology facilitates that powerful perspective. The perch is a viewpoint, argues Pratt, that emerged out of the mid-nineteenth-century explorer literature produced by men and, via male travel genres, women.[30]

Pratt points out about the travel writing genre that, in the end, for all the heroics tourists wrote into these types of "discovery," the act of discovery was anything but. Instead it "consisted of what in European culture counts as a purely passive experience – that of seeing."[31] The popular travel narrative would insure that eyes of others were disciplined to see the West Coast in the same way. Excursionists such as Maria Collis would look, but not touch, and certainly not push at boundaries. Collis also does not even share with us everything in sight. She does not acknowledge the presence of the salmon cannery villages, those important summer ports of call in British Columbia that she would most certainly have called at according to the *Queen*'s regular itinerary of fixed stops.

Fish out of Water

Emily Carr (1871-1945), a Pacific-coast-born artist of British ancestry, and an exemplary interpreter of Canada's West Coast wilderness, had a different, more conflicted sense of the western edge than easterners such as Maria Collis could ever envision. When Carr sought subjects for sketching, she increasingly chose the remote coastal Aboriginal villages of northern Vancouver Island and beyond, which she saw as emptied and desolate traditional places that had been either abandoned permanently (due to the staggering population losses from epidemic diseases brought by Europeans), or at least temporarily deserted when the villagers were away at the salmon canneries.[32] Carr drew essential inspiration from, and cautiously approached, what she assumed was a primitive culture cracking and dissolving under the inescapable threat of the modern world. In Carr's writings the canneries seem to have embodied that inescapable threat to Aboriginal culture. I believe she worked hard to avoid the appearance of personal contact with these places. In her paintings, canneries are conspicuous by their absence,[33] yet in her writings – a different genre – the fish plants to which Natives and others flocked each year for employment and social contact are figured as a highly troubling presence never far from sight.

Carr grew up in the southern Vancouver Island town of Victoria toward the end of the nineteenth century. She was born into gentry but did not choose a genteel life. Fascinated with the strangeness of bodies, Carr noted details of the cosmopolitan population she remembered from her late-Victorian childhood in "young" Victoria, where, she writes, the "Chinaman shuffled in heelless shoes with his vegetable or fish baskets swinging," and the "Indian's naked feet fell pat-pat upon the earth roads."[34] She was equally attracted to the monumental carvings she discovered in 1912 in and around the deserted Native villages of dense North Coast forest settings – fierce and sensuous carved figures of spirits such as D'Sonoqua. Carr produced in 1929-30 a powerful painting of Guyasdoms' D'Sonoqua, and later a vivid "word painting" about her:

> Now I saw her face. The eyes were two rounds of black, set in wider rounds of white, and placed in deep sockets under wide, black eyebrows. Their fixed stare bored into me as if the very life of the old cedar looked out, and it seemed that the voice of the tree itself might have burst from that great round cavity, with projecting lips, that was her mouth. Her ears were round, and stuck out to catch all sounds. The salt air had not dimmed the heavy red of her trunk and arms and thighs. Her hands were black, with blunt finger-tips painted a dazzling white. I stood looking for a long, long time.[35]

In the late 1920s, Carr's wild, lonely images and her sense of the physical vulnerability of her own aging and expanding body (not for Carr the mid-Victorian ideal of female slenderness, which symbolically represents reproductive femininity) would become the hallmarks of her late, growing, national reputation as a painter of Northwest Coast cultural landscapes, despite her modest claim to being *just* a little old lady painting at the farthest edge of her country, "at the edge of nowhere," beyond the margins of the Canadian artistic community.[36] In this respect Carr resembles another travelling female painter, the nineteenth-century English botanical illustrator Marianne North (1830-90). North sought out rough, dangerous foreign conditions for her painting trips, conditions that did not "become a lady," in order to satisfy what her biographer Suzanne Sheffield reckons was her "inner longing for freedom."[37] Her background is similar to Carr's in other important respects. Her father died when she was young, and she remained single her entire life: both factors apparently contributed to her ability to act on her "longing for freedom." North produced two autobiographies/ memoirs of her "happy life," and as was the case for much of Emily Carr's autobiographical writings, both were edited and published posthumously.[38]

In the 1930s, in her sixties and in declining health and spirits, still living modestly and still single, Carr turned almost completely away from painting coastal places and rainforest to writing about them. It is her writings that concern us here. Carr's main literary mentor, Ira Dilworth, writes that Carr's artistic mentors coaxed Carr in the 1920s to begin setting her thoughts down on paper.[39] She thereafter carried little notebooks with her in a shoulder sack and wrote in them while studying and sketching subjects for her art. It was a practice that Carr describes as "wording" her experiences.[40] Out of these inventive records and the poems and jingles she had poked away at from an early age, and with the helpful criticism of three literary women friends of hers, Flora Burns, Ruth Humphrey, and Margaret Clay,[41] Carr (both in her final years and posthumously) published a string of works of fiction and non-fiction. Only one of them, *Growing Pains* (1946), is formally autobiography. Nancy Pagh, among others, argues, however, that it is likely that every one of Carr's books can be considered autobiography within a feminist re-visioning of the genre.[42] It is a re-visioning that recently led Helen Buss to call women's attention to the more inclusive genre of memoir.[43] The related form of Carr's writing – that is, the vignette style – further contributes to her distinctive voice. Just as, in her art, she pushed the bounds of a known and acceptable late-Victorian white female artists' genre of picturesque paintings of lawns and gardens, Carr in her writing used what was normally a comfortable "lady's" framework of vignettes and then subversively introduced uncomfortable, provocative visions within it.[44] This provocative quality is evident in her stories from her northern sketching trips in 1912 and 1928, contained in *Klee Wyck* (1941).

Carr's Governor General's Award-winning first book, *Klee Wyck*, was unique among her publications in that she filled it with vignettes of West Coast Native life. In these stories, Carr represents the canneries metaphorically as protagonists, as places of irresistible temptation that trap Aboriginal people

Emily Carr in her studio; in the background, *Sunshine and Tumult*
Photo by Harold Mortimer Lamb; BC Archives, D-06009

between two worlds, or, in some cases, as places of mortal danger for them. Doubtless Carr understood cannery culture, rhythms, and routines; indeed, her creative work and artistic reputation – and certainly her writings – depended on the existence of coastal cannery villages and a substantial local network of support for her ambitious, out-of-the-way trips.[45] Before her 1928 journey, Carr had always travelled to sites in the company of a white female companion and a pet dog, and on all her local travels in the north she used

Native transport and local male and female Aboriginal guides. Maria Tippett's research shows that Carr made canneries her home base and usually lived with the cannery owner's or manager's families, some of whom were Carr's own relatives.[46] These actual places and real individuals, their true names altered or dropped altogether, arbitrarily fade in and out of Carr's "verbal portraitures."[47]

Carr wrote to one of the influential sponsors of her celebrated 1928 trip to the north, Eric Brown, head of the National Gallery, about her aborted sketching trip to the east coast of the Queen Charlotte Islands (Haida Gwaii). It had been cut short by a sudden storm and a shipwreck in rough seas. She retold the story years later in "Salt Water," an extraordinary vignette in *Klee Wyck*.[48] "Salt Water" is an unusual story for Carr in that it features a direct link between the author/narrator – Carr – and salmon cannery operations. It is also unusual because she is out of control, terrified. In this sensuous – if deeply upsetting – story of a terrible storm ("We had been scarcely an hour on the sea when the rosiness turned to lead, grey mist wrapped us about, and the sea puckered into sullen, green bulges"), the narrator is shipwrecked with her dog, a male Aboriginal guide, and his two young relatives, and is briefly stranded on the wide beach scattered with sea drift at the Haida village of Skedans.[49] Immigrant fishermen for the canneries rescue her, passing her along from vessel to vessel, "like goods," in the night until she eventually lands up sprawled on a cannery wharf.

As this uncomfortable vignette unfolds, the narrator teeters across uneven and unstable surfaces – "vague as walking a tightrope across night" – and stumbles and tumbles up and down ladders and stairs ("Salt Water," 85). She gropes in the dark – of the storm and fog, the spaces below deck, and the night. She wants to be on land but ends up at sea, seasick. She is helpless against the itineraries of the captains and crew of the fishboats, scows, and cannery packers operated by Japanese and Norwegians as she inches her way along the saltwater web, at the heart of which is a salmon cannery.

First, large, bearded, Norwegian sailors rescue her in a little storm-tossed boat and deliver her to a seiner, where she flops down onto the fish hatch and lies there, "sprawling like a starfish," until, she writes, "[the captain] picked me up like a baby and dumped me into the berth in his own cabin" ("Salt Water," 83). This is the first of several references to her bodily state as a captured sea creature: dizzy, breathless, unbalanced, manhandled. The Norwegian seine boat takes her to a "Jap" fish scow, where she will, now separated from her Native travel companions and her dog, wait for a packer boat to tow it to a cannery. She falls into a dreamlike state and "loathsome thoughts" drift in and out of her mind – the fish scow, all those fish out of water, the violence, and the "ripping knives." This flickering of images in her dream is born of an intimate acquaintance with cannery operations:

"Solitary, uncounted hours in one of those hideous square-snouted pits of fish smell! Already I could feel the cold brutes slithering around me for aeons and aeons of time before the tow ropes went taut, and we set out for the cannery. There, men with spiked poles would swarm into the scow, hook each fish under the gills. The creatures would hurtle through the air like silver streaks, landing into the cannery chutes with slithery thumps, and pass on to the ripping knives" ("Salt Water," 85).

Then a "Jap" fishboat agrees to keep her at the fish scow until she is – along with the waiting catch – collected. She was goods, "a pick-up that somebody asked someone else to dump somewhere" ("Salt Water," 86). The Japanese crew that collected her included a "curious little creature" who attended to her, helping her to navigate – "tip and roll" – her body into a minuscule bunk in the pitch-black of the ship's hold. The foreign-sounding "creature" is beyond her imagining: "Doubtless he had a middle because there was a shriveled little voice pickled away somewhere in his vitals, but his sou'wester came so low and his sea-boots so high, the rest of him seemed negligible" ("Salt Water," 90-91).

She is perhaps grateful for the presence of this formless stranger, whom she dubs "Sou'wester-Boots." He is someone with whom she no doubt identifies, somebody who is, like her, out of place. However, this comforting thought loses out to the frightening sound of the kiss of the lapping water on the thin boards of the hull against her ear, and to the frightening sights, smells, and other sensations: the look of the inky darkness of the room, with its smell of fish and tar, and the feel of the saw-like thrusts of the ship's rudder cable "playing scales" on her backbone ("Salt Water," 91-92). The scenario she describes is closer to a torture chamber than a rescue mission.

When she reaches the cannery – the antithesis of the deserted Native villages she normally gravitated to – at three in the morning, safety remains a dangerous climb away: "We came to the base of an abnormally long perpendicular fish ladder, stretching up, up into shadow so overwhelmingly deep it seemed as if a pit had been inverted over our heads." This conflation of darkness, danger, and uncertain and unstable space enjoins Carr's technophobia about the cannery itself, as she announces: "It was the wharf and the Cannery." It must have been low tide. In her floundering and terror-stricken attempts to navigate her body up the long ladder into the "giddy blackness" of the fog-shrouded wharf above, all progress is slowed by the indelible sounds of the exposed foreshore beneath the cannery, with "mud sucking sluggishly around the base of piles, the click of mussels and barnacles, the hiss and squirt of clams" ("Salt Water," 92). Her feet "slithered and scrunched on stranded things." Unseen men in the fog above her bark orders and wave lanterns, the lights of which barely penetrate the blanket of fog. "Hanging in the void," she writes, "clinging to slipperiness, was horrible – horrible *beyond words*!" ("Salt Water," 93; my emphasis). Tumbling off the top of the ladder and onto the wharf, she props herself up, "T-squared against wharf and shed ... time, three A.M. ... place, a far north Cannery of British Columbia" ("Salt Water," 93).

Carr's use of this unusual verb, "T-squared," to describe her body relative to the cannery prompted Hilda Thomas to explain Carr's choice of words. "T-squared" suggests an "aporia," argues Thomas, who says the term is "an undefined, or perhaps, indefinable, space between two parallel and equally dehumanizing lines of experience." Thomas' creative explanation, which focuses on the geometry of Carr's activated noun, T-square, proceeds, as I understand it, from a particular reading of Carr's life story and a powerful late-1980s feminist theme: the necessity of challenging the boundaries of the nature-culture divide. Thomas writes that, "on the one hand there is raw nature, on the other a reified and fragmented mechanized culture. Throughout her life Carr strove in her art to open up a human space between these two – a space in which beauty and feeling could be 'at least imaginatively experienced.' That struggle can be read as a sub-text of 'Salt Water.'"[50] It is also possible to read, in her use of "T-squared," Carr as the antimodernist technophobe that she was, or at least represented herself to be (for we are never quite sure with Carr). Even in the "Salt Water" journey to a "far north" cannery, Carr invites us no further into the compound than the wharf's edge. She is back at a place where "difference" is once again under control. She has regained the privilege of whiteness. The important part of the vignette is over.[51]

Road Kill

The final story in this trilogy concerns the great yawning mouth of the Skeena River; its regional salmon cannery centre, Port Essington; and the story of Miss Loretta Chisholm (1905-26). Chisholm was a twenty-one-year-old, white teacher who was beaten and murdered outside this town on a walk "alone." Unlike Emily Carr, a prominent older woman who was well-versed in self-representation in a number of media, including her own life writing, Chisholm was a young, "ordinary" woman, and her story is entirely reconstructed through popular sources written by observers and represented as local history. We have nothing of Chisholm's voice, only second-hand accounts, post-mortem, of her habits and dress, her modus vivendi. These evoke an identity as a girl of the New Day, a type of 1920s image of girls and women that Veronica Strong-Boag explores in *The New Day Recalled*.[52]

Chisholm's unsolved murder guaranteed her centrality in Phylis Bowman's local history of this mixed-race community on the Skeena, a river of memory, destiny, and mists.[53] Laura Cameron, in her exploration of identity and locality within the immensely obliterated Fraser Delta landscape of southern coastal British Columbia, considers the many ways that mixed-race communities memorialize (or "forget," or even miss) powerful events and places.

She joins others in arguing that using space as a context in which to write and talk about events in time has a long – and for the storytellers, a dynamic and flexible – tradition.[54] Such revisionist approaches to material history are pushing the 1980s construction of a New Western History (an exercise, in Patricia Limerick's words, of "closing the frontier and opening western history") in the United States and Canada on to the next stage.[55]

Bowman's history of Port Essington, *Klondike of the Skeena!* (1982), appears in the appropriately named "Raindrop Series" of local history booklets written and self-published by the author. Unlike the standard autobiographical, linear approach of the males among her fellow local historians, Bowman's history is a collage of stories excerpted from old newspapers and missionary bulletins and is heavily illustrated with annotated old photographs and maps. Perhaps Bowman constructed it from her personal scrapbook, for it has the look of a scrapbook.

No single event receives more attention in Bowman's revelations about Port Essington, in the main text or in the annotations, than the murder of Loretta Chisholm on a trail that led out of town.[56] At the western end of the town, beyond Cunningham Bay where the old Native village stood, an intact narrow plank walk ran above the marshy extension of the tidal mudflats. Named the Sawmill Trail, or Old Mill Trail, the walkway led out of town and out of sight of town, around the back of a small rocky promontory, past the cemetery, and through several miles of muskeg beyond it to the sawmill. The Sawmill Trail and cemetery give anyone familiar with Port Essington pause for thought. Everyone knew that the trail was a family favourite for Sunday afternoon strolls and that the cemetery was a rare isolated, private meeting spot for courting couples.[57] Even later in the century, after the sawmill burned down and the boardwalk began to rot, people still hiked out that way according to Bowman.

The cemetery's local fame – notoriety, really – derives from the brutal murder that occurred near it, just off the trail, on Sunday 23 May 1926. The young murder victim was from Vancouver. In Port Essington, where she taught school, she boarded at the home of the white net boss for one of the canneries and his wife. Prior to her recent arrival in Port Essington, Chisholm had taught at two tiny settlements in British Columbia's northern Interior. This background information hints at the young Vancouverite's individuality and willingness to occupy widened boundaries, within limits. A search party found Chisholm's body the day after she was last seen heading out on a "short" walk Sunday before breakfast and church. Off the plank walk, about a mile and a half from town, searchers followed a trail of blood. She had been dragged some fifty feet from the elevated walkway into the bush and muskeg, battered, and suffocated, a handful of moss shoved down her throat. The newspaper reports never failed to mention the bizarre details of her bodily remains: she was lying face down, with her lower body only partly clothed (some clothes torn off) and her throat plugged with moss. One boot was missing but her gloves were on. The school inspector told reporters that Chisholm was an experienced, college-trained teacher of "ability and high character, 'a real lady.'"[58] The Vancouver papers stressed this proper status even more, emphasizing that Chisholm was a graduate of the University of British Columbia and Vancouver Normal School.[59]

Her body was shipped to the regional coastal town of Prince Rupert, where the coroner's inquest and first trial for murder took place. It was here that the jury examined the remains, the coroner performed the autopsy, and the locals held a funeral. The post-mortem report left no doubt as to the scope of the bloody, gendered violence inflicted on this "real lady's" face and torso:

> There was a horizontal wound about 1½ inches in length on the left temple with blood oozing therefrom, a large swelling over the left cheek bone, about three inches in diameter, scratches on both eyelids, fractured nose with blood oozing, ragged fractures of both lower and upper jaws, the fracture of the latter extending to the left eye, marks as from human nails on both sides of the chin, extensive bruises on the neck, broken hyoid bone on the neck, depressed right lung with blood in the cavity, contracted heart, ruptured liver, and various discolorations of the skin. The mouth and throat were plugged down to the Adam's Apple with moss and there was moss in the windpipe. There was no indication of criminal assault.[60]

Chisholm had been fatally silenced in a highly sexualized way but not, apparently, raped. The medical examiner testified that had it not been for the suffocation, she would have had a "fighting chance" for recovery. Physical recovery, perhaps, but what if she had been raped (and some ambiguity exists about this fact)? One Vancouver newspaper included a coded reference to attempted rape, mentioning, for example, "strong indications that outrage had been attempted," while another interpreted the autopsy report as indicating that "the girl fought bravely and saved her honour."[61] Would the young schoolteacher have recovered from that act of sexual violence, a "fate worse than death," as Karen Dubinsky puts it in *Improper Advances?*[62]

The inquest jury found the cause of death to be suffocation at the hands of a person or persons unknown. The criminal trial produced a different verdict. The trial judge quickly sentenced an Aboriginal lad, Joseph Sankey, to death by hanging for the murder, and the judge sent the boy south to prison in New Westminster, where young Sankey served over a year in jail pending appeal of his sentence. Chisholm's remains likewise went south, to her family in Vancouver, her final resting place.

In 1928 the appeal court ordered a new trial for Sankey and a change of venue to New Westminster, where he was in jail. At the second trial, far away from the Skeena, Sankey was found not guilty and set free. The evidence against him had always been circumstantial; some of it now proved false. Sankey was *almost* a classic "suspect" of the sort that inevitably surfaced when women were murdered in the Canadian west. Lesley Erickson argues that the mythic villain – typically "Indians" and "vagrants," possibly also Eastern European "immigrants" – "like the mythic Mountie, was an essential element in the traditional narrative of Western Canadian colonization; his existence on [settler] society's margins justified the domination of middle-class values and British-Canadian systems of law and order in the culturally diverse West."[63] These stereotypical criminal elements lurking in the wilderness also served to keep proper women in bounds.

All cultures rely heavily on the separation between proper bodies and improper bodies. But there were no fixed categories to be found in the Chisholm murder case, only circumstantial evidence, open to interpretation. In addressing the issue of blame, habits and body language – stature, clothing (what is there, how it is worn, what is missing) – came into play in the public spectacle of the courtroom, which was filtered through the local newspaper and collated for Bowman's local study. The couple Chisholm boarded with, the Morrys, testified before the inquest that they had urged her to have breakfast before her walk. They said she usually took long walks alone after school for exercise, but never before on Sunday mornings, and she had never been "molested before, they believed."[64] Mrs. Morry testified at the first trial about Chisholm's condition when she set out on her walk. The picture is of serviceable dress and excellent spirits: skirt, sweater, and rain slicker, her high rubber boots turned down. Chisholm's clothes were in good condition. She wore heavy chamois gauntlets and had a barrette on her bobbed hair. On cross-examination the landlady acknowledged that the deceased was "quite strong physically."[65]

Witnesses for Sankey explained that the young man had travelled from his Port Simpson home to work in one of the Port Essington canneries; he boarded in town with his uncle and cousins. Some witnesses had spotted two white men, strangers, that Sunday morning, heading out on the Sawmill Trail ahead of Loretta Chisholm, and later saw them heading out of the area in a boat. These men were not found. Sankey was the only suspect taken into custody, and within days he was charged with the crime.[66] According to local newspaper reports at the time police detained him for questioning, Sankey was a "comparatively small man with a rather shifty appearance, darker than the average Indian."[67] In Vancouver, the story of the murder and the first trial, which found Joseph Sankey guilty, received front-page coverage that labelled young Sankey a "half-breed" Indian, a hybrid identity that conveyed more sensationalist value than would straight Indian status.[68] This misleading half-breed label was not, apparently, part of the reporting in the north, where Sankey was known.

Reports of the shocking cemetery murder and of Sankey's arrest and first trial conjure up popular images of Native men and white women and of hierarchies of race and gender similar to those Sarah Carter found were created and manipulated over time in the late-nineteenth-century prairie West. Stereotypical images of women, which women rarely had a hand in creating, helped to establish boundaries between Natives and white settlers and to justify repressive measures against Native peoples.[69] By the 1920s, however, when Chisholm was found murdered in this North Coast town, it would have been difficult to draw clear images of Aboriginal savagery, on the one hand, and innocent white, female victimhood, on the other. This was not the Canadian prairie West in the 1800s. The accused young Aboriginal was rooted in the district, a local who boarded in town with his close relatives and worked for a cannery. North Coast Native people were socially connected and largely at home in the resource towns of the Skeena district. Chisholm, on the other hand, was white and a middle-class professional from Vancouver, which meant she carried power and prestige with her; but she also was from out of town, young, and on her own, moving around from place to place, relatively transgressive, so out of place here.

At Sankey's second trial, the defence council successfully stressed the lack of bodily evidence pointing to Sankey as the murderer: "not a hair of the girl's head nor a shred of her clothing was found on the accused despite the obvious fact that a terrific struggle must have taken place."[70] Reports described the victim as five feet, five and a half inches, tall and 140 pounds; this was roughly the same size as the accused murderer, Sankey.[71] The probability that he could have overwhelmed and murdered a woman of the same size and weight was subtly open to question. The blood (on Chisholm's body and at the murder site) and blood stains (on Sankey's clothing) had been tested for the first trial and had given a more or less positive reaction for human blood, but to which humans did the various pools, drops, smears, and stains uncovered in the case belong?[72] The small stature of the young accused, his slow wit (at the first trial taken as a sign of callous indifference – "He bore the appearance of a person bluffing it out to the end"[73] – but later regarded more sympathetically), the technical inability to pinpoint the origin of blood on either the victim or the accused, and the shift away from the initial perception of Chisholm's body as vulnerable would have helped to give the young man an air of innocence at the second trial.

If Sankey gained an air of innocence in the second trial, could the same be said of Loretta Chisholm? Was Chisholm complicit in her own fate? The question appeared to hang unspoken in the air of the courtroom during both murder trials. Chisholm's "habit" of taking long walks *alone,* and *for exercise* – though never before on a Sunday morning before church – and her dishevelled state when found left the question open to speculation, although no such speculation appears in the local newspaper reports selected by

Bowman.[74] At the second trial, additional small details came to light that provide a clearer picture of Chisholm as a modern girl occupying widened boundaries: Chisholm had "worn no hat." Her raincoat was "transparent" and torn on one sleeve; her boots were turned down "at the knee."[75] Carolyn Strange, in a different context, reveals that young, single women workers in late-nineteenth- and early-twentieth-century Ontario were understood by reference to the values associated with the places they inhabited. In identifying "Toronto's girl problem," moral reformers were concerned with the unsupervised leisure time of such women, especially as many lived – like Miss Chisholm did – apart from their kin.[76] We hear this sort of generational and gendered value expressed in Port Essington in the 1920s by one of the search party who found the body, Arthur Douglas Hardy. Hardy told the inquest he had been the first in town to suspect "foul play." He testified that he "had always been scared of the girl going on her lonely walks. All kinds of characters gathered at the village in the fishing season and he did not care for his own daughters to go out alone that way. There was no regular travel on the trail."[77] We hear in the courtroom the voice of a proper father; we do not hear from his daughters.[78]

Why were these details about Chisholm's habits and dress so important to rehearse post-mortem? The public scrutiny of Chisholm after her death gave voice to this community's – and the older generation's – values concerning proper womanhood. Chisholm was no "femme fatale." If anything, she was the opposite, what Helen Buss identifies as "the new version of 'true/real' womanhood of the twentieth century, a gendering of females as active, boyish women, who are 'good sports' and companions for their men, while not competing with them."[79] She would also have been subject to the air of suspicion that Carolyn Strange discovered in Toronto in an earlier period: that young, single, working women bartered sexual favours for amusements (or were suspected of doing so). "Lurking beneath the surface of every report on women and work was a subtext (or perhaps metatext) of prostitution," according to Strange.[80] By the 1920s, panic about the freely moving female had abated in Toronto, but it was still felt by young women in the social eddies of the northern coastal reaches of British Columbia.

Were, as Hardy (the "proper father") had testified at trial, coastal cannery towns very dangerous places – and if so, dangerous for whom? Work on the canneries in preparation for the opening of the fishing season was just beginning, a point made in the very first newspaper reports of the discovery of the girl's murdered body: "As the season advances, the number of Indians and others increases."[81] One detects in this statement an example of what Erickson discovered in the prairie West: the use of coded language for the presence of criminal elements lurking in the bush in Western Canada, warnings of the danger "Indians and others" allegedly posed to proper women. The essential cosmopolitan character of this rough place spawned numerous linguistic and ethnic enclaves that were self-organized and largely autonomous. Throughout these nodes, individuals could come and go almost unnoticed when the cosmopolitan population of the townsite and Indian reserve temporarily swelled to thousands during the summer fishing season, before it shrank to a few hundred permanent residents once winter snapped back. The witnesses at trial mirrored the racialized nature of the town, with its floating population, complexity of identities, and opaque social boundaries. Star witnesses for the Crown were a ten-year-old Norwegian girl, Haldis Sandhals, and an elderly "naturalized German," a boat builder by the name of Charles Reinholt, who had returned to Essington after being interned as an enemy alien, jailed, and eventually deported from the region during the First World War.[82] Key witnesses for the defense were Sankey's relatives and a Japanese female shopkeeper. Sankey and the majority of the other Native and ethnic minority witnesses spoke through interpreters. Despite their social and cultural diversity, these individuals seemed to understand in ways that Chisholm did not that seemingly safe places were actually dangerous for women in "man's country" – places like the country lanes and berry patches that Dubinsky's research found so physically unsafe for young women in other northern rural areas.[83]

The townsfolk and the newspaper journalists who covered the story seemed relieved when the young Aboriginal escaped the gallows and went free. Reporters wrote that in the New Westminster courtroom, packed with women, applause greeted the judge's verdict.[84] There was, doubtless, a local need to smooth over the histories of violent crime. But over the years the men and women, and certainly the Native communities, of the Skeena district naturally remained edgy about the uncertainty left following the acquittal. Decades later in 1979, after Joseph Sankey died, the prominent white North Coast doctor and amateur historian/ethnologist, Dr. R.G. Large, declared an end to the mystery of Chisholm's murder. Large told the press that he had found an old story that proved an "itinerant Finn" had killed not only Chisholm, but also the victim of another unsolved murder, a young English maid in a boarding house (brothel) in the red light district of Prince Rupert. Mrs. Harry Killas (neé Esther Solomon) was found murdered 17 April 1928 – when Sankey was still in prison.[85] Large hoped that this would lift the cloud of doubt that hung over the head of Joseph Sankey and, by extension, over all Native communities in the district.

Bowman writes that Dr. Large's disclosure wrote "finis" to the unsolved murder of Loretta Chisholm, though Bowman keeps the mystery (and thoughts of Chisholm's inadvertent local boundary crossing) alive with the tantalizing suggestion that "oldtimers still wonder what really happened on the sawmill trail that Sunday morning in 1926."[86] After Sankey died in the 1960s, one former official in the case suggested to Bowman that the boy had been the murderer after all, that Chisholm had in fact been sexually assaulted (but the news concealed to spare her parents any embarrassment), and that stuffing moss down a victim's throat was "an old Indian trait."[87] After the German boat builder, Reinholt, died, a local constable apparently heard from Essington Natives that he probably was the murderer because he had given false testimony against Sankey at trial. This interesting counter-rumour also makes it into Bowman's history.[88]

Mysteries and mythmaking are the passion of local historians such as Phylis Bowman, who inevitably reproduce the dominant masculinist narratives of conquest and progress to explain life on colonial frontiers. When Bowman prepared her work of local history in 1982, Port Essington was a "ghost of a ghost town" and she was one of the few still around the area with first-hand memories of the Chisholm murder. The unsolved murders of Chisholm and Killas became central to Bowman's progressive, "man's country" representation of the northern frontier in those "exciting and colorful years": "The [Chisholm and Killas] deaths remain, as so many other tales along the misty Skeena, part of the mysterious past of those exciting and colorful years when hundreds of settlers, prospectors, miners, fishermen, loggers, and businessmen flocked to the area to open up the Skeena River Valley ... when [Port Essington] was, in truth, the 'Klondike of the Skeena.'"[89]

Conclusion

What are we to make of the stories of these women?

Maria Collis floated over the BC coastal contact zone in 1890 in the process of coming from and heading to someplace else. She brought her boundaries with her. She occupied an isolated perch, an early explorer's stance, and was buffered socially and physically by her urban, middle-age, married, upper-middle-class status. In the language of dress, she was the epitome of civility and taste. She wore a tourist costume for the occasion and maintained a tourist's gaze. She even distanced herself from most of her fellow excursionists, thus stratifying and filtering what seemed at a distance to be a collective experience. She developed no contact, no interaction, no understanding, and, it would appear, no fear. Hers is a bird's eye view. She insists on a wilderness vision of the landscape despite the obvious technoscape before her. The coast remains a safely remote colonial frontier, not a contact zone. It remains exotic and she represents it as such in her conventional adherence to the male literary travel genre and colonial narratives of the late nineteenth century.

Emily Carr resided closer to the contact zone than Collis, at the southern edge of the BC coastal region. Unlike Collis, she made her main living from observing the coastal contact zone. From her actual home she made episodic visits to the north, using, but always pushing past, tourist paths, and always, out of fear, cocooning herself with pet dogs; white female companions (chaperones), including her relatives; and local Aboriginal men and women whom she needed and trusted. Thus, her own fears and her social position, by the 1920s, as an elderly, white "spinster" prevented her from establishing much real or sustained contact with the contact zone, other than the carefully planned, escorted trips into the Northwest Coast exotic edge. This self-isolated "little old lady on the edge of nowhere" maintained crucial limits: she did not paint canneries where Natives worked and found new social experiences, preferring the near-deserted Aboriginal villages, where she kept a watchful eye on the northern rainforest that inspired her work and made her international reputation in the interwar era as an artist, a writer, and, by the 1960s, Canada's iconic "explorer-painter."

Carr's northern journeys, like Collis' northern coastal excursion, were always imbued with the sense of the right to be there. However, the largely ignored autobiographical vignette "Salt Water" shows Carr out of her depth, as "goods," which is the ultimate objectification of colonized individuals. She uses the accident to offer us a glimpse behind the mask and into a woman's terror and weakness in the face of unanticipated difference and loss of control when she slips through the boundaries into "beyond." Clearly, she found herself in the very position of personal danger she had worked so hard to avoid. She maintains crucial limits in another way. Emphasizing her age and bulky body allows her to dodge expectations of femininity; she represents herself as frail and vulnerable, but never feminine. Carr's "word painting" in this instance moves beyond words, closer to what Joy Parr argues in "Notes for a Story of Twentieth Century Canada" is the "broader base of timely knowledge" necessary for a "more sensuous historical practice."[90] Carr's depiction of the coastal landscape/seascape in this vignette is extraordinarily "real" in a sensuous manner – sounds, bulging sea, sea creatures, dirt, decay, wet surfaces, choking smells, blackness, suffocating confinement. It is more real than Collis' picture of it, with no understanding and no contact, though perhaps less real than the description of Loretta Chisholm's wounds.

Loretta Chisholm was, of the three travelling women, the only one who did not represent herself. She is also the only one of them who threw herself into the contact zone, which makes her violent murder there all the more chilling. She had the habits and appearance of one of the new liberated young women of the interwar era. At the cannery town of Port Essington, Chisholm's vocation as a teacher; her middle-class, urban status; and her home away from home as a boarder with a white family of local standing meant that in terms of female respectability, Chisholm was still in bounds, "a real lady." Her freewheeling behaviour was appropriate for her age group and her class and urban origins, but in Skeena country she was out of place, alien in the eyes and traditions of the older settled generation. What the Aboriginal communities within and beyond Port Essington would have made of her behaviour we do not know. However, she became a light-ning rod for the overt expression of racist attitudes toward them. Her mur-der allowed newspapers in British Columbia to run sensationalist articles about the charge and sentencing of an Indian "half-breed." In the interwar decades, and given the popularity of eugenics, "mixed blood" was regarded as a degenerate race. Thus, the context of a volatile rural, racialized commu-nity population made the practice of the urban New Day girl lifestyle less practical or safe, something Chisholm apparently was unable to see. In the mind of the settler community, Chisholm's walks beyond the town bound-ary – alone – suggested her transgression of the social boundaries that would have protected her from harm.

Chisholm's body image (dead body scrutinized and live body recalled) was made and remade, post-mortem, by the search party, investigators, coro-ner, pathologist, medical examiner, men and women of the jury, and the many witnesses at the two criminal trials, most of whom likely sought to satisfy settler community scrutiny as to roles and mythic villains, rather than the "truths" about this woman's real life. Her voice is silenced by a continuing older tradition of male violence and by subsequent community comments, fears, and needs. Chisholm's picked-over image is confounded – and kept alive – not only by the narratives of the mixed-race cannery town, but also by an intermediary in the telling, Phylis Bowman, the white, fe-male, Skeena-area storyteller, whose own life story as a "frontier woman" from Port Essington is (invisibly) bound up in her carefully preserved scraps of history.

Each of these stories develops ideas about the different ways in which Western women "encounter, interact, and conflict" with dimensions of a European colonial frontier. Each story raises the issue of what is seen and reported on the western edge while on the move. The range of motion, intensity of experience, and point of view in each case differs, but each raises questions of personal security and boundaries as they relate to posi-tion – the position these types of women travellers carry with them into the northern coastal area, and the point of view they establish and encounter there. Clothing and other forms of body language help them to make state-ments about their social standing, age, sexuality, and ideological positions, and positions them (and others who they observe) in the environment. Each of them had a sense of belonging, even though they were "out of place."

Acknowledgments
This chapter was prepared while I was a scholar-in-residence at the Peter Wall Institute for Advanced Studies at UBC, which provided the much-appreciated funding. Portions of the chapter have been presented at the following meetings: "Connections: From Local to Glo-bal," New Zealand Historical Association, University of Canterbury, December 2001; Pa-cific Northwest History Association, University of Western Washington, April 2003; "Contested Terrains: Gendered Knowledge, Landscapes, and Narratives," Women's History

Network, University of Aberdeen, September 2003; "Inhabiting Multiple Worlds: Auto/biography in an (Anti) Global Age," International Auto/biography Association, Chinese University of Hong Kong, March 2004. The keen eye and generous comments of Jenéa Tallentire and Arthur Ray are much appreciated, as is the invitation by Katie Pickles and Myra Rutherdale to contribute to this present collection.

Notes

1 For a discussion of "Northwest Coast," see Wayne Suttles, "Introduction," in *Handbook of North American Indians*, vol. 7, *Northwest Coast*, ed. Suttles, 1-15 (Washington, DC: Smithsonian Institution, USGPO, 1990), 1.
2 Mary Louise Pratt, *Imperial Eyes: Travel Writing and Transculturation* (London: Routledge, 1992), 4, 6-7. Pratt is from rural southern Ontario, a place connected to the colonial past in such complex ways that knowing it helped her to think about contact zones. My thanks to Katie Pickles for reminding me of this aspect of Pratt's scholarship.
3 Ibid., 7.
4 Karen R. Lawrence, *Penelope Voyages: Women and Travel in the British Literary Tradition* (Ithaca, NY: Cornell University Press, 1994).
5 Northrop Frye, *The Bush Garden: Essays on the Canadian Imagination* (1971; Toronto: Anansi, 1995).
6 Margaret Atwood, *Survival: A Thematic Guide to Canadian Literature* (Toronto: Anansi, 1972).
7 Frye, *Bush Garden*, 219-20.
8 Vicki L. Ruiz and Janice Monk, "Chapter Five: Editors' Introduction," in *Western Women: Their Land, Their Lives*, ed. Lillian Schlessel, Vicki L. Ruiz, and Janice Monk, 153-54 (Albuquerque: University of New Mexico Press, 1988), 153.
9 Frye, *Bush Garden*, 149.
10 W.H. New, *A History of Canadian Literature* (New York: New Amsterdam, 1992), 46. See also Doris Shadbolt, Map A, Map B, and "Chronology," in *Emily Carr* (Vancouver: Douglas and McIntyre, 1990), 228, 229, 219-22.
11 Bruce Braun, *The Intemperate Rainforest: Nature, Culture, and Power on Canada's West Coast* (Minneapolis: University of Minnesota Press, 2002), 181.
12 Ibid., 181-82, citing Jonathan Crary, *Techniques of the Observer: Vision and Modernity* (Cambridge, MA: MIT Press, 1990).
13 Ibid., 182-83.
14 Rob Wilson, "Blue Hawaii: *Bamboo Ridge* As 'Critical Realism,'" in *What's in a Rim? Critical Perspectives on the Pacific Region Idea*, ed. Arif Dirlik, 282-304 (Boulder, CO: Westview Press, 1993), 285-86.
15 Dianne Newell, ed., *The Development of the Salmon-Canning Industry: A Grown Man's Game* (Montreal and Kingston: McGill University Press, 1989); Dianne Newell, *Tangled Webs of History: Indians and the Law in Canada's Pacific Coast Fisheries* (Toronto: University of Toronto Press, 1993; reissued 1997); Dianne Newell, "Dispersal and Concentration: The Slowly Changing Spatial Pattern of the British Columbia Salmon Canning Industry," *Journal of Historical Geography* 14, 1 (1988): 22-36.
16 Mrs. Septima M. Collis (Mrs. General C.H.T. Collis), *A Woman's Trip to Alaska, Being an Account of a Voyage through the Inland Seas of the Sitkan Archipelago in 1890* (New York: Cassell Publishing, illustrated by the American Bank Note Co., 1890).
17 See also James Morris, *Pax Britannica: The Climax of an Empire* (Harmondsworth, UK: Penguin, 1979), cited in Sara Mills, *Discourses of Difference: An Analysis of Women's Travel Writing and Colonialism* (London: Routledge, 1991), 1. Mills makes a point of limiting her studies to writers who describe their travels in colonized countries. See also Napur Chaudhuri and Margaret Strobel, eds., *Western Women and Imperialism: Complicity and Resistance* (Bloomington: Indiana University Press, 1992).
18 Patricia Jasen, *Wild Things: Nature, Culture, and Tourism in Ontario, 1790-1914* (Toronto: University of Toronto Press, 1995), 26.
19 Lawrence, *Penelope Voyages*, xii.
20 Ibid., x-xi. See also Nancy Pagh's discussion, "Theorizing Colonial Women's Travel Writing," in *At Home Afloat: Women on the Waters of the Pacific Northwest* (Calgary: University of Calgary Press, 2001), 87-89.

21 Critical to the process of travel writing in the specific case of published explorers' narratives, but applicable to all travel writing, are the stages through which the travel narrative evolves: from initial cryptic on-the-spot observations recorded in diaries or logbooks, through to memories of the place mixed with recollections of other places and times that inform the final published account. See Daniel Clayton, "Captain Cook and the Spaces of Contact at Nootka Sound," in *Reading beyond Words: Contexts for Native History*, ed. Jennifer S.H. Brown and Elizabeth Vibert, 95-123 (Peterborough, ON: Broadview Press, 1996), 103-4, citing I.S. MacLaren, "Exploration/Travel Literature and the Evolution of the Author," *International Journal of Canadian Studies* 5 (Spring 1992): 39-68.

22 Braun, *Intemperate Rainforest*, 184.

23 Ibid.

24 Collis, *A Woman's Trip to Alaska*, 72.

25 Paug, *At Home Afloat*, 130, 98.

26 Collis, *A Woman's Trip to Alaska*, 73; Elizabeth McKinsey, *Niagara Falls: Icon of the American Sublime* (New York: Cambridge University Press, 1985); Jasen, *Wild Things*, Chapter 2, "Taming Niagara."

27 Victoria Dickenson, *Drawn from Life: Science and Art in the Portrayal of the New World* (Toronto: University of Toronto Press, 1998), 111.

28 Collis, *A Woman's Trip to Alaska*, 73-74.

29 Pratt, *Imperial Eyes*, 202.

30 See ibid., Chapter 9, which provides a powerful, critical discussion of the ideological implications of this approach.

31 Ibid., 204.

32 Emily Carr, *Klee Wyck* (Toronto: Irwin Publishing, 1941), 32, 45-51.

33 A point on which Braun concurs. Braun, *Intemperate Rainforest*, 180. But see the sketches and notations in Carr's sketchbooks from the late 1920s concerning her trips to the Skeena and Nass rivers and the Queen Charlotte Islands in 1928, and to Nootka, Friendly Cove, and Port Renfrew in 1929. See the cannery sketches and brief descriptions in Doris Shadbolt, *The Sketchbooks of Emily Carr: Seven Journeys* (Vancouver: Douglas and McIntyre, 2002), 58, 74, 78, 79, 90-92. Shadbolt has included sketches that are of cannery sites and buildings but not identified as such. See sketches, 70, 81, and possibly 86.

34 Emily Carr, "East and West," in *The Book of Small* (Toronto: Irwin Publishing, 1942), reprinted in *The Emily Carr Omnibus*, introduced by Doris Shadbolt (Vancouver and Toronto: Douglas and McIntyre, 1993), 155.

35 Emily Carr, *Guyasdom's D'Sonoqua*, oil on canvas, 1929-30, the Art Gallery of Ontario; Emily Carr, "D'Sonoqua," in *Klee Wyck*, 33.

36 Several sources exist for understanding Carr's manipulation of her own image: "Emily Carr Found Inspiration in B.C. Wilderness" (Obituary), *Canadian Review of Music and Other Arts*, December-January 1945, 34; *Little Old Lady on the Edge of Nowhere*, a film dramatization in two parts of Emily Carr's life and work, showing her canvases. The dramatic documentary was produced and directed by Nancy Ryley of the CBC, broadcast by CBC-TV on 14 and 15 September 1975, and distributed by National Film Board of Canada (both parts 57 minutes, 1975); Eva-Marie Kroller, "Literary Versions of Emily Carr," *Canadian Literature* 109 (Summer 1986): 87-98; Maria Tippett, "A Paste Solitaire in a Steel-Claw Setting: Emily Carr and Her Public," *BC Studies* 25 (1975): 33-37; Maria Tippett, "Who 'Discovered' Emily Carr?" *Journal of Canadian Art History* 1 (Fall 1974): 30-34; Braun, *Intemperate Rainforest*, 164.

37 Suzanne Le May Sheffield, *Revealing New Worlds: Three Victorian Women Naturalists* (London and New York: Routledge, 2001), 99. See Chapter 3 ("Finding a New Life: Marianne North As Daughter, Patron, and Traveler") and Chapter 4 ("Painting Outside the Lines: Marianne North's Botanical Art").

38 Marianne North, *Recollections of a Happy Life: Being the Autobiography of Marianne North, Edited By Her Sister, Mrs. John Addington Symonds* (London: Macmillan, 1892); Marianne North, *Further Recollections of a Happy Life: Selected from the Journals of Marianne North, Chiefly between 1859 and 1869, Edited By Her Sister, Mrs. John Addington Symonds* (London: Macmillan, 1893).

39 Ira Dilworth, "Preface," in Emily Carr, *The Heart of a Peacock*, n.p. (Toronto: Oxford University Press, 1953).

40   Ira Dilworth, "Foreword," in Carr, *Klee Wyck,* n.p.
41   Kerry Mason, "Emily Carr," in *The Oxford Companion to Canadian Literature,* 2nd ed., ed. Eugene Benson and William Toye, 177-78 (Don Mills, ON: Oxford University Press Canada, 1997), 177.
42   Nancy Paug, "Passing through the Jungle: Emily Carr and Theories of Women's Autobiography," *Mosaic* 25, 4 (1992): 63-79.
43   Helen M. Buss, *Repossessing the World: Reading Memoirs by Contemporary Women* (Waterloo, ON: Wilfrid Laurier University Press, 2002), who argues that in thinking about women's "autobiography," we need to pay attention to "memoir." I am grateful for the astute discussion in Jenéa Tallentire Gilley, "Daughter of Zelophehad: Margaret Bayne's Autobiography and the Framing of the Single Self," presented at the annual meeting of the Canadian Historical Association, University of Toronto, 2002.
44   I am grateful to Jenéa Tallentire for this important suggestion about Carr's use of vignettes. For a discussion of the boundaries pushed in Carr's painterly career, see Braun, *Intemperate Rainforest,* 169, and 296n10.
45   Eric Brown to Emily Carr, 19 March 1928; Carr to Brown, 27 March 1928; Brown to Thorton (Canadian National Railway), 4 April 1928, Correspondence with/re: Artists: Emily Carr, 7.1-C, National Gallery of Canada (NGC). Marius Barbeau to Carr, 12 and 22 February 1928; Carr to Barbeau, 27 February 1928, Barbeau Collection, Correspondence files, "Emily Carr," National Museum of Civilization (NMC). Her Indian guides, who also befriended her, included Fred McKay, a Nishga of the Nass River, who made her 1928 trip to Greenville possible; the Haida couple Will and Clara Russ, who took her in 1912 to important villages on the Queen Charlottes; and Albert Derrick, a Haida who took Carr around to revisit these spots in 1928 (transcription of notes by Barbeau 1947, informant W.H. Russ, Skidegate, Barbeau Papers, B-F-627, NMC).
46   At Alert Bay she lived with the Spencers and travelled with their daughter, Clara. Working out of Arrandale Cannery on the Nass River, Carr lived in a "cottage," ate meals in the cannery mess hall, and enjoyed tea times with the cannery manager, Walter E. Walker, and his wife. One of Carr's nieces, Emily English, was married to the manager of Balmoral Cannery on the Skeena; by the time of Carr's sketching trip to the Queen Charlottes in 1928, he was manager of the South Bay Cannery, which Carr made her base of operations. Another niece, Lillian Nicholles, taught school at Masset, on the Queen Charlotte Islands. See Maria Tippett, "Emily Carr's *Klee Wyck,*" *Canadian Literature* 72 (Spring 1977): 49-58, at 50, 57.
47   Tippett, "Emily Carr's *Klee Wyck,*" 53.
48   Carr to Brown, 11 August 1928 (dated South Bay), Correspondence with/re: Artists: Emily Carr, 7.1-C, NGC. Carr wrote to Brown 1 October 1928 asking if he had received the earlier letter and stressing that she had taken off an entire morning to write it.
49   Carr, "Salt Water," in *Klee Wyck,* 78-93, at 79 (hereafter cited in text).
50   Hilda Thomas, "Klee Wyck: The Eye of the Other," *Canadian Literature* 136 (Spring 1993): 5-20, at 18. I am grateful to Hilda Thomas for drawing this essay to my attention.
51   My thanks to Jenéa Tallentire for suggesting this interesting twist.
52   Veronica Strong-Boag, *The New Day Recalled: Lives of Girls and Women in English Canada, 1919-1939* (Toronto: Copp-Clark Pitman, 1988).
53   Phylis Bowman, *Klondike of the Skeena!* (Prince Rupert, BC: [s.n.], 1982); E.A. Harris, *Spokechute: Skeena River Memory* (Victoria: Orca Publishers, 1990); R. Geddes Large, *The Skeena: River of Destiny* (Vancouver: Mitchell Press, 1957); Walter Wicks, *Memories of the Skeena* (Saanichton, BC: Hancock House, 1976). In the latest work, *Spokechute: River of Memory,* E.A. Harris tells readers that his Port Essington story was in a sense a family affair. He reconstructed the story from his own memories of being a boy there; the stories his parents told, and the diaries they kept of their Port Essington days; the local history articles his mother published in newspapers when in her nineties (to celebrate the British Columbia centennial); and the snapshots she took in the 1920s with her little plain box camera. When Agnes Harris died in 1973 she was ninety-nine years old (Agnes Harris, "The Ghosts Walk this B.C. Town," *Vancouver Province,* 3 May 1958, and "Port Essington, Skeena River, B.C.," *Victoria Colonist,* 5 November 1972).

54 Laura Cameron, *Openings: A Meditation on History and Sumas Lake* (Montreal and Kingston: McGill-Queen's University Press, 1997), 76-91.
55 Taken from the title of the introduction to Patricia Nelson Limerick, *The Legacy of Conquest: The Unbroken Past of the American West* (New York: Norton, 1987).
56 Clippings from the *Prince Rupert Daily News*, 1926 to 1928, reproduced in Bowman, "A Shocking Murder Recalled," in *Klondike of the Skeena!* 35-63. Bowman also works in mention of the Chisholm murder in many of the captions to photographs, maps, and plans.
57 Bowman, *Klondike of the Skeena!* photo captions, 133, 142.
58 *Prince Rupert Daily News*, 25 May 1926, in Bowman, *Klondike of the Skeena!* 35.
59 *Vancouver Evening Sun*, 25 November 1926, 1.
60 *Prince Rupert Daily News*, 24 May 1926, in Bowman, *Klondike of the Skeena!* 51.
61 *Vancouver Evening Sun*, 25 May 1926, 1; *Vancouver Daily Province*, 28 May 1926, 1.
62 Karen Dubinsky, *Improper Advances: Rape and Heterosexual Conflict in Ontario, 1880-1929* (Chicago: University of Chicago Press, 1993), 15-16.
63 Lesley Erickson, "Murdered Women and Mythic Villains: The Criminal Case and the Imaginary Criminal in the Canadian West, 1886-1930," in *People and Place: Historical Influences on Legal Culture*, ed. Constance Backhouse and Jonathan Swainger, 95-119 (Vancouver: UBC Press, 2003), 96.
64 *Prince Rupert Daily News*, 8 June 1926, in Bowman, *Klondike of the Skeena!* 38-39.
65 Ibid., in Bowman, *Klondike of the Skeena!* 41-42.
66 *Prince Rupert Daily News*, 25 November 1926, in Bowman, *Klondike of the Skeena!* 52.
67 *Prince Rupert Daily News*, 28 May 1926, in Bowman, *Klondike of the Skeena!* 37.
68 *Vancouver Daily Province*, 25 May 1926, 1; 25 November 1926, 1; *Vancouver Evening Sun*, 27 May 1926, 1; 25 November 1926, 1.
69 Sarah Carter, *Capturing Women: The Manipulation of Cultural Imagery in Canada's Prairie West* (Montreal and Kingston: McGill-Queen's University Press, 1997); Sarah Carter, "Categories and Terrains of Exclusion: Constructing the 'Indian Woman' in the Early Settlement Era in Western Canada," *Great Plains Quarterly* 13 (Summer 1993): 147-61.
70 *Prince Rupert Daily News*, 9 June 1926, in Bowman, *Klondike of the Skeena!* 62.
71 *Prince Rupert Daily News*, 28 May 1926, in Bowman, *Klondike of the Skeena!* 39.
72 *Prince Rupert Daily News*, 16 June 1926, in Bowman, *Klondike of the Skeena!* 47.
73 *Prince Rupert Daily News*, 8 June 1926, in Bowman, *Klondike of the Skeena!* 53.
74 *Prince Rupert Daily News*, 28 May 1926, in Bowman, *Klondike of the Skeena!* 39.
75 *Prince Rupert Daily News*, 22 November 1926, in Bowman, *Klondike of the Skeena!* 49.
76 Carolyn Strange, *Toronto's Girl Problem: The Perils and Pleasures of the City, 1880-1930* (Toronto: University of Toronto Press, 1995).
77 *Prince Rupert Daily News*, 28 May 1926, in Bowman, *Klondike of the Skeena!* 39.
78 A pertinent observation from Jenéa Tallentire.
79 Helen Buss, "A Feminist Revision of New Historicism to Give Fuller Readings of Women's Private Writing," in *Women, Autobiography, Theory: A Reader*, ed. Sidonie Smith and Julia Watson, 222-31 (Madison: University of Wisconsin Press, 1998), 227.
80 Strange, *Toronto's Girl Problem*, 10.
81 *Prince Rupert Daily News*, 28 May 1926, in Bowman, *Klondike of the Skeena!* 35-36.
82 Bowman, "Introduction," *Klondike of the Skeena*, 13.
83 Dubinsky, *Improper Advances*, 35-63.
84 *Prince Rupert Daily News*, 8 June 1926, in Bowman, *Klondike of the Skeena!* 62.
85 *Prince Rupert Daily News*, 19 April, 21 April 1928, in Bowman, *Klondike of the Skeena!* 58, 78-79.
86 "Finis," Bowman, *Klondike of the Skeena!* 79.
87 Ibid., 80.
88 Ibid., 80-81.
89 Ibid., 81.
90 Joy Parr, "Notes for a More Sensuous History of Twentieth Century Canada: The Timely, the Tacit, and the Material Body," *Canadian Historical Review* 82, 4 (December 2001): 720-45, at 732.

12
The Old and New on Parade: Mimesis, Queen Victoria, and Carnival Queens on Victoria Day in Interwar Victoria
Katie Pickles

The scrapbook of the Lady Douglas Chapter of the Imperial Order Daughters of the Empire (IODE), a Canadian women's patriotic organization dedicated to promoting a British Canada, records that in 1923, and again in 1931, to celebrate Queen Victoria's birthday the leader of the organization in Victoria, Mrs. McMiking, dressed as Queen Victoria on 24 May for the Victoria Day parade in Victoria, British Columbia.[1] McMiking passed through the streets on a float commemorating the reign of Queen Victoria. The *Daily Colonist* reported that the float and the wording on the embankment in front of the Parliament Buildings – "Queen Victoria's Birthday. Born 1819. Died 1901" – was in keeping with the motto of the Lady Douglas Chapter: "To keep one hand on the traditions of the past, and green the memory of our illustrious dead."[2]

Focusing on the women who took part in the Victoria Day spectacles in Victoria during the interwar years, in this chapter I interpret the events, demonstrating how the celebrations were the embodied performance of national, imperial, and civic pride or, as Anne McClintock has put it, "nationalism as fetish spectacle."[3] I argue that the dominant narrative being performed was one of Anglo-Canadian identity, which combined older "traditional" Victorian values with those of a modern age. The construction of Anglo-Canadian identity involved the unquestioned conquest and colonization of Aboriginal peoples, viewing Aboriginal life-worlds as belonging to the past. Canada was to grow as a nation by building upon British democracy and constitutional monarchy, the Christian myths and saintly symbols of the British Isles, and economic and cultural "progress" through new innovations and technologies.

Veronica Strong-Boag has suggested that, during the interwar years, "old and new ways of thought and practice frequently dwelt, albeit uneasily, together."[4] I argue in this case study that in the interwar events performed on the streets of British Columbia's capital city on Victoria Day, women of different generations played a part in creating Anglo-Canadian identity.

Representing allegiance to the past, a generation of female imperialists was still inspired by Queen Victoria, considering her a role model. Keeping her memory alive extended to the embodied presence of Regent McMiking on parade *as* Queen Victoria. Military parades, historic floats, and flowers at the statue of Queen Victoria in front of the Parliament Buildings also invented traditions that evoked the past. Meanwhile, a younger generation of women were crowned as Queens of Agriculture, Progress, State, Benevolence, Commerce, and Sport. Emanating from a new postwar confidence for women, carnival queens existed beside the continuation of the "Victorian" traditions of female imperialists. Rather than forgetting Queen Victoria and the age that she had personified, with the accompanying values abandoned for a modern age, the old persisted, mingling with the new, especially through the efforts of loyal daughters of the empire who existed to make sure that her memory was "kept alive."

The Old

Dressing as Queen Victoria was by no means the domain of Regent McMiking alone. Applying the concept of mimesis is useful in understanding why both women colonizers and the colonized donned the costume of the Queen. Recent postcolonial scholarship has adapted the ideas of Erich Auerbach on mimesis to examine the "relation between art and imitation in the creative process."[5] The concept, "with its connecting concepts of imitation, simile and similarity," is particularly useful for the possibility of seeing repetition or mimicry.[6] When colonized peoples imitated Queen Victoria, they demonstrated a process of seeking authenticity through appropriating/embodying the colonizer.[7] Sylvia Van Kirk's study of the fortunes of five founding families of Victoria includes a photograph of Josette Work dressed as Queen Victoria. Van Kirk explains Josette Work's mimesis as an example of emulating Queen Victoria. As Victoria was "the epitome of a Victorian matron," she was Josette Work's role model. Adding another layer, Josette Work was part Cree.[8] Dressing as Queen Victoria helped Josette Work to be accepted among Victoria's elite. In an interesting twist, Regent McMiking's chapter of the IODE, the Lady Douglas Chapter, was named in memory of another part-Native woman who was the wife of a former Vancouver Island governor. In Vancouver, the Pauline Johnson Chapter was named for the Anglo-Mohawk Canadian poet.[9] Such women were claimed and celebrated for their mimesis as colonial elite. In existing as simultaneously different and autonomous, their "authenticity" allowed them to become a part of the IODE's vision for a British Canada, exemplars of assimilation, rather than posing a challenge.

At variance with colonized women who dressed as Queen Victoria to gain authenticity, this chapter is about mimesis as inventing, rather than challenging, Anglo-Canadian traditions. Displaying similarity and identifying with things British obscured difference. From a postcolonial perspective, the "appearance" of Queen Victoria so many years after her death as a part of Victoria Day celebrations can be interpreted as mimesis, the mingling of art and reality, of staged imitation through the medium of the body. It is worth noting that, in general, it was common for patriotic pageants to involve plays with historical characters,[10] and John MacKenzie has suggested that through the use of pageants, imperialism remained in popular culture longer than one might think.[11] For Britain, empire "infiltrated all areas of culture, media and society in the period between the 1870s and 1940s."[12] With some Victoria residents keen on promoting a British Anglo-Canada, patriotic performances formed an important element of the city's interwar Victoria Day celebrations. Regent McMiking as Victoria, however, went beyond being an actor in a role. I argue that her performance was an attempt to embody the virtues of the Queen and to promote a British Canada.

The Victoria Day parades were a visual display of the dominant construction of city, nation, and empire. Such patriotic displays were harnessed to elite identity and were held on the steps of the Parliament Buildings with the full institutional support of the nation-state. While the presence of the military displayed the strength of nation and empire, schoolchildren represented the nation's future, receiving training through the school curriculum and in imperial youth groups. Pomp and pageantry were the order of the day, as evidenced in the main events, which included crowning ceremonies, school sports, dances at the armouries, street carnivals, parades, and regattas. A glowing account in the *Daily Colonist* described a typical Victoria Day parade during the interwar years:

> Yesterday afternoon, Victoria witnessed what is declared by old-timers to be probably the largest parade which has ever wended its way through the city's streets. Lovely creations on wheels, having no aim but to charm the eye, beautifully bedecked vehicles for charming queens, floats designed for purposes of historical symbolism, band after band adding life to the scene with spirited selections, comic get-ups in motorcars, on bicycles, and on foot, and all the other elements which compose the traditional Victoria Day processions here, passed between the eagerly watching spectators, who crowded the route in numbers which are thought to surpass all previous records in this regard.[13]

It is important to note that participation in these public events did not necessarily imply endorsement of the ideology behind them. In her research into nineteenth-century parades in New York, New Orleans, and San Francisco, Mary Ryan notes that "social and political differences could not all be resolved by evoking attractive symbols or eliciting cheers from a holiday crowd."[14] That the holders of Anglo-Canadian identity went to such great lengths to publicize their efforts was likely an indicator that their power and prowess belonged to a previous era, which in the post-First World War years was fast being eclipsed by a more diverse and confident Canadian nation. Such fears of the declining power of Anglo-Canadian hegemony were connected to the commercial and civic interests of a place named Victoria.

In the last years of the twentieth century, the construction of national identity received much attention from scholars, alerting us to the power of "imagined communities" and the "invention of tradition."[15] In reconstructing Victoria Day, it is important to be aware that "imperialistic powers deprived colonized peoples not only of their territories and wealth but also of their imagination."[16] Indigenous narratives were silenced, erased though renamings, and then replaced with Anglo-Celtic spectacles that imposed the meanings of the colonizer.[17] In Victoria, because the provincial capital was named for Queen Victoria, imperial, national, and civic patriotic outpourings were intimately connected. Indeed, Victoria the city had more interest than other places in keeping the Queen's memory alive. It was clear to business and tourism interests that there were long-term commercial benefits to be gained by marketing the regal connection, even if it meant remaining closed for the public holiday. A large advertisement in the *Daily Colonist* in 1923 for the Hudson's Bay Company, itself tied in to Canada's history of colonization, included a picture of the late Queen and proudly stated, "Victoria Day 24 May. In Memory of England's Greatest and Most Beloved Queen 1837-1901. The store closed all day today."[18] Commercial interests hoped that tourists would flock to the city to attend the celebrations, on a pilgrimage, as it were, to pay their respects to the late Queen and celebrate national ties to Britain. An editorial in the *Daily Colonist* the same month boasted that the events would "leave a lasting impression of wholehearted pleasure on our own people and the visitors who will be with us this week."[19]

Queen Victoria and Female Imperialism

Regent McMiking became Queen Victoria as a part of Queen Victoria's legacy – twentieth-century female imperialism – whereby a generation of women was inspired by the late Queen, considering her a role model and her memory an ongoing inspiration in their attempts to advocate "empire unity" by promoting Britishness around the empire. Thus far, scholarly work on British female imperialism has focused on the Edwardian era, considered the time when imperialism in general was at its peak.[20] It makes sense to ground Canadian female imperialism in the same time period, although it continued, in a shifting form, throughout the twentieth century.[21]

As this literature shows, female imperialists in the former "white" dominions were stronger in their convictions, and clung to the idea of empire longer, than those in the imperial centre, challenging the notion that female imperialism started in the imperial centre and was subsequently distilled throughout the empire.[22] Indeed, Canada was home to the largest female imperial organization, the Imperial Order Daughters of the Empire (IODE). In 1900 the founder, Mrs. Margaret Clark Murray, a journalist, philanthropist, and wife of an influential McGill University professor, John Clark Murray, returned to Montreal from London, where she had witnessed much pro-war jingoism centred on the South African War. She decided to act upon the public outpourings of Anglo-Canadian patriotism that she sensed around her. Her intentions were to seek an opportunity to strengthen Canadian national ties, as well as imperial connections. As Julia Bush argues in her work on Edwardian ladies and imperial power, a "spiritual creed of Empire was attractive to many British women as it was to their male counterparts."[23] Canadian female imperialists were spurred on by the idea of a strong Canada within a strong British Empire, an ideology that Carl Berger attributed to some of Canada's leading intellectual men of the time.[24]

In terms of activities, initial class composition, and political affiliations, female imperialism fitted very closely with the imperial propaganda clubs, a number of which were founded at the end of the nineteenth century throughout the British Empire.[25] These were conservative movements that sought to foster social, cultural, and economic links between the different parts of the British Empire, promoting economic growth in peacetime and a loyal fighting force during wartime. Using textbooks, exhibitions, and entertainment to promote their ideas, their varied constitutions and their defensive and cultural concerns came together in the theme of imperial unity.[26] The Navy League, the Victoria League, and the Girl Guide and Boy Scout movements epitomized such organizations. The symbols of the IODE also reflected empire unity. The motto was one flag, one throne, and one Empire (referring to the Union Jack, the British monarchy, and the British empire). Likewise, the badge cast imperial foundations in metal, with the crown symbolizing the British monarchy; the Union Jack standing for Britain and empire; and both surrounded by a seven-pointed, outward-radiating star, with one point for each of the major territories of the empire. On behalf of Canada and the empire, the IODE's objectives were to stimulate patriotic sentiment, to foster common cause among women and children throughout the British Empire, to care for the dependants of military personnel, and to preserve the memory of brave and historic imperial deeds.[27]

In life and death, Queen Victoria was of key importance in the formation of groups of female imperialists such as the IODE, the Victoria League, and the Guild of Loyal Women in South Africa. Supporting the Queen was of vital importance at the time of the IODE's formation. When she founded the IODE in 1900 during the South African War, Margaret Clark Murray asserted that it was time to "stand by our Queen at all costs, to shake our

IODE membership badge. The crown symbolized the
British monarchy, the Union Jack, Britain, and Empire,
surrounded by a seven-pointed outward-radiating star,
one point for each of the major territories of the Empire.

fists if necessary, in the face of the whole of Empire, and show them what
we are made of."[28] When she sent telegrams to the mayors of Canada's provincial capitals, she asked: "Will the women of Fredericton unite with the
women of Montreal in federating as 'Daughters of the Empire' and inviting
the women of Australia and New Zealand to unite with them in sending to
the Queen an expression of our devotion to the Empire and an emergency
war fund to be expended as Her Majesty shall deem fit?"[29]

In 1901 in Britain, the Victoria League was formed as a memorial to
Victoria, who had died on 22 January, and was named "in memory of our
late Gracious Queen, and with the desire to continue the great work of
closer union throughout the Empire for which she did so much."[30] Julia
Bush has argued that late Victorian and Edwardian imperial rhetoric "drew
heavily upon motherhood, both as biological and racial actuality (the need
for healthy white soldiers and settlers) and as a symbol of the nurturing,
civilizing tasks of Empire. Queen Victoria, of course, represented the ultimate
maternal icon, the 'Great White Queen,' and 'Mother of Empire' whose loving care for her colonized subjects was as deeply imbued with superiority

and controlling power as it was with a sense of Christian duty."[31] Bush explains that, "without exception, the ladies' imperialist associations were devoted to the Queen, and then to her memory, perpetuated through her daughters' patronage of their activities. For Victoria embodied maternal imperialism at its most authoritative, and through her royal status resolved the paradoxes implied by strong female rule accompanied by a conservative outlook on gender roles. Many highly conservative ladies of the upper middle class and the aristocracy were attracted to organized female imperialism as a socially acceptable means of political self-assertion."[32]

Although it was officially non-partisan and non-sectarian, the IODE was unofficially politically conservative. As a pro-women group, however, it could expose the contradictions of labelling women as "conservative." Work by Angela Woollacott, Leila Rupp, and Fiona Paisley on interwar feminism demonstrates that there could be strong imperial undertones, as well as challenges, to feminist projects.[33] More specifically, historians have demonstrated that imperial feminism had much in common with female imperialism. Bush asserts that the "definition of imperial duty and the redefinition of womanhood went hand-in-hand," and that "Edwardian ladies, of both pro-suffrage and adamantly anti-suffrage persuasion, chose to organize actively in the Empire's cause."[34] It was, after all, in part thanks to the lobbying of the IODE during the First World War that the limited franchise had come about.[35] Tapping into a strong historical current of evoking tradition when advancing change, those seen as belonging to the "old" were active in heralding the "new."

Dorothy Thompson has gone so far as to advance the argument that Queen Victoria's strength and example unwittingly led the way to twentieth-century feminism. Queen Victoria herself was opposed to feminism, as evidenced by her concern to check "this mad, wicked folly of Woman's Rights, with all its attendant horrors, on which her poor feeble sex is bent, forgetting every sense of womanly feeling and propriety ... The subject makes the Queen so furious that she can not contain herself. God created men and women different – let them remain each in their own position."[36] But according to Thompson, although Victoria's reign emphasized the "moral authority of women in the family rather than making their presence in public life more immediately acceptable," nonetheless "the presence of a woman at the head of state worked at a deeper level to weaken prejudice and make change more possible in the century following her reign."[37]

If female imperialists owed much of their inspiration to what Queen Victoria symbolized, in her death they found even more strength as they attempted to follow in her footsteps. Julia Bush argues that with the "ultimate female imperialist icon" dead, "the leading ladies were themselves prepared to be iconized and to use their social status and high-level political connections to advance their cause."[38] Bush even suggests that the upper-class feminine influence of the female imperialists was "often able to out-trump the male-led leagues, for the ladies associations could plausibly claim to have inherited the mantle of Queen Victoria's own views on Empire."[39] As well as inspiration, these women drew self-confidence for their imperial projects from Queen Victoria. Endowed with the new valorization of the maternal importance of the private sphere, female imperialists "believed they were truly building the Empire in ways which only women knew." Female imperialists would carry on the work of the dead Queen. As Bush argues, "all the projects of female imperialism shared a little of the aura of [Victoria's] royal, and feminine, authority."[40] Such regal and matriarchal power was re-enacted on the streets of interwar Victoria.

Interwar Memorialization

On Victoria Day, paying homage to the late Queen centred on the stone statue of Victoria in front of British Columbia's Parliament Buildings.[41] Celebrations commenced with the IODE claiming its strong connections to the Queen and keeping her memory alive by placing wreaths and flowers on her monument. The *Daily Colonist* considered the opening activity "wholly fitting" and "touching," with its 1923 editorial proclaiming "an auspicious day." Evoking the old, it asserted that "it should never be forgotten that yesterday is a great holiday in memory of a great and wise Queen."[42] In 1924 the paper referred to the "holiday of holidays" and the IODE's "commemorative service before the statue of the great Queen Victoria in honour of her birthday."[43] The pro-imperial paper was still reporting the IODE honouring the memory of the Queen with floral tributes at the foot of her statue in 1931, and it stated in an editorial that "today is a day of celebration for the entire British family. It commemorates the birthday of Queen Victoria the Good and has been set aside as an anniversary for promoting and conserving loyalty and patriotism."[44]

The production of these Victoria Day celebrations occurred in the shadow of the First World War, with the purported "heroism and successes of the Great War" providing the backdrop for the events.[45] Whereas early work on war and memory, in particular Paul Fussell's *The Great War and Modern Memory,* argued for the disruptive effects of war and the dawning of new eras, recent interpretations emphasize the conservative effects of war, and its forcing, to borrow Jay Winter's phrase, a "walking backwards into the future."[46] Post-war Anglo-Canadian identity involved a good measure of continuity with past traditions grounded in connections to Britain, particularly the British monarchy. It also stressed service and sacrifice in order to preserve freedom and democracy. Jonathan Vance's argument that Canada remembered the First World War by emphasizing traditional values, continuity, and the positive results of the war experience is evidenced in the Victoria Day celebrations.[47] For example, the *Daily Colonist* declared that

"Empire Day is a time for pride in citizenship, for loyalty to and confidence in the future. It is a day, moreover, to remember the advantages of unity throughout a far flung realm with the lesson before us of what that unity accomplished in the years of emergency from 1914 to 1918."[48]

In the invention of such traditions, educating the young took on great importance, which explains why large numbers of children were typically involved in Victoria Day activities, often as a part of the school curriculum. As was typical in Empire Day celebrations around the British empire at the time, large numbers of children were involved in parades as representatives of the Sea Cadets, Girl Guides, and Boy Scouts. In 1929 "children [were] told of loved Queen" by the IODE, who held a "gathering to impress children with reverence for Queen Victoria."[49] Children sang in choirs, listened to their elders, and placed flowers at Victoria's memorial.[50] Another account reports that "the spectacle of more than 1,000 boys and girls of the senior classes of the Victoria public schools as they assembled in front of the Parliament Buildings yesterday morning was a stirring one to the hundreds of citizens who gathered to take part in the celebration ... the steps of the buildings were massed with school children, and lining the main driveway were troops of cadets, Girl Guides and Sea Cadets, who flanked the pathway past the fountain as far as the statue of Queen Victoria," its base covered with bouquets of flowers.[51] In this display of patriotism, the young, symbolically representing the future, were taught to connect the past (Queen Victoria's statue) to the present (Parliament Buildings).

The interwar parades took place in a eugenic age that saw a variety of countries throughout the Western world preoccupied with breeding, racial fitness, and renewal.[52] The connections between feminism and eugenics were strong in the interwar years, with female and male constructions of sexuality often entangled with eugenic ideas.[53] Indeed, those writing about sexuality and the social history of medicine, such as Jeffrey Weeks, Roy Porter, and Lesley Hall, suggest that the history of sexuality is related to the history of eugenics.[54] With the reality of immigrants arriving in Canada from places other than the British Isles and Western Europe, there was a continued fear of "foreigners" and new calls for assimilation and Canadianization.[55] The perceived threat posed by foreigners led to a more clearly defined sense of what qualities Canadians should have.[56] The assertion of a Canadian Anglo-Celtic race (England, Scotland, Ireland, and Wales) was enacted through a renewed antimodern interest in seasonal festivals.[57] In Victoria these celebrations were *colonial* festivals, with adulation of the "mother country" as the uniting factor. As British racial superiority had provided the central justification for imperialism, Canadian female imperialists appropriated old sentiments and created a new interwar Anglo-Canadian identity.[58]

In combining a belief in Anglo-Celtic superiority with aesthetic displays of antimodernism, the celebrations in Victoria appealed to the pageantry of a romantic and chivalrous past. Judith Smart argues that "Queen competitions for May Day, Mardis Gras and various political anniversaries or watersheds imitated mediaeval pageantry and myths to evoke tradition and continuity and sometimes to challenge authority and celebrate victories of the ordinary people." She suggests that "the popularity of these events grew with the need for symbolic unity as the forces of social and cultural cohesion weakened with industrialisation."[59] In interwar Victoria, Victoria Day events were about the construction and display of Anglo-Canadian identity. Interestingly, in the colonial context, the antimodern and anti-industrial were able to coexist with the dominant Anglo-Canadian identity. As celebrations of Victoria's birthday fell in the Canadian spring, the festivities took on a May Day identity. Preindustrial traditions, such as the maypole and folk dancing, were in evidence at spring festivities not confined to the city of Victoria. At Cumberland, British Columbia, for example "there were three poles and they were very prettily braided by the younger school children."[60]

The New

Overall, feminist historians view women's interwar position as fundamentally different to the one they held in the early 1900s. Women had the vote and full constitutional recognition, and they were entering new modern occupations: the working classes were going into commerce, factories, and department stores, and the middle classes into nursing, teaching, and universities. There was the sense of a "new day," of greater freedom, less restrictive clothing, and newly liberated flappers who were "sexually liberated and actively pursuing heterosexual relations."[61] Research into women's feminist organizing during the interwar years suggests it was a post-franchise era in which Canadian feminists had a strong sense of the history of women's changing place in society.[62] At this time, the pre-franchise women's organizations such as the IODE, the Women's Christian Temperance Union, and the Young Women's Christian Association represented an older generation of women, the "custodians of an activist tradition."[63] Meanwhile, Veronica Strong-Boag notes that, "in the 1920s and 1930s, youthfulness was celebrated to an unprecedented degree in print, on film, and on radio."[64]

It is not surprising, then, that at the front of the Victoria Day parades were the "Queens of the Frolic." While dressing as Victoria might be seen as memorializing the past, Queens of the Frolic were part of a postwar coming of age for women. They were a sight that could appear carefree and overindulgent to the older generation. As Carolyn Strange has chronicled, working girls in Toronto could be portrayed as both dangerous and in danger, partaking of the perils and pleasures of the city.[65] Throughout the Western world, the 1920s was a time when an older generation perceived a "girl problem" when young women embraced change, sought "immediate gratification and fun," and, according to Judith Smart, "embodied modernity in a literal as well as figurative sense."[66] While the potential existed for intergenerational conflict, in Victoria's interwar celebrations women of different generations converged through their mimesis as "queens" – Queen Victoria representing the recent old, and carnival queens the reborn new.

Transnationally, and with Canada as no exception, it was during the early 1920s that modern aspects of Hollywood – contest, sponsorship, glamour, and commercialism – combined with an antimodern eugenic element to spawn the modern beauty contest. Beauty pageants have been a widespread phenomenon since antiquity, with references found in Greek mythology, medieval Europe, and "Queens of May."[67] There was a rise in the popularity of contests in the Western world during the nineteenth century. Circus showman P.T. Barnum recognized the potential of beauty as competition, and in 1854 he began parading women in front of judges. It wasn't until bathing suits became acceptable, however, that "respectable" women would enter these contests.[68] Meanwhile, boosted by the development of photography, the contests took place in newspapers, parading whiteness in black and white newspaper ink. Readers could gaze at contestants from afar and vote for the woman they considered to be the most beautiful.[69]

Writing about contemporary beauty contests, Colleen Ballerino Cohen, Richard Wilk, and Beverly Stoeltje suggest that as a form of "pageantry," beauty contests position the "body as a site for naturalizing cultural precepts and enacting power." They involve allegory and symbolism, performance and semiotics, nationalism and sexuality, and are about "choosing an individual whose deportment, appearance and style embodies the values and goals of a nation, locality, or group."[70] In their discussion of the "Miss Showgirl" contests throughout the twentieth century, Kate Darian-Smith and Sara Wills see the rural Australian contests creating and representing a sense of community.[71] This was also the case with Victoria's Queens of the Frolic. In creating Anglo-Canadian identity, the interwar queens in parades and festivities in Victoria provided continuity with the old/past that was more pronounced and important than in other beauty contests of the time.[72] Inventing citizenship was an important part of the pageantry.

During the interwar years, displaying ideal citizens was particularly important in the settler societies of Canada, Australia, and New Zealand, where an older generation of women and men perceived a "girl problem" and "a growing eugenic anxiety about her sexuality and its relationship to racial fitness."[73] In Canada, such anxiety was connected to a fear of "foreigners" swamping "British stock." In a bid to secure race dominance, the IODE went to the extent in 1928 of collaborating with the Society for the Oversea Settlement of British Women (SOSBW) in a six-week cross-Canada school of twenty-five English schoolgirls. As examples of both the ideal young adult and the ideal migrant, the Anglo-Celtic schoolgirls were portrayed as "naturals" in the Canadian environment. They were shown Canadian agriculture, took part in Regina's harvest festival, and sampled Okanagan peaches.[74] Similar sentiments existed in Australia, where Kate Darian-Smith and Sara Wills have found that "photographs from the 1920s emphasise the regal and imperial themes of such tableau; themes which reflected interwar loyalty to empire, new agricultural and industrial contracts with Britain, and a heightened sense of Australia's contribution to imperial rule. These also mirrored the self-perceived role of agricultural societies, whose members had from the very first conceived their role as aiding the colonial settlement of an outpost of empire."[75] In Victoria, parading queens displayed all that was "best" in the Dominion, a modern offering to the "mother country."

Importantly, in dominions of the Empire, the monarch was the head of state. Dressing as the monarch, especially as the Queen, was a way of evoking the icon through mimesis, out of a combination of art and reality, simultaneously producing colonial unity and hegemonic settler power. Ballerino Cohen, Wilk, and Stoeltje argue that, historically, choosing men and women to represent royalty was a way of "bringing together elements of both high and low culture."[76] Queen contests were common in the nineteenth and twentieth centuries, and Judith Smart has written that "Labour Day and May Day celebrations always included Queen contests, and the festivities accompanying [Australian] Federation, Founders' Day and other such events featured local processions and floats with Queens and their maids of honour." Smart makes the pertinent point that in contrast to women's place in society, queen contests saw women command a central position, albeit symbolic and allegorical, most often representing "fertility, moral guardianship, maternalism, political principle, selfless idealism."[77] It was common to use female figures such as Joan of Arc and Britannia to represent national virtue and achievement.

In interwar Victoria, the new generation of queens met the old female imperialists through the literal presence of constitutional monarchy. Paradoxically, while beauty contests were considered immodest, a display of popular culture that challenged existing norms,[78] the civic, national, and imperial were also important, making contests simultaneously respectable. As well as being grounded in popular culture, especially through enacting regal identity, beauty contests were also respectable and linked to conservative pageantry. While Ballerino Cohen, Wilk, and Stoeltje argue that contests only went from "sideshow to citizenship" in the post-Second World War years,[79] pageants have always been about building community through the display of ideal citizens.

A component of the events in Victoria was the Citizens' Ball at the armouries. Here a carnival spirit prevailed, with revellers competing for prizes. At the 1924 ball there were prizes for best national Spanish dancer, best fancy dress character, and best Follies girl, and "high spirits, mirth and jollity rollicked hand in hand at the Armories masquerade ball."[80] The queens were guests of honour at the ball, arriving with their attendants and maids of honour, and King Carnival, "a herald announcing the fact from the bandstand in the centre of the floor."[81] Often neo-romantic and chivalrous, the spectacles borrowed liberally and lavishly from different cultures and historical time periods, inventing traditions out of the old for interwar Anglo-Canada. In an account of Queen Mona's procession, the spice of the exotic "orient" coexisted with a benevolent settler men's group, the Foresters: "Mona, Queen of the May and also Queen of Benevolence, appeared amid a splendor befitting one who held the proud honor of reigning over the city during the celebration. Her float was modelled generally on one of the state barges of Cleopatra. From her throne beneath a curving canopy Queen Mona smiled benignantly upon her subjects. The float was prepared by the Foresters, whose candidate Queen Mona was, and the colors of the order, scarlet, gold and Lincoln green, were tastefully used. The single word 'Benevolence' appeared in large letters upon the sides of the float."[82] (John MacKenzie has analyzed "the Orientalist aspects of the spectacular theatre" for "the expectations of their audiences in terms of their curious blend of excitement, escapism and education.")[83]

Less surprisingly, the popular British patriotic figures John Bull, Britannia, and Queen Elizabeth I also appeared on Victoria Day. At Beacon Hill Park in 1923 a play was preceded by a pageant, "the procession of historical characters being led by ruddy John Bull in the person of Mr Sampson, Britannia in the person of Mrs de Gruchy, and Queen Elizabeth impersonated by Mrs Hawthorne." This British section of the pageant was contributed by the Royal Society of St. George, with the red cross of St. George being carried in front. Bolstering imperial unity, the army and navy, sports, Florence Nightingale, Girl Guides, and Boy Scouts were all represented in costume. Amid the revelry, mindful of the recent war, the pageant was preceded by the singing of "The Passing of the Pessimist."[84]

Memories of the First World War, and forgetting and/or overcoming them, contributed to creating a positive fairy-tale atmosphere of revelry and wonder that was of prime importance in the celebrations. In 1923 the *Daily Colonist*, reporting on the thousands attending the holiday pageant, recorded that it

was a wonderful display of optimism, this eager crowd of age and youth which rimmed the ropes stretched about the big natural stage, and if visitors from other cities needed any proof of the existence of the optimistic spirit in Victoria they could not have found it in more pronounced form. The flower-garlanded and gleaming white columns of the Greek temple lost nothing in classical beauty in account of the rain, and the actors and other performers in the pageant and play went through with their parts with as much apparent pleasure as if the sun had been shining in its best-known Victoria manner.[85]

Drawing upon an antimodern aesthetic, queens were a way of expressing the hope, potential, and optimism of the interwar years. On display as ideal citizens, through their various crownings as queens of Agriculture, Progress, State, Benevolence, Commerce, and Sport, they embodied the civic and economic virtues of society.[86] Here, the queens were on display to herald the future economic bounty of British Columbia. Their purpose was not historically novel. Kate Darian-Smith and Sarah Wills' work on agricultural queens in Australia situates young women in traditions that "can be traced back to antiquity, where women were associated with the natural cycles of reproduction and agriculture. Social and religious traditions in western societies are steeped with rituals where women physically embody and represent human participation in nature and stand allegorically for the principles of community and country. From the Greek goddess Ceres to the May Day and harvest queens of the town festivals, women have been widely represented as symbolic of community solidarity, fertility and nature."[87] In interwar Victoria, ancient times were being evoked when the 1923 pageant included a Greek temple.

How are we to position and make sense of the Queens of the Frolic? If we can read work on the female form in monuments, as articulated by Marina Warner, which shows that there is not necessarily a correlation between symbolic and actual power, does the same hold for live women so allegorically embodied?[88] Historical context is always central in such considerations. Mona Domosh has argued that in America at the beginning of the twentieth century, Victorian aesthetic ideology and gender ideology were interconnected, with Victorian aesthetic ideology containing the "possibility of subversive meanings."[89] But the contrary argument can also be made: that live women as allegory heralded the modern-day "objectification" of women. It was just as women became "modern" and liberated that they appeared in pageants as if turned into the equivalent of "stone," as if to freeze their accomplishments. Kate Darian-Smith and Sara Wills follow this line of thought when they argue that making women "for show," including regal imagery, "belies the increasingly complex challenges to the perceptions and definitions of femininity" and that the "depiction of the 'Queen' as remote and passive masked the actuality of rural women's economic productivity."[90]

Crowning Women

How are we to interpret the crowning of Queens of the Frolic in interwar Victoria? As the preindustrial mingled with the modern and industrial in the festivities, the same was in evidence with the queens. For example, in 1923 Queen Mary (Miss Mary Brown), Queen of Industries "arrayed in a robe of white beaded georgette ... had as her maids of honor Miss Irene Craig, who bore her train, and Miss Bella Cross, who carried the crown of mauve leaves and metallic flowers. Both were attired in mauve, with hats to match." The queen was greeted on the steps of the Parliament Buildings with a naval and military guard of honour from HMCS *Patrician*.[91] Rather than clashing, flower and metal coexisted, as did the evocation of harvest festival and popular culture with official pomp and ceremony. Meanwhile, representing rural areas, and emphasizing agriculture and nature, queens came from districts west of the city. From Metchosin came Queen Connie (Miss Connie Blake) of the Earth, while Sooke was represented by Queen Jean (Miss Jean Nicholson) of the Forest. "Both were fittingly dressed to symbolize the realms over which they ruled. Queen Connie represented a corncob, wearing a costume of green and yellow." The queens were crowned by Lieutenant-Governor W.C. Nichol, who before an "immense gathering" "placed emblems of royalty on their heads."[92]

> Each coronation was greeted with applause from the spectators, and then came the crowning of Dora, Queen of the Frolic. His Honor placed the symbol of authority on her head, and as she turned with a smile acknowledging the acclaims of the crowd, another blare of trumpets proclaimed that she was *truly Queen*. When the Queens were seated on their thrones, with Queen Dora in the centre, Premier John Oliver delivered a brief address. It was a pleasure, he said, to express to Her Majesty the Queen of the Frolic the loyalty of her subjects, whose hearty desire it was that her whole life should be as happy as upon this her coronation day.[93] (emphasis added)

The young women were not, of course, "truly queen." From such accounts it might be interpreted that through the act of crowning, men and their institutions, in this case the King's representative in British Columbia and the premier of the province, were bowing down to women, "treating them as royalty." In 1924 on the steps of the Parliament Buildings, Mayor Reginald Hayward crowned Queen Mona, attended by her pages and maids of honour. In a modern time, the language of the paper was redolent of a chivalrous age: "Amid the plaudits of the multitude, the Queen drove from the city to Parliament Square, where she was received by the Mayor with an address of welcome, bestowing upon her the freedom of the city. The coronation ceremonies were a spectacular proceeding witnessed by a large throng of the Queen's subjects."[94] In 1929 it was estimated that five thousand people gathered to see Queen Clare, the Queen of May, crowned.[95] Queen Clare was the schoolchildren's choice, and Victoria High School presented her with a string of pearls.[96] Her lavish fur-trimmed robe signalled status and glamour.[97] Due to the inclement weather, Queen Clare and her attendants were unable to ride in the special float and were instead transferred to "a closed car so that she might be in the parade and the citizens not altogether disappointed."[98]

Were postwar Victorians seeking solace in Hollywoodesque glamour? Can the coronations be read as symbolic evidence of a new postwar age that valued women? Taken further, were men bowing down to women, bestowing them with the freedom of the city? Given men's domination over the public sphere, this might be taken as cruel mockery. In seeking an explanation, the appearance of Regent McMiking in an historic float as Queen Victoria is important. Queen Victoria "appeared" long after the orthodox "Victorian" age. McMiking embodied the old, a generation of female imperialists active in constructing interwar Anglo-Canadian identity. These staunch women were true to their aim of perpetuating Victoria's memory, seeking to, as they saw it, pass on her legacy. While Mrs. McMiking dressed as a queen, Queen Mona and Queen Clare were the successors more readily associated with the interwar years of overcoming the traumas of the First World War. Hence the old and the new were both embodied as queens, and both used a regal identity to construct Anglo-Canadian identity.

The concept of mimesis has provided the uniting theme through this chapter. Understanding interwar Victoria Day in Victoria requires that we move beyond viewing the events as pretend, make-believe, or ridiculous, in order to capture what was tangled up in the nexus between art and reality. Multilayered discourses drawing upon different historic time periods converged and were embodied in different generations of Anglo-Celtic women. Many years before, symbolizing the eternal body politic of the monarch, a wooden effigy formed a part of Queen Elizabeth I's funeral procession. The mortal body of the Queen was gone, but the monarchy lived on.[99] Maybe members of Canada's IODE were so sure that they themselves embodied Queen Victoria that they were passing on the mantle to the new generation of the Queens of the Frolics?

Notes

1 Scrapbook of Lady Douglas Chapter, 1919-39, reel 0286, N1 IM 7L.1, Vancouver City Archives (VCA).
2 *Victoria Daily Colonist*, 24 May 1923, 8.
3 Anne McClintock, *Imperial Leather: Race, Gender and Sexuality in the Colonial Contest* (New York and London: Routledge, 1995), 368.
4 Veronica Strong-Boag, *The New Day Recalled: Lives of Girls and Women in English Canada, 1919-1939* (Markham, ON: Penguin Books, 1988), 2.

5 Jean-Pierre Durix, *Mimesis, Genres and Post-Colonial Discourse: Deconstructing Magic Realism* (Basingstoke, UK: Macmillan, 1998), 45. See Hayden White, *Figural Realism: Studies in the Mimesis Effect* (Baltimore: Johns Hopkins University Press, 1999).

6 Arne Melberg, *Theories of Mimesis* (Melbourne: Cambridge University Press), 4.

7 "Thomas Crosby with Native woman, 'Queen Victoria,'" n.d., courtesy BC Archives, HP665; Clarence Bolt, *Thomas Crosby and the Tsimshian: Small Shoes for Feet Too Large* (Vancouver: UBC Press, 1992).

8 Sylvia Van Kirk, "Tracing the Fortunes of Five Founding Families of Victoria," *BC Studies* 115/116 (Autumn/Winter 1997-98): 149-79. Van Kirk has revealed that the Native origin of some of Victoria's founding families was obscured for decades.

9 "IODE Honors Indian Poetess," 18 March 1946, unidentified, Matthews Collection, VCA. In a formal ceremony, members annually placed daffodils, Johnson's favourite flower, on her monument in Stanley Park and then took tea. See Veronica Strong-Boag and Carole Gerson, *Paddling Her Own Canoe: The Times and Texts of E. Pauline Johnson (Tekahionwake)* (Toronto: University of Toronto Press, 2000).

10 See John MacKenzie, *Propaganda and Empire: The Manipulation of British Public Opinion, 1880-1960* (Manchester, UK: Manchester University Press, 1984).

11 Ibid., 12.

12 Ibid., 14.

13 *Victoria Daily Colonist,* 25 May 1924, 2.

14 Mary P. Ryan, *Women in Public: Between Banners and Ballots, 1825-1880* (Baltimore: Johns Hopkins University Press), 56.

15 Edward Said, *Culture and Imperialism* (London: Vintage, 1993); Benedict Anderson, *Imagined Communities: Reflections on the Origin and Spread of Nationalism,* 2nd ed. (London: Verso, 1991); Eric Hobsbawm and Terence Ranger, eds., *The Invention of Tradition* (Cambridge: Cambridge University Press, 1983); Raphael Samuel, *Theatres of Memory,* vol. 1, *The Past and Present in Contemporary Culture* (London: Verso, 1994); and Raphael Samuel and Paul Thompson, eds., *The Myths We Live By* (London and New York: Routledge, 1990).

16 Durix, *Mimesis, Genres,* 187.

17 See Paul Carter, *The Road to Botany Bay: An Exploration of Landscape and History* (New York: Knopf, 1988).

18 The *Daily Colonist,* 24 May 1923, 7.

19 The *Daily Colonist,* 23 May 1923, 4.

20 Julia Bush, *Edwardian Ladies and Imperial Power* (London: Leicester University Press, 2000); Elizabeth L. Reidi, "Imperialist Women in Edwardian Britain: The Victoria League 1899-1914" (PhD dissertation, St. Andrew's University, Scotland, 1998).

21 Katie Pickles, *Female Imperialism and National Identity: Imperial Order Daughters of the Empire (IODE)* (Manchester, UK: Manchester University Press, 2002).

22 For evidence of this argument see Pickles' *Female Imperialism and National Identity,* and "'A Link in the Great Chain of Empire Friendship': The Victoria League in New Zealand," *Journal of Imperial and Commonwealth History* 33, 1 (January 2005): 29-50.

23 Bush, *Edwardian Ladies and Imperial Power,* 2.

24 Carl Berger, *The Sense of Power: Studies in the Ideas of Canadian Imperialism, 1867-1914* (Toronto: University of Toronto Press, 1970). This occurred at a time when the economic importance of Britain in Canada was decreasing and trade with the United States was increasing.

25 W. David McIntyre, *The Significance of Commonwealth, 1965-90* (Basingstoke, UK: Macmillan, 1991).

26 MacKenzie, *Propaganda and Empire,* 148.

27 Pamphlet (IODE, 1982).

28 Speech given at Windsor Hotel parlours, Montreal. IODE Collection. Library and Archives Canada (LAC), MG 28 I 17, 18, 3, 11a, 13 February 1900.

29 MC 200 MS 1/A/1, Provincial Archives of New Brunswick.

30 Julia Bush, "Edwardian Ladies and the 'Race' Dimensions of British Imperialism," *Women's Studies International Forum* 21, 3 (1998): 277-89, at 281. See also Reidi "Imperialist Women in Edwardian Britain."

31 Bush, "Edwardian Ladies and the 'Race' Dimensions," 278.
32 Ibid.
33 Fiona Paisley, *Loving Protection? Australian Feminism and Aboriginal Women's Rights, 1919-1939* (Carlton, Australia: Melbourne University Press, 2000); Leila Rupp, *Worlds of Women: The Making of an International Women's Movement* (Princeton, NJ: Princeton University Press, 1997); Mrinalini Sinha, Donna Guy, and Angela Woollacott, eds., *Feminisms and Internationalism* (Oxford: Blackwell, 1999).
34 Bush, "Edwardian Ladies and the 'Race' Dimensions," 278.
35 See Pickles, *Female Imperialism and National Identity*, 48-49.
36 Dorothy Thompson, *Queen Victoria: The Woman, the Monarchy, and the People* (New York: Pantheon Books, 1990), 137.
37 Ibid., 145.
38 Bush, *Edwardian Ladies and Imperial Power*, 5.
39 Ibid., 68.
40 Ibid., 69-70.
41 See Mary Ann Steggles, "Set in Stone: Victoria's Monuments in India," *History Today* 51, 2 (February 2001), 44-49; and Mark Stocker, "Queen Victoria's Statues," *History Now* 7, 4 (November 2001): 5-9.
42 The *Daily Colonist*, 25 May 1923, 4.
43 The *Daily Colonist*, 27 May 1924, 1.
44 The *Daily Colonist*, 24 May 1931, 4.
45 Ibid.
46 Paul Fussell, *The Great War and Modern Memory* (Oxford: Oxford University Press, 1975); Jay Winter, *Sites of Memory, Sites of Mourning: The Great War in European Cultural History* (Cambridge: Cambridge University Press, 1995). See also Katie Pickles, "Edith Cavell – Heroine: No Hatred or Bitterness for Anyone?" *History Now* 3, 2 (1997): 1-8.
47 Jonathan Vance, *Death So Noble: Memory, Meaning, and the First World War* (Vancouver: UBC Press, 1997).
48 The *Daily Colonist*, 24 May 1931, 4.
49 The *Daily Colonist*, 24 May 1929, 7.
50 Ibid.
51 The *Daily Colonist*, 26 May 1929, 7.
52 See Lesley Hall, "Women, Feminism and Eugenics," in *Essays in the History of Eugenics*, ed. R.A. Peel, 36-51 (London: Galton Institute, 1998); and Nancy Leys Stepan, *"The Hour of Eugenics": Race, Gender, and Nation in Latin America* (Ithaca, NY: Cornell University Press, 1991).
53 Lucy Bland, *Banishing the Beast: English Feminism and Sexual Morality, 1885-1914* (London: Penguin, 1995); Greta Jones, "Eugenics and Social Policy between the Wars," *Historical Journal* 24, 3 (1982): 717-28; Angela Wanhalla, "Gender, Race and Colonial Identity: Women and Eugenics in New Zealand, 1918-1939" (MA thesis, University of Canterbury, 2001); Carol Lee Bacchi, "Race Regeneration and Social Purity: A Study of the Social Attitudes of Canada's English-Speaking Suffragists," *Histoire Sociale/Social History* 11, 22 (1978): 460-74; and Mariana Valverde, *The Age of Light, Soap and Water: Moral Reform in English Canada, 1885-1925* (Toronto: McClelland and Stewart, 1991).
54 Jeffrey Weeks, *Sex, Politics and Society: The Regulation of Sexuality since 1800* (London: Longman, 1989); Roy Porter and Lesley Hall, *The Facts of Life: The Creation of Sexual Knowledge in Britain, 1650-1950* (London: Yale University Press, 1995).
55 See Angus MacLaren, *Our Own Master Race: Eugenics in Canada, 1885-1945* (Toronto: McClelland and Stewart, 1990).
56 Ibid., and Pickles, *Female Imperialism and National Identity*, Chapters 2, 3, and 4.
57 For work on antimodernism see Ian McKay, *The Quest of the Folk: Antimodernism and Cultural Selection in Twentieth Century Nova Scotia* (Montreal and Kingston: McGill-Queen's University Press, 1994); and Donald A. Wright, "W.D. Lighthall and David Ross McCord: Antimodernism and English-Canadian Imperialism, 1880s-1914," *Journal of Canadian Studies* 32, 2 (Summer 1997): 134-53.
58 See Bush, *Edwardian Ladies and Imperial Power*; and Pickles, *Female Imperialism and National Identity*.

59 Judith Smart, "Feminists, Flappers and Miss Australia: Contesting the Meanings of Citizenship, Femininity and Nation in the 1920s," *Journal of Australian Studies* 71 (2002): 1-15, at 8.
60 The *Daily Colonist*, 26 May 1923, 7.
61 Kathryn McPherson, "'The Case of the Kissing Nurse': Femininity, Sexuality, and Canadian Nursing, 1900-1970," in *Gendered Pasts: Historical Essays in Femininity and Masculinity in Canada*, ed. Kathryn McPherson, Cecilia Morgan, and Nancy M. Forestell, 179-98 (Don Mills, ON: Oxford University Press, 1999). See also Rita Felski, *The Gender of Modernity* (Cambridge, MA: Harvard University Press, 1995); and Kathy Peiss, *Hope in a Jar: The Making of America's Beauty Culture* (New York: Metropolitan Books, 1998).
62 Strong-Boag, *The New Day Recalled*, 221.
63 Ibid., 208.
64 Ibid., 179.
65 Carolyn Strange, *Toronto's Girl Problem: The Perils and Pleasures of the City, 1880-1930* (Toronto: University of Toronto Press, 1995).
66 Smart, "Feminists, Flappers and Miss Australia," 3.
67 Colleen Ballerino Cohen, Richard Wilk, and Beverly Stoeltje, eds., *Beauty Queens on the Global Stage: Gender, Contests and Power* (London and New York: Routledge, 1996), 3. See also *Feminist Review* 71 (2002), a special issue on fashion and beauty.
68 Kate Darian-Smith and Sara Wills, "From Queen of Agriculture to Miss Showgirl: Embodying Rurality in Twentieth-Century Australia," *Journal of Australian Studies* 71 (2002): 17-31, at 18; Ballerino Cohen, Wilk, and Stoeltje, *Beauty Queens on the Global Stage*, 3-4.
69 See Liz Conor, "The Beauty Contestant in the Photographic Scene," *Journal of Australian Studies* 71 (2002): 33-43.
70 Ballerino Cohen, Wilk, and Stoeltje, *Beauty Queens on the Global Stage*, 2-3.
71 Darian-Smith and Wills, "From Queen of Agriculture to Miss Showgirl," 31.
72 Smart, "Feminists, Flappers and Miss Australia," 8.
73 Ibid., 1.
74 Katie Pickles, "Exhibiting Canada: Empire, Migration and the 1928 English Schoolgirl Tour," *Gender, Place and Culture* 7, 1 (2000): 81-96.
75 Darian-Smith and Wills, "From Queen of Agriculture to Miss Showgirl," 19.
76 Ballerino Cohen, Wilk, and Stoeltje, *Beauty Queens on the Global Stage*, 3.
77 Smart, "Feminists, Flappers and Miss Australia," 8.
78 Smart, "Feminists, Flappers and Miss Australia," 6-7.
79 Ballerino Cohen, Wilk, and Stoeltje, *Beauty Queens on the Global Stage*, 5.
80 The *Daily Colonist*, 24 May 1924, 9.
81 The *Daily Colonist*, 25 May 1923, 8.
82 The *Daily Colonist*, 25 May 1924, 2.
83 John MacKenzie, *Orientalism: History, Theory and the Arts* (Manchester: Manchester University Press, 1995), 189.
84 The *Daily Colonist*, 27 May 1923, 9.
85 Ibid.
86 *The Daily Colonist*, 27 May 1924, 1.
87 Darian-Smith and Wills, "From Queen of Agriculture to Miss Showgirl," 18.
88 Marina Warner, *Monuments and Maidens: The Allegory of the Female Form* (London: Vintage, 1985).
89 Mona Domosh, "A 'Feminine' Building? Relations Between Gender Ideology and Aesthetic Ideology in Turn-of-the-Century America," *Ecumene* 3, 3 (1996): 305-24, at 309. See also Nuala Johnson, "Cast in Stone: Monuments, Geography, and Nationalism," *Environment and Planning D: Society and Space* 13, 1 (1995): 51-56.
90 Darian-Smith and Wills, "From Queen of Agriculture to Miss Showgirl," 19.
91 The *Daily Colonist*, 27 May 1923, 11.
92 The *Daily Colonist*, 25 May 1923, 1.
93 Ibid.
94 The *Daily Colonist*, 27 May 1924, 1.
95 The *Daily Colonist*, 24 May 1929, 6.
96 The *Daily Colonist*, 26 May 1929, 8.

97 See Chantal Nadeau, *Fur Nation: From the Beaver to Brigitte Bardot* (London and New York: Routledge, 2001).

98 The *Daily Colonist*, 26 May 1929, 7.

99 Jennifer Woodward, "Images of a Dead Queen," *History Today* 47, 11 (November 1997): 18-23.

Contributors

Jean Barman is the author of *The West beyond the West: A History of British Columbia* (University of Toronto Press), now in its second edition. Her two current books are *Stanley Park's Secret: The Forgotten Families of Whoi Whoi, Kanaka Ranch, and Brockton Point* (Harbour Publishing) and, co-authored with Bruce Watson, *Leaving Paradise: Indigenous Hawaiians in the Pacific Northwest* (University of Hawai'i Press).

Robin Jarvis Brownlie teaches in the History Department at the University of Manitoba and is the author of *A Fatherly Eye: Indian Agents, Government Power, and Aboriginal Resistance in Ontario, 1918-1939* (Oxford University Press, 2003).

Sarah A. Carter has taught Canadian history at the University of Calgary since 1992. Her publications include *Lost Harvests: Prairie Indian Reserve Farmers and Government Policy* (McGill-Queen's University Press, 1990), *Capturing Women: The Manipulation of Cultural Imagery in Canada's Prairie West* (McGill-Queen's University Press, 1997), *Aboriginal People and Colonizers of Western Canada to 1900* (University of Toronto Press, 1999), and the co-authored book *The True Spirit and Original Intent of Treaty 7* (with Treaty 7 Elders and Tribal Council, Walter Hildebrandt, and Dorothy First Rider) (McGill-Queen's University Press, 1996).

Sherry Farrell Racette has a PhD from the University of Manitoba. With a background in Fine Arts, she is an experienced cross-cultural educator in the areas of Indigenous Studies and art, with expertise in the traditional arts of the Métis. She wrote and illustrated *The Flower Beadwork People: People Place and Stories of the Métis* (Gabriel Dumont Institute, 1991) and also illustrated Maria Campbell's *Stories of the Road Allowance People* (Theytus Press, 1994), Freda Ahenakew's *Wisahkechak Flies to the Moon* (Pemmican Press, 1999), and Ruby Slipperjack's *Little Voice* (Coteau Books, 2001). Her recent exhibitions include *Dolls for Big Girls* (2000) at Regina's Rosemont Gallery, and *Rielisms* (2001), a group exhibition at the Winnipeg Art Gallery.

Jo-Anne Fiske is currently Professor and Coordinator of Women's Studies at the University of Lethbridge. She is a partner in the National Network of Aboriginal Mental Heath Research, and a co-investigator in research addressing impacts of declining economy and government policies on women's caregiving obligations. She has published numerous articles in academic journals and is author of *Cis Dideen Kat – When the Plumes Rise: The Way of the Lake Babine Nation* (UBC Press, 2000).

Carole Gerson is Professor in the Department of English at Simon Fraser University, where she teaches Canadian literature. She has published extensively on Canadian literary history, and with Veronica Strong-Boag has co-authored a study of Pauline Johnson and a scholarly edition of Johnson's work. She is a member of the Royal Society of Canada and is currently co-editing volume 3 (1918-80) of the *History of the Book in Canada/Histoire du livre et de l'imprimé au Canada*.

Cecilia Morgan is Associate Professor in the History of Education Program, OISE/University of Toronto. She is currently completing a manuscript on Canadian tourism in Britain and Europe, 1870s-1930s, and is working on a study of Aboriginal peoples' travels and the transatlantic world, 1780s-1900s.

Dianne Newell is Professor of History and Director of the Peter Wall Institute for Advanced Studies at the University of British Columbia. Her five books include *Tangled Webs of History: Indians and the Law in Canada's Pacific Coast Fisheries* (University of Toronto Press, 1993). She has prepared a new book manuscript, *Islands of Work at the Rough Edge of the World*. Her new SSHRC-funded research is on the American-Canadian author-critic-anthologist Judith Merril and her intellectual circles in postwar science fiction. Dr. Newell has authored and co-authored papers on women's science fiction in *Foundation: International Review of Science Fiction, European Journal of American Culture*, and *Journal of International Women's Studies*.

Adele Perry teaches history at the University of Manitoba, where she is Canada Research Chair in Western Canadian Social History. She is currently working on gender, sexuality, and colonialism in nineteenth-century British Columbia, migration and Aboriginal policy in turn-of-the-century Canada, and transnationalism and colonialism in eighteenth- and nineteenth-century northern North America.

Katie Pickles teaches history at the University of Canterbury, New Zealand. She is the author of *Female Imperialism and National Identity: Imperial Order Daughters of the Empire* (Manchester University Press, Studies in Imperialism, 2002), the editor of *Hall of Fame: Life Stories of New Zealand Women* (The Clerestory Press, 1998), and with Lyndon Fraser, *Shifting Centres: Women and Migration in New*

Zealand History (Otago University Press, 2002). Her monograph on memory, colonial identity, and the martyrdom of Nurse Edith Cavell will be published by Palgrave in 2006.

Myra Rutherdale is Assistant Professor in the Department of History at York University in Toronto. She is the author of *Women and the White Man's God: Gender and Race in the Canadian Mission Field* (UBC Press, 2002) and is currently editing a collection of essays entitled *Duty Bound Dispatch: Nurses and Midwives in Canada's Outposts and Outports*.

Joan Sangster teaches History and Women's Studies at Trent University where she is also Director of the Frost Centre for Canadian Studies and Native Studies. She has published on Canadian working-class, women's, and legal history, including her recent monograph, *Girl Trouble: Female Delinquency in English Canada* (Between the Lines Press, 2002). She is currently researching a book on women and work after the Second World War.

Veronica Strong-Boag teaches in Women's Studies and Educational Studies at the University of British Columbia. She is a member of the Royal Society of Canada, a former president of the Canadian Historical Association, and author of *The New Day Recalled: Lives of Girls and Women in English Canada 1919-1939* (Copp Clark Pitman, 1988) that won the John A. Macdonald Prize for Canadian history in 1988 and *Paddling Her Own Canoe: The Times and Texts of E. Pauline Johnson (Tekahionwake)* (University of Toronto Press, 2000) that won the Klibansky Prize for the best Canadian book in the Humanities in 2000.

Index

Note: Page numbers in italic indicate an illustration. DIA stands for Department of Indian Affairs.

Abikoki, Jim, *141*
Abitibi (Quebec), 26
Aboriginal people: in British Columbia in 1800s, 112-13; curfews, 215-16; imperial efforts to control, 70; imperial view of immoral nature, 7-10, 56, 92, 112, 187-88, 194; increasing social marginalization, 198n19; marriage forms, 8, 115-16, 118, 132-36, 140-42, 150-55, 168; in Ontario historiography, 68; rural-urban migration, 182; use of bodies to colonize, 229; view of child discipline, 186; views of Christian conjugality, 119-22
Aboriginal women and girls: childbirth, 233-34; in correctional facilities, 181, 183-84, 199n32; as crime victims, 209-10, 217, 219, 225n30-32, 46, 227n118; delinquent, 184, 187-96; DIA power over, 8, 160-75, 176n9; DIA references to, 162-63; as equal or superior to white women, 6, 47, 55, 58; in imperial writings, 51, 58; imposition of white clothing, 10, 238-42; Johnson's stage performances, 48-51, *52*, 54, 56; Johnson's writings about, 48, 53-63; missionary efforts to domesticize, 9, 114-15, 139; missionary efforts to teach labour roles to, 5, 122-25, 139; Monture's lectures about, 73; oppression, exploitation, and diminution, 47, 51; as "other," 4; in patriotic Anglo-Canadian celebrations, 11, 273; policies, 8, 121, 137-39, 148-49, 167-70; in polygamous marriages, 132-35; power and authority of, 61-62, 112-13, 136-37, 219; regulation of political activity, 166-67; regulation of sexual activity, 167-75; relationships with white men, 116-19; and residential schools, 6-7, 90, 93-94; restricted presence outside reserves, 68; sewing for a living, 17-18, 23-24; as sexual transgressors, 7-10, 47, 56, 92, 140, 161, 163-69, 172-75, 195-96, 206, 208, 213; suspect because not subservient, 10; in United Kingdom, 4; in Western clothing, 219-20; in women's institutes, 73.
See also Métis women and girls
Adhemar, Angelique, 19
Agatooga (Inuit man), 239
age: of "delinquent" girls, 199n31; and DIA attitudes, 164; minimum for marriage, 151, 158n96
Aklavik, Northwest Territories, 231, *232*
Alberta: Mormons, 142-46, 148; Treaty 7, 147, 155
alcohol, 209-10, 224n29
Alert Bay, British Columbia, 115, 123
Allary, Catherine, 39
Allen (male teacher, Red River), 20
American Fur Company, 19, 21, 27, 31-33
American Horse (Aboriginal man), 149-50
American Philosophical Society, 76
Amyotte (Amiot), Madeleine. *See* Desnommé, Madeleine Amyotte
Anda (Tsimshian woman), 124-25
Anderson, A.S., 177n26
Anderson, Kim, 170
Anglican Church: baptisms of Aboriginal men and women, 32, 137-38; emphasis on clothing, 238-40; emphasis on health and hygiene, 229, 231; establishes

permanent villages, 113; nuns' clothing, 236; in Pauline Johnson's background, 49; in Pauline Johnson's writings, 57; schools and missions, 69, 110, 121, 123-25, 230-31; view of marriage, 118, 121, 137-38, *141;* view of mixed-race relationships, 117; view of womanhood, 112, 124-25

Anishinabe people, 168, 174, 177n22

Armstrong, Jeannette, 48

Arviat, Nunavut, 230, 233

Askin, John, 19

Ask-kaw-taphi-tak (Sitting with Earth) (Cree elder), 40

Assiniboine people, 139

Atchina (Inuit woman), 241, 243

Audubon, John J., 32, 45n90

Auerbach, Erich, 273

Augé, Marc, 91

Australia: Empire-building, 4, 277, 282-83

Backhouse, Constance, 137

Baird, Elizabeth Fisher, 42n7

Ballantyne, Robert, 27

Ballerino Cohen, Colleen, 282-83

Bannatyne, Anne McDermott, 17

Bannerji, Himani, 181, 190

Barman, Jean, 9-10, 109

Barnum, P.T., 282

baskets, 18, 22, 26-27

Bates, Jane Elizabeth, *144*

Battle of Grand Coteau, 39, 46n116

Bear's Shin Bone (Blood man), 154-55

Beaucage, Gertie, 170

Begg, Magnus, 151

Belcourt, Georges, 21, 43n28

Belhumeur (fur trader), 32

Bell, Charles Napier, 28, *30*

Bella Bella, British Columbia, 110, 113

Berger, Carl, 276

Betteyloun, Susan Bordeaux, 21, 43n30

Beynon, William, 116

Big Sisters, 182

bigamy, 145, 148

Bird, James, 20

Bird, Madeline Mercredi, 22, 43n38

Black (fur-trade family), 20

Blackfoot people: divorce, 136; marriage forms, 132, *133*, 134, 140, 143, 147

Blackfoot Reserve, Alberta, 147, 151

Blake, Connie, 286

Blanchard, Jane Bell, 20, 43n21

Blondeau, Françoise Desjarlais, 37, 39, 46n116

Blondeau, Johnnie, 46n116

Blondeau, Melanie, 37, 39-40

Blondeau, Simon, 39, 46n116

Blood people, 147

Blood Reserve, Alberta, 138, 146-47, 152, 155

Bombarde. *See* Labombarde, Nancy Kipling

Bompas, Selina, 237

Bordeaux, James, 43n30

Bordeaux, Susan, 21, 43n30

Bordo, Susan, 228

Bowen, Susan, 235

Bowman, Phylis, 247, 258-59, 263-65, 267

Boy Scouts, 276, 280, 284

Boyd, Robert, 218

Brabant, Joseph, 120

Brant, Beth, 47

Brant, Catherine, 75

Brant, Ethel. *See* Monture, Ethel Brant

Brant Historical Society, 69, 71, 85n4, 86n13

Brant, Joseph, 67, 69, 71, 74-77

Brant, Molly, 47, 63n9

Braun, Bruce, 248, 250

bride-price, 116

Britain. *See* United Kingdom

British Church Missionary Society, 230

British Columbia: Aboriginal women in Victoria, 10; colonization, 109-13, 125-26, 206-7; colonizing white women, 10-11; gold rush, 206-8, 213-14; map, *111*; mission and residential schools, 97-98, 104n18; missionaries, 7-8, 10, 110, 125-26; Northwest Coast contact zone, 246-49

Brown, Eric, 256

Brown, Lydia J., *144*

Brown, Mary, 286

Brown, R.C. Lundin, 118, 121

Brown, Wendy, 103

Brownlie, Robin Jarvis, 8

Bruce (fur-trade family), 20

Buckner, Phillip, 5

Buffalo Bird Woman, 134

Bull, John, 284

Bunn (fur-trade family), 20

Bunn, John, 27

Bunn, Thomas, 44n66

Burdett-Coutts, Angela, 110

Burnet, Jean, 228

Burns, Flora, 254

Burton, Antoinette, 4, 122, 131

Bush, Julia, 276, 278-79

Buss, Helen, 254, 263

Butler, Adelaide, 236

Butler, Judith, 5

Butler, William, 28

Calgary Stampede, 36
Cameron, James Dugald, 20
Cameron, Laura, 258
Campbell, Celia, 21, 43n29
Campbell, Margaret, 43n29
Campbell, Robert, 45
Campbell, Scott, 43n29
Canadian Handicraft Guild, 37, 39
Canham, Charlotte, 235-36
canneries, West Coast: Carr's view, 253-58, 270n46; and Chisholm murder, 258-65; Collis' view, 248-50, 252
Cape Croker, Ontario, 175n1
caps (fur), 24
Carcross, Yukon, 238
Card, Charles Ora, 144-45
Card, Zina Y., *144*
Cardinal, Harold, 167
Cardston, Alberta, 144-45
Carey, George Hunter, 215
Carr, Emily: autobiography, 10-11, 246; conflicted sense of West Coast, 252-53; as explorer-painter, 248, 265-66; paintings, 253-54; personal history, 253, 258; picture, *255*; writings, 255-58, 266
Carrier people, 113
Carter, Sarah A., 8, 262
Catholic Church: Durieu system, 113; and nuns as motherless daughters, 90, 93; nuns' clothing, 28; in Pauline Johnson's writings, 50; principles of celibacy and chastity, 104n21; principles of sacrifice and mortification, 98; representations of motherhood, 96, 98; and residential school staff and students as motherless daughters, 93; schools and missions, 19-20, 28, 92-94, 97-98, 100, 110, 112, 115; view of marriage, 118, 120, 122, 140, 152; view of mixed-race relationships, 116-17
Cavalier, Rachel, 21
celibacy: as block to demonstrating conjugal example, 118; defined, 104n21; among nuns and missionaries, 96, 100, 118
Chalmers, Harvey, 69
Chardon, Francis A., 31
Charles, John, 26
Charles, Joseph, 26
Cheadle, Walter, 34
Cheyenne people, 135
childbirth, 233-34, 244n19
children: of Aboriginal woman married to white man, 170; abuse in residential schools, 101-2, 104n14; in Blackfoot divorce, 136; as brides, 116, 151, 158n96;

in English divorce, 137; importance of clothing in colonization, 228-29, *232*, 239-40; importance of health and hygiene in colonization, 230-31; in patriotic Anglo-Canadian activities, 280; power of DIA over, 163, 165, 173, 176n9; taken over by state, 90, 92, 94, 96-98, 103n9, 182, 190; under polygamy laws, 137-38, 140, 149, 154-55. *See also* women and girls
Chippewa women, 42n7, 160
Chisholm, Loretta, 11, 247, 258-67
Chouteau, Pierre, 45
Christian schools. *See* residential and mission schools
Christie (fur-trade family), 20
Church Missionary Society: in British Columbia, 110-12; efforts against polygamy, 137; in northern Canada, 230
Clark (fur-trade family), 20
Clark, Jane Bell, 20, 43n21
Clark Murray, John, 276
Clark Murray, Margaret, 276
Clarke, John, 26
Clay, Margaret, 254
Clayoquot, British Columbia, 110
Clayoquot people, 114
cleanliness. *See* hygiene
clothing: of Aboriginal women in Victoria, 219-21; attitude of missionary women, 235-42; and Chisholm murder, 261, 263; "cowboy," 36-37; importance of indigenous forms, 22, 28-29, 36-38, 237; as marker of assimilation, 273; as marker of civilization, 10, 228-30, 235-40, 252; as marker of the exotic, 243n9; "Native," in stage performances, 49-50; photographs, *29-30, 33*; sewing role of Métis women, 5, 17, 25-27, 33-41; trading post production of, 23-26
Coast Salish women, 62
coats: Arctic, 237; capotes, 28; hide, 19-20, 23-24, 27, 32-33, 44n41, 44n42, 45n96; mackinaw, 19-20, 43n15
Coburn, Katherine, 75-77, 89n88
Cochrane, John J., 215
Cody, Buffalo Bill, 50
Colenso, John William, 137-38
Collis, Maria Septima, 10-11, 246, 249-50, *251*, 252, 265
Comaroff, Jean, 111, 197n7
Comaroff, John, 111, 197n7
Comox, British Columbia, 110
contact zones: defined, 4, 246
Conybeare, C.F., 153-54
Cook (fur-trade family), 20

Cooper, Carol, 209
correctional facilities, 181, 183-84, 199n32
Coutlée, Thérèse, 21
Cowichan, British Columbia, 110, 115, 124
Cowie, Isaac, 25-26
Craig, Irene, 286
Crary, Jonathan, 248
Cree people: marriage forms, 132-34; women sewers, 40
crime: assault, 150, 209-11, 213, 219, 227n119; Chisholm murder, 11, 247, 258-65, 266-67; drunkenness, 211-14, 216, 219; Killas murder, 264-65; prostitution, 205-12, 217-19, 224n20, 263; sexual abuse and assault, 101-2, 103n9, 104n14, 108n9, 185; whisky giving, 209, 213. *See also* polygamy
Crosby, Thomas, 119
Cross, Bella, 286
Crowfoot, 74
Cumberland, British Columbia, 281
Cumming, C., 26

Daines, Sara, *144*
Daly, John M., 161-64, 166-68, 171-73, 177n22, 177n26
dance halls: association with prostitution, 212-18; financial gain from, 215; role of Aboriginal women, 220-21
Darian-Smith, Kate, 282-83, 285
Daughters of St. Ann's, 110, 124
Davidoff, Leonore, 113
Davin, Anna, 2
Davis, John, 20
Davis, Kathy, 9
Davis, Matilda, 20
Davis, Nancy, 20
Dawson, Yukon, 235
de Cosmos, Amor, 205, 207, 217-19
de Gruchy (Victoria woman), 284
delinquents: boys, 192; "causes," 185; connections between white and Aboriginal girls, 196; defined, 183-84; sentences, 185-86
Delorme, Marie Rose, 22, 36-37, 46n112
Dempsey, Hugh, 152
Dene people, 116
Denig, Edward, 32
Denig, Edwin Thompson, 139
Department of Indian Affairs (DIA): calls for reform, 72; gender and race discourse, 162-66; marriage policies, 8, 121, 131, 140-42, 146-55, 167-70; and mixed-race relationships, 170-72, 177n36; on nomadic or camp life, 115; promotes colo-

nialism, 162; regulation of political activity, 166-67; restrictions on sexuality, 172-75; and sewing production, 37, 39. *See also* Indian agents
Depression, 173-74, 181, 236
Derrick, Albert, 270n45
Derridean feminism, 3
Deschambeau, Charlotte, 43n38
Deschamps (fur-trade family), 31-32
Deschamps, François, 31
Desjarlais, Antoine, 39
Desjarlais, Françoise, 46n116
Desjarlais, Isabella, 37, 39
Desjarlais, Lucy, 39
Desnommé, Madeleine Amyotte, 34, 40, 46n101
Desnommé, Pierre, 34, 46n101
DIA. *See* Department of Indian Affairs
Dickenson, Victoria, 250
Dickson, Robert, 19
Dilworth, Ira, 254
diseases, 209, 218, 230, 239-40
divorce: in Aboriginal societies, 136, 140-41, 167, 174; under English law, 137, 168; under United States law, 143-44
dolls, 27
Domosh, Mona, 285
Donald, Emily, 171
Doré (Métis woman), 26
Douglas, James, 113, 123
Dreaver (fur-trade family), 20
D'Sonoqua, Guyasdoms', 253
Dubinsky, Karen, 3, 260, 264
Dumoulin (male missionary), 28
Duncan, Sara Jeannette, 53
Duncan, William, 115-16, 120, 122-24
Durieu, Paul, 120; Durieu system of missions, 113-14, 120
d'Youville, Marguerite, 96

Eade, H.J., 166-67
economy: declining British partnership, increasing U.S. partnership, 288n24; in Depression, 173-74, 181; and Métis women's sewing, 5, 17-18, 26-29, 31-42; post–Second World War, 181-82; during Second World War, 182-83, 193; value of women's work, 60-61, 65n55
Edelman, Hope, 104n14
Edgar, Mary, 81
Edmonton (Alberta), 23
education: of fur-trade children, 18-19; Monture's lectures about, 67, 72-73; of non-Natives about Aboriginal people, 72-74, 85n4; in sewing, 18-23, 72, 124-25; on Six Nations Reserve, 72-73;

woman-to-woman, 18-19, 22-23. *See also* residential and mission schools
Edwards (DIA agent, Kenora), 167
Elizabeth I, Queen of England, 284, 287
England, 18
Erickson, Lesley, 261, 263
Ermatinger, Ed, 26
Esquimalt, British Columbia, 207, 209-10
Eto (Inuit woman), 240
Evans, Ephraim, 217-18
exogamy, 116

Farrell Racette, Sherry, 5
Fassovier, Antoine, 225n32
Feeman, Minnie Aodla, 242
feminism: and collective experience, 3; interwar, 278, 280-87; and power, 3; Queen Victoria as symbol of, 278; and sexual frontiers of empire, 180-81, 280; women's bodies as heart of, 3
Fernandez, Gregory, 227n120
Fidler, Peter, 23
File, Celia, 76, 78-83, 88n51, 89n77, 89n86
Findlay, Eileen J. Suárez, 224n18
Fine Day (Cree chief) 40, 132-34
Finlayson, D., 26
Finnegan, Patrick, 227n119
firebags, 24-25, 33
First World War: lobbying by IODE for female suffrage, 278; post-war pageantry, 274-75, 279, 284; veterans and wives, 175n2, 176n3
Fisher, Marienne Lasalière, 19, 42n10
Fisher, Robin, 206
Fiske, Jo-Anne, 6-7, 113
Fleming, Archibald, 239
Flett (fur-trade family), 20
Flett (Métis woman), 18
Folds, Nancy, 26
Forget, Amedée, 147-49, 151-54
Fort Benton (Montana), 27
Fort Berthold (North Dakota), 35
Fort Carlton (Saskatchewan), 20, 27, 33, 34
Fort Cass (Montana), 31
Fort Chipewyan (Alberta), 22
Fort Churchill (Manitoba), 23-24, 27
Fort Clark (North Dakota), 27
Fort Edmonton (Alberta), 24, 27, 34
Fort Ellice (Manitoba), 25, 27
Fort Laramie (Wyoming), 43n30
Fort Macleod (Alberta), 140
Fort Pierre (South Dakota), 27, 32, 45n96
Fort Pitt (Saskatchewan), 27, 34
Fort Qu'Appelle (Saskatchewan), 25, 27
Fort Rupert (British Columbia), 110
Fort St. Joseph (Michigan), 19

Fort Selkirk (Yukon), 231
Fort Union (North Dakota), 27-29, 31-32, 45n96, 139
Fort Vermillion (Alberta), 24
Fort William (North Dakota), 31-32
Foucauldian feminism, 3, 13n27, 180
Foucault, Michel, 229
Foucet, Léon, 123
France, 4-5
Frank (son of Red Crow), 152
Franklin, Sir John, 25
Fraser River, British Columbia, 110
French, Alice, 231
Frye, Northrop, 247
fur trade: children's education, 18-23; clothing production at trading posts, 23-26, 36, 41; women's role, 5, 18, 41
Fussell, Paul, 279

Gagnon, Josette, 46n115
Gardepie (fur-trade family), 31-32
Gardepie, Jean Baptiste, 31
Garrioch, Peter, 35
gender: in imperialism, 2; in initial contacts between Europeans and Americans, 5; in missionary vision and system, 112, 120; women in Aboriginal communities, 112-13, 136-37; working-class roles, 122-23, 179. *See also* men
Gerson, Carole, 6
Gervais (Métis woman), 26
Gibbons, Caroline, 233, 243
Giles, William, 213-14
Girl Guides, 276, 280, 284
girls. *See* Aboriginal women and girls; children; white women and girls; women and girls
Gladman (Métis woman), 18, 42n6
Gladman, George, 42n6
gold rush, 206-8, 213-14
Goldfrank, Esther, 134, 136
Good, J.B., 119-20
Gordon, Linda, 118
Gordon, Sarah Barringer, 143
Goulet, Louis, 35-36, 41, 43n28
Goulet, Moise, 36
Graham, J.F., 142
Gramsci, Antonio, 88n60
Grandin, Vital, 145
Grant, Johnny, 17
Gravel, Domitilde, 31
Gravel, Marguerite, 31
Gravel, Michel, 31-32
Green Bay (Wisconsin), 19
Greene, Alma, 67
Grewal, Inderpal, 136

Grey Nuns, 21, 28, 96
Grignon, Elizabeth, 19
Grimshaw, Patricia, 117
Guild of Loyal Women, South Africa, 276
Guillord, Henry, 122
Gunn, Sally, 25
Gutiérrez, Ramón A., 109

Haida people: fur trade, 208; gender structure, 112; seasonal sales in Victoria, 207; women's power and authority, 10, 62
Hall, Catherine, 110, 113
Hall, Lesley, 280
Hamilton, James, 31
Hamlyn, R.J., 26
Hammer, Elizabeth, *144*
Hardisty (fur-trade family), 20, 45n97
Hardisty, Richard, 34
Hardy, Arthur Douglas, 263
Hargrave, James, 26-27
Hargreave, Letitia, 24
Harmer, Adeline, 236
Harriet, Jane, 44n52
Harris, Agnes, 270n53
Harris, E.A., 270n53
Harris, Edward, 32, 45n90
Harris, Thomas, 216
Hawthorne (Victoria woman), 284
Hayward, Reginald, 286
health: diseases, 209, 218, 230, 239-40; health care as colonizing influence, 229-34, 241
Helmcken, John Sebastian, 209, 214
Hennessy, Rosemary, 180
Henry, Alexander the Younger, 23-24
Herring, Frances, 212
Hesquiat, British Columbia, 120
Hidatsa people, 134
Highway, Tomson, 50
Hill, Harold, 67, 85n4
Hills, George, 118-19, 121, 220
Hinds, Margery, 242
Hines, John, 138
Hinman, Jane, *144*
Hinman, Rhoda C., *144*
Hockin, E. Prudence, 236, 239-41, *241*
Hough (Victoria constable), 219
Houghton, R.C., 135
household sewing, 37, *38*
Howells, Emily Susanna, 49
Hoxie, Frederick, 84
Hudson's Bay Company: attitude toward "supernumerary" wives, 138; closure for Victoria Day, 275; clothing production, 23, 36, 41; fur-trade families, 20; soap

stores, 230; sponsorship of sewing education, 21; travel routes, 27
Huel, Raymond, 92
Hughes, Mary Salslawit, 205, 207, 219, 222
Hughes, William, 205, 219
Humphrey, Ruth, 254
Hungry Wolf, Beverly, 134-35
hygiene: as mark of civilization, 229-31, 238, 240-41; as proof of domesticity, 114, 165; as proof of moral character, 185, 188, 231

Ibey, Mary L., *144*
Illissipi (Inuit girl), 240
Imperial Order Daughters of the Empire (IODE): badge and motto, 276, *277*; feminist activities and results, 278, 281; founded, 276; keeping memory of Queen Victoria alive, 11, 272, 279-80, 287; official objectives, 276; vision of a British Canada, 272-73, 282-83
imperialism: entrenchment in early 1900s, 70; female, 2, 275-79; missionary model, 111-12; propaganda clubs, 276; significance, 4-5; view of Aboriginal women, 47, 51, 60
Indian Act, 169-70, 172
Indian agents: increased powers on reserves, 70, 162; interest in and power over sexual habits on reserve, 8, 160-65, 173-75; views on and power over marriages, 8, 139, 141, 143, 146-48, 151-55, 167-72, 176n9
Indian Hall of Fame, Six Nations, Ontario, 69
influenza, 230
Ingham (female teacher, Red River), 20
Inkster (fur-trade family), 20
Inuit people, 237-38
Inukpuk, Johnny, 242
Inuvialuit people, 230, 232
IODE. *See* Imperial Order Daughters of the Empire
Iroquois people: Monture's lectures, 72, 75; women's power and authority, 62

Jasen, Patricia, 249
Jasper House (Alberta), 27
Jenny (Haida woman), 213-14
Jenny (Tsimshian woman), 219
Jews, 207, 215
Johnson, E. Pauline: appearance, 48, 51, *52*, 53, *55*; championed Aboriginal women, 47-48, 54, 57-59, 63; personal history, 48-49, 63n9; posthumous impact, 69, 71, 77, 83, 288n9; stage

performances, 48-51, *52*, 54, 56; traversed two worlds, 6, 48-49; views on religion, 50-51; writings, 48, 53-63
Johnson, Evelyn, 63n9
Johnson, Jacob (Tekahionwake), 49
Johnson, Sir William, 49
Jolly, Margaret, 125
Jones, D.J., 26
Joseph (Catholic Aboriginal man), 122
Judith Basin (Montana), 36

K., Julia, 166-67
Kainai people, 132, 134, 136, 152-55
Kamboureli, Smaro, 51
Kane, Paul, 24
Kaplan, Amy, 181
Keating, William, 19, 22
Kelm, Mary-Ellen, 3, 229
Kenadqua (Aboriginal woman), 121
Kendi, Mary, *241*
Kennedy, Charles, 96-97
Ketchie (nun), 21
Kewinaquot (Odawa chief), 42n10
Killabuck (Inuit man), 239
Killas, Esther Solomon, 264-65
Kincolith, British Columbia, 110-11, 113, 119, 124
King, Thomas, 50
Kinzie, Julia, 42n7
Kipling, James (John Ram), 31-32
Kipling, Nancy, 31-33, 40
Kipling, Ram, 31
Koennecke, Franz, 172-73
Kurz, Rudolph, 28-29, 32, 139

Labombarde, Alex, 29, 32-33, 45n90
Labombarde, Nancy Kipling, 28-29, 31-33, 40
Laframboise, Josette, 18
Laframboise, Madeline Marcot, 18-19
Lagrave (Grey Nun), 21-22
Langmore, Diane, 118
language: of class, 197n7; of DIA about Aboriginal women, 162-63; media in Victoria on Aboriginal women, 205-6; use of term "squaw," 47, 62-63, 162, 164, 176n8, 205, 212
Large, R.G, 264
Laronde, Judith Morin, 34
Laronde, Louis, 34
Laroque, Rosalie Laplante, 38, 46n115
Larpenteur, Charles, 31-32
Lasalière, Marienne, 19, 42n10
Lasalière, Pierre, 42n10
Latham, Ruth, 230-31
Lawe, John, 19

Lawrence, Karen, 246, 249
League of Indian Nations, 70
Legal, Emil, 152
leggings, 24, 27-28, 34
Lejac Residential School, British Columbia, 97-98, 104n18
Lewis, Richard, 216
Lewis, Robert J., 161-64, 167-69, 171-74, 177n22
Limerick, Patricia, 259
literacy, 18-19
literature: on colonial encounters, 5; contribution of this book, 1-2; on metropolitan power, 4-5; on position of Aboriginal peoples, 4, 72, 74, 85n4; on role of Aboriginal women, 5-7; on role of domesticity and family, 7-9; on women's bodies in Canadian contact zones, 9-11
Loft, Bernice: appearance and attitude, 78-79, 82-83, 89n77; as Canadian, 87n32; expertise, 79-80; financial struggles, 80-83, 88n51; not friendly with Monture, 83-84; friendship with File, 76; personal history, 69-71; public appearances, 68, 70-71, 78-81; traversed two worlds, 6, 69, 79-82, 84
Loft, Elizabeth Ann Johnson, 69-70
Loft, Frederick Ogilvie, 69
Loft, William De-wau-se-ra-keh, 69-71, 80, 82-83
Logan (male settler), 20
Logan, Barbara, 20
Lomas, W.H., 125
Lorde, Audre, 3
Lowman, Mary, 20
Lyman, Francis, 157n58
Lytton, British Columbia, 110

McClintock, Anne, 2, 208, 229, 272
McClung, Nellie, 60
McColl, Ebenezer, 140
McDermott, Annie, 20
McDonald, A., 26
McDonald, Allan, 147
Macdonald, Sir John A., 145, 157n58
McDougall, Eliza, 45n97
MacFie, Matthew, 206-7
McGillivray, Joseph, 26-27
McGirr, M., 147
McIvor, Madeline, 124
McKay (fur-trade family), 20
McKay, Fred, 270n45
McKay, Nancy, 25, 44n52
McKenzie (fur-trade family), 20
MacKenzie, John, 4, 274, 284

McKenzie, Kenneth, 32
McKenzie, M., 154
Mackenzie, William Lyon, 228-29
mackinaw coat, 19-20, 43n15
McKinsey, Elizabeth, 250
McLean, J.D., 152
McMiking (IODE member), 272-73, 287
McTavish, George Simpson, 25
Manchester House (Saskatchewan), 23
Mandelbaum, David, 40, 132
Manitoulin Island, Ontario, 161, 171
Maracle, Lee, 48
Marcot, Jean Baptiste, 18
Marcot, Madeline. *See* Madeline Marcot
  Laframboise
Marcot, Migisan, 18, 42n10
Marcot, Thérèse, 18-19, 42n10
Marguerite (Swampee woman), 42n2
marriage: DIA policies, 8, 121, 131, 140-42,
  146-55, 161, 167-70, 177n21; first in
  southern Alberta, 140; as form of con-
  tainment, 174; forms among Aboriginal
  people, 8, 115-16, 118, 132-36, 140-42,
  150-55, 168; mass, 119; minimum ages,
  151, 158n96; missionary efforts to en-
  force, 119-22, 168; mixed-race, 7-8,
  116-19, 121, 177n36; negative effects of
  Indian Act, 169-70, 172; picture of wedding group, *141*; staple of missionary
  program, 7-8, 115-16
Marsh, Donald, 230-31, 233
Marsh, Winifred Petchey, 233, 237-38
Martha (Inuit woman), 240
Martin, Helen, 49
Martin, Kathleen, 231
Martin, Milton, 67, 85n4
Mason, Philip, 208
Maxidiwiac (Hidatsa woman), 134
Mayer, Frank Blackwell, 35
medicine. *See* health
men: relative merits of white and Aboriginal husbands, 171-72; roles in missionary vision, 112; value of polygamy, 135;
  various uses for women in Victoria,
  206-17; white men, minimum age for
  marriage, 158n96. *See also* gender
Mercredi, Madeline. *See* Madeline
  Mercredi Bird
Metchosin, British Columbia, 286
Methodist Church: missions in British Columbia, 110, 112-14, 124; moralizing on
  dance halls, 217; view of marriage, 119,
  135, 138
Métis women and girls: in correctional
  facilities, 188; delinquent, 184; sewing
  education, 16-17, 21-22; sewing for a

living, 5, 17, 25-41. *See also* Aboriginal
  women and girls
Metlakatlah, British Columbia, 110, 113,
  115, 119, 123
Michilimackinac (Michigan), 18-19
Middle Woman No Coat (Blackfoot
  woman), 134
Mike (Inuit man), 241, 243
Miles, Robert, 26
Milton, William, 34
mimesis: defined, 273; to establish
  Anglo-Canadian traditions, 273-75, 283,
  287; to establish authenticity, 273
mission schools. *See* residential and mission schools
missionaries: celibacy as block to demonstrating conjugal example, 118; clothing
  of, 28, 235-39; in colonization of British
  Columbia, 110-12; culture of motherhood, 94; emphasis on health and hygiene, 229-32; in Johnson's writings, 50;
  as saviours of Aboriginal women, 116;
  view of Aboriginal women, 8, 10,
  112-13, 217-18; view of marriage, 7-8,
  115-22, 134-39, 168; view of women's
  domestic role, 113-15; view of women's
  role in labour, 122-25
Missionary Society for the Church of England, 230
Mitchel, Charles, 225n30
Mitchell, David, 18
Mitchell, Elizabeth, 18, 42n7
mittens, 24, 28, *29*, 34, 237
Mittleberger, W., 26
mixed-race children: difficulties integrating, 48-49; in Johnson's writings, 53-54,
  56
mixed-race relationships: in DIA views,
  170-72, 177n36; in missionaries' views,
  7-8, 116-19, 121
mixed-race women: in fur trade, 23-26;
  occupy border spaces, 48; sewing education, 16-17, 21-22
moccasins, 24-25, 27-28, 31-32, 34-35
Mohawk people, 87n32
Monk, Janice, 247
Montreal, Lower Canada, 18
Monture, Ella, 83
Monture, Ethel Brant: appearance and
  attitude, 67, 74-76, 78; as Canadian,
  87n32; expertise, 72; financial struggles,
  76-77; not friendly with Loft, 83-84;
  personal history, 69-71, 86n10, 86n13;
  on position of Aboriginal people in
  Canada, 72; public appearances, 67-68,
  71-75, 78; reluctance to write about self,

77-78; traversed two worlds, 6, 67, 69, 76-77, 84; writings, 73, 76-77, 89n88
Monture, Gilbert, 83
Monture, Wilbur, 69
Monture-Angus, Patricia: on Johnson, 47
Moodie, Susanna, 3, 228-29
Moore, John H., 135
Moore, Mary, 18, 42n6
Moose Factory (Ontario), 18, 24-26
Morgan (superintendent at Six Nations), 78-79
Morgan, Cecilia, 6
Morice, A.G., 116
Morin, Judith, 34
Mormons, 142-46, 148
Morris, Edwin, 45n90
Morrys (couple in Chisholm case), 261
Moses, Elliott, 67, 75, 84n4
motherless daughters: in Aboriginal narrative, 102; both children and staff at residential schools, 93-94, 96-97; defined, 104n14; nuns as, 90, 95, 101; psychological effects, 94, 101
mothers: in Aboriginal narratives, 93, 99-100; in Catholic narratives, 93-96, 98; federal allowances, 161; of girls who become nuns, 90, 95; in Johnson's writings, 59-61; loss of, and identity formation, 94; loss of, and violence by nuns, 94, 104n14; in polygamous relationships, 134-35; in psychological narratives, 94, 101; Queen Victoria as ultimate role model, 273, 277-78
Mud Lake Band, Ontario, 172
Murray (fur-trade family), 20

Na'hor (Hawaiian man), 211, 225n44
Nanaimo, British Columbia, 110, 124, 205
Navy League, 276
Nawash Reserve, Ontario, 160, 175n1
Nellie (Inuit woman), 238
New Westminster, British Columbia, 110, 211
New Zealand, 277, 282
Newcombe, E.J., 147-48, 152
Newell, Diane, 10-11
Neylan, Susan, 109
Nichol, W.C., 286
Nicholles, Lillian, 270n45
Nicholson, Jean, 286
Nightingale, Florence, 284
Nisga'a people, 209
Nlaka'pamux women, 118
Nolan, Marguerite, 20-21, 43n23
Nolin, Angelique, 20-21, 43n23
North, Marianne, 254

Northwest Exploring Expedition, 34
Northwest Territories, 10
nuns: in British Columbia colonization, 110; chastity, 100-1; clothed in Aboriginal dress in Red River, 28; life of sacrifice and moral discipline, 95-100; as motherless daughters, 90, 93-94, 101; relationships with Aboriginal children, 7, 96-100; role in constraining Aboriginal girls' sexuality, 92; sewing education for girls, 21-22

O'Connor, Hubert, 103-104n9
Odawa women, 18
Ojibwa women. *See* Chippewa women
Okalik, Annie, 233-34, 243
Okanagan Valley, British Columbia, 110
Okenese, Marguerite, 31-32
Oliver, John, 286
Ontario: colonization, 8, 68, 163, 183; resource development post–Second World War, 182; training schools, 180, 182-83, 185-95
Ontario Agricultural Hall of Fame, 69
Ontario Association of Agricultural Societies, 69
Ontario Training School for Girls (OTSG): aims, 182-83; founded, 9, 182-83; ideal of domesticity, 185-87; ideal of moral and feminine training, 187-91; ideal of work ethic, 192-95
Oronhyatekha, 74
OTSG. *See* Ontario Training School for Girls (OTSG)
Owen, Robert, 115

pad saddles, 32, 34, *35*
Padlimiut people, 230, 233
Paget, Amelia, 37, 39
Paisley, Fiona, 278
Pangnirtung, Nunavut, 234, 236, 239-41
Paquin, Julien, 168
Parry Island Reserve, Ontario, 166
Parry Sound, Ontario, 161, 171, 177n22
Pagh, Nancy, 250, 254
Peace River, British Columbia, 236
Peigan people, 147
Pembina (North Dakota), 21, 27-28
Perry, Adele, 7, 208
Phillips, Ruth, 50
Pickles, Katie, 11
Picotte, Honore, 45
Pierson, Ruth Roach, 3
Pike, Warburton, 34-35
Plains Aboriginal people, 8, 132-42, 146-55

Plaited Hair (Blood man), 148-49
Plante, Antoine, 46n115
Poitras, Celina Amyotte, 40
Pollock, Della, 80
polyandry, 155n1
polygamy: among British Columbia peoples, 116, 120-21; defined, 155n1; dissolution of, 137-39; missionary efforts against, 116, 120-21, 135-37; among Mormons, 143-46; picture of Blackfoot women and husband, *133*; among Plains peoples, 8, 132-42, 146-55; political policies against, 8, 121, 131, 140-42, 146-55; as threat to nation, 145; in United States, 143-45
polygyny, 135, 155n1
Porsild, Charlene, 235
Port Essington, British Columbia, 258-59, 261, 263-66
Port Simpson, British Columbia, 110, 113-14, 116
Porter, Roy, 280
potlatches, 116-17, 128n31
Pottinger, Betsy, 26
Prairie du Chien (Wisconsin), 42n7
Pratt, Mary Louise, 4, 109, 246-47, 249
Prince Rupert, British Columbia, 264
prostitution. *See* sex trade
Provencher (Catholic priest), 20-21
Pruden, Caroline, 20
public health movement, 229
Pulsipher, John, 142, 149

Qu'Appelle Industrial School, 39
Quebec, 5
quillwork, 37-40
Quirt, Bessie, 237

Racette, Josette Desnommé, 46n101
Rae, John, 25
Rae, W.G., 26
Rama Reserve, Ontario, 177
Rankin, Sophie Thérèse, 19
Raybold (Methodist white woman), 124
Red Cormorant Woman, 43n30
Red Crow (Kainai Chief), 132, 134, 152
Red River Settlement (Manitoba): female education, 20-21; sewing, 17, 20-22, 27-28, 33, 43n33; on travel route, 27-28;
Reece (Anglican white woman), 124
Reed, Hayter, 146-47, 149-50
Reinholt, Charles, 264-65
religion. *See* Anglican Church; Catholic Church; Methodist Church; missionaries; nuns; residential and mission schools; United Church

Rem, John, 31-32
Renton, Jane, 18, 42n6
residential and mission schools: as anthropological places, 91; education in domestic skills, 19-22, 115, 139; harsh or traumatic experiences for children, 90, 92, 94, 97-98, 101-104n9, 182; impact on Aboriginal women, 6-7, 90, 93-94; impossibility of "true story," 90-91; positive experiences for children, 96-97; both staff and children as motherless daughters, 93-94, 96-97; used to entrench imperial control, 70, 94; view of immorality of female students, 92; as way of preventing polygamy, 148-49, 151. *See also* training schools
Rhoda (Inuit girl), 240, 243
Riel, Louis, 48
Riel Rebellion, 70
Rilling, Catherine, *144*
Roberts, Charles, 19
Robertson, C., 26
Robinson, Alfred, 23
Robinson, Harry, 64n19
rogans (baskets), 18
Rollstone/Ralston, Catherine, 49
Roman Catholic Church. *See* Catholic Church
Rouleau, Arthur, 36
Royal Commission on Aboriginal Peoples, 181
Royal Commission on Bilingualism and Biculturalism, 72
Royal Society of St. George, 284
Rubenstein, Ruth P., 44n61
Ruiz, Vicki, 247
Rupp, Leila, 278
Russ, Clara, 270n45
Russ, Will, 270n45
Russell, Lynette, 4
Rutherdale, Myra, 10, 118
Ryan, Mary, 274

saddles, 32, 34, *35*
St. Boniface (Manitoba), 20-22, 43n28
St. Joseph (Manitoba), 19, 21, 43n28
St. Paul (Minnesota), 21, 35
Salslawit, Mary, 205, 207, 219, 222
Sampson (Victoria man), 284
Sandhals, Haldis, 264
Sangster, Joan, 9
Sankey, Joseph, 260-61, 264-65
Sausier, Carol, 239-40
Sauvé, Charlotte, 17, 42n2
Sauvé, Jean Baptiste, 42n2
Schindler, George, 42n10

Schindler, Thérèse Marcot, 18-19, 42n10
Schmidt, Louis, 28
Scotland, 18
Scott, Duncan Campbell, 39, 51, 155, 160, 164
Sea Cadets, 280
Second World War, 182-83, 193
Secwepemc people, 113
Sehwahtahow (Cree woman), 23
Semmens, John, 135, 138
sewing: area of female expertise, 19, 23, 124; education in, 18-23, 72, 124-25; for a living, 17-18, 23-42
sex trade: association with dance halls, 212-18; concept of prostitution, 224n16; demand for, 224n20; DIA actions against, 172-74, 178n42; labour training to avoid, 194; in Victoria, 123, 206, 208-11, 214
sexual abuse: by clergy, 103n9; long-term effects, 101; and removal of girls instead of perpetrators, 185; in residential or mission schools, 101-2, 104n14
sexuality: Aboriginal girls and women as transgressors, 7-10, 47, 56, 92, 140, 161, 163-69, 172-75, 195-96, 206, 208; beauty pageants and queen contests, 11, 273, 281-87; demonization of marginalized groups, 224n18; and eugenics, 280, 282-83; freedom before marriage, 136; in Johnson's writings, 54-56, 58-59; medical, legal, and social context, 180-82; mores after Second World War, 189; in Plains societies, 136; and presence or absence of mother, 94, 100-1; subtext for all women, 263; training school efforts to restrict and define, 187-91, 194-96
Sheepshanks, John, 117
Sheffield, Suzanne, 254
Shingle Point, Yukon, 236
Sidney, Angela, 238-39, 243
Sidney, George, 238
Siksika people, 140, *141*
Simpson, George, 18, 25-26
Sinclair, Harriet, 20
Sinclair, Phoebe, 27, 44n66
Singing Before (Kainai woman), 152
Sisters of Charity. *See* Grey Nuns
Six Nations of the Grand River Reserve, Ontario, 69-71, 75
smallpox, 218
Smart, Carol, 93
Smart, James, 152
Smart, Judith, 281-83
Smith, Charley, 36
Smith, Marie Rose Delorme, 22, 36-37, 46n112

Snell, James G., 143
snowshoes, 25, 35
Society for Oversea Settlement of British Women, 282-83
Society for the Propagation of the Gospel in Foreign Parts, 110
Solomon, Esther, 264-65
Songhees people, 10, 207-10, 218
Sooke, British Columbia, 286
South African War, 276-77
Southesk, Earl of, 28, 33-34, 46n103
Spence, Nancy Kirkness, 26
Spencer (fur-trade family), 20
Spivak, Gayatri Chakravorty, 116
"squaw," 47, 62-63, 162, 164, 176n8, 212
Star Blanket (Cree chief), 153
Steine, Charles, 225n31
Stenhouse, Anthony Maitland, 145
sterilization, 179
Stewart, A., 26
Stocking, George, 208
Stoeltje, Beverly, 282-83
Stoler, Ann Laura, 13n27, 180
Stó:lō people, 119
Storrs, Monica, 236
Strange, Carolyn, 263, 281
Stringer, Sarah (Sadie), 232, 235-36, 238
Strong-Boag, Veronica, 6, 258, 272, 281
Stuart's Lake, British Columbia, 110
Sutherland, Agnes, 96, 99
Sutherland, Neil, 229
Swampee women, 17
Symington, Fraser, 176n8

Tagish-Tlingit people, 238
Tait, Mary "Florida" Monkman, 33-34
Tait, Philip, 34
Tastewich, Baptiste, 34
Tate, Charles, 114
Tate, (Mrs.) Charles, 114
Taylor, Samuel, 25, 44n52
Tekahionwake (Jacob Johnson), 49
Thibido, Augustus, 34
Thomas, Hilda, 258
Thomas, Nicholas, 125
Thompson, Dorothy, 278
Thorne, Susan, 197n7
Tippett, Maria, 256
Tomlinson, Alice Woods, 124
Tomlinson, Robert, 111, 119
Toronto, Ontario, 281-82
Traill, Walter, 24-26
training schools: ideal of domesticity, 184-87; ideal of feminine purity, 186-91;

ideal of work ethic, 192-96; reform agenda, 180. *See also* residential and mission schools

travel writing, 249-52, 265, 269n21

Trim Woman (Kainai), 136

Trivett, Samuel, 138

trousers (hide), 24

Truthwaite (fur-trade family), 20

Tsimshian people: efforts to change gender structure, 116; efforts to collect into villages, 114; efforts to teach work skills to, 123-24; fur trade, 208; gender structure, 10, 112, 116; lack of marriage form, 118, 121; missionary teaching of women, 115; seasonal sales in Victoria, 207; sex trade, 209, 219

tuberculosis, 230

Turner (missionary), 240

Umaok, Susie, 237

Umaok, Thomas, 237

United Church, 117n26

United Kingdom: celebrated in Canada, 274, 279-81; colonization of Africa, 196n3, 200n46; as contact zone, 4; decreasing economic partnership with Canada, 288n24; educational centre for fur-trade children, 18; propaganda clubs, 276-77; as source of Canadians, 4-5, 280-81; view of underclass, 229; working class in, 196n3

United States: increasing economic partnership with Canada, 288n24; Loft's life and presentations in, 70, 80, 87n32; Monture's life and presentations in, 69, 72, 75, 87n32; Mormons, 142-43; polygamy, 142-43, 149-50; postcolonialism, 198n24; stereotypes of Aboriginal women, 164

urban areas: Aboriginal migration to, 182-83, 195

Utley, Robert, 149

Valverde, Mariana, 229

Van Kirk, Sylvia, 5, 273

Vance, Jonathan, 279

venereal diseases, 209

Venn, Henry, 137

Victoria, British Columbia: dance halls, 211-18, 220-21; history, 206-7; missions, 110, 124; moral gratification through use of Aboriginal women, 217-21; press, on Aboriginal women, 205-6, 210-11, 219; regulation of Aboriginal women, 215-16; roles of women, 205, 207, 219-22; sex trade in, 123, 206, 208-11,

214; shanties, 210-11; Victoria Day celebrations, 272-75, 279-87

Victoria, Queen of Great Britain and Ireland: death, 277-78; female imperialist role model, 11, 272-73, 275, 278-79, 283, 287; inspiration for women's groups, 276-79; maternal role model, 273, 277-78; memorialization, 11, 272-74, 279-81, 287; opposed to feminism, 278

Victoria League, 276-77

Vincent (Métis woman), 18, 42n6

Vincent, Thomas, 42n6

Wallace, Paul, 76

Ware, Vron, 2

Warner, Marina, 285

watch pockets, *33*

Watson (missionary), 238-39

Weeks, Jeffrey, 280

Welsh, Charlotte, 17, 42n2

Welsh, Norbert, 17

White, Nanny Governor, 26

White, Richard, 144

White Pup (Blackfoot man), 151

white women and girls: in agreement with racist practices, 2, 181; belonging out of place, 10-11; in correctional facilities, 181, 187-88; domestic training, 182-83; as domesticated, 113-14, 164-65; imperialist efforts, 2, 275-79; imposition of clothing taste on Aboriginal women, 10, 238-42; integral to colonial encounter, 1, 181; need for help in winter, 10, 236-38; as observers, 246, 248, 252-58; obsession with fashion, 228; as superior to Aboriginal women, 7, 81-82, 124, 181; as travellers, 249-52, 265; as victims, 258-67; wearing Aboriginal clothing, 237-38

Whitefish River Band, Ontario, 169

Whitehead, Margaret, 114

Whiteman, Lucy Desjarlais, 39

Whitlock, Gillian, 3

Wikwemikong, Ontario, 161, 168

Wilk, Richard, 282-83

Williams Lake, British Columbia, 110

Willis, Jane, 234

Wills, Sara, 282-83, 285

Wilson, James, 148, 152-54

Wilson, R.N., 132

Wilson, Rob, 248

Winnipeg, Manitoba, 45n81

Winship, George, 28

Winslow, Arthur H., 70

Winslow, Dawn Marie, 70

Winter, Jay, 279
women and girls: beauty pageants and queen contests, 11, 273, 281-87; "in between" (cross-cultural), 5; conjugal role, 115-22; delinquent, 183-85; domestic role, 113-15, 164-65, 184-87; in fur trade, 5; integral to colonial encounter, 1; labour role, 122-25, 192-95; minimum age for marriage, 158n96; moral and feminine role, 187-91; role in fur trade, 18; roles in missionary vision, 112-13; suffrage, 278, 281; and value of polygamy, 134-35. *See also* Aboriginal women and girls; children; gender; white women and girls
women's bodies: at heart of feminism, 3; labouring sites of power relations, 192, 195; as metaphor for nation, 9
Women's Christian Temperance Union, 281

Women's Institutes, 69, 73
Woolf, Mary L., *144*
Woollacott, Angela, 278
Work, Josette, 273
working-class people: boys' and men's training, 179; in correctional facilities, 181-96; expectation of work ethic, 192-96; gender roles, 122-23, 179; girls' and women's training, 9, 182-87; interwar years, 281; root of domestic disorder and immorality, 114; in United Kingdom, 196n3
Wright, Francis, 115

Yale, British Columbia, 110
York Factory. *See* Fort Churchill (Manitoba)
Young, E.R., 138
Young Women's Christian Association, 281
Yukon, 10